Media and Politics in a Globalizing World

Alexa Robertson

polity

The right of Alexa Robertson to be identified as Author of this Work has been asserted in accordance with the UK Copyright, Designs and Patents Act 1988.

First published in 2015 by Polity Press
Reprinted 2016, 2017

Polity Press
65 Bridge Street
Cambridge CB2 1UR, UK

Polity Press
350 Main Street
Malden, MA 02148, USA

ISBN-13: 978-0-7456-5469-0
ISBN-13: 978-0-7456-5470-6(pb)

Library of Congress Cataloging-in-Publication Data
Robertson, Alexa.
  Media and politics in a globalizing world / Alexa Robertson. -- 1
    pages cm
  ISBN 978-0-7456-5469-0 (hardback) -- ISBN 978-0-7456-5470-6 (paperback) 1. Mass media--
Political aspects. 2. Press and politics. 3. Elite (Social sciences) 4. Globalization. I. Title.
  P95.8.R63 2015
  302.23--dc23
                                                                              2014025712

Typeset in 9.5 on 12 pt Utopia by
Servis Filmsetting Ltd, Stockport, Cheshire
Printed and bound in the United States by LSC Communications

The publisher has used its best endeavours to ensure that the URLs for external websites referred to in this book are correct and active at the time of going to press. However, the publisher has no responsibility for the websites and can make no guarantee that a site will remain live or that the content is or will remain appropriate.

Every effort has been made to trace all copyright holders, but if any have been inadvertently overlooked the publisher will be pleased to include any necessary credits in any subsequent reprint or edition.

For further information on this topic please visit the companion website, mediapolitics.net

For further information on Polity, visit our website:
politybooks.com

Contents

Preface

In 1980, a political satire was broadcast on British television about a cabinet that had embarked on a new era of 'Open Government'. In one episode of *Yes Minister*, a state visit from the president of an African country is eagerly awaited, when the minister, Jim, sees a television news report that says there has just been a coup d'état in 'Buranda'. He tells his aide to get the foreign minister on the telephone. The aide asks whether the call should be scrambled, so it can't be overheard. The minister tells him not to bother – 'it's not secret, it's on the news!' Once the call is placed, it turns out that the foreign minister, Martin, hasn't heard about the coup. Martin asks how Jim knows about it. 'It was on the news', replies Jim, growing increasingly alarmed. 'Didn't you see? Don't you know? You're Foreign Secretary, for God's sake!' Martin explains that his television set is broken. When Jim expresses surprise, and asks about Foreign Office telegrams, Martin explains: 'They always come in later. I get all the foreign news from TV.'

In the real world outside the minister's fictitious government office that year, globalization had yet to make itself felt. The word was seldom used in popular parlance, scholarly articles or university course catalogues. The globe was neatly divided into East, West, North and South. Ronald Reagan was about to be elected US president and the temperature of the Cold War between the United States and the Soviet Union was dropping. The first Islamic Revolution had just taken place and Saddam Hussein was a friend of the Americans and British. European countries had no common currency, several of those countries did not officially exist, and only whites were eligible to vote in South Africa. People protesting throughout the world against nuclear weapon deployment, mobilized by mimeographed flyers and word-of-mouth, were dismissed by presidents, prime ministers and the press as naive and irresponsible, and urged to go back to their couches and let elites take care of the running of the world.

Just over three decades later, 'globalization' generated almost 47 million hits on Google. The line that had once clearly demarcated East and West had been erased, the presidents of both South Africa and the USA were black, formerly communist states had become democratic republics, and right-wing extremism had taken the place of communism as the political bogeyman of Europe. Even when the tenth anniversary of 9/11 was observed, the major threat on the political agenda was not violent conflict (be it the nuclear war of a bygone, bipolar world or the suicide bombs of the war-on-terror decade). It was global financial collapse. The anti-regime protests of young Arabs, tweeting to each other and the world on their smartphones, was lauded by political elites and media commentators everywhere. And government had become open in a way that could not have been dreamt of even by the authors of television fiction in 1980, as the publication in September 2011 of more than 250,000 uncensored diplomatic cables by WikiLeaks made painfully obvious.

Unlike previous disclosures by the (in)famous whistleblower, 'Cablegate 2' happened without the collaboration of journalists working for mainstream media organizations in the UK, Spain, Germany, France and the USA. The documents were unedited, prompting the global broadcaster Al Jazeera English (AJE) to publish an appeal on its website to 'crowdsource Cablegate'. Explaining that its journalists wanted help finding the stories contained in the documents, AJE listed three links to the cables, with instructions to viewers to copy-paste what they found most interesting, and submit them for journalists to write up (AJE 2011a). Less than two years later, Edward Snowden would show that state agencies were also exploiting communications technology, to monitor the actions of citizens much more efficiently than citizens could monitor the actions of governments.

It would seem that rather a lot has happened in the past few decades. How did we get here from there – and where, exactly, are we?

Exploring answers to such questions is what this book is about, even if it does not claim to provide definitive answers. It concerns the relationship between media and politics in a world that is globalizing, if not globalized (because the process is not complete). The relationship in focus is evolving in significant ways – some indeed argue that it is being transformed. To be able to assess such claims, however, that which is new must be placed in its historical context. The tension between change and continuity is a red thread running throughout the chapters that follow.

The context of inquiry

The world has long been interconnected. Early accounts of globalization tended to treat it as something unprecedented, symptomatic of the late twentieth and early twenty-first centuries. Among the many volumes that have been published on the topic since 1980, however, a good many point out that exchange between different governments, economies and cultures can be traced back to the 'new imperialism' of the late 1800s, or even earlier, to the age of the explorers, or further back in time to the heyday of the Vikings. But there is a widespread understanding that, in recent decades, historical interconnections have become radically intensified, and a myriad of new ones have sprouted and encircled the planet like a vine grown out of control. There has been a qualitative change in the world that people have to function in: simply put, it has grown both bigger and smaller. Correspondingly, there has been a qualitative change in how people go about dealing with it. (That would be politics.)

Politics has always been about communication. Pharoahs, emperors and absolute monarchs were skilled practitioners of the art of the media spectacle, and representations of collective action and identity are to be found on the medium provided by the stone of the Lascaux caves where Paleolithic artists portrayed the community's 'others'. But in popular and academic discourse, the relationship between political and media actors is often portrayed as having been revolutionized in recent decades.

Despite popular parlance – the tendency to speak of them in singular form – 'the media' have never been a monolithic force. And the plethora of actors, institutions and technologies invoked by the collective term are morphing at such a rate that they defy containment in traditional analytical categories. What 'the media' actually are is consequently far from clear. The word 'media' tends to be used without reflection, by scholars and laymen alike, which prevents us from making sense of media power and the changes taking place so rapidly in the worlds we inhabit – be they physical, virtual or imaginative. Understanding what 'the media' are, and being able to analyse their political role, are intertwined tasks. It is work that must start in a globalized environment characterized by rapid technological change, rather than end there, as has tended to be the case with many works on the subject.

At one time, broadcast media were considered to be the unifiers of the nation, especially in countries with strong public service broadcast traditions. Particularly in relation to events beyond the borders of the country, or when the nation or the values associated with it were under threat, media depictions of politics and the world contributed to what Benedict Anderson famously called the 'imagined community' of the nation. Under globalization, the most urgent challenges to the nation have come to be shared by others; decisionmaking is decentred and deterritorialized; and new actors have taken to the stage of politics. National public service traditions have been pummelled by economic liberalization, de-regulation and global media flows. Broadcasting gave way some time ago to narrowcasting, the national audience became fragmented, and citizens became consumers. It became increasingly apparent that political and social life are media-saturated, and that something often referred to as 'media logic' is the metronome setting the tempo at which events in these realms unfold. The power struggle continues between media and political actors – the struggle for control over information flows, and the struggle for power over images of politics. It is by no means clear that once voiceless challengers using 'new' media are winning this battle: there is evidence that the initative has been reclaimed by familiar elites. New forces have emerged to occupy new positions of power, but established actors have also been quick to exploit new technologies to reinforce their positions.

Globalization and the digital revolution have thus had consequences for the way we understand the media–politics relationship, for the issues that require attention, and for the conceptual repertoire most suitable for such scholarly work. The starting point for what follows is this contemporary setting – an environment understood better in terms of dynamic rather than static relationships. Actors on all levels of all manner of societies are now faced with new challenges, but also new possibilities, because of the way media technologies are developing, and because of the way they are being used. This book is meant as a companion, or perhaps 'rough guide', for the reader embarking on a journey through this turbulent landscape of change.

About this navigation device

Many accounts of media and politics sensibly focus on a single country – usually the United States or Britain. But the nature of the media–politics relationship differs from one culture to the next, and those cultures can be local, national or transnational. Empirical accounts of specific settings, case studies, and books replete with nutritious facts and figures provide useful precision and detail, but are not always amenable to generalization. It can be hard to know what to do with the insights generated by such nationally grounded scholarship when it comes to understanding larger processes. The German sociologist Ulrich Beck (2006) has warned against 'methodological nationalism', and for good reason: if we want to understand the world we live in, then the nation is no longer the natural starting point. The flip side of the coin is that ambitious overviews and attempts to paint 'the bigger picture' can often be too general, abstract or theoretical to be helpful to scholars seeking to place a given media–politics relation in a wider context. The middle route charted in this book is inspired by comparative explorations, across culture (comparing specific national settings and mapping differences between national and transnational settings) and time (probing the tension between continuity and change). The intellectual destination is a vantage point from which it is possible to see (and understand) general patterns, by learning from specific instances.

The aim of the book is to provide an analytical approach – a way of thinking about, studying and doing research on media and politics in a globalizing world – rather than a reference book full of information. It is meant to stimulate questions and suggest an attitude towards how to go about looking for answers, but does not purport to provide the latest facts and figures (which change daily, and can be found online). Employing a problematizing approach, theoretical generalizations about 'the media' are interrogated with the help of examples from different cultures and different levels of society. In this way, the reader is encouraged to use empirical analysis to critique the claims encountered in scholarly literature and popular discourse about media power. By operationalizing abstractions like 'the media' and 'politics' into identifiable actors whose actions can be analysed and explained, the intention is to chart a course through a conceptually burdened area of inquiry (theory) and show how notions about the media–politics relationship can be studied in practice (empirical research).

The two media artefacts with which the book begins – a television programme from 1980 and a website from 2011 – can serve as pedagogical 'portkeys' to the academic realm where scholars from different disciplines try to make sense of this evolving relationship. They are simple examples, but they are also primary source materials, and under their impetus, it is possible to arrive at insights into a tangle of real-world and theoretical problems. To the reader who is unfamiliar with the metaphor, it should be explained that portkeys are everyday objects in the world of Harry Potter. Although easily overlooked, they transport the user to the relevant destination upon activation (which happens when they are grasped). At first, feelings of vertigo can be experienced, as the ground falls away and the destination is approached through a confusing whirlwind of impressions, but with practice it is possible to land gracefully. It is hoped that the commonplace artefacts and illustrations which open each of the following chapters will be useful in transporting the reader from the ground of everyday mediated experience through the sometimes turbulent clouds of theory, and that he or she will learn to land on his or her feet.

Reader dashboard

As this is a sprawling, confusing (and wonderfully stimulating) subject, a strategy is needed to ensure coherence. The one provided in this book is a litany of central questions that frame each chapter.

What's the problem? This could be theoretical. (What is 'mediatization' actually, how could it be recognized if stumbled across in an alleyway on a dark night, and how can it be operationalized so as to help explain what is happening in a specific context? This is one example of a theoretical problem.)

It could be empirical or relate to something happening IRL, in the 'real' world. (What's the difference between a video sequence filmed by a young demonstrator in Kiev's Independence Square on her smartphone and uploaded on YouTube, and a report filed from the same place by a CNN reporter? What's the analytical difference between crowdsourcing, citizen journalism and professional newsgathering in such situations?)

Or it could be ethical or normative. (Is public-service broadcasting, which is relatively sheltered from market forces, better for democracy than commercially funded broadcasting, which is usually thought to be relatively free from state control? Is the freedom of speech facilitated by the internet a good thing, even when people like Anders Behring Breivik can use this facility to spread anti-democratic propaganda across cyberspace before committing mass murder of political opponents at home in Norway?)

How can these ideas be tested empirically? This is an important question, because only by putting concepts, claims and ideas to the empirical test can we critically assess their usefulness.

What is new, when it comes to the features of a given phenomenon (say, a technological development that brings media users from all over the world together in a single site), and what is just a new twist on a situation that has prevailed for a long time? (The telegraph deterritorialized communication more than a century ago, so some would argue that it is just that more people are now communicating in that mediated space.)

What is the general pattern (of media globalization, for example) and what are the cultural exceptions to it? (Russians are among the world's most active internet users, but overwhelmingly visit sites in their own language, so while their blogosphere is heavily trafficked, Russians tend to stay within the confines of their own country, even when travelling through cyberspace.)

Who does a certain state of affairs (e.g. file-sharing) matter to? Who are the stakeholders (the copyright-holders, the media-users who want to access the file, or the policymakers trying to deal with regulation in a digital landscape with porous borders)?

The book is divided into three parts.

Part One presents what could be called 'the big picture'. The introduction (chapter 1) explicates the tricky question of what 'the media' are, and where to look for politics if a state-centric focus is to be avoided. Ways of thinking about the interconnections between media and politics in such varied contexts are set out and questions posed that should be kept in mind while considering the media–politics relationship from different actor perspectives. Chapter 2 is about media power seen through the prism of continuity and change. It revolves around the political roles traditionally ascribed to 'the media' and how they are being transformed by economic, and not least technological, developments. Some of the metaphors associated with these roles – like the watchdog, agenda-setter and manufacturer of consent – emerged in particular political and academic cultures, and may fit the situation in other cultures about as well as the glass slipper fitted the feet of Cinderella's stepsisters.

Part Two zooms in to look more closely at the detail of the larger canvas painted in the first part of the book (or the terrain mapped out, for those who prefer metaphorical consistency). The media–politics relationship involves a struggle for power and control over information, and over understandings of how the world works. It is a relationship that looks different depending on the perspective of a given stakeholder. Each of the four chapters of Part Two considers the media–politics relation through the eyes of one set of actors – elites, journalists, activists, and 'the people formerly known as the audience', as Jay Rosen (2006) famously called us. Not only do things differ according to vantage point ('where you stand depends on where you sit'), the scholarly literature on these different sets of actors tends to have different theoretical points of departure. Part Two reviews the different perspectives, then explores how power entails different things for different stakeholders in the media–politics relationship, and how the balance is being affected by technological, economic and political developments.

Part Three focuses on several key debates. One has to do with mediated conflict (chapter 7), another with what has been called 'infotainment' (chapter 8) and a third with the phenomenon scholars seek to capture using the notion of 'mediatization' (chapter 9). The problems and potential of media freedom in heterogeneous societies are the focus of chapter 10.

Pressing the printed equivalent of the 'home' button, the concluding chapter returns the reader back to the main menu, suggesting intellectual sites to foray. A Research Guide is included at the end for the reader who is interested in embarking, or continuing, on such a journey.

The book is intended as a rough guide through a rich landscape of academic debate and real-world developments. There is no yellow brick road: it is easy to get lost, and there can be a point in doing so (depending on whether one would rather explore Oz or keep close to the ground in Kansas). But two red pins on the map are perhaps in order to indicate where this particular tour is headed.

The first red pin is the concept of hybridity. It is key to the argument and structure of the book. We live in not just a world of multiple media devices, but one in which media formats and genres overlap and merge, and the line between politics and the media is increasingly difficult to distinguish. The point is not to try to corral events and issues into tidy analytical categories, and certainly not to confine them to one academic discipline or another, but to acknowledge and explore the interactions.

The second red pin is placed on the map by the 'fortress' (to use the English translation of the popular Danish political drama *Borgen*) occupied by political elites. Many accounts of media and politics under globalization are informed by political economy perspectives that critique market forces and lament the inferior media products that they spawn. While these perspectives are represented at strategic places throughout the following chapters, and their concerns are often well founded, this book does not set out to critique the media, but to analyse the power relations between actors in that 'field' (to use Bourdieu's term) and those in the realm of politics. Journalists the world over pay a high price to get the news out. A problem returned to throughout the book is how states and political elites are using media technology to regain the upper hand, thought momentarily to have been ceded to non-elites, to cement and increase their power. To the extent that there is a villain in this piece, it is not Market Forces (the golem of Murdoch and Fox that haunts many other accounts of political communication), but the panopticon.

For further information on this topic please visit the companion website, mediapolitics.net

Acknowledgements

Andrea Drugan at Polity suggested this book. She persuaded me that it was needed and that it should have the globalized, digital environment as its point of departure, rather than its endpoint, and was always encouraging and constructive when dealing with whatever critical concerns were voiced (as often as not by me). From her amazing stable of experts, she provided full-on and insightful reviews at every step of the work, from the first outlines of the book, to the first chapters, and then to the final manuscript. A major vote of thanks is due to those eight anonymous reviewers for their constructive feedback. Thanks also to Lauren Mulholland and Joe Devanny, for their editorial assistance in the early stages of this work, and to Elen Griffiths who oversaw its completion. Thanks also to Leigh Mueller for meticulous attention to detail at the copy-editing stage. I am very privileged to have been able to work with an editorial team that invests so heavily in the review process, while giving rein to their authors.

At about the same time as Andrea and I started to talk about this book, a network of political scientists and media scholars from across Sweden known as 'MIM' began to plan a research programme on mediatization under globalization. Both these pursuits forced me to look at, and find words to capture, the 'big picture'. As someone who feels more comfortable with keeping her head down and close to the empirical material, this did not come naturally, and I am grateful for the intellectual space provided by the MIM network, and especially Ulf Bjereld and Marie Demker, to help me accomplish the gymnastic feat of keeping my head up and ear to the ground (for unfolding events to pick up and dissect).

Brainstorming sessions with Alexandra Segerberg and Lance Bennett were particularly invigorating, and some of my best thinking was done while talking with Alexandra on the train or walking with Lance along the Stockholm waterfront. The advice at the end of the book on how to get started on a research project was worked out over the course of several years with Alexandra, a much valued colleague with whom I have had the pleasure of seeing many a solid research paper over the finish line in time.

After many years in academia, I finally found my intellectual home at the Department of Media Studies in Stockholm (IMS) as work on this book began. Seminars there, with in-house colleagues and international scholars, have provided an important source of information and ideas ever since, and the opportunity for critical dialogue. This book could not have been written without the stimulating working environment you have provided and the friendship you have offered. Tack skall ni ha!

Other friends have been important to this venture, either by providing continual encouragement and enthusiasm, by offering a berth when I was doing research, or quite simply by expressing the (in my view unreasonable) conviction that this project was possible. Karen Sorensen, Virginia Budd, Matt Baird, Emelie Dahlström, Tamar Gutner, the other Bologna *amici* and music friends: thanks for asking how it was going, and for listening to the long answers. I promise to talk (and write) about other things now.

Special thanks to my students, past and present. This book has been written with you and your successors in mind. It is people like you who make teaching so energizing and research meaningful. I would particularly like to acknowledge the alumni who so promptly replied to a message soliciting experiences of the media in working and private life. These busy and successful people took the time to respond thoughtfully, sometimes eloquently, and often at length. Master's students at IMS have left a particular mark on this book, by doing interviews and fieldwork that they have graciously let me re-use, by following up on class discussions with clips and written accounts of their own cultural takes on the issues we have been discussing, and by helping me think through the issues dealt with in the book. I'd like to mention Nika Bender, Julia Fenckart, Luiza Chiroiu, Diana Andreea, Rebecca Schmidt and Leone Serrander here, and Emma Dahlin for helping me develop a course on politics and popular culture, which improved chapter 8.

Thank you, finally, to my family. Although this book draws on what I have taught and done research on for many years, the actual writing of it fell outside my duties at Stockholm University, and I had to take time off work to ensure that it was finished before Twitter was as relevant to prospective readers as shortwave radio or black-and-white television. This of course did not mean less work, just less pay, and I am grateful to my husband Claes, who fortunately has a Real Job Outside the Ivory Tower, for making this practically possible. He and our children put up with my absences, both physical and mental, with good grace. Nick and Clarie have also been invaluable sources of insight, although they may not be aware of it. Without young people in your lifeworld, it can be difficult to stay abreast of the most recent developments in media technology, or what programmes must be watched, and to maintain a sense of how these things matter to how young people make sense of the world. Clarie is the mistress of the insightful question and a living example of the dissolving border between private and public mediated realms. It is a delight watching her develop into a good scholar. Nick is a repository of insights into the world of political comedy, which he is more than willing to share, and was great company during the final throes of revision. I hope that both of you wonderful people will help me ensure the book remains a living thing, and reasonably up-to-date, for a while at least. Whether or not you're up for that, I dedicate it to you.

PART ONE

1 Introduction

Five weeks had passed since Tunisian fruitseller Mohamed Bouazizi set fire not only to his own body, but also to the tinder of frustration and democratic yearning smouldering on the streets of the Arab world. Tunisia was observing the first of three days of national mourning for the people who had died in the 2011 uprising that resulted in the hasty exit of President Zine al-Abidine Ben Ali. The veteran BBC World reporter Lyse Doucet walked her viewers down 'the Fleet Street of Tunis' and into the premises of the country's oldest state-run newspaper, where staff had just divested themselves of their editor-in-chief. The excitement in the reporter's voice was unmistakable. 'What a difference a week makes in Tunisia', she said, and grinned; 'You can hear the sound of protest wafting through the windows.' All the people discussing politics so heatedly would have been arrested a week before; overnight, journalists had found themselves free to think when they wrote. 'You can't underestimate how extraordinary all of this is', she told her global audience, and promised that 'from this, a new Tunisia will emerge' (*BBC World News*, 21 January 2011, 9 p.m. CET).

As it turned out, considerably more than a week would be needed to achieve a stable democracy in Tunisia and the neighbouring countries to which the revolution spread, and journalistic freedom was in many places shortlived. But few would disagree that people had found themselves acting in a radically changed political landscape. They were not alone. The social and political upheaval that came to be known as the 'Arab Spring' threw into sharp relief the impact of technological developments that were equally radical, which posed challenges to the journalists covering the revolutions, and to the scholars who study the work of those journalists.

The Arab Spring is a portkey that opens on the key concerns of this book: political and media change in a world of transcended borders, challenged elites and difficult publics.

The Arab Spring is a good example of how political change and developments in media technology go hand-in-hand. There is continuity in such change: the Protestant Reformation went together with the invention of printing, and the French Revolution and Revolutions of 1848 were accompanied by the rise of journalism and the mass press. But this portkey also places the person grasping it before a vista of change, showing how political developments can only be contained within national settings with difficulty, and how local events, like a fruitseller dousing himself with petrol and striking a match, can become global issues. It shows how journalists are being challenged by the need to cover processes that are unprecedented in their significance and scope, and in the speed with which they unfold, and to do so under conditions of information blockage and physical danger. And it is an instance of how people have become accustomed to witnessing the live coverage of history, present in time if not space. As Silverstone so elegantly put it, media technologies 'both connect and disconnect, but above all act as bridges or doors, both open and closed, to the world' (Silverstone 2007: 18).

Scannell (2004) notes that news coverage is usually retrospective in nature. The original event has already taken place, and the work to be done is that of sense-making. If that applies to journalism, it is particularly true of scholarship. Where journalists have cultural narratives to fall back on, however, the scholar has theoretical frameworks (which are of course also narratives, of sorts) to help make sense of new data. In such a context, we would be well advised to follow the advice of Hoskins and O'Loughlin (2010: 187) and 'think imaginatively about how we can represent the phenomena we are interested in'.

The first task is to specify what that is. What is globalization and where does politics take place in a globalizing world? What is – or rather are – 'the media'? How should we approach the task of comparing mediated political interactions in different settings? How should we go about making sense of what is happening to that interaction in the face of technological and other sorts of changes? There is, finally, the matter of how such large questions can be related to specific instances like the Arab Spring. Put another way, how can the general be related to the particular?

Globalization and politics

'Globalization' is the word most often used to describe how the world has become increasingly interconnected at all levels in recent decades. Since the mid-1980s, scholars have studied how such driving forces as economics, technology, politics and cultural change have contributed to the globalization process, and they have argued about how it is best understood. Some differences of opinion stem from which of those driving forces scholars have been most interested in. Others can be traced back to the various theoretical perspectives which have informed the work of those scholars. More than a matter of theory, globalization is something that can be observed in the world around us – in the financial crises that result in people losing their jobs and homes; in the spread of epidemics; in the trafficking of drugs and people that spills across borders; in the activities of the multinational corporations whose products we buy; and not least in the media products we consume. It is a process that has consequences for citizens, for society, for states and for the world community.

Globalization is the process whereby polities, economies, institutions and actors at all levels of society become increasingly connected across national borders. The word first found its way into a dictionary in 1961, but the process that word describes was not established as an object of scholarly enquiry until the mid-1980s. Up to that point, academics tended instead to talk about internationalization or international relations, until it became apparent (to some at least) that the post-cold-war world differed in distinctive ways from earlier periods. Whereas internationalization refers to how the activities of states become increasingly intertwined while remaining attached to the national territory, globalization refers to a qualitative change in social relations that are played out in the world as a single place. What makes globalization different from international relations is that the actors involved in these relations are no longer exclusively states.

One way of understanding this is to pose the question: what does it mean to say that something is globalized? Football can serve as a heuristic here. Fans in Thailand, for example, commune with fans on the other side of the world in real time when they all watch Liverpool play Champions League matches. When the Thai government bid for 30 per cent ownership of the team in 2004, it had strong popular backing. Although it did not end up being owned by Thailand, Liverpool could nevertheless be considered a global team (and is indeed acknowledged as a global brand): of the forty-nine players on its 2011 squad, only fourteen were English nationals. Other players came from places as far-flung as Australia, Spain, Denmark, Slovakia, Brazil, Argentina and Uruguay. The world's most international activity is also the most local, with strong feelings of attachment to neighbourhood and nation living on, despite the fact that football players and trainers work in a borderless global market (Ahlin 2004).

Football is a good heuristic because it incorporates several of the key dimensions of globalization. It is as much about big business as it is about sport, entertainment and current affairs: the economic is one dimension. Football also has to do with institutions and transnational organizations. On another level, it has to do with identities – pulling, ironically, away from the global to the national, ethnic and local. And communications technology is an essential part of the contemporary football phenomenon, as people on every continent can, and do, follow regional and world championships simultaneously, leaping from their couches or mats in glee or brandishing their fists in the air in frustration over a goal experienced throughout the planet simultaneously. This is a banal example of what is referred to in the globalization literature as 'time–space compression'. And the everyday nature of football is also part of what makes it a useful metaphor when seeking to understand globalization, because the phenomenon is something that concerns ordinary people and everyday life as well as political elites and world affairs.

Looking for politics in a globalizing world

Politics and the political are understood as broad, generalized phenomena in this book. Following Mouffe (1997), they are not seen as having to do with a certain sort of institution (like parliament or the national congress), or a specific sphere (such as the public one), or level of society (the national, for example). The political is instead conceived as 'a dimension' that 'determines our very ontological position' (Mouffe 1997: 3).

When they claimed that 'politics is everywhere', Charles & Smith (2010) meant that it is to be found in global, national, local and domestic settings. Boundaries that seem permanent and inevitable, if not natural, 'turn out to be subject to contestation and, sometimes displacement' (Charles & Smith 2010: 527). This is not new to the global era, however.

Government policies, and particularly neoliberal ones, are among the driving forces of globalization. Aided and abetted by the IMF, the WTO and the World Bank, political decisionmakers at the end of the last century facilitated the deregulation of capital that is a prerequisite of economic globalization. Two decades later, their successors, struggling to manage the global financial crisis, imposed new regulations to staunch the haemorrhaging of economies that were more intertwined than ever. Political actors have sought to both re- and de-regulate media as well as financial flows, as will be seen in chapter 3.

Politics in a globalizing world: Rajendra Pachauri, head of the United Nations Intergovernmental Panel on Climate Change (IPCC) speaks to the press at the Copenhagen Climate Conference on 17 December 2009. Photograph: Trevor Snapp / Corbis.

The stretching and deepening of the connections within networks of NGOs and civil society actors such as the Red Cross, UNICEF, Amnesty International, environmental movements, digital action networks (and, on a murkier level, terrorist organizations and drug and prostitution cartels) is politics.

Politics can also be found in the development of universal values and norms and the spread of democracy to places it has not previously existed, or from which it disappeared for a while. Scholars interested in this dimension of politics have written about the spread of a cosmopolitan culture that is based on a liberal notion of people's equal worth, regardless of where they live, and a growing awareness of the world as a single place, with a globally shared collective future. This is not necessarily, or at least not always, an altruistic reflex. Rather, it stems from the insight that the main risks and problems facing us in the global era defy national borders; that we share these problems with people elsewhere; and that we must find common solutions to them.

There is a scholarly problem here too, given that there are many versions of democracy in a globalizing world and that its political systems are many and hybrid. While it is useful to revisit political theory to recall ideals and classic incarnations (be they direct, representative or liberal democracy), it is equally important to keep an empiricist's eye on the realities of the political systems that prevail throughout the world IRL. Under globalization, these have morphed, so that fewer and fewer can be unproblematically labelled 'democratic' or 'authoritarian', and more and more are 'messy mixtures' of these political forms (Chadwick 2011). It has thus become increasingly common, in the field of comparative politics, to refer to 'pseudodemocratic' or 'hybrid' regimes. In some countries in Africa, Asia and Latin America, free and fair elections, while enshrined in the constitution, take place in settings in which there is also widespread corruption or coercion by religious or military elites, or where those in power simply ignore the rules. This was spectacularly illustrated by the 2010 presidential elections in Côte d'Ivoire, where incumbent Laurent Gbagbo refused to honour the outcome and to cede power, with months of violent conflict as the result.

While citizens might be free to vote for the candidate they prefer, an election could nevertheless be considered unfair if journalists cannot report on the issues at stake without risking their jobs or their physical safety, as is the case in what have been called 'repressitarian' regimes (such as Iran, Singapore and the Caucasus). But even in states universally considered to be democracies, the 'war on terror decade' provided ample evidence of how contested the notion of 'undue intrusion' can be, with even more coming to light in the subsequent Orwellian decade of the Snowden revelations that the US government was spying on its own citizens and those of other states. In multicultural societies characterized by conflict between people of different ethnic origins and religious persuasions, the legal limits on freedom of expression are also often sorely tested. The media–politics relationship is riddled with tensions related to these problems. As Sklar points out, what we are talking about is an increasingly complex form of political organization, and democracy in any one country is 'at best, a composite fragment. Everywhere, democracy is under construction' (Sklar 1987: 714). Chadwick thus has a strong case when he urges us to think in terms of hybrid political – and, as will be seen, media – forms, because hybrid theory makes it possible to see how democratic and authoritarian political practices 'intermesh and simultaneously coevolve' (Chadwick 2011: 5).

On a more general level, citizens' political involvement has been threatened by 'depoliticization'. Splichal uses this word to refer to a process whereby 'the responsibilities of political institutions are delegated to politically independent regulatory agencies or private or semi-private organizations'. Issues that were once subject to formal political scrutiny are relegated to market-driven regulation; government has been replaced by governance; and the people affected by these decisions have very limited possibilities for participating in and consenting to them (Splichal 2009: 397).

When looking for politics in a globalizing world, we consequently have to pay attention to what is happening outside official realms – on the streets and in the chatrooms where activists challenge the status quo, and in less turbulent corners of the private sphere, where fragmented audiences produce as well as use media messages. Not least, attention must be paid to the boundary that once used to divide these spheres into public and private, and to how it is contested. The private sphere manifests itself in public in the personal networks that are playing a more prominent role in large-scale protest (Bennett et al. 2008; Walgrave et al. 2011), in the public communication of civil society organizations (Segerberg & Bennett in review) and in the way 'ordinary' people engage with society, politics and each other (of which more in chapter 5). As Bennett (2010) put it, democracy has become a crowd-sourced activity. The development of transnational spheres of governance, on the top or in the centre, and global networks of social movements, on the bottom or in the periphery, have rendered problematic the connection between citizenship and the nation-state that was long taken for granted in political theory (Stevenson 2003: 6).

Politics, then, is played out in settings that are increasingly difficult to classify. To be a citizen is to be a member of a political community, but what does that mean in a globalizing world where the global and the local overlap, and in which national sovereignty is challenged on a daily basis? Globalization has changed the relationship between *demos* (the collective subject of representation, i.e. the political community or citizenry) and *ethnos* (the imagined community of membership and affiliation, which has historically been the nation). States of the twenty-first century have lost the exclusive power to protect the public interest effectively, in that it is no longer entirely their remit to regulate. Relations between dominant actors and their antagonists are changing in significant ways.

To understand politics as relating to public affairs makes sense – as long as it is possible to distinguish the public from the private, and to be clear about what publicity (as in public-ness) entails in contemporary settings (of which, more below). But to think of politics as synonymous with democracy is misleading, as it always has been, although perhaps for new reasons. Authoritarian states threatened the classical liberal separation of state and civil society (essential to the theory and practice of democracy) by keeping the private sphere under surveillance. The problem now is not only that democratic states like the US and UK have been shown to engage in similar practices, but also that it has become a much more complicated matter to determine what is public, in the sense of something held in common, and accountable. Both within and beyond states, power has become decentred and authority fragmented. Put simply, it has become 'extremely difficult if not impossible to know who decides what, and how it is decided' (Splichal 2009: 396).

Rather than trying to establish what politics is, and where it is to be found, the position taken in this book is that it is more helpful to think in terms of power, both in the sense of 'potential' and 'constraints'. One benefit of such an approach is that it makes it easier to relate the realm of the political to that of communication. But if it is difficult to define globalization and politics, it is much more challenging to be clear about what is hidden behind the term we read, hear and use countless times each day, often unthinkingly – 'the media'.

What is 'the media'?

'The media' is a catch-all term for the plethora of technological forms, institutions and actors that facilitate communication, and the texts thereby produced. By technological form is meant the medium itself (newspapers, radio, television, computer, tablet or mobile phone). An institution can be something specific (like the European Broadcasting Union or the *Times of India*) or general (a social sphere). The category of 'media actors' is a sprawling one that includes anyone involved in the production of media texts – journalists, editors, producers, scriptwriters, cameramen, bloggers and tweeters (in some instances, at any rate) and the people who own or run media organizations (in some instances, again – the Berlusconis and Murdochs of the world, but perhaps not the public of public service). In this book a 'media text' refers to anything produced by these actors, be it a photograph, newspaper article, news broadcast (or news report within a broadcast), online op-ed, blog, film or YouTube clip, or other such artefact.

But these are all nouns and if it is to be of any assistance when analysing the relations that concern us, a scholarly definition requires verbs, or at least an idea of how the nouns are connected to each other. Thompson provided this in his classic theory of media and modernity, where he set out that mass communication is 'the institutionalized production and generalized diffusion of symbolic goods via the fixation and transmission of information or symbolic content' (Thompson 1995: 26). The reader may be forgiven for feeling none the wiser, so a moment devoted to unpacking this admittedly somewhat difficult phrase is one well spent.

What Thompson seeks to grasp is phenomena (in the plural) that have emerged historically. When charting the development of media technology ('the fixation and transmission of information or symbolic content'), he draws on the work of the medium theorists, chiefly Harold Innis, Marshall McLuhan and Joshua Meyrowitz, who focus on the characteristics of a particular form of transmission. Their interest is in how a given medium constitutes or shapes a distinct environment that encourages people to communicate in one way rather than another. While there are problems with McLuhan's famous adage that 'the medium is the message', it is easy to relate to the idea that people communicate differently, and package their thoughts differently, depending on whether they are writing a letter to their grandmother relating their experiences of doing research in a distant city, posting pictures of a recent trip on Instagram, or comparing notes about demonstrations against cutbacks with friends and acquaintances on Facebook or Twitter.

Content – even the way we think and experience things – is thus structured by particular media forms that socialize and condition their users. The 'content structure' is stretched out in a specific way, reflecting the spatial and material conditions of the system for 'transmitting the information or symbolic content'. As a broadcasting system changes, for example, so does the content structure and so, thus, does the conditioning of television viewers (Couldry & McCarthy 2004). Given the contours of the news environment that have evolved since McLuhan (1964/2003) published his thoughts on the media, and not least in recent years, it is worth thinking about the consequences of some 'transmissions' having become abbreviated (tweets and mobile alerts), while others have been extended (conventional television programmes tending to have longer items, and newspaper stories being hyperlinked via online news sites to external sources and archives for those who want in-depth follow-up).

Thompson also pulls into his definition the institutions that seek to make use of those technological developments, for some sort of gain (symbolic or financial). 'The media' thus refers to an industry as well as a technological form, involves commodification and a recognition that media forms have a value. An example of how both symbolic and economic valorizations can be involved at once is 'samizdat', the Russian word for self-publishing that has been incorporated into other languages to designate the dissemination, at times clandestinely, of literature disapproved of or banned by the government. After a decade of almost total freedom of speech in Russia following the dissolution of the Soviet Union in 1991, the state began to tighten its control over the Russian media significantly. In recent years, people have consequently turned to a digital samizdat – the heavily politicized Runet (the Russian-language sector of cyberspace), which had a monthly audience in 2013 of 63 million (www.gemius.com). The political communication that circulates on the Runet has symbolic value – as does the network itself. But it is also a commoditized space with economic value. According to the Association of Communication Agencies, the online advertising market in Russia rose 40 per cent in 2010 to 26.7 billion roubles, the equivalent of £580 million or $940 million. Companies entering the Russian social media market learned to 'poach' leading bloggers (Rozhnov 2011). In effect, this turns media actors, known for their symbolic capital, into commodities, or gives them 'economic' as well as 'symbolic' valorization, to use Thompson's terminology. The different forms of valorization can be completely entangled, posing an empirical challenge to media scholars and students.

Another characteristic of mass communication, according to Thompson (1995: 18) is that it 'extends the availability of symbolic forms in time and space'. Other scholars than the medium theorists have given some thought to how the advent of broadcasting changed people's relationship to space, and not least the space of politics. First radio, then television, made it possible for people living in different parts of the country to experience events that were taking place far away – events that unfolded in public, but which were followed from the privacy of the home (Couldry & McCarthy 2004; Scannell 1996; Williams 1974/2003).

To be able to speak of mass communication, in Thompson's theory, the symbolic forms must be publicly circulated. But mass communication is also characterized by a 'structured break' between the production of media messages and their reception, i.e. the flow of messages. Thompson argues that people on the receiving end have limited or 'strictly circumscribed' possibilities of intervening in or contributing to the processes in which the messages and symbolic forms in these flows are produced. Production, he writes, takes place in the absence of input or 'cues' from receivers. The audience or public has relatively little power, and readers and viewers are 'left to their own devices'.

Thompson's account of the media and modernity has become a classic, and for good reason: few others have so meticulously dissected the complex of components, dimensions and processes concealed by the seemingly innocent word 'media'. He does not seek to describe conditions prevailing in the early 1990s, when the book was written, but a historical development dating back centuries. As such, his theory could be expected to be reasonably durable. In some ways it is, but in other respects, technological developments of the past two decades have rendered some of his claims problematic.

After a shelflife of approximately seventy years, the term 'mass communication' has become inappropriate (Simonson 2010). It has long been burdened with unfortunate associations, because the word 'mass' harkens back to the problems highlighted by the pessimistic theorists of the Frankfurt School, who saw people as ideological dupes of political propaganda and of the greed of media industries (to be discussed in more depth in chapter 5). Whether or not 'mass' has ever been an accurate adjective, and whatever one's ideological take might be, the rise of niche marketing and replacement of broadcasting with 'narrowcasting' made the notion of mass communication outdated, if not irrelevant. But it is perhaps the digital revolution and explosion of social media, rather than economic forces, that pose the most serious challenge to Thompson's account.

The 'moment of accelerated change' which we are said to be experiencing has brought with it multiple interfaces, an altered relationship between the recipients of media messages and those seeking to benefit from their commodification (such as advertisers), and in many countries the restriction of the purview of broadcasters that once enjoyed a monopoly (Urrichio 2009: 61). Social media can be thought of as cultural processes (Williams 1974/2003), because they are interactive and perpetually updatable rather than fixed (Booth 2010). Their processual nature is captured by the notion of 'Web 2.0', described by O'Reilly as being a way of making people part of a 'global brain' (Sreedharan et al. 2011), but is also discernible in the impact of Twitter. Five years after the micro blog was launched in 2006, over 70 million tweets (messages of no more than 140 characters) were being sent daily. Its contribution to the processual nature of current media forms stems from the fact that there are always many people using Twitter, especially at major events, making fact-checking possible. Social media – both in their form and in their use – render profoundly problematic Thompson's claims that mass communication involves a structured break between the producers and receivers of media messages, and that receivers can contribute little input to the production and dissemination of information.

So much for this potted conceptual history, and its discontents. In the chapters that follow, an attempt will be made to avoid referring to 'the media' in general terms or in the singular, and instead to be specific about which aspect of the phenomenon (or phenomena) is in focus, be it a given medium or media form, media institution, media actor or media text. Users of this book (in itself a text which, it is to be hoped, has both symbolic and economic as well as pedagogical value) are encouraged to do likewise. But when doing so, it is important to bear in mind that even these specifications are generalizations of sorts, given claims that we live and operate in a 'convergence culture' (Jenkins 2006, 2007) in which the borders between different media forms, institutions, actors and texts have become hopelessly blurred. There are good reasons for heeding Chadwick's call to think of these, and the politics with which they interact, in terms of hybridity. In the intellectual forays of chapters to come, there is cause to follow his advice and think less in terms of 'either/or' and more in terms of 'not only, but also' (Chadwick 2011: 10). This applies not least when thinking about what for a while were termed 'old' and 'new' media.

Making comparisons

Distinctions between 'old' and 'new', and between media forms, institutions, actors and texts, are not the only ones to have become blurred. Distinctions between the various phenomena that political and other social scientists study have also grown fuzzier as globalization proceeds apace. As Beck argues, it is no longer sufficient to approach the task of understanding society through the portal of one's own country. Comparative analysis is required, between different national and political cultures, and across the local/national/global interface.

Gunaratne (2007) suggests that researchers compare communicative interconnections between the many subsystems within a single 'living system' (for example, a nation-state), several living systems (for example, the nation-states constituting the European Union) or 'lower hierarchical levels' (interaction between journalists and local politicians, for example, or in Scotland, the Rio de la Plata or the Maghreb). He maintains that it is unsatisfactory to study communication in the world system without considering the nested hierarchy of national societies beneath it, as the whole is more than the sum of the parts (Gunaratne 2007: 268). But the opposite is arguably true as well. It is becoming increasingly difficult to understand what happens in national settings without paying attention to communicative practices that transcend them.

Hallin and Mancini have demonstrated how dangerous it is to make generalizations even about media institutions within the same political union, given the distinctly different traditions governing the interaction between political systems and media cultures. Their argument (to be presented more fully in chapter 3) is that continental European media systems fit uneasily in the largely Anglo-Saxon accounts of how media and politics interact, and in their classic anthology of 2004 (updated and extended in 2011) they introduce alternative versions more suited to different settings.

A conceptual repertoire developed by the socio-cultural anthropologist Arjun Appadurai has been drawn on when making comparisons across institutions and actor categories. Appadurai (1996) argues that globalization should be seen as consisting of five scapes: financial, technological, ethno/migrations, ideological and media. These scapes are thought to be both related to and distinct from each other, in that they have their own separate dynamics. Scholars have found this a useful idea because states may have, or acquire, more power in one scape than another. It also makes it possible to deal with developments that mean media systems can be characterized both by state intervention and by conformity to the rules of the global capitalist economy.

In a similarly comparative frame of mind, Norris and Inglehart (2009) argue that national societal values intervene in the 'cosmopolitan flows of information' washing over borders. These culturally distinct 'firewalls' affect the extent to which different countries become integrated into the cosmopolitan flow. The firewall metaphor is helpful when analysing the contraints imposed by media technologies and institutions on the dissemination of symbolic forms, to use Thompson's terminology. The result of action taken by Chinese authorities to control the flow of digital communication, for example, has been referred to as the 'Great Firewall' (Curtin 2010). Straubhaar points out that actors like the BRIC nations (Brazil, Russia, India and China) are emerging global media powers that have more clout in certain contexts than others, and has made a compelling case for the need 'to disentangle what is national, what is global and what is perhaps most clearly seen as transnational'. He calls for comparisons that attend to how such media powers build on a strong home base, as well as on an important regional or cultural–linguistic-market one (Straubhaar 2010: 258–9). Parameswaran also emphasizes the importance of finding ways to understand 'the crisscrossing, converging, and sometimes colliding, historical and political contingencies that shape the contours of global and local media, even in neighbouring countries' (Parameswaran 2010: 288).

How then should the task of comparing media–political interactions in different settings be approached? Systems theory can be revisited, as suggested by Gunaratne; survey data used that reveal differences between the values of individuals in different countries, as by Norris and Inglehart; or consideration given to how economic and political actors promote and undermine each other's work in media capitals or regional contexts, as Straubhaar and Parameswaran encourage. Hallin and Mancini's analytical framework can also be used to compare journalistic traditions and media institutions in different countries according to their degree of commercialization, autonomy from political pressures, professional ethos and so on (of which more in chapters 3 and 4).

A given interaction could also be addressed using questions first posed in the Preface. What's the problem? Is it understanding the relative influence of global economic trends and how they are tempered by national traditions, or by constraints imposed by the state? Or the inapplicability of prevailing models, based on western values but deployed as if universal, to the practice of journalism in, say, Africa (Shaw 2009)? Or the trouble the Hungarian government ran into when trying to enact a restrictive new media law in 2011, opposed by European officials who said it ran counter to the democratic values of the EU? Whose problem is it (the Hungarian government's or the EU officials'?). And should the problem be understood as something qualitatively new, or the latest development in a situation that has prevailed for some time?

Continuity and change

Many questions arise in the wake of changed circumstances. What are the general features of continuity and change in the relationship between journalistic and political 'fields' (to use Bourdieu's term)? And what about changes in the relationship between stakeholders – between media actors and those who wield political power, on the one hand, and between media actors and media users (audiences and publics) on the other?

Some time ago, Stevenson (1999) asked how best to characterize the relationship between the practice of politics and a society that is increasingly 'symbolic'. One way of answering is to pick up the threads unravelled above and continue thinking about what technological change has done to space. Couldry (leaning on Henri Lefebvre) has written that all social and cultural change involves transformations of 'social space'. With the expansion of space that came with broadcasting came the expansion of experience, and people found themselves inhabiting a mediated referential world which was qualitatively new. Television, while embedded in the domestic space of the home, brought faraway things into focus (literally 'seeing far', at least in German). Over time, and with lightning speed in recent years, this referential space has expanded and become mobile. The world now fits in our pocket, in the tiny screen that follows us to school, to work, to the beach and to the revolution, with apps that bring us our friends, old television programmes, our internet bank, and a live news feed from Damascus. The space that was once simple, restricted and homogeneous has become hybrid, multilayered, heterogeneous and specialized (Couldry 2008: 385; see also Chadwick 2011; Gurevitch et al. 2009; Meyrowitz 2009; Urrichio 2009).

A distinction that is becoming increasingly blurred, in the wake of technological change and the freer flow of information, is the one between media and democracy (which is not identical to the one between media and politics). Another evolution that has already been mentioned involves 'the people formerly known as the audience', who have been the focus of much media research, and who in the guise that has interested political scientists could be called 'the people formerly known as members of the public'.

C. W. Mills famously defined 'the public' in contrast to the 'mass'. For a public to exist, according to his conception, there should be a reasonably even balance between the number of people expressing opinions and the number on the receiving end of those views. Communication flows must be structured in such a way that it is possible to respond immediately and effectively to opinions vented in public, and opinion formed in such communicative exchanges should readily find an outlet in effective action. Finally, the institutions of government and of those in authority should not penetrate the public, which is more or less autonomous in its operations (Mills 1956/2000).

Whatever they are to be called (and by corollary, whatever role they are conceived as playing in the media–politics interface), 'ordinary' people's relationships with elites and with 'traditional' media actors are changing, and roles are being recast, because of the new practices in which they are engaging. 'Sofalizing' and 'two-screening' are among these. The terms refer to the online activity around television content that takes place on a companion device connected to the internet, such as a laptop, iPad or smartphone. The industry has become aware of the fact that people continue to use the television to get television content (which is shared), while engaging in interaction about that content and other things through social media activities (which are often private, or at least protected by the user, as anyone with a teenage daughter will know). Two-screening means that social media are not making live television obsolete, it has been argued. They are making it essential. People throughout the developed world are engaging in 'social TV', characterized by a 'powerful relationship' between television and social media (Rippon 2011; Thinkbox 2011). The phenomenon of digital storytelling is another example of people's adaptation to new media forms, and one that poses an additional challenge to Thompson's claim that the structured nature of communication flows means that we have 'strictly circumscribed' possibilities for contributing to the processes in which messages and symbolic flows are produced and circulated in public. The media practices of ordinary media users are thus forcing adaptation on the part of political elites, media actors and the media industry – and in the thinking of scholars who study their interaction.

Politics on street and screen

The 'global village' is an oft-invoked metaphor for a world that evolving media forms and practices have turned into a community in which everyone is within reach, and whose activities are visible to all. The term was coined in the early 1960s by McLuhan, who thought that 'cool' or electronic media (especially television) were returning people to a shared culture that resembled that of the village. Half a century later, the 'global' part of the metaphor is still a futuristic vision, for while technological developments may well have rendered the globe a single site rather than a collection of far-flung countries and continents, not everyone has a berth in the village. The number of internet users rose from 10 million in 1993 to 665 million in 2003, but there were fewer than 2 million computers in the less developed countries by then. Granted, things have changed in the last decade. By 2011 there were 2 billion internet subscribers and 5 billion mobile phone users worldwide, and more than half of them were in developing nations, according to Hamadoun Toure, head of the UN telecommunication agency. But the highest density of online surfers in the population continued to be concentrated in Europe, the Americas and Russia – despite the surge in the number of users in the Asia/Pacific region to 857 million, the mobile phone revolution in Africa, and the high density of digitally connected people in the Arab world.[1] And with this, still grasping the portkey of the Arab Spring, we found ourselves landing in a 'scape' whose contours are shaped by parallel and mutually reinforcing changes in media and politics.

The ongoing struggle between the people who took to the streets of the Arab world in 2011 and their rulers has reflected differences over the most desirable form of government, widespread unemployment and corruption. But it has also – significantly – been a struggle for control over information. Facebook was hailed by many as a catalyst for the uprisings. It was on Facebook that the video showing Bouazizi burning himself to death was posted, and via Facebook that subsequent demonstrations were organized (Freedland 2011). Soon after the first protests began in Tunisia on 10 December 2010, the government stepped up its habitual website blocking, and began harvesting passwords and user names of bloggers, reporters, political activists and protesters (Anderson 2011). Egyptian authorities subjected journalists to arrest and physical attacks, began jamming mobile phone communications wherever protesters gathered, and blocked Twitter. When television crews were banned from filming at Tahrir Square – the epicentre of the Egyptian protests – on 25 January 2011, correspondents on the ground filed reports by phone and then used the Cribble Live service to convert them to MP3 audio files and publish them before they could be blocked (Gahran 2011). Hundreds of thousands of tweets about events in and around Tahrir Square were sent out in the course of a few intensive days in late January and early February 2011. Twitter was a unique tool for channelling dissatisfaction and mobilizing opposition by disseminating information to a large number of people both on Tahrir Square and in the rest of the region and world beyond. When the Egyptian authorities ordered leading internet suppliers to shut down Facebook, Twitter and even the internet itself between 27 January and 2 February, supporters outside Egypt created provisional networks with the help of telephone chains and SMS messages. But soon, when the internet was up again, protesters were confronted by another problem, which had also dogged their counterparts in Tehran and Moldova in 2009 and would continue to plague activists throughout the Arab world in the coming years: the army had created its own Twitter account, and was using it for counter-information (Barkman 2011).

A few months after the uprisings began, Google's chairman, Eric Schmidt, warned that the use of social media by Arab democracy movements could result in harder crackdowns on internet freedoms in the region and elsewhere. As the technology grows more pervasive and as 'the citizenry becomes completely wired', governments stepped up their efforts to regulate the internet as they did with television (BBC 2011b). Schmidt was speaking from professional experience: Google had been in regular conflict with the Chinese state for years over its attempts to limit public access to its services, and Google executive Wael Ghonim had been arrested by Egyptian authorities during the February 2011 uprising. Three years later, in the post-Snowden context, Schmidt's concern was to reassure users in democracies as well as repressive states that government control of the internet would not encroach further into their private lives.

What conceptual issues do these developments raise, how can they be researched empirically, and what avenues of discussion do they open for the rest of this book?

An example of the difficulties involved in containing politics in national settings, and something to think about: whose responsibility was it to rescue the 200 Nigerian schoolgirls kidnapped by Boko Haram in May 2014? Protesters in New York suggest it was a matter for the world, and not just the Nigerian government. Photograph: M. Stan Reaves / Corbis.

The Arab Spring is a reminder that political change and changes in media technology are companions, and that such changes pose a challenge to journalists and scholars as well as to political elites. It is a compelling illustration of the fact that politics can now be contained in national settings only with difficulty – of how local occurrences and problems can become global media events. As to the question of where politics takes place in a globalizing world, the Arab Spring answer is: on the street and on the screen.

To think about

The Arab Spring is a portkey that allows comparisons of media–politics relations on different dimensions and between different stakeholders. It involved relations between national governments and their publics – relations that had strong communicative elements. It involved connections between those publics (comprised of activists, 'ordinary people' and smartphone-wielders) and global publics who were obviously in mind when tweets and blogs were posted in English – connections with which Silverstone would have felt more comfortable than Splichal, given that the addressee was amorphous and what was required of that collective recipient of the communicative action even less clear. But through this communication, and the live coverage provided by national and global networks, the events of the Arab Spring involved some sort of relation between the people on the streets of the Arab world and political elites in other countries and in transnational fora, who called on Ben Ali, Mubarak, Gaddafi, Assad and Saleh to relinquish power. One thing to think about is how politics in a globalizing world can be found in the development of universal values and norms (like freedom of the press and of assembly) and the spread of democracy to places it has not previously existed.

It is also to be found in the growing awareness of the world as a single place. A football match experienced simultaneously at different ends of the earth was cited earlier as an example of the time–space compression that is characteristic of globalization. The moments when the eyes of the world were focused on Tahrir Square represent another enactment of this, and an opportunity to reflect on what media technology is doing to social space and our relation to political events. Another thing to think about is which other examples and moments can be used to illustrate and understand this phenomenon.

There are, it has been noted, different versions of democracy in the world. The people who followed the Arab Spring could no more fit in Tahrir Square or Pearl Roundabout than into the *agora* of ancient Athens, but new media technology allowed billions around the world to be there in real time, if not in real space. While they will only ever have indirect accounts of Pericles' justification for the Peloponnesian War, they could follow, with Egyptians on the ground, the beleaguered President Mubarak's address to the nation. What does that mean for democracy in a world where technology transcends borders but people still only get to vote in national (or at most European) elections?[2]

Eyewitness accounts disseminated through cyberspace (or, as Thompson would put it, the generalized diffusion of information and symbolism) about the crackdown, and violence against protesters and demonstrators, put civil liberties, intrinsic to the notion of liberal democracy, in the limelight. Few who followed the events of the Arab Spring were likely to think that the right of Tunisians, Egyptians, Bahrainians and others to freedom of speech and assembly were not on the agenda. What began to evolve in the wake of the protests of 2011 was a hybrid in political, Chadwickian, terms. Democracy may or may not be crowdsourced, but the global network of social movements that emerged so spectacularly, and its communicative practices, certainly problematized the connection between the repressetarian states of the *ancien régime* and the citizens of the Arab world and other places to which democratic uprisings spread. How is control to be conceived, and what sort is desirable, in such a world?

What will the newsrooms of places like Tunisia look like tomorrow, and how much difference will a year or two make (metaphorically speaking)? What communicative spaces will remain open and which will close? Cottle (2006b: 428) cautions that sustained analysis is needed of how media actors adopt different 'performative stances' through time when responding – reflexively – to mediated crises and conflicts. This is something else to think about.

Another is what happens when revolutionary events unfold on television, in real time – what Dayan and Katz (1992) have famously called 'the live broadcasting of history'. This is more than a question of journalistic strategies for filling a slot when there is a news blackout, deciding whether to use crowdsourced footage that cannot be independently verified, or indeed how to report at all when being deliberately targeted by security forces. At stake is rather a larger epistemological question pertaining to truth claims in 'snowballing narratives', and the ambivalent role of media professionals who both observe and construct events that they are inescapably part of. There will be an opportunity to think more about this when the role of journalists, and their perspective on the media–politics relationship, is in focus in chapter 4.

The public sphere that became engaged in following and discussing the Arab Spring can be thought of as transnational or 'postnational'. The addressees of communications relating these events could reasonably be described as 'an amorphous mix of public and private transnational powers that is neither easily identifiable nor rendered accountable' (Fraser 2007: 19). One more thing to think about is what this might entail. The notion of the public sphere, and how it is being challenged by the sort of developments outlined above, is a key concern of the next chapter.

2 Power in Media Societies

In 2007, WikiLeaks founder Julian Assange and his associates had a problem.[1] They had set up a non-profit media organization dedicated to bringing information 'of ethical, political and historical significance' to the attention of the public while keeping the identity of their sources anonymous. They had announced their determination to reveal injustices that had been kept from public view by governments around the world. But the public was not getting the information. The scoops were going largely unnoticed by mainstream media.

By 2010, that had changed. Professional journalists acknowledged that WikiLeaks had become a source they needed to monitor regularly. And it was someone else who had a problem – the US government. WikiLeaks became a household name when it posted a video filmed from an American helicopter gunship over Baghdad during the Iraq War. The 17–minute version of *Collateral Murder*, which showed a group of civilians and two Reuters employees being gunned down by the American soldiers, whose conversation made it sound like they were playing a computer game, went viral on YouTube. This disclosure differed from the climate leaks in that it was edited by WikiLeaks: if nothing else, the name framed its contents in a way that sent a powerful political message, and the video release was widely seen as an attempt to set the global news agenda.

Worse was yet to come, from the perspective of political elites around the world, and in Washington in particular. A few months later, the Assange team leaked documents relating to five years of the war in Afghanistan to three leading publications, whose journalists were by now working together with the whistleblower: the British *Guardian*, the American *New York Times* and Germany's *Der Spiegel*. Before releasing the documents to the general public, Assange asked the Pentagon for help in removing the names of people who could be physically harmed by the disclosures, but was turned down. In November 2010, WikiLeaks and leading media in five countries (this time including *El País* in Spain and *Le Monde* in France) simultaneously published the first 200 of over 250,000 diplomatic cables from US embassies throughout the world. What came to be known as the 'Cablegate' material included documentation of widespread corruption in the Tunisian government, and many observers thought the disclosure was a contributing factor in the ousting of Tunisian President Ben Ali.

'Cablegate 2' followed in September 2011, as related in the Preface. The fact that no attempt had been made this time to remove the names of the people who could be harmed by the disclosures incurred the censure of former allies in the mainstream media. These were not the only disclosures and would not be the last, although the 'cause' was hampered by internal dissension, economic difficulties, and Assange's decision to become a fugitive rather than stand trial for rape in Sweden. WikiLeaks continued to accept 'restricted or censored material of political, ethical, diplomatic

Wikileaks founder Julian Assange, at New Media Days 09, 17 November 2009.
Photograph: Peter Erichsen, www.newmediadays.com.

or historical significance' uploaded to the site's dropbox, which was said to be easy to use and to provide 'military-grade encryption protection'.

> Submitting documents to our journalists is protected by law in better democracies. For other countries, the electronic drop box is there to offer help and protection. (wikileaks.org)

As well as posing a problem to governments across the world, and to its journalistic collaborators, WikiLeaks posed a scholarly problem to those interested in understanding the media–politics relationship, and how that is changing as a result of developments in media technology. How are phenomena like this organization to be understood, and sense made of the developments that brought it into being, its zenith and its nadir?

In this chapter, it will be suggested that one way forward is to link empirical analysis of the actions of such players (and the technology which makes them so influential) to scholarship on the political roles traditionally ascribed to media actors and institutions, and on power. Apart from those mentioned above, the stakeholders in this chapter are people and organizations who seek to protect freedom of information, on the one hand, and actors less enthusiastic about the upsurge in transparency movements on the other – the political elites of polities characterized by porous national borders, who are the focus of chapter 3.[2]

Understanding power

Carpentier (2011) has identified two basic models of power: the causal and the strategic. The former builds on Weber, who defined power as related to the likelihood that one actor in a social relationship is in a position to get its way, even in the face of resistance, and on Dahl's linear-causal model of power (A can get B to do something that B would not otherwise do). Bachrach & Baratz drew attention to power-wielding among elites working in backrooms, working where the public could not scrutinize, and thus contest, their agendas. To gain analytical purchase on this, they developed the idea of a 'second dimension' of media power (Bachrach & Baratz 1962). Lukes (1974/2005) added a third dimension, by drawing attention to the ability of the powerful to shape people's preferences without them being aware of it.

The strategic model, associated with theorists like Foucault, treats power as something that is practised rather than possessed. Power relations, in this view, are multidirectional rather than linear, and can move (Carpentier 2011: 140). Resistance is thus part of the exercise of power, rather than external to it or helpless in the face of it – an idea that will be returned to in chapter 5. Related to this is the notion of discursive power (which in turn is related to concepts such as representation, ideology, hegemony and meaning, which will feature later in the book). Gramsci, with his notion of hegemony, and theorists like Raymond Williams, E. P. Thompson and Stuart Hall, around whom the field of cultural studies emerged, seek to unveil the power relations responsible for the majority of people consenting to the inequalities imposed on them by the dominant class. Meaning is central to the way Laclau and Mouffe theorize the power of discourse, which is understood as a structure which contains meaning, but within which meaning is constantly negotiated and thus constantly under construction. Theoretical ideas about discourse and representation allow for human agency – the possibility that people can develop strategies that mean they need not remain fixed in the power relations in which their class or economic situation has positioned them.

J. B. Thompson, encountered in the last chapter, used the notion of 'symbolic power' to designate the power of media actors to 'intervene in the course of events, to influence the actions of others and indeed to create events, by means of the production and transmission of symbolic forms' (Thompson 1995: 195). Livingstone views media power as an interactive process. It is not something that only the producers of messages possess: the power to make meaning out of those messages resides in the people who receive them (Livingstone 2005: 42). Couldry (2005: 194) theorizes it as 'a society-wide phenomenon' which everyone is involved in sustaining; something to be found on all levels, 'in ownership structures, hierarchies and political alliances of media corporations, as well as in access and reception' as Biltereyst and Meers (2011: 430) put it.

Media power: the three roles

'The media' (in their various incarnations) can be said to play three broad political roles, or sets of roles. The ability to perform these functions well is thought to be an indication of the health of the polity, not least when it comes to the communicative rights of the members of a given political community. These are also broad conceptualizations of media power. In chapter 4, these roles will be broken down and different perceptions of them discussed in more detail, but it is helpful to relate what is to follow to these more general categorizations.

The first role: information-relayer

Fundamental to communicative rights is the right to information. The first political role that media actors play is that of 'information relayer'.

In early accounts of the media–politics relationship, it was argued that the press was needed so that information about the running of the country could be relayed from those charged with governing it to the people they governed. The people were, in turn, expected to partake of the information so that they could fulfil their civic duties and make the right choice on election day (given that there was one).

A number of metaphors have been used over the years to describe how journalists and the media institutions they work for can go about playing this role. One is 'gate-keeping'. First coined by White in 1950, the concept has been built on, criticized and tweaked by several generations of media researchers. The idea behind the metaphor is that there is a sea of events outside the newsroom, that will not all fit into the daily newspaper, radio bulletin or television news broadcast. Gatekeepers are positioned at different points in the flow of information, letting some events through, first to news agencies, then to newsrooms, while excluding others as less newsworthy. In the newsroom, additional gatekeepers decide which events (now taking form as telegrams from wire services) will get into the paper or programme, and which will make it onto the first page or into the headlines. This function is both essential (if

The gatekeeper in the age of global news: the Al Jazeera English (AJE) newsroom in Doha, November 2011. The news organization was founded with the intention of reversing the flow and challenging Western gatekeeping values. Photograph: Witty Llama, Wikimedia Commons.

newspapers are going to be kept to readable length, and affordable, and news broadcasts within the confines of an hour or less) and problematic. Particularly when many people are injured or killed in natural catastrophes or acts of violence, assessments of relative worth have been called into question. One quantitative study of television reporting of natural disasters showed that

> the globe is prioritized so that the death of one Western European equaled three Eastern Europeans equaled 9 Latin Americans equaled 11 Middle Easterners equaled 12 Asians. (Adams 1986)

Why is this so and why do media gatekeepers allow saturation coverage of some events (such as the attack on US cities on 11 September 2001, the Asian tsunami of 2004 or Hurricane Sandy in 2012) but leave the gate only open a crack on others (like the war in South Sudan, famine in Niger, or floods, typhoons and earthquakes in Pakistan, the Philippines and China)?

The metaphor of the 'agenda-setter' has also been used to describe the information-relaying role. In a classic article, McCombs and Shaw (1972) hypothesized that 'the media' set the political agenda, and influence the salience of attitudes towards political issues. This did not mean that journalists told people what to think, but rather what to think about, as put in one of the first accounts of media influence on foreign policy (Cohen 1963). One dimension of this first role, then, is the ability, or perhaps responsibility, of media actors to draw public attention to issues that should be on the political agenda. Media workers in Sweden have campaigned for years to get the foreign ministry to pressure the Eritrean government into releasing the Eritrean-born Swedish journalist Dawit Isaak, who was arrested in 2001 for demanding democratic reforms, and when this book went to press was still languishing in jail. At regular intervals, Swedish newspapers publish a photograph of Isaak in a prominent place, and their websites sport banners indicating how many days, hours, minutes and seconds he has been imprisoned, with reports asking critical questions about what the foreign ministry is doing to secure his release. This is one example of agenda-setting that relates directly to the media–politics relationship.

Another familiar metaphor is the 'watchdog'. Apart from conveying information from the elites at the top to the people at the bottom, the ideal expressed with this term is for journalists and news organizations to act as a check on powerful institutions and individuals. The UK parliamentary expenses scandal of 2009 is a classic example, as is the legendary Watergate scoop of *Washington Post* reporters Carl Bernstein and Bob Woodward, which ended with the impeachment of Republican President Nixon. Since then, the suffix 'gate' has been used to signal the misuse of political power, and ensuing media scandals in which watchdogs snarl and bite at the heels of perpetrators. As will be seen in subsequent chapters (4 and 10), journalists in many political contexts behave as watchdogs only at great personal risk.

All three of these metaphors emerged in liberal democratic settings, and have in particular been used in accounts of press–politics relations in the US. There are cultural variations, even between liberal democracies. One scholar adjusted the watchdog metaphor somewhat, after having established that British journalists perceived themselves to be not just watchdogs, but bloodhounds, their career choice influenced by their being drawn to the excitement of the hunt. The role perceptions of

The watchdog. Leading Spanish Socialist Angel Luna arrives at a court in Valencia to face bribery charges and a waiting press pack, 22 November 2010. Photograph: Xaume Olleros / Corbis.

their German counterparts, on the other hand, resulted in Köcher (1986) concluding that a more apt moniker was 'missionaries'.

The second role: arena

The second political role is a service provided not so much by media actors as by media institutions and forms. Media outlets (newspapers, channels and websites) are thought to promote the pluralism that is necessary for healthy polities by providing a place for different actors to be heard (Lilleker 2006; Price 1996). Here, 'the media' refers to a site. It is the place, as Dahlgren (1995) so nicely put it, 'where public sphering gets done'.

The concept of the public sphere comes from a book written by the German philosopher and sociologist Jürgen Habermas in the 1960s that became influential beyond the German-speaking world when translated into English years later. What Habermas (1962/1989) had in mind was a hypothetical space between the private realm of the family and the realm of the state – a space inhabited by citizens who shared ideas and information that mattered to their political choices. Essential to this ideal are public media that provide a platform for the expression of free speech, widely accessible to citizens and interest groups (Davis 2007: 17). In this second role, media actors host and curate a space for rational debate on the issues and policies affecting society and the political community. The concept is now often used in such a way that it seems media outlets have become the public sphere, as opposed to a resource for citizens to use when discussing political affairs in that sphere.

Political theorists argue that a public sphere and a sovereign power must correlate with each other. This is because of the normative requirement that the public sphere serve both as a forum for citizens' deliberations, and as a medium for the mobilization of public opinion (Splichal 2009: 394). Conceptions of the public also mean that this sphere should be free of interference from political authorities, as explained in chapter 1. Those authorities do interfere, though, and sometimes the interference is well meant. The EU has long promoted the development of a European public sphere, in which feelings of affinity can be nurtured and the democratic deficit of the EU rendered – well, less deficient. There are, it is lamented, 'few meeting places where Europeans from different Member States can get to know each other and address issues of common interest' (EC 2006).

A number of scholars have argued that if the same European or EU news is covered in different media outlets in Europe at the same time, it would be possible to say that a European public sphere existed (see, for example, Trenz 2004: 292). According to this view, the European public sphere is a 'pluralistic ensemble' of issue-oriented publics and, like Brigadoon in the old musical, the sphere comes into being when all of those publics think and talk about the same thing at the same time. Sceptics argue that it would be necessary for the same news agenda to prevail in all European languages, and for people to think of themselves first and foremost as EU citizens, and only secondarily as members of nations, for a European public sphere to exist (Schlesinger 2007, 2003). Others point out that if a common language, a common nationwide media system and citizens with a common identity were preconditions for a national public sphere, then few states could be said to have one.

The debate about a European public sphere, and the process of Europeanization of which it is a manifestation, are good examples of globalized politics, and of the complications that arise when the borders between familiar political entities and media roles become blurred. Policy elites have found it problematic that there is a lack of European media (something different from national media in European countries), and that the European media that do exist are not up to the mark. Even if some journalistic responses to the Eurocrisis complicated this claim (see, for example, the joint publication in 2012 by the *Guardian, El País, Gazeta, La Stampa, Suddeutsche Zeitung* and *Le Monde* of a series called 'europa' aimed at helping Europeans understand each other)[3], Schlesinger is not alone in his scepticism (Axford & Huggins 2007; Brüggemann 2005; Frydén Bonnier 2007; Kleinsteuber 2001; Machill et al. 2006; Semetko et al. 2000; Splichal 2006). Elections to the European Parliament often give sceptics ammunition, as campaigns tend to be matters of domestic rather than European politics, election coverage in most countries is correspondingly national in focus, and turnout is poor. At the same time, increasing numbers of Europeans (in EU- and non-EU-member states alike) follow the Eurovision Song Contest when it is broadcast live on television, and the number of votes cast for the 'best' melody continues its steady climb to unprecedented levels. When the contestants took to the stage in the finals in Copenhagen in 2014, more than 170 million people watched the same event at the same time in the same communicative space.[4] The Eurovision Song Contest is a reminder that politics has a cultural dimension, which is overlooked at one's peril. This insight has a bearing on the third media role.

The third role: culture-bearer

Culture-bearer is an unwieldy moniker for the agents that discursively weave together the different threads that are the fabric of multicultural societies. As well as weavers, these actors can be thought of as translators, who ensure that people in a given political community have a shared conceptual vocabulary, and have a common repertoire of values and understandings on which political action can be based and decisions justified. In some countries, journalists consider it their job (and are expected) to act as nation-builders. This third role relates to the *ethnos* first mentioned in chapter 1 – the imagined community of membership and affiliation.

This third role is a profoundly political one, although not always evident, because it is ideological and concealed in discourse. This kind of power resides in the stories we are told about ourselves in media and popular culture texts – the powerful discourses that shape everyday life. Rather than attending to what goes on in the Kremlin, on Parliament Hill or in the Palacio Nacional, scholars interested in what is designated here as the third role look to everyday discourses and practices to see how phenomena like television provide 'materials to be worked on' when people construct their identities (Barker 1999: 7; see also Couldry 2001, 2008; Davis 2007; Schirato & Webb 2003; and Stevenson 2003).

Television in particular, despite the incursion of social media, continues to help 'define' society insofar as it gives us the language and symbolic repertoire to help us make sense of, and agree on, the terms in which we speak about the world around us (Orgad 2012; Robertson 2010a; Stevenson 2003:11; Street 2001). Before television, radio too played such a role. According to 'media archaeologist' Urrichio, radio was developed for specific purposes, providing 'the electronic nervous system for the nation – its publics and events – with the unspoken utopian or dystopian hope that all hearts would beat as one' (Urrichio 2009: 69). Concepts deployed by scholars interested in this sort of power, imbued in this sort of technology, include 'mediatized ritual' (Cottle 2006b) and 'media events' (Dayan & Katz 1992; Couldry et al. 2010).

While literature drawing on concepts associated with the first two roles – and in particular, that of information-relayer – assumes there is some sort of reality external to media texts, scholars interested in the third role make no such assumptions. Nor is it a coincidence that verbs like 'construct' pepper their writing. The point is not that journalists and the authors of other media texts about politics fabricate their stories (although there are, of course, some colourful examples of them doing so). The idea is, rather, that the narrative act itself – the work of putting events and processes into words, or pictures – results in such mediated stories meaning one thing rather than another. To paraphrase Cohen, media power may reside not in telling us what to think, or even just what to think about, but rather *how* to think about it. Technological developments, moreover, have made it increasingly difficult to distinguish between events that are external to the media, and their mediated existence. Making such analytical distinctions, or appreciating why they cannot be made, is a task that will be returned to in chapter 9, and the debate on mediatization.

Media roles and power in flux

Perhaps the most challenging aspect of technological change is encapsulated in the term 'convergence', which refers to not only the technological and economic merging of media forms and outlets, but also their organizational, systemic and structural coalescence (Marsden & Verhulst 1999). That said, references to convergence usually have to do with the technological changes that digitalization forces upon the media and communication industries (Herkman 2012: 371). Or, as one influential thinker put it,

> Media convergence is more than simply a technological shift. Convergence alters the relationship between existing technologies, industries, markets, genres, and audiences. Convergence alters the logic by which media industries operate and by which media consumers process news and entertainment. Keep this in mind: convergence refers to a process, not an endpoint. (Jenkins 2008: 15–16)

Given the task set in this book of assessing the degree of change as opposed to continuity, the question becomes: to what extent are the roles traditionally ascribed to media actors and institutions, and the power relations that go with them, changing under convergence?

Changing features of the information-relayer role

An example of the changing nature of the first, 'information-relayer' role is that practitioners of 'old' media are now using 'new' media, with the technologies facilitating those roles converging in hybrid systems. In 'old' media like newspapers, radio and television, there are physical limits to the time and space that can be taken up by stories of the political world. Once information is in digital form and disseminated on the internet, it is out of anyone's control, and there are no limits to cyberspace. This has serious consequences for the gatekeeping power of mainstream media organizations. Similarly, the work of the watchdog is being outsourced or, as it is sometimes put, democratized. An example of this is what occurred on a US subway in 2009. When rail transit officers shot and killed a man, several passengers recorded the event and uploaded the documentation to YouTube. The videos sparked protests and were used as evidence in the trial. In Sweden in 2013, a witness filmed while an unarmed, drunken man was set on by a police dog and sustained thirteen blows from a policewoman's baton. The witness sent the film to the country's largest newspaper, where it was published online and on paper, resulting in a public and political outcry. In the world of ubiquitous mobile phones and CCTV cameras, potential watchdogs are everywhere – for better or worse.

On a more general level, it can be said that a shift has occurred in the locus of information-relayal. A media system grounded in the network society has not only a centre, from which news flows (symbolized by a given country's Broadcasting House), but also a periphery, where information circulates spontaneously, without the need for amplification by mainstream media organizations (Katz & Scannell 2009). This does not mean that established media institutions, charged with playing the traditional roles outlined above, have abdicated or been forced off the pitch by new media players. It does, however, mean that they are losing ground (Dayan 2009,

2010). This affects the traditional media roles, the way they are played, and their impact (Antony & Thomas 2010).

In a similar vein, commentators like Rosen (2006) have written of a shift away from journalism as the production of news (or truths) towards journalism as the management of a process in which news emerges and is transformed over time (sometimes referred to as the 'democratization of truth'). Once a closed, linear process, the making of news has become 'cyclical' and transparent. News items are distributed as they emerge, and are altered continuously in collaboration with the consumers of that news.

The changing contours of the public sphere

There is a widespread view that the internet and related technologies could renovate 'the place where public sphering gets done'. It was mentioned above that Europeans are disinclined to take part in elections to the European Parliament but are enthusiastic about voting in the Eurovision Song Contest. The same applies to people the world over who pay (their telephone providers) to vote in the various national editions of *Idol* and *Star Academy*. Similarly, it is often remarked upon that in most countries in the twenty-first century, voters are apathetic, disillusioned and generally uninterested in conventional politics – but at the same time keen on blogging, keeping abreast of the news online, and networking (Papacharissi 2002, 2010). Globalization itself, it has been argued, gives rise to a new kind of public sphere, or at least the need for one. It has already been mentioned that, while policies formed, and decisions taken, at all levels in the globalized world have an impact on people's lives, citizens have had trouble finding a space to reflect on this collectively, and on suitable courses of action, beyond the framework of the nation-state. One strongly stated argument is that the internet is changing this, by increasing the 'feasibility of citizens' participation in public discourse beyond national boundaries' (Splichal 2009: 392). The idea is that a new kind of public sphere is taking shape under globalization that could improve on traditional national ones, by furnishing citizens with the tools and space to realize their personal right to communicate.

But there are problems. In conventional conceptualizations of public opinion, the state and the public act as clearly defined antagonists in the national public sphere. The 'public' of emerging transnational public spheres is not clearly defined, and it lacks an 'addressee' (the transnational counterpart to the state). Questions are thus being asked about how contemporary public spheres could effectively fulfil the democratic function set out in Habermas' original conception (Fraser 2007). If opinion is formed in a global public space about political problems shared across national borders – global warming, financial collapse, the civil liberties of fellow human beings born in other countries and so on – then who is to heed it, and in what forum?

Publicity or 'publicness', the defining principle of the public sphere, has itself been transformed, it is argued (Gurevitch et al. 2009: 170). This is a matter not just of technology, but also of economic imperatives. The newspaper, for example, is said to have been commodified in the late nineteenth century, and was transformed from a cultural organization to an industrial product, its valorization shifting from the symbolic to the economic, to use Thompson's terminology. Kant understood what has been translated as freedom of the press (or 'pen') to be freedom of the citizen to publish with the aid of the press, as opposed to the freedom of the publisher to make a profit. The commodification of the newspaper has thus been identified as a manifestation of the radical change in the nature of publicity that took place in the late nineteenth century. That nature is under constant construction. The earlier ideal of reasoned debate taking place in a setting outside the walls of the home has been overshadowed by the notion of publicity as ensuring that someone or something attracts a lot of attention, or information about a product (Splichal 2009: 403). The public of the public sphere is different from the public of public relations.

The 'third role' in flux

When it comes to strengthening the fabric of society, or perhaps ensuring that it does not unravel, it can be observed that propaganda, spectacle, information control, and the use of verbal and visual narratives to maintain social cohesion are distinctive features of the contemporary landscape. In some respects, this is familiar. Classic media events starring presidents swearing the oath of office, and heirs to European thrones on their way to the altar, have centuries-old precedents. The difference is that the pomp and circumstance are now followed live by millions of people, far from the capitals in which they take place. Katz & Scannell (2009) acknowledge that, even if the shift from centre to periphery reflects a parallel shift in power, the same traditional media, elites and opinion leaders continue to set the agenda and shape the discussions that take place in the public sphere. Gurevitch et al. (2009) have also concluded that the television–politics relationship that emerged in the 1960s is by and large that which continues to prevail in the digital era.

In other respects, this role is also in flux and many societies find themselves at a point of transition. In the same season as one of the aforementioned royal weddings (of Britain's Prince William to Kate Middleton) took place, violence spread from London, scene of the nuptuals, to other cities. The disturbances reflected how disaffected young Britons had become from the society that such spectacular events are meant to keep strong. A parallel fragmentation has taken place in the institutions relaying these events – i.e. the institutions whose role it is to maintain social cohesion. Broadcasting was characterized in earlier periods by media institutions at the centre that articulated grand narratives of the nation-state and the family. This has been replaced by more heterogeneous and hybrid media systems in which the periphery is comprised of networked audiences in possession of the communicative means of production and distribution (Gurevitch et al. 2009).

The phenomenon of WikiLeaks is symptomatic of the way traditional roles are changing, and an example of the empirical challenges posed to the theories of power and ideals about media roles that structure much scholarship in this field.

Making sense of WikiLeaks

WikiLeaks was unequivocal in its stance that transparency creates a better society, reduces corruption and strengthens democracy, not just when it comes to government actions, but in all institutions of society and in the corporate world as well (WikiLeaks 2010). As Assange argued:

> Transparency should be proportional to the power that one has. The more power one has, the greater the dangers generated by that power, and the more need for transparency. Conversely, the weaker one is, the more danger there is in being transparent. (quoted in Sifry 2011)

The 'second dimension' of power mentioned above refers to the ability of elites to work in back rooms and take action and make decisions away from the scrutinizing gaze of the public. It is precisely this sort of power that WikiLeaks challenges – the sort typically maintained by 'conspiratorial interactions among the political elite'. Sreedharan et al. (2011) have noted that the WikiLeaks antidote to this 'conspiracy' – mass leaking – bears a close resemblance to what has been called 'mass self-communication'.

The term is used by Castells in a work about communicative power in a society that is understood to be structured around digital networks, based on the exchange of information, and global. A key group of powerful actors in the network society is comprised of what Castells calls 'switchers', who control the connecting points between various strategic networks. They could, for example, control connections between political leadership, media, and technology networks and use this control to produce and spread particular political-ideological discourses (Castells 2009: 46). Discourses 'shape the public mind' via the networks that organize socialized communication, according to Castells. Through these networks, actors trying to change the way society works can launch alternative projects and publicize values that challenge the 'powers that be' and transform people's consciousness (2009: 53).

WikiLeaks can be thought of as a Castellian 'switcher'. In its heyday, it controlled strategic information obtained from sources in military (and other) networks; leaked it to media networks; and deployed it in a way that gave rise to a heavily politicized discourse. This political-ideological discourse undoubtedly changed many people's minds about the way the world works, or confirmed their distrust of established institutions. It certainly posed a symbolic and very real challenge to many political establishments. WikiLeaks exercised a qualitatively new form of power because its advanced technological infrastructure enables 'very small groups and even individuals to project substantial organizational power' (Chadwick 2011: 20). Information-relayer *par excellence* – gatekeeper, agenda-setter and watchdog are all appropriate metaphors here – WikiLeaks also formed an arena of sorts, and in the ideological discourse that arose in that arena, an 'us' crystallized in contradistinction to the 'others' who witheld information, attempted to shut down servers and put pressure on the organizations that served as intermediaries between WikiLeaks and the people who wanted to support its work, for example by donating funds through PayPal.

How exactly the relations between WikiLeaks and the mainstream news organizations it worked with are to be understood is a question that requires empirical analysis (as do a mapping of the pattern of power relations within WikiLeaks itself and the power plays that resulted in Assange's collaboration with Kremlin-backed channel Russia Today). Assange solved the problem that opened this chapter by initiating collaboration with professional journalists. When early scoops failed to garner the attention he and his associates had hoped for, collaboration with the *Guardian* in particular proved a solution. Edward Snowden turned to the same newspaper when he decided to let it be known that the US was spying on its own citizens and those of other states. This is a good illustration of the periphery–centre dynamic mentioned earlier, and of how news circulating in the periphery can continue to require amplification by established actors in the centre. Comparative research is needed here too, as it is clear that not all of the mainstream media outlets reacted in the same way to such behaviour. Some of the actors involved, powerful players in their own networks, claimed that WikiLeaks had always been treated as an outsider and that they had the upper hand throughout their 2010 collaboration. The executive editor of the *New York Times*, for example, said:

> we have treated Julian Assange and his merry band as a source . . . the relationship with sources is straightforward: You don't necessarily endorse their agenda, echo their rhetoric, take anything they say at face value, applaud their methods or, most important, allow them to shape or censor your journalism. (quoted in Chadwick 2011: 26)

And it is clear that, in its early years, WikiLeaks had no power over these established actors, who published its material in unspectacular ways, and without attributing it by name. But by 2011 the situation was reversed, and WikiLeaks published the 'Cablegate 2' documents without going through its mainstream partners. This time, the 'mass self-communication' did get the attention of the public.

The impact of WikiLeaks, as Chadwick writes in a rich and insightful piece, has much to do with new sorts of practices based on the convergence of 'new' and 'old' media. These integrative practices are indicative of a hybrid ecology in which professional investigative journalists combine forces with volunteer activists. The hybridization of 'established institutional power and distributed network power' is also in evidence (Chadwick 2011: 35). WikiLeaks describes itself as a media organization, but Chadwick suggests that it is more than that: it is a website, an e-mail list, a technological infrastructure, a publishing business, a lobby, a group of dedicated activists and a transnational network of hackers, among other things (Chadwick 2011: 21).

The WikiLeaks phenomenon is thus a portkey not only for making sense of changed roles and power relations, but also for dealing with the challenge of conceptualizing 'the media' themselves, continuing work begun in the last chapter. And it is a useful portkey to grasp when thinking about the 'public' part of the the 'public sphere' and how understandings and use of the notion of 'publicity' are changing with technological evolution and political praxis. Splichal urges us to retrace our steps, and use the notion of 'publicity' as it was originally intended – i.e. the personal right to communicate in public; surveillance of the public over government; and mediation between the state and civil society (Splichal 2009: 404). The radical transparency movement of which WikiLeaks was, for a few years at least, the most spectacular manifestation reinvents publicity in all these senses, and will keep political theorists, public sphere scholars – and hopefully ambitious students – busy for some time to come.

To think about

WikiLeaks raises empirical, theoretical and ethical questions. Were its disclosures – like those of Edward Snowden – acts of public service? How important is the watchdog role when seen in a context of radical transparency – what is the price of knowing what governments are doing and saying, and is it a reasonable price to pay?

Like WikiLeaks, the media–politics relationship in general involves a struggle for control over information. It has been said that soft power is out, and that the name of the game is now 'smart' power. Implicit in almost any discussion of power is not only how it is used, but also how it can be misused; not only what it can do for actors, but also how it works against actors who have unequal power resources. Another thing to think about is how different the relationship can look from the perspective of different stakeholders, and how the tension between the use and misuse of media power differs in different cultural settings.

Part Two reviews the perspectives of different sets of actors with different vantage points, and explores how media power entails different things on different dimensions of the media–politics relationship. Questions and concerns about power will also be returned to in subsequent chapters, not least in chapter 6, as networked politics have thrown a number of the issues related to media and activism into sharp relief. When stopping to think about where to look for politics in a decentred, globalizing world, it is instructive to reflect on where power is located in digital flows.

PART TWO

3 Political Elites

In May 2011, leading French politician Dominique Strauss-Kahn was arrested in the US in a blaze of negative publicity. His public disgrace resulted from allegations that he had sexually assaulted a hotel maid when she came to clean his New York suite. Prosecutors later dropped charges, but only after the story went global, and people everywhere were treated to a view of the IMF chief doing the 'perp walk' – the US ritual in which an arrested suspect is paraded before reporters and paparazzi so they can take the photos that are their livelihood. DSK, as the former finance minister was widely known, saw his prospects of running for the French presidency in 2012 fade with the US rape case.

It was suggested earlier that a helpful way of understanding politics is to think of it in terms of power, both in the sense of 'potential' and in the sense of 'constraints'. When looking at the media–politics relationship from the perspective of political elites, an awareness of both is often translated into a quest for control – in particular, over information flows and images.

Chapter 1 drew on Thompson's classic theory of media and modernity, which suggests, among other things, that a 'transformation of visibility' has taken place. Political

Top French politician and managing director of the International Monetary Fund, Dominique Strauss-Kahn, is arrested in New York in May 2014 after allegations of sexual assault. Photograph: © ERIC GAILLARD / Reuters / Corbis

leaders have become familiar because we see them regularly on television, and have learned to think of them as figures in a shared world that is visible to everyone. In English, the word 'public' has morphed and is now generally associated with that which is visible, rather than what is held in common.[1] According to Thompson, this has introduced a qualitatively new kind of fragility into the political system. While politicians desperately try to control their visibility, it tends to 'slip from their grasp' and work against them (Thompson 1995: 119–20, 123, 141). Publicity, or public visibility, is thus a two-edged sword that political elites must learn to wield with skill.

That spring day in 2011, the media-savvy DSK lost control of his visibility. He is far from the first member of the political elite to suffer such a fate. What is interesting for the purposes of this book is how the episode threw into sharp relief the differences between two political and media cultures, highlighting the control that politicians in one of those cultures had exerted over journalists. Questions were raised in the global public sphere about the appropriateness of that national norm system, and about the dividing line between private and public.

It was, namely, an open secret amongst French reporters that DSK had a reputation for womanizing. But his alleged proclivities remained under-reported until the New York arrest because of France's strict privacy laws, and because of the code of conduct the French media corps has imposed on itself to avoid litigation. When DSK was made head of the IMF in 2007, one French journalist in particular was concerned that the behaviour of 'the Great Seducer' would cause problems in a global institution based in North America, where a different public moral order prevails. Jean Quatremer failed to get the newspaper he worked for, the left-leaning *Libération*, to carry his piece on this, but he published it on his blog. He was then accused by colleagues of having broken a taboo, and was put under pressure from DSK's aides to remove the story.[2] Only when the US rape charge made headlines in the Anglo-Saxon media could French journalists run stories about the French politician having allegedly sexually harassed the New York maid and other women (including journalists), by quoting foreign media reports. As a correspondent for Britain's *Guardian* newspaper explained, the right to privacy under French law is absolute: 'Nothing takes precedence over it, not a public interest argument, not freedom of expression, nothing.'[3] In the American setting, by way of contrast, press freedom is given priority – both legally and culturally – over the right of the individual to privacy. These differences obviously have political implications when the individual in question holds public office.

When setting out to explore the media–politics relationship from the perspective of political elites, the DSK saga is a useful portkey for several reasons. It is a good illustration of the transformation of visibility, and the conditions of radical transparency that prevail under globalization (a phenomenon dealt with from a somewhat different angle in chapter 2). It problematizes claims about unidirectional flows of power, whether conceived as being exerted by political elites over media actors, or vice versa. It is a good illustration of the globalization of politics, given that the scandal surrounding the head of an international institution was widely seen as scuppering his domestic political ambitions. And it is a reminder of the different shapes that the media–politics relationship can take in different cultural settings.

The problem in focus in this chapter is how to win and maintain control over the content and dissemination of messages that matter to politics. It will be argued that this is a familiar struggle, dating back centuries, but also one that has changed in significant ways in the digital age. General patterns can be discerned, and will be summarized in the thick of this chapter. But the DSK portkey, and other illustrations that will crop up along the way, are empirical evidence that there are cultural exceptions to these general patterns (even within the same political community) that need to be addressed, for, as the adage would have it, the exception can prove the rule. The stakeholders in focus are the political elites who try to establish and maintain control over political communication – and, more specifically, those in leadership positions, with the responsibility for political decisions, or who aspire to such positions. But the technology now at the disposal of such elites raises serious questions when it comes to the other actors to be explored in this part of the book – journalists, publics and activists – and to the implications for democracy. Something to think about is whether media-technological developments are giving such actors more freedom from control by elites, or conversely giving elites more resources for control. The chapter begins with an outline of media-related challenges typically confronting political elites – be they a disgraced IMF head, a European Commissioner, a South African opposition leader, a Swedish foreign minister, a Russian leader, an Ecuadorian president, a US admiral or a pope.

Scholarly points of departure

In a well-known text, the adviser to an Italian premier alerted his employer to the importance of maintaining a patina of decency in the eyes of an increasingly powerful public, to avoid being associated with any measures that would make him unpopular, and to invest in image politics, striving 'to demonstrate grandeur, courage, sobriety and strength'. The adviser was not Miti Simonetto, former Prime Minister Berlusconi's spin doctor: it was Niccolò Machiavelli, the Renaissance civil servant and scholar (Machiavelli 1532/1978: 102, 112–13). In the years that elapsed between the zenith of the Medici in Renaissance Florence and that of Berlusconi in Mediaset Rome, and particularly in the past few decades, a library's worth of works on political communication has amassed. Image politics is only part of the story.

A seminal article published in 1981 by Gurevitch and Blumler maps out interactions between 'two sets of mutually dependent and mutually adaptive actors' (Gurevitch & Blumler 1981: 479). Other well-known contributions to the project of theorizing the relationship between political leaders and journalists have expanded the conceptual repertoire to include models of 'indexing' (Bennett 1990), 'political contest' (Wolfsfeld 1997), 'cascading' media–state relations (Entman 2004) and foreign policy – media interaction (Robinson 2002).

Models like this have tended to be formulated with national politics, and often with a particular polity, in mind. Arguing that such theories, largely Anglo-Saxon, do not fit well with how political and media actors interact in Europe and beyond, Hallin and Mancini (2004, 2011) introduced a set of models to facilitate not only generalizations, but also comparisons of different traits. Among these are professionalism, part of which relates to the degree of journalistic autonomy from political institutions and actors; pluralism of parties and publications; and 'political parallelism', which has to do with the associations between media outlets and political parties, and to the nature and intensity of such associations.

The 'Liberal' model in the Hallin–Mancini framework is most reminiscent of the US system, which is characterized by the dominance of market mechanisms, but it has also been applied to Canada, Australia, the UK and Ireland. In these countries, the free flow of information is, in theory, seen to take precedence over state involvement. Northern European countries such as Germany, Sweden and Denmark have a different, 'democratic corporatist' system, in which public and commercial media coexist, but with a state that is more interventionist even in its championing of media autonomy, as will be seen at the end of the chapter. The countries of southern Europe, grouped around the Mediterranean, belong to the third 'Polarized Pluralist' model. The media institutions and actors of these countries tend to be integrated more closely into party politics, and conform to a different tradition of journalistic professionalism from that of other countries, with actors from what Bourdieu would call the political field moving in and out of the journalistic field, and vice versa. Journalists in such systems, and the organizations they work for, generally advocate particular political ideologies, and the state actively intervenes in their sector (Hallin & Mancini 2004: 298). The France of DSK has been placed somewhat uncomfortably in this third model. It is not important for the present discussion how well it fits: the point is that Hallin and Mancini provide a framework that facilitates an understanding of the contrasting reactions to the DSK scandal in terms of more general political-cultural patterns.

Apart from differences between political cultures, scholars have also remarked on differences over time, and three 'ages' of political communication have been distinguished in the post-World War II period (Blumler & Kavanagh 1999). In the first age, political communication was a top-down affair. Information originated with the parties, and members of the press took their queue from agendas set by political elites, and the way those elites framed political issues. In the second age, the rise of television, and its establishment in homes throughout the West, changed the nature of communication and the behaviour of communicators. Scholars noted that it was journalists and the owners of media organizations who were now setting the agenda, with politicians having to learn to compete for mediated space. Television also enlarged the audience to include people who had not previously followed politics. By the time it became apparent that a third age had begun, characterized by media abundance, that audience had become fragmented and neither political parties nor mainstream media were in control of the message any longer. Scholars are not agreed as to whether we are still living in a third age, which has developed more radically than Blumler and Kavanagh could have envisaged years ago, or whether we have entered a qualitatively different 'post-broadcast' age, characterized by 'the end of television' (Katz & Scannell 2009).

Sampedro (2011) argues that the relationship between politicians, journalists and other stakeholders is more contentious. It is also inherently unstable. This is because power relations are always contingent and because the relationship is in a state of constant mutation (as one 'age' and its predominant technology succeeds another). Political communication is now said to be in a state of crisis, the victim of new trends and challenges emanating from cyberspace. But digital technology is not the origin of the crisis or of the challenges facing elites, Sampedro maintains: it only emphasizes features of the relationship that have long been in place, and which have long been problematic. Three traits of the current political communication environment are central to the research agenda of the scholars who study its mutations: the fact that information flows are now transnational; scepticism about a single, unified public sphere; and the technological empowerment of 'ordinary' citizens (2011: 431).

But this chapter is not about scholars: it is meant to open a vista on the relationship between media and politics when seen from the vantage point of political elites. What are the challenges confronting them? Are the problems they encounter the result of changed political and media landscapes, or are they perennial, pre-globalization headaches, familiar from any age in which political elites have had to manufacture consent?

Problems faced by political elites

Political elites the world over face problems dealing with uninterested, cynical, volatile or rebellious publics; with the demands of what is often referred to as 'media logic'; and with what seems to be an increasingly uncontrollable information flow.

Difficult publics

Most countries experience elections – to anyone following global news on a regular basis, it can at times seem as though there is always one taking place somewhere – but the way they are experienced differs substantially. Contrast, for example, that familiar news shot of a ballot box in an empty room in a Western European country, into which one or two dutiful citizens struggle to cast their vote for the European or national Parliament, with the image of long queues of people unused to being given a voice, and the turbulence that ensues when that voice is ignored – be it in Iran, Kenya, Côte d'Ivoire or Russia. Even in reasonably quiet democracies, elites have been challenged, over the course of the past generation, by the changing nature and inclinations of electorates, or what at times appear to be difficult publics.

During the first 'age' referred to above, people in democracies throughout the world tended to vote in predictable ways, either for the party that represented their social class, or for the one that represented their values, or both (the two being often intertwined). The second 'age' was characterized by dealignment. People voted in unpredictable ways, choosing issues rather than platforms, and making decisions based on the appeal of leaders' personality traits rather than the track record or manifesto of the party headed by those leaders. This was to the extent that people continued to vote at all: in the second age, the uninformed voter was replaced by the cynic as the villain of the piece.

The busy voter is perhaps behaving rationally when he or she questions the incentives of reading, digesting and comparing party manifestos, given that the costs incurred in such work are much greater than what is to be won from casting a vote every few years (Street 2001: 195). It is not surprising that the impression political elites made on people became more important during the second 'age' than before, characterized as it was by an increasing abundance of information and the primacy of the 'cool' medium of television. One problem facing these elites has thus been how to make those impressions favourable, or indeed to capture the attention of the public and keep it long enough to make any impression at all. The task has not been made easier by an increasing tendency for potential voters to be sceptical about the claims and promises of politicians, and cynical about their intentions. Concepts such as 'video malaise' (Robinson 1976) and a 'spiral of cynicism' (Cappella & Jamieson 1997) reflect attempts to theorize such developments.

In the third 'age', publics became cynical not just about politicians and their policies, but also about the way they are conveyed. Politicians have found themselves compelled to deal with more spaces of mediation than ever before, and with expectations that they master the art of cross-media communication. The irony of the new media ecology is that some populaces have become dealigned and disengaged by information overflow, while others have exploited new technology to join forces and mobilize in ways that have posed substantial problems to political elites the world over – in North Africa and the Middle East, in the tender or pseudo-democracies established in the wake of the Soviet Union, in debt-ridden capitals whose financial districts have been besieged, and in countries that once aspired to EU membership.

It is no coincidence that these problems have coincided with different ages in political communication, intimately connected as they are with the different media forms that have characterized each. The challenges posed by difficult publics are often associated with the media they use.

Media logic and moguls

The notion of 'media logic' is often – confusingly – invoked to refer to different driving forces. At times 'media logic' designates the constraints imposed on political communicators by new technological forms and formats ('the medium is the message'). At others, it is used to refer to the economic interests of media owners, which influence the proclivity to provide some sorts of news rather than other (better or more favourable) ones. Some national leaders have been vociferous in their critique of this tendency. Ecuador's leftist President Correa, for example, complained that conservative business interests used their economic influence (not least ownership of leading media) to attack his 'progressive' government, while Argentina's President Cristina Kirchner found her room to maneouvre curtailed by the powerful Grupo Clarín, which has enjoyed a virtual monopoly over the country's media since the days of the right-wing dictatorship (Watts 2013). At the other end of the political spectrum, France's right-wing former President Sarkozy was equally unhappy with the economic dominance of Google, and juxtaposed the world of politics (legitimate) with that of media corporations (not representative of the people) in an address to the G8 forum (the informal but exclusive group of seven leading industrialized nations and Russia):

> the States we represent need to make it known that the world you [Google] represent is not a parallel universe, free of legal and moral rules and more generally all the basic principles that govern society in democratic countries. Now that the internet is an integral part of most people's lives, it would be contradictory to exclude governments from this huge forum. Nobody could nor should forget that these governments are the only legitimate representatives of the will of the people in our democracies. (G20–G8 2011)

In other settings, leaders as different as EU Media Commissioner Viviane Reding, Pope Benedict XVI and the US Navy's Admiral Roughead spoke publicly of the challenge posed by new media forms and outlets. The EU has found itself compelled to find ways of 'filling' new technologies with content that is novel and exciting, and of dealing with the paradoxical situation in which consumers have increasingly limited choice, and access to less culturally diverse products, despite the explosion in the number of media outlets (Reding 2009). The former Pope (speaking on the feast day of St Francis de Sales, the patron saint of journalists), decreed that digital technology was ushering in a period of 'vast cultural transformation', and acknowledged the unprecedented opportunity it afforded. The problem, as he saw it, was that the 'truth' was becoming that which receives most attention, rather than what is actually right (an interesting distinction if ever there was one). Fortunately for the Vatican, his successor, Pope Francis, quickly proved to be capable of attracting media attention and to have considerable communicative prowess.

Like the pontiffs, US admirals are seen (by themselves at least) as heads of a global organization, the work of which is transformed by digital media. The US Navy, according to Admiral Roughead, has had to come to terms with the demand for radical transparency. Speaking to naval officers now faced with the challenge of having to communicate with 'an audience of audiences' (in that every individual is connected to a networked audience of their own), Roughead said that leaders in hierarchical organizations were anxious about relinquishing control over the message.

> Separate from the technical concerns about things like network security, this is a concern over losing exclusive 'rights' to your brand, your image, or what people might say about your organization. But in today's media environment of user-generated content, 'control' is an illusion.

The challenge, as he saw it, was to navigate between the public and the personal, and to find a balance between accountability and empowerment (Roughead 2011). How well those charged with US security have succeeded in finding that balance would become hotly debated the world over in the years that followed the 2011 speech.

However credible the admiral's words, the DSK case demonstrates that navigational skills such as these are required of leaders regardless of whether they command a fleet of ships or risk drowning in negative publicity. Difficulties negotiating the blurred border between public and private persona became acute during the second age of political communication, dominated by the 'logic' of television. In earlier periods, few people had been able to see their leaders close up. Print journalists met the president or prime minister in his offices – and in some cultures worked and socialized with him – and passed on his words as dictated. Once press conferences started being televised, reporters no longer had to ask permission to quote leaders. And, through what McLuhan (1964/2003) called the 'cool' electronic media, they were demystified, their stubble and sweat (and, as women began to infiltrate the upper eschelons of political power, various other flaws) seen close up.[4] As Meyrowitz (2009: 44) puts it, television 'humanized' the image of political rulers, and lowered them to the level of the common person. It encouraged the 'personalization' of politics, placing the focus on individual politicians and their characteristics rather than the policies they stood for, or the forces that shaped those policies (Campus 2010; Patterson 2000). It is sometimes argued that political leaders have been forced to become celebrities (Street 2001: 195), but whether or not they have, and in which cultural and political contexts, is an empirical question.

The ascent of television has nevertheless meant that political elites lost control over their images or 'brands', as Admiral Roughead would say, and made them victims of the new sort of visibility to which Thompson referred. According to Ellis (2009a: 113), politicians have had to submit themselves to the same 'regime of understanding' as any other television performer. This has meant that the political process has been transformed into the business of gaining trust – of getting people's confidence, rather than necessarily getting it right.

Information flows

As mentioned in chapter 1, there is now a sense in which other public spaces are encroaching upon television's historic management of public visibility. It is no longer just television – its formats and logics – to which politicians need to adapt. In the digital landscape, the 'viral energy' of social media and the world of Wiki constitutes 'a new flow of incessantly circulating publicity in which reputations are enhanced and destroyed, messages debated and discarded, rumors floated and tested' (Gurevitch et al. 2009: 170).

New sorts of media technology and outlets require new sorts of regulation. In 1989, when the European Commission launched its Television Without Frontiers policy, the challenge European elites faced was to regulate media production and distribution at a time when satellite broadcasting was showing how porous national borders were, and when national media policies were being pushed off course by the communications revolution (Sakr 2008: 278). A decade later, the question was no longer how to influence the media companies that offered consumers a pre-defined schedule. The focus of control had instead become the consumer, and the question was what rules should apply to media products supplied at the request of users, who could now decide not only what to watch but also when to watch it. Apart from on-demand media, policymakers have found themselves having to deal with file-sharing, hate-group blogging, the circumvention of privacy laws by Twitter, and a host of other predicaments that few regulators could have foreseen. Elites involved in government and governance are finding it increasingly difficult to control the global communication infrastructure, not least because it is being rebuilt before their eyes.

Digital media pose a special kind of challenge to national governments, because of what Kumar (2010) calls their 'borderless architecture'. Google – in some respects as powerful as a nation-state – began disseminating previously classified satellite images of national territory in 2005, resulting in complaints (most of them futile) from politicians in Australia, the Netherlands, South Korea, Thailand and, not least, India and Pakistan, as Google Earth complicated the territorial dispute surrounding the Kashmir province (Kumar 2010: 163). National sovereignty has been challenged in other ways too. As discussed in chapter 2, WikiLeaks showed how vulnerable states have become now that information can spread with the use of servers beyond their reach.

Digital technology has given new power to old practices, and to states that have long engaged in the practice of covertly targeting dissenters from locations outside the country. Syria, for example, incited violence against regime critics at home when the conflict broke out in 2011, from government websites hosted clandestinely in Canada – violating Canadian foreign policy in the process.[5] Social media have also

Vladimir Putin is booed by the audience when taking to the stage to congratulate the
Russian victor at a wrestling match in November 2011. Russian Channel One edited
the footage so only the cheers that greeted the former Russian prime minister could
be heard on television, but the boos reverberated throughout cyberspace. Photograph:
premier.gov.ru. Reproduced under Creative Commons licence.

exacerbated the fragility discussed earlier in the book – the loss of control when leaders' visibility slips from their hands and their misdeeds and mishaps are amplified.
Once publicized on national television (where many state actors could control the
image), these gaffes now travel virally throughout the globe, as Vladimir Putin experienced shortly before the 2011 elections to the Russian Duma. Apparently thinking
he would enhance his strong-man image through association with martial arts and
victorious fighters, Putin climbed into the ring and grabbed the microphone after a
fight between a Russian and an American (which the former won). Crowd-sourced
video indicates that Putin was caught off-balance by an unexpected chorus of boos
from the audience, and stumbled over his words. Russian state television's Channel
One broadcast the footage after editing it so that only cheers could be heard. But the
booing reverberated throughout cyberspace, courtesy of YouTube and members of
the difficult public who had captured and posted the moment.

Elite strategies for control

In Brussels, the working day for an EU Commissioner begins with a rundown, at the
morning meeting, of what journalists are reporting, nationally and globally. *What are
the major issues we need to be aware of just now*, she asks herself? *Is there any criticism
we need to respond to? How are we to maximize attention surrounding a given issue
or proposal soon to be presented? Shall we write a debate article, book an interview,*

or arrange a meeting with selected correspondents to get off on the right foot? These are among the questions that the Commissioner and her staff discuss and deal with.[6]

In Germany, about 650 people work for the Federal Press and Information Office, which answers directly to the chancellor. Like the Brussels people, the German office employees have to inform the government about what is being reported around the world, keep their fingers on the pulse of public opinion and communicate to that public the objectives of the government. But as politics in 'democratic corporatist' Germany means coalition politics, the parties seek public support for their respective stances and vie for stronger positions using political communication as a weapon – battles that 'are fought out in the media' (Sanders et al. 2011: 528). In 'polarized pluralist' Spain, the parties have long worked with a strongly partisan press, and there is no counterpart to the German office. Spanish government communication has tended to be reactive, rather than proactive. In the UK of the 'liberal' model, on the other hand, every ministry has a director of communication, who heads a team that works to ensure that policy is communicated to the wider public with a government 'spin' on it. 'Special advisers' brief ministers, on the one hand, and journalists, on the other, in a bid to retain the 'power of definition'. While legislation has been introduced to make legal distinctions between governmental and partisan political communication in Spain and Germany, the UK has opted for 'guidelines' and codes for good practice (Sanders et al. 2011: 534–7).

In South Africa, Lindiwe Mazibuko was elected leader of the the Democratic Alliance in 2011, becoming the first black woman, and the youngest person, to head the parliamentary opposition. She used a PR firm to help her with her campaign, drawing fire from some quarters and praise from others, who considered her strategy to be an indication of a 'modern, global approach to politicking' (Gilbert 2011).

These examples are indicative of different strategies for dealing with media logic, difficult publics and information flows. Ultimately, they all have to do with gaining control of the narrative.

Strategies for dealing with difficult publics and media power

Efforts to gain control of the narrative have been associated with a variety of concepts and strategies: the professionalization of communication, the packaging of politics, spin, PR, image-making, and celebrity politics (as in the sort of politics featuring politicians who become celebrities in their own right, not the sort featuring celebrities who pursue political or humanitarian agendas, of which more in chapter 8). Some strategies, for instance interactive newsmaking or interview control, are aimed at journalists. Some, such as 'going personal', are aimed directly at the public. Sometimes, such as when it comes to reshaping narratives, the aim is to reclaim the power of definition from activists and demonstrators. There is a good deal of continuity involved in many of these strategies – image politics has been around since the days of absolute monarchs like Elizabeth I of England and Louis XIV of France. But there have also been significant developments. As heads of state from Washington to Moscow, foreign ministers in Stockholm and ayatollahs in Tehran have demonstrated, one way of dealing with the power (and 'logic') of established media institutions is to bypass them, and communicate directly with people using social media.

Professionalization is associated with the second 'age' of political communication. As parties became less successful at forging and maintaining the link between publics and politics, political elites began instead to exploit television for this purpose, adapting their behaviour and messages to its formats. Politicians became more 'professional' in their dealings with journalists, and they began to devote resources to the employment of other professionals in a bid to exploit media logic to their own ends – hence the PR firms and spin doctors. Corner (2003) writes in this context about 'the political shop' and elite use of the media as the space of 'demonstrable representativeness'.

'Packaging' refers to the idea that politics are marketed and sold to political consumers like other products in a commercialized environment. Critics see such strategies as leading to the trivialization of political arguments, and a situation in which appearances matter more than policies. Some argue that professional communication strategies are essential in an age of increasingly complicated politics and in complex globalized settings, and are thus a service to the public (Coombs & Holladay 2007). But there is good cause for concern that packaging has led to a lack of transparency, because information from governors to governed has become so highly controlled (Street 2001: 185).

From the flora of techniques described in the literature on political marketing, a few recur as the most effective in various national contexts (Campus 2010; Franklin 2004; Louw 2005; McNair 2006). First and foremost is creation and maintenance of an appealing image – work called for by Machiavelli and in which political leaders

The photogenic First Ladies Michelle Obama and Carla Bruni were widely seen as key components of the images of the Obama and Sarkozy presidencies. White House photo by Chuck Kennedy. Photograph: From the Official White House photostream / Wikimedia Commons.

have invested considerable effort and resources throughout human history. What is more unique to the second and third ages of political communication is how the images that elites have sought to cultivate (at least outside North Korea) are less those of gods who rule by divine right or by virtue of inherently brilliant traits, and more those of 'the "person next door", with low-key style, self-deprecating humor, and (at least feigned) humility' (Meyrowitz 2009: 45). Politicians have become 'recognizable performers, but also intimate strangers' (Stanyer 2007: 72). Skilful image-makers develop a cult of familiarity, with details of their private lives strategically exploited in the construction of political identities. This is true even in countries with jealously guarded privacy like France. The DSK rape case illustrated not that the private spheres of French elites are out of bounds, but that those elites are meant to be in control of the public performance of those private lives. While François Hollande had some trouble with this during his second year in office, a telegenic 'first lady' could be said to have been a key component of the image of the presidency of his predecessor, Nicolas Sarkozy.

Second, political elites in democratic states, and in many pseudo- or non-democratic ones as well, try to establish a direct link with the public, to turn them into followers (Louw 2005: 179). Television was used to good effect by various leaders in this context – Ronald Reagan was the past master of the art of forging emotional connections with Americans through skilful use of television cameras – but politicians the world over have exploited the technology of Facebook and Twitter more recently to connect directly with the public.

Sarah Palin, once thought to be a contender for the White House, has over 3 million 'friends', according to her Facebook pages, and even the foreign minister of a small European country like Sweden has been able to boast over 280,000 'followers'. During the pro-democracy uprisings in 2011, Swedish Foreign Minister Bildt used Twitter (twitter.com/carlbildt) to reach his Bahraini counterpart, Khalid bin Ahmed al-Khalifa, who had 32,000 followers himself at the time. (Al-Khalifa used Twitter to spread the Bahraini monarchy's views on the pro-democracy uprising, but that is another story.)

A third political marketing strategy that recurs in the literature is the creation of media events, or the propensity to use such events to enhance a leader's image. News management is also used to ensure that the timing, location and presentation of events that do not originate in the media, and whose exploitation can be used to make a leader look good, conform to media formats (Iyengar & McGrady 2007: 133). This is not new – J. F. Kennedy's 'Ich bin ein Berliner' speech of 1963 is a classic example – but it is a technique that has come to be deployed on a more regular basis, with more skill, and more interactivity. Just as Kennedy used the Berlin Wall to highlight the freedom his America claimed to represent, by juxtaposing it with the brutal containment of East Germans behind a heavily policed barricade, many Western leaders leapt to associate themselves with pro-democracy uprisings abroad. British Prime Minister David Cameron and French President Sarkozy, for example, rapidly convened a heavily publicized conference on the future of Libya after the fall of Gaddafi.

Iconic moments can be used by political elites on both sides of the barricade to redefine the narrative. The image of a young student standing unarmed in front of a tank during the Tiananmen Square protests in China in 1989, for example, has been used to tell a variety of stories. Many are familiar with how it was used to represent the forces for peaceful change pitted against those of violent oppression; the individual pitted against the machine; and a new generation challenging the old guard. But the Chinese Communist Party used images from the same protests – including photographs taken by Western journalists – to tell a different story. The official Chinese narrative was a romantic myth of heroic soldiers who saved the nation by restoring order in Beijing, and the Chinese people from disruptive acts (Becker 1996: 190).

The image of the Chinese student and the tank became a global icon, entering the collective political imagination around the time media globalization took off. Two decades later, protesters throughout the world mounted challenges to established political elites with the aid of media technology that the Chinese students of 1989 could not have dreamt of (of which more in chapter 6). But the technological revolution of the intervening years has not just aided dissenters. It has also, significantly, enhanced the power of states to control political opponents, troublesome populaces, and other competitors on the global political playing field. These resources have been deployed to gain control over information flows in a world of porous borders.

Strategies for controlling information flows

The world depicted in classic works on political communication is by and large that of (Anglo-Saxon) domestic politics, in which politicians confront reporters and, as said, struggle with them and their opponents to control the narrative. The world depicted by those who seek to understand communicative power in global settings is somewhat different. Erik Bettermann, the director general of Deutsche Welle, the German global broadcaster, has said that 'the internet is no longer just a tool for dissidents and activists – but for dictators as well' (DW 2011). Jake Appelbaum, of the (in)famous Tor Project (www.torproject.org), describes the global space as a world of small fiefdoms. 'Every Ayatollah has his own website', the computer security researcher (and hactivist) told members of NGOs and the public, years before anyone had heard of Edward Snowden; 'You are the bad people to someone somewhere.'[7]

Appelbaum is a controversial figure, but most would now agree that there is reason to be worried about 'backdoors' and other routine accessing of data on someone else's computer without their permission or knowledge. Technological advances have made it possible to trace the origin of anonymous sources and take measures against people who think differently from those in power. State-run organizations in the Middle East and China have used the internet to 'keep the public in line and separated from the outside world' (DW 2011; see also Slaughter 2012[8]). Just weeks before Bettermann issued his warning about internet control, the Iranian government reported it would be replacing the worldwide web (the 'www' of internet addresses) with an 'Iranwide web', effectively disconnecting the country's online community (Rhoads & Fassihi 2011). Similar measures have been taken by the governments of Cuba, Myanmar and North Korea.

It is helpful to think in terms of two broad sets of strategies for controlling information flows: regulation, and repression.

Barely a generation ago, people in most of Europe and elsewhere had access to one or two publicly funded, and in many countries state-controlled, radio and television channels. That changed in the 1980s, not (just) because of technological advances, but because of decisions taken by governments. Deregulation started in the early 1980s in the UK under Margaret Thatcher, and spread quickly eastwards, to France where advertising crept into all broadcasting, and to Italy, where media mogul and party leader Silvio Berlusconi levelled the distinction between media and political empires, and beyond.

Political actors have sought not only to de-regulate (at home) but to re-regulate (in the global marketplace). Since the early 1990s, the EU has tried to 'europeanize' the communications of its member states in a bid to stem the 'free' flow of largely US media products. It has done so through legislation, cultural regulation and the introduction of protective measures (Heikkilä 2007; Robertson 2014). In other parts of the world, elites have similarly tried to govern information flows either through legislation, or by backing alternatives to established US and European media outlets. These include Telesur in Latin America, the Kremlin-backed global broadcaster Russia Today, and Al Jazeera, the channel widely seen as a bid by the ruling Al Thani monarchy to make the tiny state of Qatar a foreign-policy giant in the region (Figenschou 2013; Robertson forthcoming 2015).

Political elites regulate to promote what they see as being in the public interest (such as a plurality of voices in multicultural societies) and to curb what they see as harmful to society (such as child pornography) or what they quite simply judge to be a threat. At times, this causes cross-border tensions and disagreements between friends. Canadian regulators rejected a move in February 2011 to repeal a law that forbids lying on broadcast news, in order to prevent an influx of US-style channels like Fox News and right-wing talk radio. This is an example of cultural regulation, or perhaps even protectionism, to safeguard the Canadian model of liberal democracy. About the same time, Hungary was forced to make changes in the new media law it had enacted in January 2011, because of EU censure. The law would have punished broadcasters, newspapers and websites with heavy fines for coverage deemed unbalanced by the state. As Hungary had just taken over the rotating presidency of the EU when the law, seen by critics as an attack on free speech, went into effect, the issue had international repercussions. Politicians in Germany and Luxemburg were among those who expressed concern that the law would make it difficult for the EU to criticize countries like China and Iran, or place demands on candidate countries, when it came to their restrictive media practices. The right to freedom of expression was also at the heart of the debate around the Stop Online Piracy Act (SOPA), that was put before the House of Representatives in the US the same year. After what came to be known as the 'nerd lobby' pointed out the extent of advance censhorship the Act would involve, and the English version of Wikipedia, and thousands of other websites, went offline in an anti-SOPA protest in January 2012, plans to draft the bill were postponed. As examples such as these show, the media landscape often resembles a battlefield on which business interests, developers of technology and other stakeholders struggle with policymakers to gain the higher ground.

Regulation still exists in material, as well as legislative and virtual, form. Tawil-Souri (2011a) has documented how Israeli authorities have managed to confine Palestinians in Gaza not just with barricades and barbed-wire fences, but also by controlling the telecommunications infrastructure. The Israeli military banned the use of telephone lines for sending e-mails after the First Intifada in 1989, and, as late as 2011, the Palestinian digital network still relied on the infrastructure in Israel, where the switching nodes are situated. Gaza has in effect been cut off from the outside world and from Palestinians elsewhere in the country, 'sealed through both real and virtual walls' (Tawil-Souri 2011a: 3). Tawil-Souri and others (Andrejevic 2007; Boyle 2003; Schiller 1999, 2007) have warned that digital enclosures are taking shape in other places, and that the 'commons' are shrinking, as states gradually shift to more comprehensive regimes of control.

President Mubarak failed when he tried to retain control of Egypt by taking it offline in January 2011. But governments elsewhere have succeeded in disconnecting mailers, surfers, bloggers and tweeters, or have used the technology to frighten them. Text messages appeared on the mobile phones of people gathered on Independence Square early in 2014. 'Dear subscriber', the SMS said, 'you have been registered as a participant in a mass protest' (Wolodarski 2014). Regimes resisting democratic reform throughout the Middle East and in Moldova have spammed protester hashtags and traced their messages to dissenters who have subsequently been jailed. The crackdown by the Iranian government on the 'Twitter Revolution' of 2009 has been the subject of many pieces, and much attention has been paid to China's measures to silence opponents, and its quarrel with Google over the hacking of Gmail accounts. Saudi Arabia rivals China in its (successful) efforts to filter problematic content, blocking websites of which it disapproves at their gateway or prosecuting individual users (Kumar 2010: 167). It was thus with some concern that observers noted the purchase by Saudi Prince Walid bin Talal of a 'strategic stake' in Twitter for $300 million in December 2011.

Censorship has existed for hundreds, indeed thousands, of years. It has continued throughout the three ages of political communication, or perhaps been 'reborn' (Glanville 2010: 3). 'Not only does the internet make it possible for authoritarian regimes to monitor their citizens' activities as never before', Glanville notes, 'it has also made censorship acceptable, even respectable, in democracies.' The internet is not the Wild West – its present incarnation is the result of legal, political, economic and social decisions – and governments everywhere are prepared to exploit its resources to retain control over a turbulent media landscape. Critics have expressed concern about a tendency to invoke child protection, counter-terrorism and intellectual property rights as pretexts for filtering and blocking websites and for covertly collecting and storing personal data about members of the public. The scholarly literature is increasingly peppered with references to the panopticon, and to ideas of Gilles Deleuze and Michel Foucault about the *dispositif* that keeps publics under surveillance and in check. Mobile technology has given the affluent of the world the possibility of working and communicating wherever they are. But as anyone who has taken a photo on their mobile phone and plugged it into their computer or uploaded it on a cloud will know, a programme can immediately pinpoint where and when the picture was taken, and millions of people find themselves 'tagged' in images making the rounds in cyberspace beyond their control. As Appelbaum wryly puts it: a smartphone is a tracking device you can also use to make phone calls. Add to this such quotidian features of modern life as biometric ID cards, CCTV cameras, body scans at the airport and software cookies, and it becomes clear that not only the likes of DSK have trouble managing their visibility: the blurring of the border between private and public works for, as well as against, political elites. Technology can empower political elites, as well as constrain them, just as it can all the other actors in the media–politics relationship.

To think about

One evening, when Silvio Berlusconi still had a firm grip on Italian politics, Swedish audiences were surprised to hear the newsreader on the advert-free SVT network announce that it was time for a commercial break. Across the screen flickered multiple images of the smiling Italian prime minister, surrounded by scantily clad veline, with a banner informing Swedish viewers that Berlusconi controlled 90 per cent of Italian television channels and had become prime minister after a massive media campaign. The news item was about an advert that Swedish Television had been airing to persuade people to pay their licence fees. The message of the 'Free Television' campaign was that, without support for public broadcasting, Sweden would find itself at the mercy of a Berlusconi and a privatized, trivialized media. The news angle was that Sweden's ambassador to Rome had been called to the Italian foreign ministry, where a formal complaint about the campaign had been lodged. Italian parliamentarians publicly objected to the Swedish public broadcaster having been allowed to criticise the government of a fellow EU member state. The head of SVT defended the advert, and pointed out that the Italian reaction underlined its message – that there were political cultures nearby in which politicians thought it their right to tell media companies what they could and could not broadcast. The Swedish minister of culture agreed, and said that politicians had no business getting involved in editorial decisions, whether or not the company was financed with public funds. The squall blew over within a week, but the incident highlighted just how different relations between political and media actors in two different cultures can be, even within the same political union.

Berlusconi eventually left the Quirinal Palace, and, in the wake of his resignation, European political elites debated whether moves should be taken to prevent a similar monopoly in the future. It was pointed out that the EU sets high standards for countries applying for membership, but fails to compel countries already in the union to guarantee the plurality of voices thought vital to a healthy democracy. The European Union lacks legislation and regulatory mechanisms for this because member states want to retain control over their own media systems. One thing to think about is which course is the most appropriate. Another is where control should be located – within or beyond the state?

Like the DSK story recounted at the beginning of this chapter, the Berlusconi–SVT spat can work as a portkey to open up a bundle of problems. This bundle contains an empirical problem: how is the relationship between political and media actors to be explicated? And there is a normative one. Where should the line be drawn between public and private – when it comes to ownership, when it comes to visibility, and when it comes to the tension between the needs of political elites on the one hand to ensure national security, and, on the other, to protect the freedom of the individual to personal integrity? Crossing other boundaries, how much pressure should be put on national governments by other states – be they friend or foe – and by transnational bodies like the EU and UNESCO, to ensure common ethical denominators? (These issues will be returned to in chapter 10, but should be kept in mind in the meantime.)

There are sound reasons for arguing that state control over national media systems is diminishing (Sampedro 2011: 433), but also that states remain resilient (if increasingly insolvent) and that the power of political elites in national settings has grown rather than diminished, in tandem with technological advances. There is also a significant degree of continuity in the business of 'image politics'. Corner's invocation of a staged photograph of US President Theodore Roosevelt, taken in 1886, is a useful reminder that the business is not a recent invention. But there are important dimensions of change here too: specific kinds of political persona are now required, and the 'performance' has changed in terms of scale and in the consciousness with which it is strategized (Corner 2003: 67–8).

Something else to think about, when it comes to the professionalization of politics, is who really has the power in public relations, and whether PR is always a 'bad' thing. To say that someone is professional has a good ring to it, while 'PR' tends to be pronounced with a moue of distaste, at least by academics and people outside the industry. What is the best way to think about the work involved in communicating to stakeholders and (where these are not identical) the public? And what sense is to be made of the fact that it is not just politicians who need public relations firms, but also that the reverse is increasingly true? As one PR consultant explained, politicians have access, system knowledge, experience in political analysis, the ability to think strategically and knowledge of framing (Allern 2011: 132). A question to be returned to in chapter 5 is whether the professionalization of political communication and technological developments have disempowered citizens, as suggested by Hamelink (2007) and Wring (2005) or whether they have given non-elite groups a chance to compete for control of the narrative (Cottle 2003).

Political communication research is said to be at a turning point, in the face of the unprecedented changes which both political elites and the scholars who study them, must address. According to some (e.g. Barnhurst 2011), the field has remained methodologically and theoretically cautious. The times call for more adventurous approaches. Certainly, there is a wealth of empirical material to mine, cases and affairs to explicate, and comparisons to be made, for the adventurer who wants to explore the perspective of the political elite in more depth.

4 Journalists

This chapter's portkey is not a metaphor. It is a real object, lying small and flat and quiet on the table, and need not even be grasped for the user to plunge headlong into confusing, colliding worlds.

One tap of a finger and two prominent Swedish journalists are having an argument, each brandishing the image of a different newsworld. The publicist and former editor-in-chief of *Svenska Dagbladet* is lamenting the demise of quality journalism. Not only has the space allotted to politics in both his paper and its larger rival *Dagens Nyheter* shrunk to half its size since the mid-1990s. Mats Svegfors is incensed because money saved by using less paper (broadsheets having become tabloids and news being increasingly consumed online) has not been reinvested in content. The journalist corps has been decimated, more job cuts are on the horizon, and the reporters whose business is words are lower down in the food chain than the layout artists who prioritize pictures. 'The demand for critical, independent journalism is disappearing fast', warns the man who once ran the conservative broadsheet; 'Commercialization and the supremacy of economism ooze from every pore of society.'[1]

A voice from the liberal *Dagens Nyheter* objects. Fewer words being devoted to coverage of national politics in an outward-looking country is not evidence that today's journalism is inferior to yesterday's. Turning for support to Mark Twain (the novelist who began as a newspaper man, and who famously quipped 'I didn't have time to write a short letter, so I wrote a long one instead'), the editorialist arguing with Svegfors points out that the length of a text is no measure of its quality. A research report is cited in defence of the view that there is as much 'hard news' in the daily paper now as then, and less of a preoccupation with personalities than in the 1960s. Nordic journalists are no longer cowed by the powerful, and newswork has become professionalized where it once was politicized.[2]

Another tap on the portkey, and the Swedish voices fade. In their place, two women are discussing media and politics in Johannesburg (and on the live stream of a global news channel). Ory Okolloh, co-founder of the open crowdsourcing platform Ushahidi, is saying that new media technology is playing a pivotal role in Kenyan politics, making elections more transparent, freer and fairer.[3] Swipe to Ryan Gallagher's revelation in the *Guardian* that new technology is doing quite the opposite – that defence contractor Raytheon has secretly developed software capable of predicting the future behaviour of Facebook, Twitter and Foursquare users, to the considerable interest of security forces who are everywhere keen on following activists' movments.[4] Another tap, and media mogul Rupert Murdoch (whose Twitter feed is closely followed for clues as to what is afoot in his global Newscorp empire) is tweeting with British Labour MP Clare Short about the possible disappearance, from page 3, of the *Sun*'s notorious topless women, who are 'so last century'. #Vatican is saying a new pope will soon be named, following Benedict XVI's shocking resignation (major news outlets have put the live reactions coming in from Catholics and other audience members around the world at the top of their websites), although it is understood the announcement will come from a chimney and not from @Pontifax. A tap and a swipe, and a journalist is debating with commenters about the politics of representation, and the decision of *The Impossible*'s Spanish director to focus on a Western family in his portrayal of a global catastrophe that killed tens of thousands of Asians. His voice is almost immediately drowned by tweets about the three Baftas that Ben Affleck has just claimed for an American–Iranian hostage crisis film that has representation issues of its own. Two more taps, and a link posted by a Friend many longitudes away in Minnesota, who in turn is a Friend of Barack Obama, summons up a picture posted on the president's Facebook timeline declaring that 92 per cent of Americans support universal background checks for gun sales – a strikingly different picture of US opinion from that reflected by the European newspapers and television programmes that are another tap or two away. Going 'home' by activating the button at the bottom of the portkey, the world disappears and the voices discussing mediated politics grow silent.

The places just visited will be familiar to most readers. But as ever, when attempting to understand the media–politics relationship, the quotidian is a useful starting point for scholarship. These dialogues touch on economic threats to quality journalism, the impact of technology (empowering or enslaving?), changing journalistic role conceptions and news values, the tension between politicization and professionalism, and the question of whether newswork is abetted or undermined by crowdsourcing. Instances were encountered of audience views being swiftly incorporated into an unfolding news story, and of political elites bypassing established media channels to disseminate their narrative and imagery on social media networks. Journalists working for 'old' media were blogging and tweeting, and political issues were represented differently by media based in different countries. A journalist in the North longed for a lost golden age, while one in the South expressed excitement about a brave new world. A media user exercised her prerogative to withdraw her attention, and switched off the cacophony of voices and views.

The reporter's classic investigative queries provide the structure for this chapter. Answering the 'who' and 'what' questions involves the groundwork of conceptual clarification, which is a precondition for fruitful discussion and particularly necessary if the objective is to make comparisons. An attempt to present a systematic overview of the problems confronting journalists is a response to the question of 'why?'. As for 'where?', it will be argued that, while global, if not universal, patterns are discernible, there are important differences between national cultures, making it unwise to generalize about how journalists relate to politics in different settings.

It could be said – and often is – that journalism has long been in crisis. What is qualitatively new? Under the heading of 'when?', it will be argued that the power of the journalist can be understood in terms of both continuity and change. As the example of Machiavelli served to remind us in the last chapter, the relationship between the politically powerful, who have sought to control the narrative, and those whose business is to relay it, has always been fraught, if not downright conflictual. The answers provided in what follows may well lead, as usual, to more questions, about which the reader is invited to think at the end of the chapter.

In India, the world's largest democracy, the media landscape is a 'vast and loud space', with eighty-seven news channels and countless newspapers. But how to cover an election riddled with religious as well as economic strife? Al Jazeera English / *Listening Post*, 12 April 2014. Photograph: Goutom Roy / Al Jazeera English / Wikimedia Commons.

Who? What? Getting a conceptual grip

Who is a journalist and what is journalism? The question is surprisingly seldom posed, and the answer is not self-evident. It can be grand. As one practitioner put it, the purpose of journalism is to

> convene large audiences around salient events and debates to feed the public discourse. It's about bearing witness to events on behalf of people you don't know, with the promise not to deceive them, and to verify facts before publication. It's about revelation and investigation calculated to hold power to account and make influence reveal itself. And to do all of this in the public – not private or section – interest. (Marsh 2011: 50)

Others see journalism in more banal terms: as 'something you do', a job or a craft. It is variously conceived as a practice or a profession; an institution or an industry; an occupational ideology or a culture (Boudana 2011; Deuze 2005; Manning 2001). Danish journalists see their work as being about selection and construction and trading; as a race or a power game (Gravengaard 2012). Researchers who studied news production in the 1970s found it to be a regulated and routine process of manufacturing, and described news organizations as factories that required regular deliveries of raw material to be processed and delivered to consumers in the form of a standardized and familiar product (Cohen & Young 1973; Golding & Elliot 1979).

If news has been likened to fast food (a uniform product that quickly feeds the cravings of some but is unlikely to nourish), equally distasteful metaphors have been used to portray the people who make it. As well as factory workers driven by routine rather than rational thought, they have been characterized as bloodhounds or vultures, and in the wake of the UK phone-hacking scandal, the decades-old image of reporters represented as 'pigs in raincoats' was revived.[5] One correspondent, describing the behaviour of his counterparts covering the US Republican primaries in 2011, didn't mince his words:

> Journalists gorge on the red meat of this dramatic narrative, gnawing on the bare bones of the results, chewing over their implications. The candidates' flaws and foibles, abilities and indiscretions are put under a blazing spotlight. Who will sweat and crack? (Mardell 2011)

Quite different descriptors from pigs, bloodhounds and vultures come to mind, however, when one visits the website of the Committee to Protect Journalists (cpj.org) or stands in front of the long, high wall in Washington's Newseum, inscribed with the names of more than 2,000 reporters and photographers from around the world, all killed while trying to do their job. The images of celebrities like Bob Woodward and Carl Bernstein of Watergate renown or the murdered Anna Politkovskaya and Veronica Guerin, who continued to report despite repeated threats to their lives, also carry associations other than porcine, be they hero or martyr, or perhaps both.

Decades ago, Cohen (1963) suggested a distinction be drawn between journalists who considered themselves neutral observers, and those whose self-perceptions were of participants in the political process. The distinction remains a touchstone in scholarly work on journalistic identity, and has been tested, developed and tweaked by subsequent generations of researchers. It has been established that journalists see themselves variously as disseminators (neutral) and interpreters (objective if not neutral) of political information, as adversaries whose job it is to be critical of government and business interests, and as agenda-setting mobilizers of the public. More recent research has documented other fault lines. 'Interventionist' journalists are described as socially committed and assertive, unlike those who espouse neutrality, impartiality and detachment. Loyal journalists, who see themselves as partners of ruling elites, have a markedly different view of the media–politics relationship from watchdogs who openly challenge those in power. Some understand themselves as speaking to citizens; journalists, on the other hand, with a 'market orientation' address consumers (Hanitzsch 2011: 481). It has been established that journalists frequently see themselves as filling several of these job descriptions, and playing multiple roles (Donsbach & Patterson 2004; Johnstone et al. 1976; Weaver & Wilhoit 1996).

In many scholarly accounts, journalists are lumped together with the institutions and organizations they work for and referred to collectively as 'the media' (and formerly as 'the press'). This is unhelpful. News outlets are sometimes privately owned, sometimes publicly owned and sometimes owned by the state or the government of the day, and even when these owners are well intentioned, the interests of news organizations and journalists 'are not quite aligned' (Ryfe 2009: 208). Anyone interested in understanding power relations should thus maintain an analytical distinction between the two sets of media actors. Technological change has made the task of defining the journalist difficult enough without involving owners and institutions.

In sum, there is no straight answer to the deceptively simple question of what journalism is and what journalists are and do. In fact, this is at least in part an empirical question, for reasons that will be discussed in what follows.

Professional cultures

Particularly when comparisons are in focus, it is useful to think about journalism as a cultural practice. Those who do so research its character and performance in specific contexts (Carey 1992; Coman & Gross 2012; Hanusch 2009; Lauk 2008; Weaver 1998; Zelizer 2005). Being a member of a given journalistic culture means being guided by collective, and often tacit, knowledge, and the conscious or unconscious recourse to particular practices.

Professionalism is a key concept here. Functionalist sociologists conceive of this as a process in which a collective identity is acquired, defined and redefined; in which a consensus emerges around the definition of roles; and which involves group control of its members (Mellado & Humanes 2012: 987). One German scholar has written about 'professional milieux', which he envisages as arenas in which practitioners 'struggle over the dominant view on journalism's primary social role' (Hanitzsch 2011: 478). This sort of struggle can be glimpsed in current discussions about the increasing, rather than diminishing, need for professionals in a convergent world of crowdsourcing, in debates like the Swedish one at the beginning of this chapter, in the watchful eye kept by national unions and international federations of journalists on working conditions of their members and counterparts in newly minted democracies, and in the soul-searching that follows scandals in ancient ones, like the British phone-hacking and *Newsnight* kerfuffles of 2011–13.[6]

Professionalism is bound up with the independence or autonomy of journalists in their dealings with both state and market. Influenced by Bourdieu (2005), a generation of scholars has come to think of journalism as a field structured by the forces of autonomy and those which encroach upon it. Where there is greater professional autonomy, political and economic forces will be less influential (Benson & Hallin 2007; Benson & Neveu 2005). While this terrain differs in different political and media systems, the 'liberal' model of journalism native to Anglo-Saxon countries (Hallin & Mancini 2004, 2011; see chapter 3) was for many years the yardstick by which professionalization was measured. Where journalism is understood in these terms, the role of the professional is by and large that of the information-relayer. To be able to provide the public with balanced and accurate information, and to be a fearless but discriminating watchdog, freedom of information and expression in the polity must be respected and guaranteed by an independent judiciary, and the journalist must be unencumbered by pressure from political or business elites. In other words, professionalism and autonomy go hand-in-hand. Apart from the size of the paycheck, there is thus a generic difference between being a professional journalist and being a professional footballer or hockey player. What defines the professionalism of athletes is the fact that they are bought and sold and paid to promote the interests of whoever has most recently acquired their services. What defines the professionalism of journalists is precisely the fact that they are not.

Professional autonomy has become the touchstone of journalism in its ideal form (Deuze 2005; Mellado & Humanes 2012), and while scholars like Hanitzsch might find themselves able to discern emerging professional milieux on a global level, others have documented significant national differences between 'sacerdotal' and 'pragmatic' journalistic cultures. In the former, politics has a special status, national politics are considered self-evidently newsworthy, and political elites are prioritized news sources. In pragmatic news cultures, on the other hand, journalists are generally sceptical of political and economic elites, and of the information that emanates from the halls of power, and, instead of taking their cue from the political establishment, adhere strictly to shared news values (Esser 2008: 400). More space is given to oppositional voices in countries that are accepting of uncertainty and where relativist positions on what is thought to be true are more likely to be adopted (Hanusch 2009: 617). Sacerdotal and pragmatic news cultures can be found in different newsrooms in the same country – organizations and institutions have cultures too – but national differences are important to attend to, especially when claims are made, by writers working within a critical political economy tradition, about the homogenization said to result from global commercialization trends.

Objectivity and bias

Another ideal continually invoked by journalists from quite different cultures is as old as the profession itself (Schudson 1978, 2001). While familiar enough to be taken for granted, the notion of objectivity needs to be interrogated in the context of increased recourse to user-generated content. Objectivity involves certain truth claims (Boudana 2011; Carpentier & Trioen 2010), and the idea that there is a world of events and political or social relations that can be faithfully reflected in journalistic accounts. This is the epistemology behind the first media role discussed in chapter 2, and is often evident in how journalists talk about what they do and what they value.

The World Press Photo Award – the biggest and most prestigious of all news photography competitions – is rich primary source material for research into journalistic perceptions of objectivity. Because the organization that selects the year's best images, and gives the award its name, was founded in 1955, the motivations for choosing award-winners also yield insights into how the profession's take on objectivity has varied over time. One of the prize-winning images of 2011 depicted the drama of the thirty-three Chileans trapped underground when the mine they were working in collapsed. Journalists from all over the world gathered with their cameras at the pithead, but the winning image was captured by one of the miners, not a professional. While the picture wasn't better, in aesthetic terms, it was judged to be closer to the 'truth' of the experience. As one of the judges put it

> Proximity will win out in the end. It was proved by the miners' pictures. It was proved by the London bombings and telephone pictures on the tube train. The really strong, point-of-action kind of one-off news images that come from any medium are the ones that are going to be the most memorable.[7]

The understanding behind such words, and the decision of the jury, is that the camera does not lie. The closer a person is to an event, the better their chances of capturing it faithfully, and thus of providing objective reports. It could be argued, however, that being so close entails being part of the story and the inevitable adoption of a subjective rather than objective viewpoint. In an age of crowdsourcing and valorized proximity, subjectivity is thus eliding with objectivity in current parlance. Whether taken by a professional with an expensive camera or by an ordinary person with a mobile phone, however, photographs are not intrinsically honest and often far from neutral, as illustrated by other examples from the World Press Photo Awards to be discussed later in this book.

The journalist who fails to report in a 'neutral' or 'balanced' way is criticized – by media watchdogs, politicians, members of the audience and, not least, by students taking media courses – as guilty of bias. Often used unthinkingly, the term is a catch-all for quite different things. McQuail (2010) distinguishes between 'partisan bias' (which is present when the views of different sides are accounted for, but the journalist makes it clear which party or cause has the preferable stance), 'propaganda bias' (when only one side is reported), and 'unwitting bias'. As the name suggests, committing this particular sin is not a deliberate act, but rather the result of standard operating procedures and a reflection of what is instinctively known to be the stuff of news in a given journalism culture. Van Dalen (2012) has established that this sort of bias (which he calls 'structural' rather than 'unwitting') guides journalists to pay more attention to some politicians (such as the president or prime minister) than others (such as opposition parties or grassroots activists). Given that polities have different power structures, this sort of bias will also vary from country to country. In the US, for example, politicians from the third-largest party get vastly less coverage than Democrats and Republicans (some readers may even find themselves resorting to Google to find out which the third-largest party in the US is). In European countries with systems of proportional representation, on the other hand, the third-largest party, however small, may wield considerable parliamentary power, be represented in the government with ministerial positions, and thus figure more prominently in journalistic accounts of politics.

The fourth sort of bias identified by McQuail is much more difficult to grasp empirically, but arguably that much more powerful. 'Ideological bias' refers to assumptions about the way the world works, and value judgements associated with them, that are so taken for granted that they are rarely questioned or even made manifest. Familiar from the third role played by media actors that was presented in chapter 2, this sort of bias has a conserving effect, in part because 'journalists tend to view the world through the eyes of the dominant culture' (Hanusch 2009: 615). These ways of seeing are not learned at schools of journalism or in the newsroom. Sanders et al. (2008) found, in a cross-national study, that the attitudes of journalism students are shaped by shared cultural understandings of what journalism is and how it is practised that are acquired long before the start of their training. The prevalence and power of such ideological bias means that any universal claims about journalistic norms and values – whether they are made by scholars or by journalists themselves – should not be taken at face value.

Why? Problems confronting journalists

If journalism is envisaged in the Bourdieuian way – as a field – then journalists can be seen as trying to defend their turf on a battleground, with powerful forces converging on them from different directions. Technological, political and economic forces, and the problems they bring in their wake, help explain why journalism is said to be in a state of crisis.

Problems related to technological change

Digitalization has created an insatiable need for new material. In earlier times, newspapers had a finite number of pages and were published once a day at most, and radio and television news broadcasts had fixed time slots. Digital delivery systems have radically expanded the size of the news hole and wreaked havoc on fixed publication schedules. The news junkie's kick is a headache for the journalist expected to provide the fix. Media professionals are compelled to develop new editorial routines and publishing formats on a continual basis and, as mentioned, the news is never finished (Barnhurst 2011: 576). Media professionals face competition from laymen who no longer need a passcard to a building staffed by trained technicians and furnished with expensive equipment to gather and publish news online. What Mortensen (2011: 13) calls a 'landslide' of visual information on current world affairs, the result of crowdsourcing and citizen photojournalism, must be vetted and curated.

In the early weeks and months of the 2011 Arab uprisings, journalists made avid use of crowdsourced material. Official sources were unreliable and governments took active, and often violent, steps to prevent their own and foreign journalists from reporting. Amateur images were a necessary alternative, and often part of the story (Robertson 2013), which is why the unfolding of these events on screen served as the portkey for the first chapter of this book. By the time the uprisings had developed into civil war in Libya and Syria later that year, however, journalists found cause to be more sceptical of the raw footage posted on YouTube and submitted to their online sites. As Bennett-Jones (2011) put it, old-fashioned government efforts to control media coverage were 'outflanked by a sassy opposition that has shaped what the PR experts would call "the narrative"'.

Established broadcasters have learned to compare the weather in a picture they have been offered with the weather reported by meteorologists for that day and place. They have to ask people who know Homs or Deraa if they recognize the buildings in the footage. And if the voice of the person filming a sequence is audible, they have to find someone reliable to confirm that the accent is right. Mohammed Safi, the head of programming at Al Jazeera, noted during the Israel–Palestine conflict of November 2012 that a point had been reached when the Middle East was 'being depicted by each and every person inside the region'. When authoritarian regimes controlled political imagery and communication, individuals lacked a voice, he said, but 'now everyone is their own reporter'. Rather than taking a weight off the shoulders of the professional journalist, this poses a new challenge. It has become more important than ever for broadcasters to have 'people on the ground', according to Safi – to be able to sift and contextualize the voices from the street, and the pictures from the cameraphone.[8] New technologies and possibilities have thus been accompanied by new problems.

Problems originating in the political realm

Natasa Skaricic had worked for twenty years as a professional journalist when she was fired on the grounds that the government of Croatian Prime Minister Sanander had found her 'unsuitable'. At the time, she was involved in an EU project on health care corruption and was one of the authors of the first book to be published about corruption in the Croatian health system. Together with fifty other journalists, intellectuals and activists, she had launched an initiative against censorship in Croatian media. Journalism in the newest EU member state is troubled in several respects: still recovering from the problematic way war crimes were reported in the 1990s, it has been heavily influenced by economic interests. Health journalism suffers particularly from corruption, in Skaricic's experience, because the government, journalists and editors cooperate with the health and pharmaceutical industry and are granted privileges in return. Professional and objective reporting on health care was made practically impossible by a united industry front, and gatekeeping by a few powerful people in key (and intersecting) positions.[9]

Political elites' strategies for controlling information flows, dealt with in the last chapter, constitute significant problems for journalists, and they are dependent on the judgement and competence, and in some cases the good intentions, of those responsible for regulation – for making media policy – in changing technological and economic settings. Some of the problems that can be filed under this heading are relatively benign. Others are malignant. There is a continuum that stretches from dependence on politicians for material (given the aforementioned insatiable need for new material and increasing time pressures), through spin and disinformation, to clientelism and physical intimidation, and ultimately the threat to life. Not only newspapers are dying: journalists have increasingly become the targets of government and security forces. Between 1992 and 2014, over 1,000 journalists were killed throughout the world – 616 of them murdered with impunity, and, in March 2014, 167 journalists were in prisons throughout the world, jailed for trying to do their job.[10]

Scholars of journalism and political communication have documented a variety of limits on professional autonomy emanating from the political realm (Blumler & Gurevitch 1995; Hallin & Mancini 2004). Cook (1998) has gone as far as to argue that journalists do not just cover politics, or even act as megaphones for the powerful: they work for outlets that are political institutions in their own right. Reporting has been institutionalized as part of the political process, he claims, at least in the US. Already well placed to be the focus of news attention, for reasons outlined earlier, the 'newsworthiness' of powerful political actors is enhanced by the fact that, in many countries, the funds they have at their disposal to finance political communication vastly exceeds the resources of journalists (Ettema et al. 1987/1997; Hanitzsch & Mellado 2011; Preston 2009; Shoemaker & Reese 1996; see also spinwatch.org).

In new and hybrid democracies, and in non-democratic states, the authorities give journalists 'guidance', be it formal or informal. Reporters working for independent and opposition media outlets operate in contexts in which political actors control licensing, airwaves and internet service providers, and libel laws are misused 'to threaten journalists with prison and media outlets with bankruptcy' (Freedman 2012: 50–1). The threats do not always work, and the guidance is not always accepted. In 2013, journalists at the influential Chinese *Southern Weekly* went on strike in protest against the 'dictatorial' behaviour of the Guangdong provincial propaganda chief, deemed inappropriate in an era of 'growing openness'. The action garnered a massive wave of attention, and the line between guidance and interference became the subject of renewed negotiation.

The second media role outlined in chapter 2 – that of arena – assumes that political actors all have access to a common space in which they can set out their messages and arguments, like goods on display in a marketplace. What Wolfsfeld (1997) has called the 'principle of cumulative inequality' ensures that some have access to large, well-lit display windows in the most attractive commercial district, while others have to hawk their wares, at least metaphorically, out of the back of a used car. While differential access to the media arena is a problem for political actors, the problem for journalists is the reverse: they have very different levels of access to politicians. In keeping with their information-control strategies, some political leaders will only agree to answer questions in controlled settings such as press conferences, or have questions answered by spokespeople who serve as gatekeepers. Quite a while ago, it was noted how some politicians deflected attention from weaknesses in policies and political performance by appearing in entertainment settings or on local media, where journalists have less experience or clout, leaving their spokespeople to deal with the tougher questions posed by 'beat' journalists (Rosenstiel 1993). The practice has been refined in the intervening two decades, and adapted in a growing number of countries.

A problem for journalists in Mediterranean states associated with the polarized-pluralist model, in many new (and often hybrid) democracies in Central and Eastern Europe and Russia, Latin America and Africa, is that of 'clientelism'. In some cultures, the combination of political parallelism, instrumentalization of public and private media and clientelism – 'PIC' – is unbeatable. Journalists in such settings face pressure from two sets of owners. The first is comprised of business elites with domestic and foreign economic interests other than media ownership. The second is made up of local and national politicians who often have business dealings on the side (Coman & Gross 2012: 469; Hallin & Papathanassopoulos 2002).

Even in political settings that are not burdened by clientelism, corruption or state-censorship, there is the problem of spin. Political elites, it has been noted, like to blame decreasing levels of trust in government and the political system on cynical reporting. Content analyses abound which demonstrate that journalists regularly depict politics as a game and elections as horse races, and focus on exposing the machinations of politicians rather than their policy alternatives. But it takes two to tango. As Brants et al. (2010: 27) have observed, cyncism does not begin with content: it originates in the relationship between politicians and journalists. When they are met by spin doctors and prevented from accessing accurate information because smokescreens have been erected in a widespread PR culture, many journalists find it hard to do a proper job, and an adversarial stance follows naturally.

Economic problems

Conglomerate ownership, staff cuts at news outlets the world over, and a continuing decline in the number of foreign correspondents are among the worrisome trends cited when the crisis of journalism is discussed (Edmonds 2009). A recurrent buzz-word in this context is 'cannibalism', used to denote the financing of free online news sites with revenue generated from print publications, leading to speculation that newspapers are financing their own destruction (Smedsrud 2011). Journalists are used to working under pressure, but economic problems have been added to familiar sources of stress, and the employees left after newsroom cutbacks are required to do more and different things – often less skilled tasks than their training and previous experience warrant. The sources of concern can also be sources of confusion. The clo-sure of newspapers is said to be a symptom of crisis, but so is the exploding number of news outlets: the argument here is that, through the inevitable competition, the pro-liferation of outlets reduces the leeway for newsmaking to be revitalized by creativity or enterprise (Manning 2001: 52). In both instances, economic interests are identified as the problem.

At the beginning of this millennium, the European Federation of Journalists (EFJ) was already warning that 'aggressive commercial policies' were being pursued by transnational corporations at the expense of maintaining journalistic standards, 'threatening pluralism and undermining journalists' professional and social rights' (cited in Stetka 2012: 438). Public service broadcasters have conceded that they too are operating within a market discourse (Larsen 2010: 271) and media owners are pushing for more content on more platforms with fewer staff (Reinardy 2011: 33). The global financial crisis did not exactly improve things. When the EFJ announced in November 2012 that it would join trade unionists across the continent in a day of protest, public broadcasting was due to be privatized in Portugal, and those Greek journalists still in work had seen their salaries cut by 35 per cent. (Unemployment among Greek journalists that year exceeded 30 per cent. In June 2013, the govern-ment shut down the state broadcaster ERT and laid off 2,700 journalists to save money.) In Spain, a third of the staff of *El País* found itself threatened with redun-dancy. In Norway, the Schibstedt group cut a quarter of its journalists and the Sud-Ouest Group announced plans to do the same in France. Major public broad-casters like the BBC, France Télévisions and RTVE were among those 'cutting costs' and downsizing. 'All across Europe, thousands of journalists have lost their jobs or are forced to continue working under precarious conditions', with both quality reporting and media pluralism hanging in the balance, the Federation warned (EFJ 2012).

The issue of media pluralism is a reminder that tidy distinctions cannot always be maintained between political and economic constraints. As outlined above, politicians may have business interests and economic elites often have political ambitions – Silvio Berlusconi is a striking example, but not the only one. Journalists are vulnerable to corruption and interference from political and business elites in many African countries, starved as their media infrastructures often are (Josephi 2010).

The departure point for a significant strand in media research has long been that mainstream media actors reproduce ideologies that shore up the economically pow-erful (Manning 2001). It is a view more often rehearsed than demonstrated by solid empirical analysis, which is a problem. Whether or not one shares the assumptions of political economists, and whatever the owner–journalist relation in a given set-ting, it is worth reflecting on how often 'the market' is referred to as if it were a force of nature, especially under globalization. When it is, the economic problems that circumscribe journalism are correspondingly depicted as inevitable and unstop-pable. They are not. Whatever one may think of Svegfors' characterization of the state of contemporary journalism, he is right when he says that any erosion of it 'is not necessary, as it is often made out to be. It is the result of concrete decisions taken by individuals in positions of power and responsibility' (Svegfors 2013).

Where? Cultural variations

Journalists in newsrooms all over the world espouse the ideal of objectivity, and international journalism research has yielded many studies that show how journalistic orientations and practices converge under globalization. As Hanitzsch and Mellado (2011: 408) put it, 'similarities in professional routines, editorial procedures, and socialization processes exist in countries as diverse as Brazil, Germany, Indonesia, Tanzania, and the United States'.

That said, just as many studies document significant – if not 'huge' – differences between countries, and more disagreement than agreement as to the relative importance of different journalistic roles (Esser et al. 2012; Fröhlich & Holtz-Bacha 2003; Herkman 2012: 370; Kalyango & Eckler 2010; Sanders et al. 2008; Weaver 1998). Ethics are a case in point. Journalistic ethics in the UK can be interpreted in a variety of ways, partly because the ethical codes of the National Union of Journalists are formulated in broad terms and fit on a single page. The Pressekodex that governs the work of German journalists, by way of contrast, is twenty-four pages long, contains sixteen principles, and is thus considerably more constraining (Hanusch 2009: 622).

While journalists the world over grapple with the sort of problems sketched above, the particular way that their work is affected by increased commercialization or growing cynicism, for example, differs from one political system to the next, and in countries with different models of media and politics. In Anglo-Saxon states, where majoritarian electoral systems return parliaments and congresses that cement adversarial relations, news coverage tends to be correspondingly conflictual. Conflict is also reflected in political reporting in consensus democracies like Sweden and the Netherlands, but this tends to focus on differences between parties rather than between government and opposition, and the relationship has been described as one of 'critical professionalism' rather than the 'perpetual state of mutual hostility' said to prevail in North Atlantic polities (Djerf-Pierre 2000; Schönbach et al. 2001; Van Aelst et al. 2010; Van Dalen 2012). A significant amount of research on media cynicism centres around US elections. But European election campaigns are different (and shorter), with less professional campaign management, and thus different (and lesser) manifestations of media cynicism. Cynicism is also more often documented in countries where the 'liberal' system prevails, as the proclivity of political actors to use PR is more pronounced and their relationship with journalists consequently less harmonious than in countries characterized by clientelistic relations (Hallin & Mancini 2004, 2011; Van Dalen et al. 2011: 149). In the latter, information 'is treated by those in power as a private resource' (Poletti & Brants 2010: 332) and the journalistic tone is 'sacerdotal' rather than 'pragmatic'. Because of state intervention and the fact that all the main quality newspapers in Italy were owned or controlled by industrial groups at the end of the first decade of the millennium, Italian media have gained a reputation for serving the interests of the politicians and entrepreneurs that control them (Poletti & Brants 2010: 333). In countries such as Chile, Russia, Turkey and Uganda, journalists working for private media companies experience higher levels of political influence than elsewhere, because so many media outlets are owned by politicians and friends of politicians (Hanitzsch & Mellado 2011: 418).

The homogenization of journalistic milieux (usually conceived of as the spread of the liberal model) is not as inevitable as sometimes suggested. Lauk (2008) maintains that Central and Eastern Europe contain a broader variety of journalism cultures than older democracies. After the fall of the Berlin Wall, media professionals from Western countries travelled east to help journalists in newly liberated countries establish their professions. They were not particularly successful, although not necessarily for the wrong reasons. The assumption seemed to be that if you took away propaganda journalism, nothing would be left, and that Western traditions would be written on blank slates. But these countries had strong journalism histories. Polish journalism, for example, has deeply rooted traditions of professionalism, advocacy and political engagement that have prevailed in the face of the global encroachment of the liberal model and its 'fact-centred' journalism (Lauk 2008: 195).

Journalists in newer democracies have experienced confusion as to how to behave in settings where familiar relationships no longer apply, but new ones have yet to be established. They sometimes find themselves working in what has been called a 'normative vacuum'. Many journalists in former Warsaw Pact countries find themselves engaged in nation-building processes, and their work is characterized by an enlightening and instructive tone (Freedman 2012). While the number of journalists (and the media outlets they work for) in Indonesia has risen exponentially since the country began its transition to democracy in 1998, they continue to see themselves as part of the national project, dedicated to a model of 'developmental journalism' such as that which prevailed throughout the Suharto years, with the duty of the journalist stipulated as being to work for 'the good of the society'. In practice this means not rocking the political boat (Pintak & Setiyono 2011). This of true of many African journalists too, who also differ from their Western counterparts insofar as their reporting focuses on the community or civil society, rather than the individual (Shaw 2009: 501).

Not only political systems are hybrids, in globalizaed societies: political communication cultures are too (Pfetsch & Voltmer 2012: 390). But cultural differences remain tenacious, and continue to matter to the media–politics relationship. They are context-dependent and contingent on specific historical circumstances (Zelizer 2005). 'Universal' trends of negativity, sarcasm and lack of trust, just like 'universal' values of objectivity and professionalism, are in fact culturally defined concepts (Boudana 2010; Esser 1998; Josephi 2010; Poletti & Brants 2010: 331). This is both an obstacle to comparative research, and a reality that necessitates it.

When? Continuity and change

There is evidence of continuity in all three problematic areas outlined above. The experience of technology impacting on journalistic professionalism is not new. In Zelizer's analysis, the way journalists reconstructed their story of how the murder of purported Kennedy assassin Lee Harvey Oswald was covered in the US media in 1963 was in fact a discourse about the relation of journalism to technological change (in that instance the introduction of television: Zelizer 1993: 203–4). When it comes to politics, Poletti & Brants (2010: 330) suggest that claims of increasingly derogatory journalistic attitudes towards politics and politicians have made scholars blind to 'old partisanship in new clothes'. Furthermore, journalists have always been dependent on established, and indeed entrenched, political sources. Rather than decreasing under conditions of radical transparency (WikiLeaks and all that), it has been argued that this dependence has in fact increased, in step with cutbacks. Journalists are now outnumbered by officials in most countries (Ryfe 2009). Economic difficulties are a more enduring feature of the media professional's working life than is often acknowledged in the current debate, and journalists have always had to work hard to attract and keep the attention of the public. Newsrooms themselves are conservative forces that ensure continuity in key respects, socializing journalists into the use of standard operating procedures and traditional news values. As Ryfe (2009: 199) puts it, 'resistance to change among reporters is institutional and cultural'.

Having said that, there is ample evidence of significant change.

Upon retiring as world affairs correspondent in 2011, Paul Reynolds reflected on the shock he had experienced nine years earlier when he moved to BBC News Online. 'I found that I was in direct contact with the public. Horror. This had not happened before', he wrote. Writing online means

> the piece sits there in front of the reader. It is not something they might have half-heard over the airwaves. And they can contact you immediately. They do.

And journalists can respond and adapt. They do.

While the habit of juxtaposing 'new media' and 'old' mainstream media has proven hard to kick, the distinction is unhelpful and inaccurate. The people working for established media outlets across the globe – be they newspapers, radio or television – do so in digital environments. Whether it is the *Times of India*, Paraguay's *Ultima Hora* or *Sudan TV*, it is online, on Facebook and on Twitter. Journalists work on something that is no longer a product, but a process; no longer something that is 'hard' but something described as 'liquid' (Deuze 2008). Their position in society, as well as what they produce, has also become ephemeral and contested by a plethora of different media outputs (Harrington 2011: 41). As will be seen in chapter 8, these include media forms like comedy and satire.

One response has been to make the contributions of readers, listeners and viewers part of the news narrative, in ways different from the conventional vox pop. The 'Comment is Free' site of one British newspaper is an example of the 'democratization of news'. The journalistic position it reflects is that

> the traditional newspaper model of comment – half a dozen highly-paid stars – is not the only valid one. If it's in the *New York Times* and it's 'foreign', you will, by and large, get the views of either Roger Cohen or Tom Friedman. Both are wonderfully perceptive writers, but it seems a limiting proposition that theirs are the only voices worth hearing, whether on Africa, the Middle East, China, Iran, Venezuela or Russia. Comment is Free, by contrast, publishes more than 1,000 pieces a month by a wide range of people, not many of them traditional journalists. They are politicians, lawyers, doctors, priests, rabbis, teachers, soldiers, businesswomen, academics. (Rusbridger 2009: 22)

Another example is the 'Global Village Voices' of Al Jazeera English, which encourages viewers 'from regions that are not often heard in traditional western media' to use webcams or cameraphones to contribute their take on stories covered on the channel. Nigerian readers take seriously the 'report yourself' tagline of a New York-based opposition news outlet, and contribute thousands of eyewitness accounts to Sahara Reporters. Its founder Omoyele Sowore says they are reporting news 'that is too important to be left to a journalist' and cover topics that local media cannot or

The chapter's portkey in action. Photograph: © Ramin Talaie / Corbis.

choose not to, in a country ranked 112 out of 180 in the press freedom index published by Reporters without Borders in 2014. Such practices have implications for the 'ordinary people' in focus in the next chapter.

To think about

This chapter ends where it began, with voices discussing mediated politics. In some languages 'vote' and 'voice' are the same word. In others, the job of both politicians and journalists is to 'represent' us, although representation is conceptualized quite differently in political science and in media and cultural studies. As explained by a pioneer in the latter field, 'we give things meaning by how we represent them – the words we use about them, the stories we tell about them, the images of them we produce, the emotions we associate with them, the ways we classify and conceptualize them, the values we place on them' (Hall 2007: 3). One thing to think about is how journalists manage the voices we encounter when navigating the political world with the sort of portkey that opened the chapter.

Many other questions present themselves, as compelling as they are frustrating. When studying media representation, how is the journalist to be distinguished from the others who distribute information that has a bearing on politics? What is the difference between a witness who films a protest in Tunis, Bangkok or Kiev on her mobile phone and uploads it on YouTube, and the CNN correspondent who files a report from the same place? Have professionally trained journalists become redundant in a functionalist sense as well as in a practical one (i.e. increasingly unemployed), or are they needed more than ever, to help us navigate the newsworld encountered at the tap of the portkey – a space that is light years from McLuhan's

Gutenburg Galaxy? And how does the researcher approach the task of investigating the content produced by journalists, and its impact?

This chapter has focused on national cultural differences. It is instructive to think about whether the responsibilities of journalists have changed under globalization. For and to whom should they now report? Should they behave as watchdogs defending the public from the abuse of political and economic power, always on the lookout for misdeed and ready to critique? Or is it their responsibility to put their discursive and symbolic power to work in the construction and maintenance of political community, especially as their cohesion is threatened?

Development journalism, with its emphasis on nation-building at the expense of political critique, may well seem inappropriate, if not downright illegitimate, to readers in 'developed' countries. But the most important political problems of the day transcend national borders (be they financial crisis, climate change, trafficking or migration). Transnational organizations and institutions exist to deal with such problems, but unlike states they lack a *demos* – a political community of citizens to be represented in one way or another. In such a setting, is it inappropriate that journalists engage in community-building, and contribute to the development of what Beck (2006) called 'cosmopolitan outlooks'? Researchers and theorists working within the critical political economy paradigm would answer the question differently from those more interested in cosmopolitanism and the discourse on 'global imagination' (Robertson forthcoming 2015). That debate opens onto another scholarly world, replete with food for thought.

A reporter for Radio Azadi (RFE/RL's Afghan Service) interviews a citizen in Helmand Province, Afghanistan. Photograph: Agent021 at English Wikipedia. Wikimedia Commons.

5 The People Formerly Known as the Audience

It is towards the end of the Great Depression of the 1930s, and the family is gathered around the radio in the living room. They might be listening to Hans von Kaltenborn's report from Spain in the throes of civil war, or from the Czech Republic that is falling to Hitler, or to Orson Welles' deadpan news report that the Martians are invading, or to the farm broadcast or football semi-finals on public service stations in Canada and Ireland, or to a play sponsored by an American soap company, but they are listening together, within the walls of their home.

Then it is the end of the noughties – July 2011, to be more precise – and the family is in the car. The radio is on and the parents are listening to the breaking news that a bomb has gone off in the government quarter in Oslo. The man and woman in the front seat are asking each other whether the reporter said that eight people

In broadcasting's infancy, the whole family gathered around the receiving set in the evening to listen to news and entertainment. A farm family from Hood County, Oregon. Photo courtesy of National Archives and Records Administration / Wikimedia Commons.

had been killed, or whether it had been ten, when their teenage daughter offers, from the back seat, the information that a man has opened fire on young campers on a Norwegian island. Because she has been deep in her iPhone habitat and not listening to the radio, her parents correct her, and patiently explain about the bomb in the Norwegian capital. But she insists on her unbelievable horror story, and provides updates: now there are dead bodies all over the island; now there are helicopters circling overhead; now terrified adolescents are throwing themselves in the water and trying to escape. The girl's mother knows about the 'War of the Worlds' broadcast, and how people believed Welles' wild radio story of invading Martians, panicked, and threw themselves into cars to flee the city, and has a moment of déjà vu: information can so easily be distorted in a crisis. Only later is her daughter's story confirmed. When right-wing extremist Anders Behring Breivik launched his attack on Norwegian democracy, the adults had been listening to a live radio broadcast. The teenager, on the other hand, had been following the tweets of her cohorts, who were connected to the young activists in the afflicted country through far-reaching social media networks.

The portkey opening this chapter is a journey through time, but it has to do with space. The family members of the 1930s were used to consuming media messages in the same room, while those of 2011 remember getting the news of the Norwegian massacre not just because of the unfathomable events they were trying to take in but because it was so unusual for them to consume news together. Over the years, something has happened to social space, and developments in media technology are intimately related to this change. Technology is inert, however: the changes to be dealt with intellectually have to do with the ways people use the devices that convey news of the world, and what those practices mean for their relation to space, to politics and to the people affected by those politics.

The man that Anderson (1983/2006) has sitting down with his nineteenth-century newspaper enacted his membership of the imagined community of the nation when he read, but he did so alone in his room, or at his breakfast table, and took in the news passively. The family gathered around the radio, and later in front of the television, listened and watched together, and talked to each other about what they had taken in. A few decades later, families (at least in developed countries) would still be consuming the world in the privacy of their homes, but they would be doing it in separate rooms, on individual devices, no longer required to tune into the same channel and thus no longer liable to discuss those mediated messages with each other. In the twenty-first century, mobile technology has taken people out of their homes, and while they continue to consume media messages privately – on their own hand-held devices and with headphones – they are increasingly doing so in public settings. And in these public spaces, they are using the same technology not just to take in messages about the world, but to record and disseminate such messages themselves, routinely enough for their actions to be unreflecting, like those of journalists in the last chapter who commit acts of unwitting bias.

There is considerable disagreement over what to call the people in focus in this chapter. Whether they – that is, we – are conceived of as citizens or consumers, publics or audiences, media-users or 'prosumers', or any of the other names given to 'the people formerly known as the audience' (Rosen 2006), determines what is expected of this set of actors, and shapes understandings of their role in the media–politics relationship. Knowing what to call this category of actors is a problem for scholars – theoretical as well as empirical – because conceptualizations guide what we see, how we think about what we see, what questions we choose to ask and how we go about looking for answers.

Scholars are not the only ones faced with problems on this front. As will be recalled from chapter 3, politicians face the challenge of getting these people's attention and support, and 'difficult publics' vote in unpredictable ways, to the extent they vote at all. The access to digital media technology these people enjoy also means that politicians must find new ways of controlling what they want people to know and see, and it means that the task of the journalist is both less clear and more difficult. For the 'ordinary' person, the problem is finding a way to deal with information overflow, and of not succumbing to compassion fatigue when news of a massacre in Norway overshadows a famine in Somalia and a multitude of natural catastrophes, or the fatigue that results from attempts to keep up when one revolution follows another in repressitarian states. As citizens, people are on the receiving end of spin and asked to make decisions as to who should represent them in polities where professional communicators throw more and heavier spanners into the democratic works. The global financial crisis strengthened feelings of exclusion aroused by economic disempowerment and the increasingly unrepresentative nature of government, even in formal democracies. According to some scholars, people also suffer from the problem of political ignorance. As commercial media driven by the search for profits proliferate the world over, civic roles are being undermined and people prevented from understanding the power relations that shape their lives. As Kaitatzi-Whitlock (2011: 460) put it:

> Political ignorance limits citizens' ability to judge, decide, or calculate action on politically induced outcomes, a situation which amounts to depoliticization. In effect, political ignorance renders citizens incapable of living their civic lives or benefiting from rights, let alone participating in 'self-government'.

The following account begins with the conceptual problem, reviewing the different names given to the 'ex-audience' and the intellectual baggage that comes with each label. An overview of the academic debate follows – of the different ways scholars working in different traditions conceive of the relationship between message senders, the messages themselves, and the people for whom they are intended. Questions about the tension between continuity and change are then posed before returning to the question of power. Are we better understood as active makers of meaning empowered by media technology, or as unpaid labourers in the service of unelected economic actors, who reward us with increased levels of political ignorance and thus deprive us of civic influence?

You talking about me?

The way people are mirrored in the literature might not give them an excuse to pull a gun, but depending on whether a scholar comes from, say, political science or media studies, and assumes either that an individual will reach for a ballot or for a remote control, a person might be tempted to mimic Robert de Niro's taxi-driver, and wonder who scholars are talking about.

Citizens and voters

Some literature refers to the actors in focus in this chapter as citizens, who have the right to choose their political representatives and the civic obligation to vote and to keep themselves well informed. A citizen is a member of a political community and usually to be found in the data generated by pollsters. There is some truth in the wry observation that citizens really only come into being at election time, when the political establishment summons up a citizenry or electorate by making claims about what it wants. In terms of the media–politics relationship, the need to be supplied with information is the most interesting characteristic of the figure conceived in this way. Political knowledge is 'indispensable' to the citizen and essential to democracy, it has been argued, and is 'a civic fortification of the public interest' (Kaitatzi-Whitlock 2011: 460).

Sometimes researchers manage to locate people who match the citizen job description. One recent study found that young Jordanians are avid news consumers who rely on newspapers, television and interpersonal sources, and who explain their consumption in civic terms. As one respondent put it, he followed the news 'because I am a part of this world, and it's important for me to stay updated about every detail in this world' (Martin 2011: 724). Far away in small-town Sweden, librarians also expressed their relationship to the media in civic terms, when interviewed by a researcher about how they related to news reports of distant others.

> The awful thing about TV news is that you stop thinking. I mean, I've almost stopped looking at the news because of that. I think there is report after report after report, and I don't have a chance to react. So I much prefer to watch, you know, slower programmes and reportage . . . when you keep up, like.... For me it's important to react. Because I think sitting and being spoon-fed and not reacting . . . well, you feel numbed. (Robertson 2010a: 70–1)

It is precisely such failings, and the gaps in citizen's knowledge, that have proven most interesting to researchers, and for rather a long time too. 'The low level of public information about politics has been documented with monotony ever since sample survey techniques developed', complained Converse half a century ago; 'Not only is the electorate as a whole quite uninformed, but it is the least informed members within the electorate who seem to hold the critical "balance of power"' (Converse 1962: 578).

Rather than the political or media establishment, the 'uninformed voter paradigm' blames citizens for this problem, and measures their knowledge levels against an ideal model, based on public-choice theory, according to which people have complete information and clear preferences. They are sometimes also blamed for contradictory research results, as people answer pollsters' questions even when they have failed to pay attention to the information provided by elites and journalists (Zaller 1992).

Unlike the ideal citizen in the model, real people have to deal with contradictory demands and navigate a flood of confusing information. Their acquisition of it can thus never be complete, nor their preferences entirely clear. Critics of the paradigm have also pointed out that the surveys used to document the failings of the 'uninformed voter' have been better at measuring opinions than knowledge, and that what knowledge is tapped into is narrowly conceived. Scholars such as Neuman et al. (1992: 13, 15) have argued – and to some extent demonstrated – how people use 'schema' or simplifying maps to organize political facts and figures into a meaningful whole. A research focus on the ability to recall facts and figures can obscure the political cognition inherent in the deployment of such maps, and underestimate voter comprehension and the consistency of their views. Nevertheless, notions of an imperfect citizen continue to influence current scholarship on political knowledge (of which more below) and are evident in derogatory commentary on the decisions of people who vote for a Sarah Palin or a Beppe Grillo. This unfavourable view was most pithily expressed by former British Prime Minister Winston Churchill, in his infamous quip that the best argument against democracy is a five-minute conversation with the average voter.

Other scholars have more understanding for the citizen's quandary, and instead of blaming ordinary people for imperfections in the political system, acknowledge that they cannot fulfil expectations without being respected by political elites and recognized as legitimate players in the political process (Dahlgren 2009). Coleman and Blumler argue that citizenship in digital democracies needs to be envisaged, and enabled, in three ways. Beyond membership in national political communities ('legal–judicial citizenship') is a second citizenship ('political') which involves active participation and the potential to influence outcomes in democratic ways. Information is essential to this mode of citizenship. The third ('affective') mode is in play when feelings of civic belonging, loyalty and solidarity are mobilized (Coleman & Blumler 2009).

Scholars who conceive of citizenship in political, affective and cultural terms, and not simply civic ones, focus on the right to representation rather than the obligation to acquire what elites consider to be essential political knowledge. While the uninformed voter paradigm concerned American politics, for the most part, and was imbued with political conservatism, the scholarly praxis of linking of culture to citizenship began in the UK, on the critical left. Marshall (1950/1992) argued that the civic phase of citizenship was but one of three in its history, which began with the eighteenth-century Habermasian public discussions referred to in chapter 2. It was added to, but not replaced by, the political phase of the nineteenth century and, later, by a social phase. The fourth, cultural, phase of citizenship is theorized as being bound up with (public service) television. (The alert reader will have noticed a parallel here between Marshall's history of citizenship and the different ages of political communication described earlier by Blumler and Gurevitch.)

In several works, Stevenson (1999, 2003) has argued that, under globalization, it is more important than ever to think in terms of cultural citizenship. A citizen in this vision has the right not only to representation in Parliament, Bundestag, Duma or Assembly, but also to mediated representation. Cultural citizenship exists when everyone in a given society has access to the semiotic materials 'that are necessary in order to both make social life meaningful, critique patterns of domination, and allow for the recognition of difference under conditions of tolerance and mutual respect' (Stevenson 1999: 61).

Citizenship seen this way has more to do with political power than civic obligation.

Members of the public

In some scholarly discussions, the actor in focus in this chapter is conceived as a member of 'the public', a notion that has evolved over time. The space in which this public is to be found is sometimes singular and national (Garnham 2000), sometimes fragmented and plural (Mouffe 1997), sometimes transnational (Trenz 2004) or global (Stevenson 2003). Some see the public as autonomous in relation to the prevailing authorities (Mills 1956/2000), while others see publics (in Russia, for example) as convened by political elites (von Seth 2011). In other accounts, the public comes into being when someone imagines it (Coleman & Ross 2010) or when it is constructed (Dekavalla 2012).

What all conceptions have in common, however, is the idea that a public cannot exist without communication. Part of Mills' (1956/2000) definition of citizenship is the stipulation that communication be organized in such a way that any opinion expressed in public can be answered effectively. For this reason, public service broadcasting has occupied a central position in many accounts of political communication (Larsen 2010: 269). Esser et al. (2012: 250) note that a defining feature of public service broadcasting in Europe is its ability to capture 'inadvertent' viewers, because news programmes tend to be aired during prime time, so as to capture the attention of more citizens (including the less motivated) and not just more consumers (which is thought to be the strategy of commercial programmers). Comparative studies have found that those countries with the most conducive settings for capturing inadvertent viewers are Belgium, the UK, Israel, the Netherlands, Norway and Sweden, where people have a high number of access points to news coverage on both public and private channels. Before the Greek public service broadcaster was put on austerity ice in 2013, it and its Portuguese counterpart offered a rich supply of news, but 'lagged behind' in viewership shares and scheduling diversity. Inadvertent viewers were found to be a rarer species in Italy and Spain, where major channels tend to broadcast their main news bulletins only once, and at competing times (Esser et al. 2012: 263–5)

The notion of 'media publics' (Herbert 2005) refers to the ideal situation that prevails when viewers of a given broadcast argue about its content, with the best argument winning, rather than that of the most powerful person. The Habermasian ideal thus continues to influence conceptualizations of the role and power of members of the public (as well as those of the media actors who furnish the public sphere with resources for rational discussion). But technological and economic developments have posed some challenges to this idea. In an analysis of how digital technology is impacting on citizen roles and, indeed, on what happens to public space in an era of convergence, Papacharissi (2010) argues that is difficult to maintain the distinction between public and private that is central to Habermas' conception. Another problem is what is perceived by scholars on the critical left – including Habermas himself – as the 'indissoluble' tension between capitalism and democracy. In opposition to the figure at the heart of the Habermasian conception of democracy, the person who is reliant on commercial media outlets for information is thought to be addressed not as a citizen, but as a consumer.

Audience members and consumers

Unlike many political scientists, media scholars tend to treat the people in focus in this chapter as members of the audience rather than of the electorate, as consumers of media products (be they informative or entertaining), and most often as viewers. Like publics, audiences can be imagined, but they are imagined by media industries rather than politicians: the key concept of consumption situates them in relation to economic rather than political actors. Audiences do not occur naturally and their members do not choose to join one: they 'come into being around specific media technologies and texts (or genres) at particular social and historical moments and they need to be understood in relation to these dynamics' (Gillespie 2005: 1).

Three broad phases are commonly identified in the literature on audiences too (for example by Livingstone 2005: 45). The first phase is that of the 'simple' audience (associated with face-to-face, direct communication that takes place in public and is often highly ritualized), and the second that of the 'mass audience' (which is highly mediated and spatially – even globally – dispersed, comprised of people who often receive media messages in private settings). The third phase is that of the 'diffused audience' (which is strongly dispersed and fragmented, yet at the same time embedded in or fused with all aspects of daily life), of which more later.

In the historical moment of globalization, people are widely seen as belonging to global consumer audiences rather than national communities of citizens. This affects not only the *demos* but also the *ethnos*. What Europeans have in common, when it comes to communicative space, opined Schlesinger in 1993, is actually American television rather than anything European, because the US is the source of the audiovisual products 'that most easily traverse any European national barriers' (cited in Richardson & Meinhof 1999: 6). European-produced programmes, on the other hand, were thought to offer much more limited scope of audience identification. The question is whether this is still the case, fifteen years on in the process of European integration.

The media-affected

The point of departure for research on 'media effects' is that media power is greater than people power. The people in this scholarly context are voters (uninformed) and audiences (passive). The majority of public interest and public funding, not least in the US, has been concentrated on experimental research examining the short-term effects of media exposure on behaviours or attitudes. The problem with such a research focus is that it can generate results that can be used as evidence of any problem. 'Whichever way one looks at it' says Livingstone (2005: 22), 'it seems that the media can be shown, under specific circumstances, to have a variety of modest and inconsistent effects on some segments of the population'. While contemporary scholars do not live in a proverbial ivory tower, cut off from the rest of the world, and are rightly expected to make a social contribution with their research, it is a problem that their findings can be interpreted differently by policymakers, depending on the political goals. But political elites, and the editorialists who try to set their agendas, tend to be less interested in contextualization and qualifications than the scholars who produce the results they cite.

In studies of politics, effects are demonstrated by statistical correlations between 'the issue agenda, preferences, perspectives, and assumptions of the audience, and some corresponding measure of relative emphasis in the media' (Neuman et al. 1992: 9). A typical finding is that those who watch a great deal of television tend to exhibit higher levels of mainstream and stereotypical thinking, or that agenda-setting correlates with issue salience (the more news coverage of a given policy issue, the likelier people are to find it important). Comparative research has established that there are significant national variations in levels of news exposure and knowledge, giving rise to the idea that 'political information environments' can have an effect on citizen involvement and political knowledge (Esser et al. 2012: 248).

Changes in the media landscape, not least the proliferation of outlets, have resulted in considerable scholarly debate about the strength and direction of media effects. On one side of what Tworzecki and Semetko (2012) refer to as the 'malaise versus mobilization debate', some argue that 'media logic' (not usually helpfully defined) is transforming traditional political competition into an image-centred spectacle of 'video-politics', with citizens becoming spectators in the process. On the other side of the debate are those who see media developments (both technological and institutional) as leading to the fragmention of large, diverse audiences into a multitude of smaller, more mobilized groups. As the 'mass media' disappear, and with them the mass audience, the power of media effects is thought to be on the wane (Tworzecki & Semetko 2012: 408). The trend is far from universal, however, and scholars engaged in empirical research are careful not to overgeneralize. Media effects are, it is said, relatively weak in established democracies, but stronger in newer ones, where people lack 'a lifetime' of personal experience with the institutions and traditions of the democratic system. In post-communist East-Central Europe, for example, the combination of a short (or, in the case of countries like Poland, uneven) experience of democracy, 'underdeveloped' political parties and 'tabloidized' politics creates a space for media outlets to play an 'outsized' role in agenda-setting and opinion formation, according to Tworzecki and Semetko (2012: 409).

While some have their eye on political circumstances when explaining media effects, others blame technology. Sunstein (2001b), for example, insists that the increasing use of digital media results in selective exposure effects. The 'Daily Me' debate (Negroponte 1995) revolves around the hypothesis that people tailor their media consumption to their own personal tastes and views, opting out of the collective conversation upon which democratic negotiations about just distributions are predicated. These ideas are influential and often repeated, but viewed with scepticism in some quarters. According to Bimber, for example, there is no empirical evidence to support the claim that people are using new media environments to 'wall themselves off' from messages they find politically challenging (Bimber 2012: 118).

Gratification-seekers

The arguments of Sunstein and Negroponte are in the same vein as those of scholars who argued some time ago that media effects depend on the 'uses and gratifications' of people's interactions with media products and technology. The objects of study of scholars such as Katz et al. (1973–4) are not passive recipients of media messages, but people who demand and expect media artefacts and devices to serve particular functions, and who are relatives of the 'hunter-gatherers' Meyrowitz (1985) saw emerging in the dawn of the digital age. Particularly influential in the 1970s, uses and gratifications theory focused on the behaviour of consumers rather than voters. It sought to explain general motivations (why people might choose entertainment rather than informative fare) and the more gratifying aspects of some media practices as compared with others (why many people spend more time watching television than reading), rather than why people were more attentive to some messages than others and how they made use of those messages (Neuman et al. 1992: 12). It is nevertheless worth being acquainted with the theory, which has been revisited in the context of proliferating technologies. Ostertag, for example, has developed the ideas of the older research generation in a 'critical uses-and-gratifications' framework which pays more attention to issues of power and control in broader social and political settings (Ostertag 2010: 598).

The 'active' audience

Notions about media effects tend to assume a linear flow of influence from the content of media messages to the knowledge, views and understandings of the people on the receiving end. Uses and gratifications theory concedes that the audience is more active than does the effects tradition, but only when it comes to making choices, not making sense. In 1980, Hall proposed a different way of theorizing influence that was cyclical rather than linear and focused on the processes of putting meaning and information in communicative packages (encoding) and opening the packages upon delivery (decoding). What is important about the 'encoding–decoding model' is that it can accomodate unequal power relationships between senders and receivers, who occupy different positions in the social structure. In Hall's account, media producers tend to be powerful, be they journalists working in privileged positions in mainstream outlets (for example), or the elites whose hegemonic views are reproduced in mediated accounts of politics and society. But the model also allows for the possibility that audiences will resist this structural (and, Thompson would say, symbolic) power.

Media messages, according to Hall's model, can be decoded from dominant, negotiated or oppositional positions, depending on whether a member of the audience accepts (unthinkingly or otherwise) the elite understandings generally encoded in, for example, news and current affairs broadcasts (a dominant or preferred reading), receives the messages in a 'yes – but' frame of mind (negotiated) or opposes the framing of the message ('it's not at all like that!'). Such a model posits that some members of the audience may be passive, or that many 'read' media texts passively (as in unquestioningly), in the way their producers intended ('preferred reading'), but it also allows for more 'active' audience activity – for people to engage with a news report, question the way it is framed or the words used to describe political actors or social groups, and compare it with their own experience.

At one end of the research field, as noted, is the scholarly discourse that treats people primarily as citizens to be informed, and which furrows its metaphorical brow when they do not behave rationally (sometimes referred to as the 'liberal-pluralist' paradigm). At the other end is the 'critical' or 'radical' discourse on audiences which positions them as consumers, 'vulnerable to political manipulation and commercial exploitation by the culture industries' (Livingstone 2005: 11). One scholar occupying the middle ground is Katz (1980), who charted swings between these two dominant views and responded with a 'two-step flow' hypothesis that takes into account people's weapons of self-defence. Media messages are not consumed in a vacuum: personal experience and the friends and family members and colleagues with whom media messages are discussed help 'mediate media effects'. Katz sees the audience as more active than passive, for two reasons that relate to Hall's insights. First, people have to interpret what they see, read or hear before decoding can take place. Second, their knowledge and experience, and the things that may be worrying or interesting them at the moment, serve as tools in the work of interpretation.

The notion of the audience as 'active' has come to dominate cultural studies research on television reception, which is understood as 'a set of socially and culturally informed activities'. The 'active audience' paradigm treats audiences as 'plural, diverse and variable' (Livingstone 2005: 31) and the media texts they consume as 'polysemic', or carriers of many potential meanings. Viewed in this way, differently constituted audiences will thus 'work' with different textual meanings, and meaning will consequently always be unstable and in flux (Alasuutaari 1999; Barker 1999: 110–12). Scholars guided by such views of the actors in focus in this chapter are more interested in people's identities than in their knowledge or opinions. When studying the media–politics relationship, this entails an interest in whether people think of themselves primarily as members of a local, national or transnational political community, or as part of a class or an ethnic or gender minority, or as having overlapping identities, rather than whether they know which country holds the EU presidency at any given time, or the name of the Education Minister.

The people as participants: citizen journalists and prosumers

In a popular sketch, British comedians Mitchell and Webb play two television news presenters who interrupt their own broadcast to announce that Earth has just been attacked by a vastly superior alien force and is about to be annihilated. After briefly recounting the facts, they turn to the camera and ask for input from viewers.

> So: a massive and unstoppable alien invasion threatens the earth. What's your reaction? Are you affected by the end of civilization as we know it? What's your perspective? Maybe you live on Earth or know someone who does. E-mail us with your thoughts on your imminent molecular evaporation at bbc.co.uk/ emergencyapocalypse.[1]

This spoof is in fact an astute comment on the trend whereby broadcasters treat their viewers as shapers, rather than receipients, of the news story – as the people who were once the audience but are now more than that. Not everyone resorts to Rosen's unwieldy moniker to express this evolution. Abercrombie and Longhurst (1998) coined the notion of 'diffused audience' to encapsulate the qualitative change they perceived to have taken place in people's relationship to media technology, mediated messages, and space. The diffused audience does not come into being when an economic actor decides that will happen: media use constitutes the very existence of people in media-rich (and media-middling) societies. From this scholarly perspective, digital developments have eliminated the distance between those who perform and those who watch: audience members now have the skills and resources to be cultural producers in their own right. In the world of diffused audiences, media institutions do not put themselves between the 'performer' and the person on the receiving end of the performance. Diffused audiences 'are both local and global, local in actual performance, global in that imagination . . . is a crucial resource in the performance'. Communication is direct and the difference between public and private performances is eroded, according to Abercrombie and Longhurst (1998: 192).

More recently, Anstead and O'Loughlin (2011) have deployed the notion of 'viewertariat' to talk about how viewers engage actively with political issues by providing real-time commentary on Twitter while watching current affairs programmes on television. Building on Chadwick's notion of hybridity, discussed in chapter 1, they bring a different meaning to the notion of 'active' audience, by pointing out that watching television involves not just mental but also communicative activity. They make a good case for the importance of thinking in qualitatively new ways about access, acknowledge that members of the viewertariat constitute a pluralistic network, and opine that 'viewertariat activity can enrich democratic deliberation' (2011: 458).

This possibility is an undertone in much that has been written, in recent years, on 'citizen witnessing' and 'citizen journalism'. In an influential anthology, Frosh and Pinchevsky (2009: 10) highlight how things like smartphones have made possible a 'complex of relations' with global reach, 'between ordinary people, and between ordinary people and media organizations'. To some, such practices – be they referred to as witnessing, crowdsourcing or citizen journalism – are changing the role and self-perception of the audience and contributing to the emergence of a new sort of 'active citizenship' (Harcup 2011; Mortensen 2011). The argument is that these new trends in media technology and use are empowering people in their relationships not only to political elites, but also to media elites and established journalists (Couldry 2003). The 'technopolitics thesis' posits that the internet, blogosphere and interactive social media provide new opportunities to make political processes public (Sampedro 2011: 433). But as Flew and Wilson (2010: 132) point out, little is actually known about what is going on, as polemics dominate the discussion on citizen journalism. Here is a task for the empirical research agenda.

In chapter 2, it was argued that 'old' media institutions continue to wield power, despite the inroads of digitization, and that the relationship of the audience to that power is important to study. A 'dispersed' approach to this is useful. Such an approach builds on the Foucauldian insight that it is necessary to consider the ways that many different sorts of activities, involving people on every level of society, 'contribute to sustaining particular power relations' (Couldry 2005: 194). 'Media power' is not just something that the actors explored in chapter 4 enjoy, or the institutions and companies that own their outlets: 'it is a society-wide phenomenon which all of us, in various ways, are involved in sustaining' (Couldry 2005: 195). To deal with the insight, and the developments that lead to people 'doing more things in more places and in relation to more interconnected media than previously', Couldry proposes the notion of the 'extended' audience (Couldry 2005: 219).

Some argue that what is at issue here is a qualitative change; that power has shifted to the ex-audience. A group of theorists, with media scholar Henry Jenkins (2008, 2010) at the forefront, have sought to characterize the contours of a new 'participatory culture' that they see as having emerged in the 'Web 2.0' phase of societal digitization. Technological advances, they argue, have produced a participatory culture comprised of 'prosumers', i.e. people who produce as well as consume media texts and forms. Neither passive nor manipulated, prosumers are creative and more active than the audience conceived of by cultural studies scholars, as they use media technology and texts in often unanticipated and unintended ways. YouTube, Facebook and Twitter are democratizing platforms, in this account, putting audience members on an equal footing with traditional elites (Benkler 2006; Kendall 2008). While some quibble that the ability to generate content is nothing new (home video cameras have been around for a long time, and people were compiling their own playlists on cassette tape long before iTunes came along, as every Nick Hornby afficionado knows), there is widespread agreement that the ability of ordinary media users to distribute as well as create content is something qualitatively new (Napoli 2010: 509). These ideas have political import, given Jenkins' critical utopian conviction that people will eventually 'be able to participate within the democratic process with the same ease that we have come to participate in the imaginary realms constructed through popular culture' (Jenkins 2008: 245–55).

Audience as commodity and workers

In contrast to those who look at 'the people formerly known as the audience' and see citizens re-activated by technological advances (e.g., Coleman & Blumler 2012; Dahlgren 2009), 'media publics' that can influence both markets and governments by indicating their preferences (Herbert 2005) or powerful 'prosumers' (Jenkins 2008), scholars working within the critical political economy perspective view this figure as victim rather than actor; as used, even abused, rather than empowered. Ordinary members of the public or audience suffer, in this reading, from 'a media-induced affliction' stemming from commercialization, capitalism and neoliberalism. These scholars are sceptical of talk about the 'active audience' and are critical of the failure of research related to the concept to deal with 'deep structural changes in national and global media systems' (Bittereyst & Meers 2011: 416).

When such scholars write of 'the media', they have an industry in mind, rather than a technology or political actor or discursive force. Commodification is thus a key concept in their accounts. Smythe (1977) argued that the audience is a commodity itself, produced by the industry and then sold to advertisers. Audience members are doubly exploited, in this view, as they work for advertisers without pay, learning to spend their money in ways shaped by market forces rather than their objective needs. Jhally (1982) and Livant (1982; Jhally & Livant 1986) expanded on this idea with the suggestion that audiences once worked for media programmers who then turned them over to advertisers. More recently, Napoli (2010) has suggested that, in the digital era, the audience works without pay to create as well as consume media products, for both media organizations and advertisers. Kaitatzi-Whitlock (2011) is even more critical. In her view, ordinary people are ignorant rather than creative, and their very ignorance is a commodity. She is troubled by the perceived inability to distinguish between information that is valuable, and that which is worthless or perhaps even harmful. The information overload that results from the proliferation of media outlets and content explosion undermines people's cognitive capacities, she argues, and renders impossible an awareness of their real (as opposed to perceived) interests:

'knowledge gaps in public affairs, notably about prevailing power relations, generate powerlessness and frustration, thereby debilitating individuals' (2011: 461).

A rose by any other name?

Citizens, voters (dutiful or uninformed), members of the public, consumers whose behaviour is shaped by economic forces, individuals who form a diffused or extended audience, or part of the viewertariat that adapts to new technology rather than to market forces: these actors have been given many names. While Shakespeare has contributed a good deal to our understanding of society and politics, his famous line about a rose smelling sweet, whatever it is called, does not apply here. The words used to describe any given actor matter to the way the relation of that actor to power is theorized, the sort of research questions that scholars pose and, as a consequence, the sort of evidence they produce.

Powerful people?

A central task of this chapter has been to shown that the people receiving media messages and using media technology have been conceived in very different ways, as has their place in the communication process. The liberal-pluralist tradition sees that process as linear, with producers sending messages that are received passively (if at all, in the case of the uninformed voter). In this conceptualization, the people in focus in this chapter are at the end of the communication process. Scholars working within the cultural studies paradigm, in particular, see the process as circular rather than linear, and audiences as part of the process rather than its endpoint. The power of those people to resist or appropriate messages is an empirical question. They are granted potential agency in this research approach, but not assumed to use it. Given that scholars who espouse the concept of an active audience do research within the critical tradition and tend to have hearts that beat on the left, they harbour no illusions that the power of the media industry and traditional elites is on the wane. The communicative flows of participatory culture are multidirectional, with patterns of influence difficult to chart, far less document. Perhaps they are best thought of as the Baudrillardian 'blizzards' that Stevenson (2002) associates with postmodern media theory.

Different perceptions of the place, practices and power of 'the people formerly known as the audience' have normative implications. A camerawoman once interviewed on a documentary gave an insightful and revealing answer, when asked how important it was to understand what she filmed.

> It's very important. But there's a difficulty in understanding, because understanding isn't unbiased. Understanding has a political viewpoint as well. Every time we film something we film what we know, how we want to film something, what we're prepared to see.[2]

The quotation works just as well - if not better - if the word 'film' is replaced with 'analyse', and is one thing to keep in mind.

Differences in views of the role of ordinary people in the media–politics relationship are explained in part by differences in scholars' assumptions, epistemologies and 'understandings', but also in part by the fact that times and circumstances change. It can be difficult to disentangle the two. When it comes to changing circumstances, Gillespie (2005: 4) points out that 'technologies empower or disempower audiences and transform the nature of their media experiences', and that audiences themselves change as society does. The power to resist messages, to feel represented in media discourse, to be an active participant and to produce as well as consume is not independent of the circumstances in which individuals or their societies might find themselves. It matters whether the number of people going to university is waxing or waning (and of course whether the university has the resources and autonomy to do its job properly) or whether those of university age find themselves without hope of employment in countries crippled by austerity measures or long-term poverty. It matters whether their country is undergoing a transition to democracy or retreating from it. As 'the people formerly known as the audience' change, for whatever reason, the ideas and assumptions that guide the study of those people necessarily change too.

As ever, both continuity and change are involved. Warnings that ordinary people are at threat from commercialization and colonized by market forces have been issued for decades. Indeed, the alarm was raised as early as 1944 by Adorno and Horkheimer, who had fled their native Germany – a country where radio was used with ruthless efficiency for political control by the Nazis – only to find themselves in a United States where the 'culture industry' was manipulating the populace into passivity in the interests of capitalism. While the threat has existed for some time, the point being made by critical scholars, especially from the political economy camp, is that people in more countries have become vulnerable to it.

Another familiar feature in the discourse on audiences – be it scholarly or popular – is the regular recurrence of 'moral panics' (Cohen 1972). With each new technological development, concerns are expressed that media-users will suffer, become more passive or violent, more isolated ('bowling alone' as Putnam (1995) put it) and finally – like the little girl in Spielberg's *Poltergeist* – end up losing themselves in the screen. Elite concerns inevitably lead to calls for media regulation to protect vulnerable publics, which in many cases amounts to censorship, as mentioned in chapter 3. It can be instructive to follow discussions taking place within the European Union, for example, regarding legislation to prevent child pornography, which critics maintain is in fact a disguised attempt to limit other freedoms. Critics of Jenkins' optimistic view of the liberating and democratizing potential of digital technology also have the power of governments and established institutions in mind. As Herkman (2012: 373) points out,

> highlighting the utopian dimensions of converging media culture discounts those traditions, institutions, structures and practices that tend to maintain continuities in media culture and politics. In spite of the increasing number of connections between politics, popular culture and individual lifestyles, as well as the growing popularity of the internet and social media, there are still astonishingly stubborn traditions and habits in political communication.

Has new technology made people more powerful? New media technologies may lead to more transparency and public outrage. But neither that technology nor that outrage can by default change policy. Despite the open circulation of visual testimony that US soldiers were torturing and abusing Iraqi prisoners of war in the Abu Ghraib

prison, thanks to mobile phone technology and democratizing distribution platforms, and the global outcry that followed, US government policy did not change. Nor
is there convincing evidence that new technologies have resulted in a situation where
the public has achieved autonomy in relation to established institutions (Splichal
2009: 399–400). Once the dust had settled after the Occupy Movement of 2011–12,
the argument gained weight that a movement without an established organization
behind it did not threaten states, but rather was in their interests. Autonomous
mobilizations can be ignored.

And yet there are clear indications of change. Television – still the primary source
of political information for most people in many countries (Esser at al. 2012: 250)
– continues to diversify, and with it the audience. It is becoming more segmented,
globalized and fan-based (Livingstone 2005: 44). The mass culture engendered by
capitalism was characterized by standardization, commodification and conformity, and revolved around the nation. By the end of the twentieth century, people
were consuming media that were increasingly owned and controlled by large-scale
transnational companies – 'genuinely global institutions' with only minimal ties
to national cultures (Stevenson 1999: 3). Whether or not one agrees that television
remains the central medium in most societies, or finds it most useful to think in terms
of 'post-broadcast' polities (Prior 2006; Wilson 2011), the internet has not righted
the balance. Critics have pointed out that it is not a free, democratic space, but one
in which opinions and facts are mixed, and in which commercially funded search
engines, rather than professional journalists, sort relevant information, and 'push
users to advertisers or sites or preselected, best-paying companies, as in the case of
Google' (Kaitatzi-Whitlock 2011: 473).

The jury is still out and the evidence ambiguous. Digital media are increasing
people's exposure to different and less mainstream views, on the one hand, and, on
the other, narrowing people's outlooks (Negroponte and 'the Daily Me' again) and
making it possible to sidestep collective information-exchanges by the political community, be it local, national, regional or global. In 'post-broadcast' contexts, a gulf is
deepening between the information-rich and the information-poor.

> To news junkies, politics has become a candy store. Others avoid news altogether.
> Political involvement has become more unequal, and elections more polarized as a
> result. (Prior 2006)[3]

On the one hand, then, the proliferation of personal media is seen as having the
potential to empower people and enhance their knowledge of and participation in
politics while, on the other hand, undermining the preconditions for shared political cultures and public communicative spaces. This is of interest to 'critical audience
studies', which pay attention to 'individualization, privatization, fragmentation,
commercialization and consumer culture' and examine them in the context of a digital world, without losing sight of familiar power relations. Biltereyst & Meers (2011)
make a good case for seeing us in our relation to the state (as citizens or members of
the public), and to the public sphere (as active, engaged and sometimes resistant), as
people who inhabit private spaces (pleasure-seeking audiences who are creative in
their identity work) and as part of the economy (audiences as commodity or consumers). The research task they identify 'is to examine the intersection of these spaces'
(Biltereyst & Meers 2011: 423).

Given the media-saturated environments in which millions of people throughout the world exist, it is unavoidable that 'the people formerly known as the audience' are viewed in a context of active use of media technology and texts. For the scholar coming to the study of the relationship between media and politics from the political science end of the academy, it can seem somewhat strange to think in terms of culture (and indeed to consign 'ordinary people' to the ranks of 'political actors' to be studied in manifestations other than aggregate opinion data). And yet the influence of culture on media use is important. Herbert (2005: 99) makes a convincing argument for the necessity of considering 'the interaction between audiences and media forms in a variety of cultural contexts'.

To think about

With the increase in leisure time (and unemployed time and delayed transitions to adulthood) and more free information, are people in a position to be better informed than ever before? This is one thing to think about. Another is what it means when, in an age of radical transparency, ordinary people as well as journalists can play the role of watchdog, making sure that governments are not abusing their power. Is the evidence of this more convincing than that which supports the opposite view – that people have not become freer and more powerful, but are increasingly and more comprehensively enslaved, and assaulted by forces intent on increasing political ignorance? Are we being empowered by technology or colonized and socialized by the corporate forces that control the internet?

Something else that bears thinking about is what it means to live in a mediated, globalized world. The communities to which we belong – at least those we experience directly – have been extended by media globalization, it is often argued. Our ideas of shared moral worth and our identities must thus be constantly revised and adapted. What does it mean to be a Scot or a Swede or a Slovenian in the context of the EU? Where do the moral obligations of a Canadian or Chilean reside? In an age when global media provide a steady stream of news of children suffering war in Syria, famine in Africa, and female genital mutilation (FGM) in an alarming number of countries, we cannot exclude the requirement to feel empathy for and responsibility towards distant others. To be a citizen is to be a member of a political community, but what does that mean in a globalizing world where the global and the local overlap, and in which national sovereignty is challenged on a daily basis?

6 Activists

Three images reflect changing mediations of protest in different decades and different places.

The first image represents the protester as a small child steadied by adult hands. It is from a typical press report of the demonstrations of October 1983, when 3 million people took to the streets of Europe to demand an end to the arms race, and to draw attention to how life-threatening decisions were being made by political elites who were unaccountable to them. In mainstream media accounts, protesters were depicted as naively involving themselves in matters over their heads, although different national prisms refracted those images differently (Robertson 1992).

The protester in the second image is still young, but has come of age. Optimistic rather than naive, this figure is depicted as belonging to a world that speaks in a single voice. The image circulated in print and broadcast media in February 2003, when at

From left to right: the face of the peace movement in *The Times*, 2 April 1983, photograph Martin Langer (Robertson 1992); young Germans protesting in Stuttgart against the Iraq War on 16 February 2003, photograph Thomas Niedermüller, www. niedermueller.de; Occupy Toronto protesters on 15 October 2011. Photograph: Kelly Finnamore / Wikimedia Commons.

least 6 million people in sixty countries demonstrated against the imminent invasion of Iraq by the US and its allies. Despite national differences in news reporting, protesters in this discourse were, by and large, portrayed as legitimate political actors by European press and television.

The third image has shed all traces of the carnevalesque and depicts a serious and powerful political actor, named 'Person of the Year' by *Time Magazine* in 2011. The issues are legion, as is the protester, but calls for democratic accountability in a global setting top the list. According to the caption accompanying a photo montage inside the magazine, the protester is not just raising his or her voice, but actually changing the world.[1] This activist's challenge to political authority is followed closely in rolling news coverage, often fed by the activist's own pictures and testimony, injected into the mainstream news flow by social media.

The three snapshots, grouped together in the same frame of mediated activism, serve as the portkey for this chapter for several reasons. Their juxtaposition as in a triptych (the frame of visual narratives of politics more often seen in churches) throws the differences between the three snapshots into sharp relief. They are significant in themselves, but when placed side-by-side and compared, they highlight larger changes in power relations under globalization. The triptych is a useful heuristic when thinking about changes that have been taking place in the media–politics relationship, and why it is instructive to compare mediated response of and to activism across time, space and culture.

This chapter is about the influence of media forms and texts on political activism, and attempts by scholars to grasp and understand the relationship between media technology and journalists, on the one hand, and protesters, on the other, in the context of social and political change. Two sets of problems are in focus.

The first is the empirical or 'real-world' problem faced by activists seeking to influence political outcomes. This in turn involves the challenges entailed in managing and coordinating mobilization, controlling the information flow and shaping the narrative so as to garner and retain popular support, and to resist the attempts of entrenched political and economic actors to divert the flow of information and reshape the narrative.

The second set of problems is theoretical, and confronts scholars who seek to explain how naive citizens become powerful political actors. New concepts and theories put forward by scholars not yet encountered in earlier chapters, or merely bumped into in passing, offer assistance. The chapter will briefly review scholarship on political engagement and participation, the concept of 'mediation opportunity structure', and the analytical framework of connective action, and revisit the key concepts of the public sphere and power, to consider how they have been reworked by scholars of political activism.

It will be argued that, of all the vantage points through which the media–politics relationship is viewed in this book, it is here that change is most clearly in evidence, and in this context that arguments that there is a qualitative difference in power relations in the digital media age are most convincing. The chapter begins with an overview of examples of significant moments in the media–activist relationship – a brief potted history, if you like, of the relationship that needs explication. The scholarly approach to the theoretical (and analytical) problems in focus in the chapter is then presented, in an overview of leading scholarship on the topic. The chapter ends, as ever, with things to think about. How much has really been changed by globalization and digital technology? And are technological developments entirely good for political engagement?

What's kicking off, and where?

'What's going on?' asked BBC journalist Paul Mason in 2011, in an influential blog, that later become a book (Mason 2011),[2] noting that something was 'kicking off everywhere'.

> We've had revolution in Tunisia, Egypt's Mubarak is teetering; in Yemen, Jordan and Syria suddenly protests have appeared. In Ireland young techno-savvy professionals are agitating for a 'Second Republic'; in France the youth from banlieues battled police on the streets to defend the retirement rights of 60-year-olds; in Greece striking and rioting have become a national pastime. And in Britain we've had riots and student occupations that changed the political mood.

While 2011 may have been the year of the protester, it wasn't the kick-off. Political activism is far from new (one need look no further than the reports, filed by the first-century Greek journalist Plutarch, of the anti-Roman mobilization led by Spartacus to be reminded of that), and both E. P. Thompson (1968) and Habermas (1962/1989) acknowledged that the political activism of nineteenth-century labour movements – not least their discursive activity in discussion groups and study circles – contributed to the development of the public sphere and its expansion beyond the boundaries of the bourgeois elite. A century before the Tunisian fruitseller Mohamed Bouazizi set himself and the Arab world on fire, Emily Davison, who had graduated from Oxford University with first-class honours but was denied the vote, died from her injuries after throwing herself in front of the English king's horse, to publicize the cause of women's rights. Spectacular acts such as these, by the publicity-savvy Suffragettes warrant – and have received – volumes of their own, but certain key moments in the intervening century recur in the literature, and they are worth rehearsing.

Mediated protest over time

The affluent 1960s and 1970s saw the blossoming of a colourful riot of protest groups in the West. Among those that left an indelible impression were the civil rights and anti-Vietnam movements in the US and the anti-nuclear (energy and weapons) movement in Europe. Groups from the 'civil–social periphery' learned the 'lessons of images' in these years, with Greenpeace the star pupil. Its founders set off in an old fishing boat from the Canadian city of Vancouver in 1971, bound for a US nuclear testing site off the coast of Alaska, intent on 'bearing witness' to what the Americans wanted hidden from view. Subsequent spectacular protests aimed to draw the attention of the world to environmental crimes. For the next quarter of a century, the issues of environment and armaments remained intertwined, and when the anti-nuclear-missile protesters of the first portkey-snapshot took to the streets of Europe in the early 1980s, environmental activists kept them company (DeLuca & Peeples 2002: 139; greenpeace.org/usa/en/campaigns/history; Herbert 2005: 105; Robertson 1992). Anti-war mobilization resulted in a Nobel Peace Prize in 1997 (for the Campaign to Ban Landmines) and the mass mobilization against the Iraq war glimpsed in the second portkey-snapshot.

The turn of this millennium saw the burgeoning of protests with a different target: global economic injustice. In the last days of 1999, political and economic elites convened in Seattle for a meeting of the World Trade Organization (WTO). The city had been chosen by the Clinton administration for symbolic reasons, as the 'high-tech capital of the present future' (DeLuca & Peepels 2002: 125), but grassroots activists from around the world contested that imagery with a counter-spectacle of their own. The Seattle protests migrated to other cities and countries. Wherever G20 leaders met, protesters were on site to greet them – in Washington, Pittsburgh, Toronto, London, St Andrews, Prague, Quebec City, Salzburg, Genoa or Seoul. A decade and an ongoing global financial crisis later, calls for economic justice had not abated. Los Indignados took to the streets of sixty cities and mobilized a significant portion of the Spanish population in well-publicized mobilizations that remained independent of the organizations that customarily convened such protests, for example opposition parties and unions.

In 2009, demonstrations against election outcomes in Iran and Moldova caught the attention of mainstream media and publics the world over, who were soon referring to them as 'Twitter' revolutions because of how the protesters organized themselves. The 'Facebook' revolutions of North Africa followed less than two years later, although when the dust had settled it became clear that economic injustices were as much a catalyst as media technology. In all these events, however – regardless of whether environmental, anti-war or economic concerns were foregrounded – the role of media technology was highlighted and became the object of discussion and scholarly enquiry.

Apart from differences across time, there are differences between political and cultural settings worth noting.

Mediated protest across the globe

In old democracies such as Italy, feminists used social media to militate for the ousting of former Prime Minister Silvio Berlusconi. When it appeared that the 'Rubygate' scandal (involving allegations that the elderly premier had purchased sex with the under-age immigrant 'Ruby') would leave Berlusconi unscathed, the 'Se non ora, quando' (If not now, when?) initiative mobilized against the man who had for years controlled the Italian media, and public depictions of women (as scantily clad and intended to gratify men). Demonstrations on 13 February 2011 were organized via blogs, Facebook appeals and video messages posted on YouTube, and attracted a million participants. In the view of Elisa Davoglio, the poet and blogger who was one of the initiators of the event, social media were essential to the mobilization. Without the internet, protesters could never have countered the version of reality broadcast by mainstream media under Berlusconi's control, she emphasized.

> A Berlusconian truth is 'if it's not on TV it doesn't exist. He didn't count on the parallel reality called the internet.[3]

In the United States a year later, the proposed Stop Online Piracy Act (SOPA) was nipped in the bud by a 'nerd lobby' of internet activists. The Act, promoted by a well-financed Hollywood lobby, was set to 'sink digital pirate ships' by bolstering copyright legislation. Both Republicans and Democrats supported the proposed legislation until internet activists began reading the fine print more carefully and spread the word about what they had read. SOPA, they discovered, would subject the internet to censorship in advance – broadband service providers and search engines would be required to prevent people from surfing to certain sites, and Facebook and Twitter would be required in advance to ensure that no user published files or links to copyright-protected material. Opponents opined that SOPA would give the US powers over the internet as far-ranging as those wielded by Chinese authorities (Forssberg 2012). In a bid to stop the legislation before it went into effect, net activists mobilized Google, Facebook, hundreds of law professors and human rights organizations, and, on 18 January 2012 coordinated a massive anti-SOPA protest, closing down the English-language version of Wikipedia, among other things. SOPA never became law.

In India, the brutal gang rape and murder of a young student in early 2013 sparked an outcry and the establishment of a movement for the protection of women and promotion of gender rights in a country where sexual abuse is habitual and the rate of prosecution minimal. Unusually, the protests garnered support from beyond the well-educated activist middle class. Headlines in major newspapers suggested that social media were playing a key role in a country with 65 million Facebook users and an estimated 35 million Twitter accounts. The *Times of India* reported that nineteen-year-old Sambhavi Saxena had tweeted 'to India and the world' that she was being illegally held 'at Parliament St Police Station Delhi w/ 15 other women. Terrified, pls RT'.

> Twitter hashtags like #DelhiGangRape #StopThisShame #DelhiProtests #Amanat #Nirbhaya #Damini have served as anchors to inform, educate and galvanize mass support. Significantly, virtual protests through hashtags such as #theekhai (Hindi for All is well) sought to humiliate and punish the lack of sensitivity and inactivity of ageing politicians. It is instructive to note that whilst two-thirds of the Indian population is under the age of 35, the average age of an Indian politician is 65. In the wake of the Mumbai terror attacks, the growing urban, young and middle class elite have demonstrated that they are agitated and feel under-protected. And they demand change. (Barn 2013)

In new, problematic or 'hybrid' democracies like Russia, digital media have proven essential sites of opposition in recent years. In the run-up to the 2012 presidential election, which many felt was rigged in favour of Vladimir Putin from the outset, liberal opposition groups hung a massive anti-Putin banner across the river from the Kremlin. It was quickly removed, but not quickly enough to prevent photos of the action being taken and disseminated to millions across Russia, thanks to the blog of activist Ilya Yashin. Given that Russian television is carefully controlled by the political establishment, the blogging platform Zhivoy Zhurnal (LiveJournal) has become a central site of opposition to the power of the state to control public opinion. It has also become the generic term for blog in Russian, and is used by 44 per cent of bloggers in the country (Greenall 2012).[4]

Blogs have proven to be an important platform for opposition activists in Africa as well. In Kenya, bloggers such as Ory Okolloh (kenyanpundit.com) and Erik Hersman (whiteafrican.com) disseminate information and views which the mainstream media dare not carry (Kalan 2013). Two internet sites – Ushahidi and Uchaguzi – provided Kenyans with a platform for crowdsourcing attempts to rig election outcomes and incite ethnic hatred both in 2009 and 2013.

In non-democratic settings, protest has come to be closely associated with the revolutionary prowess of media technology. Burma is one of many countries where mainstream media are tightly controlled. Information about repression, human rights violations and pro-democracy struggles reach the diaspora via digital media. Burmese exiles scattered throughout the world have also used the internet to mobilize – successfully enough to persuade the US government to ban new investments in Burma (Dutta & Pal 2007: 205). The 'Twitter' and 'Facebook revolutions' in the Middle East and Arab world have already been noted, but the opportunities afforded the Syrian opposition by mobile digital technology – and activists' skill in exploiting them – are worth special mention. From the onset of the struggle to overthrow the repressive Assad regime, opposition activists ran 'an unexpected, brilliantly executed and brave campaign to film the repression and put it online', as one observer put it (Bennett-Jones 2011). Images bearing witness to the violent response of security forces, filmed in some cases with cameras disguised as pens, were posted on the internet, where they were picked up by mainstream news organizations and members of the global public. Smuggled into the country, such technology – together with the satellite phones, foreign SIMD cards and even, it was rumoured, small portable sat dishes – helped the opposition counter the Assad regime's 'old-fashioned effort' to control media coverage and 'shaped what the PR experts would call "the narrative"' (Bennett-Jones 2011).

In instances of protest and political engagement such as these, groups located on the civil–social periphery, and thus lacking instrumental power, resort instead to what Habermas (1996) calls their 'communicative power', performing spectacular acts to attract the attention of mainstream media and, increasingly, sidestepping such channels of communication and disseminating their points of view via digial media. An understanding of the media–activist relationship involves attention to practices on several levels: the framing of protest by political elites, and in mainstream media; activists' self-representations; their use of digital media to mobilize and organize action; and 'media and communication practices that constitute mediated resistance in its own right' (Cammaerts 2012: 118). Both continuity and change are in evidence in these practices. Protest artefacts tend increasingly to be personal testimonies and images posted on internet platforms. Decades ago, the women camped outside the US military base on England's Greenham Common tied domestic items (a garment or toy belonging to their child, for example) to the fence they were prohibited from scaling. Digitally or physically shared, such artefacts embed symbols and understandings, and, through them, discourses of political dissent are culturally transmitted over time, 'feeding the struggle and contributing to the construction of a collective memory of protest' (Cammaerts 2012: 125). There is continuity in such communicative action but there are significant features of contemporary activism – such as the movements for global justice – that set them off from earlier forms of protest. They are global in mindset as well as scope, for example (Juris 2004). Activists consciously link their local demonstrations to protests taking place elsewhere. Moreoever, they are 'informational' in the sense that Castells (1996) uses the term to describe societal forces organized around flexible, decentralized networks.

When observing that things were kicking off all over the place, Mason wondered: 'What's the wider social dynamic?' Answering this, and the question of political ramifications, has been the preoccupation of many scholars in recent years.

Scholarship on mediated political activism

An important social dynamic – or perhaps absence of it – that recurs in the literature is electoral decline. As mentioned earlier on, there is widespread concern, particularly among political scientists, that people are no longer participating in traditional politics to the extent they once were, and are decreasingly likely to belong to established political parties or social movement organizations. Young people, in particular, are thought to be uninformed about what elites consider to be relevant issues, and are perceived as being politically apathetic. More optimistic scholars point to new forms of engagement, new views as to what are the relevant things to know (what 'Occupy' stands for rather than the name of the minister for trade). In focus in such optimistic accounts are not civic cultures of duty-bound citizens, but an 'uncivic' society in which networks are the key organizational form, issue associations have replaced political parties, and lifestyle coalitions abound (Bimber 2012; Dahlgren 2009; Ward & de Vreese 2011: 400).

Another significant dynamic is the changing relationship between engagement and the communication of politics. Social movements have always been dependent on media outlets to mobilize political support, to legitimate and validate their demands, and to do more than preach to the choir (Gamson & Wolfsfeld 1993). Most are agreed that something is happening on this front – that the relationship is dynamic. There is less agreement as to how that change is best characterized. Scholars disagree, for example, over whether young people, even (or perhaps especially) if they are active online, are disengaging (Coleman & Blumler 2009; Dahlgren 2009; Ward & de Vreese 2011) or whether new technologies are reviving and enhancing political participation, facilitating 'expressive' political acts and making it possible for people to frame their concerns on their own terms, rather than with recourse to the frames elites use and promote (Berger 2011; Bimber 2012; Zukin et al. 2006). Whatever the dynamic, the context is, in most countries, that of late modern society organized by 'fluid' digital networks (Benkler 2006; Castells 2000).

Political engagement and participation

Classic definitions of political participation refer to activities by citizens to influence the selection of their representatives in government, or what those representatives do. Participation or engagement of this sort is sometimes referred to as 'minimalist', and exemplified by the campaigner who canvasses on behalf of his or her candidate. In contrast to minimalist participation, associated with institutionalized politics, the 'maximalist' variety has to do with 'the political' in a broader sense. Carpentier (2011) and Dahlgren (2009) include social and cultural aspects of civic life in their accounts of such engagement. The aforementioned disagreement as to whether political engagement should be regarded with a frown or with a gleaming eye can be partly attributed to some scholars focusing on minimalist, and others on maximalist forms. The distinction between 'the civic' and 'the political' is worth drawing. Given that undemocratic practices are rife in the sphere of formal democratic institutions, particularly under globalization (a recurrent criticism of the EU), broad groups of citizens, far from feeling themselves represented, are excluded from the spaces and discourses of the politics that impact on their lives. This, it could be argued, was at the heart of the protests captured in the portkey-triptych – even the image from the 1980s – and is clearly the core sentiment in the anti-WTO and anti-austerity protests of later years. A reticence to act on feelings of civic obligation need not signal a disinclination to engage in politics.

People are supposed to be represented by politicians and journalists, in government and in media reports. As representation in one sense changes or is challenged, the other sort of representation is affected. When the credibility of elite gatekeepers comes into question, Bennett et al. (2012: 127) suggest that political communication ends up following different gatekeeping rules (such as those of crowdsourcing), using different formats and sources (such as those of user-generated content), distributed in different ways (horizontally, over digitally mediated networks, rather than vertically, from the political and media centre to the periphery). Political communication and participation are thus shaped in tandem.

Digital media make it easier and less costly, in personal terms, to participate. The hands holding those of the child in the 1983 image of protest probably put mimeographed leaflets through people's letterboxes or handed them out on the street before the day of the demonstration. When Solidarnosc was defying the power of the Polish Communist Party in the early 1980s, the Swedish labour movement supported Polish activists by shipping printing presses and reams of paper across the Baltic. Three decades later, the Swedish aid agency was providing pro-democracy movements in developing countries with digital media equipment and funding (SIDA 2012). Instead of one-to-one communication (a flyer thrust in the hand of a passer-by) or ploys to catch the attention of mainstream media, in the hopes a message would be amplified using conventional channels (vertical or top-down communication), activists using digital media can communicate horizontally 'among themselves' (Bimber 2012: 117). The messages may still be homemade, but when disseminated on Facebook, the effect is of stuffing a flyer into dozens or hundreds of letterboxes with one click – or millions, when #Gezi is retweeted – without paying for costly photocopies.

Technology does not exist in a vacuum. While digital media may lower the cost of engagement, they do not necessarily make it meaningful to become involved in every political-cultural setting. There may have been 771 million mobile phone subscribers in India in 2011, with an urban tele-density of 143 per cent, but Illavarasan nevertheless found Indian youth to be apolitical. Despite being networked, their perceived inability to effect political change in a system experienced as endemically corrupt left them disinclined to use their digital resources to participate in the world's largest democracy (Illavarasan 2013: 297). Nor has technology had a significant impact on civic engagement in Singapore, despite it being among the most ICT-developed countries in the world, with a mobile phone penetration of 137 per cent in 2009. Zhang (2013) puts this down to the fact that Singapore is an authoritarian democracy, with a political culture that invites apathy for quite different reasons from those rehearsed by Putnam (1995). Given that mainstream media outlets are controlled by the authorities and that there is limited physical space for debate and discussion, the very act of going online to get alternative viewpoints is associated with higher costs, not reduced ones. Studies of youth (in)activism in both Singapore and Bangladesh serve as reminders that the contribution of digital media to political engagement is shaped by contextual factors and by culturally specific understandings of political engagement, and 'is limited by the historical trajectory of political development' (Ullah 2013:282; Zhang 2013: 268). Differences in political structures need to be taken into account, and the windows of opportunity they open or keep closed.

Mediation opportunity structure

Cammaerts points out that it is not only political structures that constrain activists. He offers the concept of 'mediation opportunity structure' to theorize how activists are both enabled and constrained 'in the current ultra-saturated media and communication environment' (Cammaerts 2012: 118). The concept connects insights from social movement research and mediation theory – two sources that are seldom combined.

The concept of 'political opportunity structure' is used by social movement researchers to explain how the structure of the world beyond the control of activists affects how they mobilize, and their chances of success. Cammaerts notes that this literature tends to mention the role of media and communication opportunities only in passing, as 'peripheral factors'. Some of the structures that constrain action are indeed 'inherent to the media itself', however, so, parallel to the political, he discerns a 'media opportunity structure'. It defines the extent to which movements are able to access, and get their message across in, the mainstream media, and their 'degree of cultural influence' over public discourse. The structure affects how protest movement members can perform the political, or the repertoires of contentious action available to them.

Different historical periods have different repertoires. Tilly (1986) identified a 'feudal' repertoire of parochial protest actions aimed at local dignitaries in the mid seventeenth to mid nineteenth centuries. A 'modernist' repertoire emerged later, when protests became national rather than local, and more autonomous in their organization. *Migalki* – the flashing blue lights that allow high-ranking officials to ignore ordinary traffic rules – have come to symbolize the abuse of political power to Muscovites, and one of the many things that made daily life harder. In 2010, they appropriated the symbol and manifested their discontent by taping blue buckets to their own cars, driving slowly, and filming *migalki* miscreants. Flash mobs of pedestrian protesters followed the convoys of bucket-topped autos, and people wearing blue buckets, plastic cups and even washing-up bowls gathered outside the Russian government headquarters. The protests of the Blue Bucket brigade suggest that 'feudal' actions have not necessarily been subsumed by the 'modern'. Indeed, such contentious performances may well occupy a central place in image-saturated societies.

Be that as it may, Cammaerts argues that available repertoires of contentious actions are determined by the mediation opportunity structure. It is both empowering and constraining:

> an ultra-saturated media and communication environment provides ample opportunities for activists to resist, to exert their agency, to self-represent themselves and

to defy the structural constraints. At the same time, activists also have to take into account these structural constraints inherent to mediation such as a mainly negative bias of mainstream media. (Cammaerts 2012: 122)

The concept can be explored on three analytical levels. The first analytical dimension is that of the media opportunity structure and can be accessed by studying mainstream media representations of protest. The second level is that of the discursive opportunity structure and involves analysis of self-mediation strategies – activists' discursive work to produce and disseminate counter-narratives that are independent of those of political and media elites. The third level is that of the networked opportunity structure. The object of analysis in this instance is the 'resistance practices' that are mediated through (presumably digital or 'new') technology (Cammaerts 2012: 122).

From collective to connective action

While the opportunities provided by networks are one dimension of a larger mediation process in Cammaerts' account, digitally networked action (DNA) is at the centre of influential work by Bennett and Segerberg (2009, 2011, 2012, 2013). In trying to make sense of the dynamics of large-scale protest movements such as those mobilizing in the shadow of the global economic crisis, Bennett and Segerberg have discerned digital action networks with two organizational patterns.

The first way of organizing engages new participants by disseminating, through social media, action themes that are easy to personalize and pass on. An example which figures largely in these studies is Put People First, which mobilized 35,000 people for an anti-G20 march through London in March 2009. To this could be added the example of Global Citizen, a 'learning and action tool' designed to increase the number of people engaged in the movement to end global poverty, and to increase their effectiveness. Using 'the power of education, communication, advocacy, campaigns and the media', Global Citizen encourages people to take action in conventional ways (by calling or e-mailing their representatives), in ways familiar from the literature on political consumerism (buying Fairtrade products) and in ways that exploit the power of digital action networks (by sharing videos about extreme

Depictions on activist websites of how communication technology can amplify the voices of citizens protesting against global economic injustice. Sources: www.putpeoplefirst.org.uk, www.globalcitizen.org/AboutUs/AboutUs.aspx?typeId=15. Reproduced with permission.

poverty on participants' own social networks). The website itself is personalized, and recommends content 'based on types of issues and actions you've already taken, and what you're likely to be interested in' (globalcitizen.org).

The second broad organizational pattern is typified by Los Indignados and the Occupy Movement, with technology platforms taking the place of established political organizations. Rather than handing out leaflets bearing the slogans and arguments of the Campaign for Nuclear Disarmament, for example, or an environmental party or movement, the political demands and grievances of participants in these organizational groupings travel through social media encased in personalized accounts. This, Bennett and Segerberg maintain, is new:

> Compared to many conventional social movement protests with identifiable membership organizations leading the way under common banners and collective identity frames, these more personalized, digitally mediated collective action formations have frequently been larger; have scaled up more quickly; and have been flexible in tracking moving political targets and bridging different issues. (2012: 742)

What Bennett and Segerberg want to draw attention to is the difference between the logics of these kinds of collective action networks, and 'the role of communication as an organizing principle'. The conceptual framework they have developed to make sense of this is called 'the logic of connective action', as distinct from the logic of collective action familiar from previous literature on social movements.

'Personal action frames' and 'collective action frames' are the central concepts in this analytical framework, which includes a three-part typology of large-scale action. At one end of the spectrum is the ideal type of collective action: large-scale action networks that depend on organizations to 'broker' mobilization. Such networks and organizations use digital media to mobilize and manage participation. At the other extreme are 'self-organizing' connective networks. Here, communication technology is not just a resource, but an agent. Personal action frames (as opposed to the collective action frames disseminated by organizations in the first, ideal type) are used to unite people across diverse social networks. In between these two types is a hybrid. Actors from formal organizations are present in this third type, but they take a step back, and use social technologies to enable 'loose public networks' to form around personalized action themes, rather than projecting the collective identities, agendas and brands of the organizations (Bennett & Segerberg 2012: 748–57).

Despite the interest shown in the 'Twitter' and 'Facebook' revolutions associated with protests in Iran, Moldova, the Arab world, Turkey and elsewhere, a significant proportion of previous research on social movement mobilization is nevertheless about contentious politics in democracies. A strength of the analytical framework proposed by Bennett and Segerberg is that it incorporates similarities between activism in different political settings – liberal Western democracies, authoritarian regimes in the Arab world, or Chadwickian hybrid systems – where digital media technologies play a key role in the organization of protest (Bennett & Segerberg 2012: 743–4).

Revisiting the public sphere in the context of activism

The concept of the public sphere crops up in rather a lot of scholarship on mediated activism.[5] As will be recalled from chapter 2, this sphere is conceived of as coming into being when engaged citizens discuss matters of mutual political concern, and as existing somewhere between the private sphere and the state. It is in this space that public opinion is formed and expressed – opinion that serves both to legitimate and to check the power of the state. While recognizing that this privileges rational dialogue, Habermas is unhappy with the turn away from text and the increasing incidence of media spectacle. And yet spectacle is an intrinsic part of much activism – not just the carnivalesque aspects of protest (of which the painted faces of the young demonstrators in the second triptych-snapshot are a typical manifestation) but also the more dramatic iconography of 'colour' revolutions, or the ubiquitous Guy Fawkes mask, or the donning of funeral garb and hoisting of symbolic coffins by the doctors and nurses who wanted to draw attention to cutbacks in the British National Health Service in 2013. Why, then, does so much scholarship on activism return to the text- and rationally based concept of the public sphere, given that it has been heavily criticized?

The answer, it could be argued, is that activism is perhaps the most obvious manifestation of political participation, and participation is central to the Habermasian ideal. Another reason is that protest opens a space – be it on street or online – where people express their views, question how state power is being used, and demonstrate their disagreement with each other or those who make decisions. It is in the protest march that the limits of the acceptable are pushed, picketed and policed. Two reworkings of the original notion of the public sphere are instructive to reflect on in this context.

The first is to be found in an influential book by Benkler (2006), who argues that digital media make public discourse more democratic by opening up a 'networked public sphere' to non-elite discourse. Thanks not only to technological advances, but also to economic organization and social practices, people are 'free' to take a more active role than in previous epochs – freer not just from the state, but from the market. The networked information economy 'offers a genuine reorganization of the public sphere', Benkler argues. The commercial imperatives of the pre-digital era's mass media organizations constrained the limits and health of the public sphere. This problem is being solved by the emergence

> of a networked public sphere [which] is attenuating, or even solving, the most basic failings of the mass-mediated public sphere. It attenuates the power of the commercial mass-media owners and those who can pay them. It provides an avenue for substantially more diverse and politically mobilized communication than was feasible in a commercial mass media with a small number of speakers and a vast number of passive recipients. The view of many more individuals and communities can be heard. (Benkler 2006: 465)

Benkler's optimistic take on the opportunities afforded by the network are often contrasted with those of Sunstein (2001a, 2001b), who, it will be recalled from chapter 5, takes a pessimistic view of the impact of digital media on democratic participation. Instead of a vital and empowering networked public sphere, Sunstein sees micropublics that have the radicalizing tendency to polarize society into groups who listen only to the like-minded, and who become deaf to the voices of others. Concerns that this is happening are reflected in the stance taken by political elites like UK Home Secretary Theresa May, who in May 2013 outlined measures for tougher pre-emptive censorship of internet sites. After a white soldier was stabbed to death in a Woolwich street by a black Englishman said to aspire to membership of a militant Islamist group, the Home Secretary vowed to forge on with a controversial communications data bill to prevent what she called the radicalization of British Muslims. Whether 'Benkler's dream or Sunstein's nightmare' provides the best description of what awaits the inhabitants of the network society depends, at least in part, on the degree of freedom allowed for online speech, according to Etling et al. (2010: 1226) – an issue that will be returned to in the book's penultimate chapter.

The second reworking of the classic public sphere notion that is helpful when seeking to understand mediated activism is the notion of the 'public screen' put forward by DeLuca and Peeples (2002). The focus of their hopeful account (like Benkler, they have a gleam in their eyes, in contrast to Sunstein's furrowed brow) is television, or a more broadly defined screen, rather than (or in combination with) social media. The sort of changes in technology and culture addressed by Benkler (and countless others who have figured in this book so far) have, according to DeLuca and Peeples (2002: 127), 'transformed the rules and roles of participatory democracy'. Where Robert 'Bowling Alone' Putnam and Jürgen 'Refeudalization' Habermas see the predominance of television (and other) screens in political settings as threats to engagement, DeLuca and Peeples maintain that 'decline is not the only possible narrative'. New forms of participatory democracy come into focus when viewed through 'the prism of the public screen', a concept that

> takes technology seriously. It recognizes that most, and the most important, public discussions take place via 'screens' – television, computer, and the front page of newspapers. (DeLuca & Peeples 2002: 130)

Building on medium theorists (such as Innis, McLuhan and Meyrowitz, see chapter 1), they argue that new technologies result in new 'modes of perception'. Like Bennett and Segerberg and, to some extent, Cammaerts, they think that new media are accompanied by new forms of social organization.

In striking contrast to the rational argument on which the Habermasian public sphere is founded, the mode of perception enabled by the public screen is one of 'distraction'. This is not a lack of attention, but a ceaseless circulation of images and words that creates a new space for visual political discourse, for spectacle in a positive sense, and 'a transformation of citizen participation' (DeLuca & Peeples 2002: 127). This account rests heavily on an analysis of how the activism of Seattle tactically exploited television as well as digital media ('Seattle witnessed the enactment of forms of activism adapted to a wired society': DeLuca & Peeples 2002: 125), and returns to the issue of power. In recognizing the dominance of corporations and new technologies, activists acknowledge that a shift has taken place, in world politics, when it comes to where decisions are taken and in where sovereignty resides.

The times, are they a-changing?

The key argument in such accounts of mediated activism – and indeed of contemporary politics – is that political discourse has become largely visual. In keeping with the third media role presented at the beginning of the book, the idea is that images create as much as they represent reality. They are 'where collective social action, individual identity and symbolic activity meet – the nexus between culture and politics'

(DeLuca & Peeples 2002: 133). Spectacles and image events are used reciprocally by established actors and their contentious opponents to shape public views and to demonstrate accountability. For DeLuca and Peeples (2002: 134), it is a matter of 'critique through spectacle, not critique versus spectacle'.

This is not to say that activists and dissidents must do all their own media work. Established outlets have an increasing tendency (although more empirical research is needed to confirm this) to report favourably on social movements and protests, particularly if they emerge in contexts distant from the reporting country. Some years ago, Cottle (2008: 855) observed how much has changed since mainstream media were documented as reporting protests using law-and-order frames, 'labelling protesters as deviant, and de-legitimizing their aims and politics by emphasizing drama, spectacle and violence'. Bennett and Segerberg (2012: 742) are among those who have since been able to confirm this, in the case of Put People First and Los Indignados. There are, as ever, differences across media culture as well as media age. One need only compare reporting of the Syrian uprising or anti-government protests in the Ukraine in 2014 on CNN, BBC World, Al Jazeera English and Russia Today, for example, to be assured of this (Robertson forthcoming 2015).

Mediations of protest, such as those comprising the portkey opening this chapter, can serve as points of entry into comparative analyses of mediated protest – across time, space, culture and media technological form. Such analyses contribute to the study of change in the intersecting realms of politics under globalization, and in the rapidly evolving media landscape in which that politics is played out. Central to each is representation, a concept used differently by political scientists and media scholars. While elites work across borders to deal with problems that can no longer be contained within national settings or solved by measures taken at the national level, the people they represent can only participate formally in politics by voting nationally (to the extent that their country has free and fair elections). Journalists are supposed to represent the public too, but, as discussed in chapter 4, those publics have changed. People can make their voices heard in the way they always have, by taking to the streets to protest against decisions and developments that affect their lives. What is different about globalized politics is that such protests are increasingly transnational, and protesters now perform for a global public. In an age of economic globalization and 'informationalism', the emergence of resistance identities is inevitable, according to Castells (1997). This is a universal take on what is admittedly a global phenomenon, but, as della Porta and Mattoni have pointed out, the Arab Spring, the European Indignados and the Occupy Wall Street protests 'were embedded in different political, social, cultural and economic interests'.[6] National and cultural differences in mediated activism should not be overlooked in the excitement around the globalization of protest and the spread of universal technologies. The way protest is framed in newscasts aimed at global, national and local publics, and how such reports give voice to dissenters and engage people watching live television, co-present in time but not space, has a bearing on democracy, however conceived, and on politics in a globalizing world.

To think about

Is the changing face of activism – insofar as it has been changed by digital media – a good or bad thing? When people express their outrage at injustices by retweeting or commenting or changing their Facebook status, are they engaging in active resistance and perhaps even contributing to the building of collective identities and the increasingly global awareness of the need for change? Are the arguments of Benkler, DeLuca and Peeples and other optimists more convincing than the scepticism of a Sunstein, and of critics like Morozov (2009), who claim that the internet has spawned a passive, rather than active, form of engagement, easily dismissed as click- or slacktivism? Or is Cammaerts (2012: 128) right when he defends clicktivism on the grounds that it is a viable practice for people whose lives are too overloaded for 'active' activism?

Another thing to think about is whether digital media technology is making things better or worse for activists. As mentioned earlier in the book, the 'colour' and 'Facebook' revolutions have not only highlighted the positive, empowering potential of mobile communication technology. When someone takes their iPhone to the revolution in their pocket, they are increasingly likely to be taking security forces with them. Such technologies are as useful for surveillance as they are for communicating (Considine 2011). The whole world is watching, in a way the anti-war demonstrators who chanted these words outside the 1968 Democratic National Convention in Chicago could never have imagined.

PART THREE

7 Mediated Conflict

It is a striking and controversial image. Her gaze lingers after the details of the most recent attack or atrocity have been forgotten. This chapter's portkey is a photograph of a young Afghani whose nose and ears were cut off with the approval of the Taliban when she ran away from an abusive marriage. When taking the picture, South African Jodi Bieber said 'I thought to myself, as a photojournalist, and as someone who is bringing my own opinion into my photograph, I was at conflict.'[1]

There are other conflicts involved. Bieber's photograph of Bibi Aisha was published on the cover of *Time Magazine* with the caption: 'What happens if we leave

A visitor at the World Press Photo Exhibition in Amsterdam in April 2011 looks at the portrait of Bibi Aisha taken by South African photographer Jodi Bieber. Photograph: Sylvia / Xinhua Press / Corbis.

Afghanistan', drawing criticism that the image was used in American news coverage for political reasons. The issue of how conflict is to be reported has to do with the relationship between media actors (be they photographers and correspondents on the ground, editorialists in the home office, or the outlets they work for and the people and organizations who own them) and military and political actors (the last two not entirely easy to distinguish between in times of war).

Bieber's portrait of Aisha was one of the winners of the 2011 World Press Photo Award, first mentioned in chapter 4. As will be recalled, the motivations for the awards, as well as the images themselves, yield insights into how journalistic views of objectivity have evolved over time. Jury members talked about how the closer a person is to an event, the better their chances of capturing it faithfully, and thus of conveying an objective report. It was argued, however, that being so close inevitably entails adopting a subjective viewpoint. In an age when proximity is valorized, and people become used to following violent conflicts unfolding in real time on 24/7 news channels, the distinction between objectivity and subjectivity has become confused. Bieber has spoken of how her photograph earned her criticism as well as the coveted prize:

> A woman, a woman academic, sitting in a university in the UK, said I objectified Aisha by showing her as beautiful. Then you had a Rabbi in a synagogue somewhere in the world saying this is how Muslims are. If you look at it, everyone used it for their own political motivation.[2]

Bieber was herself motivated to help Aisha, and to use the image and her own channels of communication to support a human rights organization, Women For Afghan Women (jodibieber.com).

Aisha's penetrating gaze, and concerns about proximity and engagement, stand in stark contrast to the infamous analysis offered by Baudrillard, who made the rhetorical claim that the Gulf War did not take place. In a collection of three essays first published in the press (in *Libération* in France and the *Guardian* in the UK: Baudrillard 1991/1995), the French theorist argued that, because of the striking inequality of the combatants (the victorious US forces engaged the Iraq ground forces from the air, rather than in direct confrontation), and because the world's only access to the conflict was through stylized propaganda imagery, the war was in fact a media construction. In the imagined world of the 'simulacra', he claimed, people 'prefer the exile of the virtual, of which television is the universal mirror, to the catastrophe of the real' (Baudrillard 1991/1995: 28). While not suggesting that wars are imagined, Thussu has had similar mediated tendencies in mind when critiquing war reporting:

> The representation of war on television has evolved in the past decade in parallel with the globalization of infotainment, demonstrating a tendency to use entertainment formats, including video/computer-game style images of surgical strikes by intelligent weaponry, arresting graphics and satellite pictures, and a 'chat-show'-style use of 'experts' (Thussu 2009: 115)

In the one account, journalists bring people so close to a conflict that the objective and the subjective meld together, and they are compelled to meet the gaze of Aisha, and think about how they might act. In the other, television keeps them at home, not so much out of harm's way as paralysed on the couch, controlled by the mechanism of 'collective stupefaction' and amusing themselves to death.

It is often said that media logic emphasizes the negative and feeds on (and fuels) conflict; indeed, textbooks teach students of journalism that this is partly what defines news.[3] The litany includes negative campaigning (which voters apparently dislike but from which politicians seem to find it difficult to refrain), quarrels and crises in reality shows (of which viewers apparently never tire, and which teach them that to be human is to compete), and hate radio (be it in the US, where it only occasionally leads to bloodshed, or Rwanda, where it stoked the flames of genocide). As the last chapter showed, media technology and mediated representations of activism are central to the political conflicts that bring people to the streets and into confrontation with governments the world over; as the next chapter will outline, popular culture teaches viewers much about war and the 'clash of civilizations'. Some of the authors who feature in this chapter are concerned that media organizations profit from war, and that this affects the accounts of conflict we are given.

Claims that media actors and organizations thrive on conflict are often couched in universal terms, but like so many other aspects of the media–politics relationship, these are empirical questions, and claims must be assessed in relation to specific situations. There are cultural variations in the centrality of conflict reporting just as there are cultural variations in the centrality of conflict in politics itself: one need only compare the architecture of the British House of Commons, with its built-in confrontation, with that of the German Bundestag, Swedish Riksdag or European Parliament, for example, to be reminded of that. The focus of this chapter, however, is global. What Kaldor (2001) calls 'new wars' emerged with globalization, and are globalized conflicts even when combat takes place in a specific locality (such as Syria or Mali). War is no longer necessarily waged between states, and the distinction between war, terrorism, large-scale violation of human rights and other sorts of violent crises becomes blurred. New wars are associated with identity crises and reflect experiences of powerlessness on the part of people who suffer from, or have been sidestepped by, globalization (Kaldor 2001: 75).

In this context, all actors in the media–politics relationship, regardless of their vantage point, are faced with problems. The problem facing political elites is familiar from earlier discussions in this book: it is to control the information flow and 'the narrative'. The need to get their understanding of a given conflict situation across, and to persuade the public it is the right one, is a problem shared by activists – whether they are mobilizing to oppose an intervention or calling for action to safeguard the lives and human rights of distant others. When it comes to military stakeholders, the scholarly literature contains contradictory views. Some argued as recently as 2009–10 that practices surrounding soldiers' use of blogs and social media platforms to share photos and videos from the field were in flux and had caught military institutions like the Pentagon off-guard (Christensen 2008; Wall 2010). Others insist that, at least since the declaration of the 'war on terror' by former President Bush in 2001, the military have been honing their information-management skills and strategies (of which more below). A member of the US military who served in Iraq explained,

> We didn't view the news media as a group of people we were supposed to schmooze.
> We regarded them as an environmental feature of the battlefield, kind of like the rain.
> If it rains, you get wet. (quoted in Moorcraft & Taylor 2007: 49)

The 'ordinary' people on the receiving end of mediated accounts of conflict must deal with an increasing flood of conflict news, and decide for themselves whether to meet Aisha's gaze or to surrender to Baudrillardian stupefaction. Their understandings can be shaped – or impeded – by bias, and they can become victims of obfuscation (Liebes 1997; Philo & Berry 2004, 2011). And, as mentioned elsewhere in this book, they have also been subjected to increasing surveillance by state authorities, aided and abetted by refinements in communications technology (Greenwald 2013). Ethnic and religious minorities (especially Muslims in many Western countries) grapple with problems that range from being misunderstood to being mistreated or killed as a result of mediated accounts of 'new wars' (Banaji & Al-Ghabban 2006).

But journalists face problems too, some of them grave. The obstacles to accurate reporting they must overcome can be daunting. They often have to report live, without a clear picture of what is going on in the warzone or bomb scene in which they find themselves (Gokul 2011: 270; Moorcraft & Taylor 2007: 44). They are subjected to increasingly professional information management by military establishments (Jensen 2011; Smith 2009; Winseck 2008). They have to cover increasingly complex wars on continually pruned budgets that are in many cases balanced by owners more concerned with profits than pedagogy (Freedman & Thussu 2012; Thussu 2009). And they are increasingly considered legitimate targets. Between 1992 and June 2013, 186 journalists were killed in combat or crossfire, in Iraq (53), Syria (28), Bosnia (13), Russia (12), Somalia (12), Israel and the Occupied Palestinian Territory (10), Afghanistan (9), Georgia (7), Yugoslavia (6), Lebanon (5) and elsewhere (cpj.org). As one veteran correspondent warned over a decade ago,

> the new insidious development is that because of the impact of our real-time capability to bear witness immediately, we are being actively targeted by warriors, warlords, and forces of even the most highly developed governments who do not want us to see what they are doing. (Gowing 2003: 233)

There is evidence of this other than the testimony of journalists and their interest organizations (such as Reporters Without Borders and the Committee to Protect Journalists, mentioned in chapter 4). The infamous *Collateral Murder* video published by WikiLeaks provided some. As will be recalled from chapter 2, it documented the shooting of Reuters journalists – one of whom died – by a US helicopter crew in Iraq. One of the charges for which former US army soldier Bradley (now Chelsea) Manning was sentenced to life imprisonment, was that (s)he leaked the video to the whistleblower.

The different views of mediated war reflected in Bieber's actions and Baudrillard's words are among many disagreements that can be encountered in the literature on mediated conflict. Often, a case is made in such unequivocal terms that contradictory accounts can be a source of confusion. In what follows, an attempt will be made to navigate the minefield, by signposting seminal events, key concepts and influential arguments.The relationship between journalists and the organizations they work for, on the one hand, and campaigning military and political elites, on the other, is an evolving one. If current debates – both within scholarship and in public discourse – are to be comprehended, familiarity with that evolution can be useful. A timeline is offered for this purpose, followed by an overview of selected scholarship. Its concepts and claims can be related to the three media roles presented earlier in the book, be they the tension between the information-relayer's obligation to be objective and the demands of journalism of attachment (the first role), the contention that 'the media' are increasingly becoming the site of war (the second role), and (when it comes to the third role) the view that conflict reporting can reinforce the political community – imagined or otherwise, but often national – by pitting a 'them' against 'us'. Despite compelling claims made by both those who argue that journalists bring people too close to the battle (offending their sensibilities or overwhelming them with compassion fatigue) and those who argue that entertaining news reports shield people from the horror of conflict, they are not infrequently assumptions or impressions that need to be put to the empirical test. As will have become clear by this stage in the book, the answers to such questions inevitably vary according to situation and cultural context.

A potted history of media–military relations

The world has always been a conflictual place, but some argue that conflict has become endemic in recent decades, given the fragmentation and asymmetrical power structures that globalization processes entail (Resende & Paes 2011: 215). No fewer than 396 armed conflicts were documented in 2012, including 18 wars and 25 limited wars. The Heidelberg Institute for International Conflict Research (2013) classified 43 of them as 'highly violent conflicts' and another 165 as 'violent crises'. Given that these are the figures for a single year, the thought of how many wars have been fought in the past century is a sobering one. While news organizations are thus often criticized for being preoccupied with violent conflict, there is at least as much scope to criticize them for ignoring dozens, if not hundreds, of armed disputes. Of this legion, a number of key conflicts recur in the scholarly literature on the media–military relationship.

The American Civil War of the 1860s, the Spanish–American War of the 1890s and the Spanish Civil War of the 1930s have all been credited with being the first photojournalist or media war, although Robert Fenton brought home photo-documentary evidence from the front lines of the (first) Crimean War in 1855 (Griffin 2010: 10, Miller 2011: 206). It is, at any rate, often recalled that newspaper baron William Randoph Hearst telegraphed his illustrator in Cuba, where rebels were fighting Spanish colonialists, with the famous instruction: 'You furnish the pictures, I'll furnish the war.' It has been suggested that coverage of the global war on terror resonates in many respects with the journalistic traditions established in conflicts of the nineteenth century (Miller 2011: 206).

In both World Wars, when national survival was at stake, journalists tended to behave as 'patriots with pens' (Moorcraft & Taylor 2007: 39). Certainly the military establishments of the Great Powers went to considerable lengths to train and use photographers and motion-picture cameramen when mobilizing for war, and did so successfully (Taylor 1991). During the Cold War, Herbert Schiller (1969) expressed concern at how communications and military spending were becoming entwined, a warning echoed later on by Dallas Smythe (1981). Official transcripts contain evidence of this. In March 2011, Secretary of State Hillary Clinton told the US Foreign Policy Priorities Committee that the US was 'paying a big price' for dismantling its international communications network, that 'our private media cannot fill that gap' and that Al Jazeera English was 'winning the information war'. The dismantled network had been set up in the Cold War, after Navy Secretary James Forrestal told Congress that

> diplomatic and military affairs are so vitally dependent upon the comprehensive-ness, efficiency, reliability, and security of international communications that the continuation of private competition in such communications can no more be ration-alized than could the administration by private enterprise of the diplomatic and military affairs themselves. (quoted in Winseck 2008: 420)

Vietnam is known as the first 'television war' and is often thought of as having been largely uncensored. Images of US soldiers returning home in body-bags (so the story goes) influenced opinion at home and turned the tide of support against the war. Then President Richard Nixon later said that 'television showed the terrible human suffering and sacrifice of war . . . the result was a serious demoralization of the home front' (quoted in Robinson 2012: 343). Research by Hallin (1986) and others has shown that the 'Vietnam Syndrome' is a myth, however, and that the American media were not critical of the war effort until a relatively late stage in the conflict. Reporters who tried to file stories about the victimization of Vietnamese civilians in the late 1960s and 1970s were resisted by mainstream media outlets and in some cases even blacklisted. It was only when schisms began to open between political elites, the government and the military that media reports became critical, and even then only some were (Griffin 2010: 14).

The 'new Cold War' era of the early 1980s (the period of the first snapshot in the activist triptych of Chapter 6) saw East–West tension manifested in a series of international conflicts. It began, though, with an old-fashioned imperial war, when British Prime Minister Thatcher sent troops to resist Argentinian efforts to reclaim the Falklands Islands in 1982. Only twenty reporters were allowed to travel with the task force, always in the company of 'minders'. Reporting in the conservative and tabloid press was notoriously jingoistic and government efforts to summon up a national 'we' that supported the war were, by and large, successful. The US government learned from this, and strictly controlled the access of reporters to the military interventions in Grenada (1983) and Panama (1989). These information-control successes in turn left their mark on the media policy of the first Bush administration during the inva-sion of the Persian Gulf in 1990–1. By that time, the word 'press pool' had become a key concept in media–military discourse. The Pentagon carefully controlled the infor-mation flow, allowed access only to carefully selected reporters, decided where they could travel and what stories they could report on, and reviewed their reports before they were published. This 'First Iraq War', as the Persian Gulf conflict subsequently came to be known, was also the first satellite war. Public and media discourse on the conflict was characterized by a fascination for satellite technology – both that used by the military to drop 'smart' bombs in a purportedly bloodless war, and that used by journalists to file live reports from the scene of the conflict. Afterwards, many journal-ists reflected soberly on what had happened, and conceded that the often starry-eyed preoccupation with technology had obstructed the work of getting the facts and pro-viding an accurate and balanced account of events. As Gerbner (1992: 8) put it,

> We saw portraits of the technology – advertisements for smart planes, tanks, missiles, and other equipment in the dress rehearsals of what they are supposed to do in

combat, but we rarely, if every, saw them in action. Indeed, it was as if there was no other side.

It is thus also to this conflict that many scholarly critiques of media and war can be traced back, as well as the recurrent claim that Western media organizations are guilty of homogeneous, 'techno-war' coverage (of which more later).

The visual documentation of the Iraq War of 2003 reprised that of the 1990–1 Persian Gulf conflict: it was heavy on video-game graphics that emphasized the superiority of Western technology and gave a 'sanitized' impression of professional control of the conflict situation. But while the Pentagon's 2003 communication policy was similar to that of earlier conflicts in its restrictiveness, it contained one key change. Instead of a press pool, it invited selected journalists to travel to Iraq and live and work alongside or 'embedded' with Allied troops. Reports of the 2003 intervention consequently showed more of the chaos of war than those filed by correspondents who had been confined to briefing rooms in 1990–1. The war reported by the embedded journalists was nevertheless, and necessarily, seen from only one side, and resulted in war coverage that has been critiqued for its uniformity and misinformation (Griffin 2010: 31–3; Thussu & Freedman 2003; Thussu 2009). According to the former BBC News Director Richard Sambrook, embedding changed everything.

> War coverage will never be the same again. We can't put the genie back into the bottle . . . war coverage is changed forever. (quoted in Bryne 2003)

CNN became a household name during the Persian Gulf War, when its reporters filed live reports from Baghdad during the first hours of the American invasion. Subsequently, the notion of a 'CNN Effect' was routinely invoked to refer to global media influence in post-Cold-War conflicts in the 1990s, and a 'something-must-be-done school of journalism' urging governments to take action to mitigate humanitarian crises in countries such as Somalia (1992–3) and particularly in Bosnia (1995). In the decade following the attacks on New York and Washington on 11 September 2001, however, a new notion began to feature in popular and scholarly parlance: the 'Al Jazeera Effect' (Seib 2008). This refers not just to the establishment and increasing prominence of the Doha-based news channel, to whom Osama bin Laden sent videotaped messages[4] and whose offices were bombed by US forces in the Iraq War, but more generally to the emergence of 'new' media and alternative sources in reporting of global conflicts. Whereas the 'CNN Effect' described the influence of media reporting on governments, the 'Al Jazeera Effect' is about the influence of new media (technologies and outlets) on mainstream media, not least Western-based 'global newsrooms', seen as too acquiescent in their faithful reporting of information channelled through NATO governments and the military (Robinson 2012: 351).

Despite Sambrook's claim, many argue that it was George W. Bush's subsequent declaration of war on terror that 'changed everything' (Entman 2003; Freedman & Thussu 2012). Visual warfare took a new turn, at this point, with the global circulation of amateur images of torture taken at the Abu Ghraib prison in Iraq, the hanging of Saddam Hussein (2006), the terrorist attacks in London (2005) and Mumbai (2008), and the violent repression of anti-government protests such as mentioned earlier in the book (in Myanmar in 2007 as well as Iran in 2009).

Following the Arab uprisings and outbreak of civil war in Libya and Syria, the importance of such new technology in the dissemination of information and, in particular, images of war has preoccupied a significant number of scholars in both political science and media studies (although Mortensen is right in saying more attention needs to be paid to this 'radical shift in the news coverage of war and conflict': Mortensen 2011: 6). In striking contrast to the slick and sanitized imagery that dominated reporting of the two Iraq Wars, these conflicts are intimately associated with grainy, jerky footage captured by amateurs on their own mobile phones, sometimes sent to professional news organizations for further dissemination, but often uploaded directly to Facebook or YouTube, and with the concepts of 'citizen photojournalism' and 'media witnessing' (Andén-Papadopoulos & Pantti 2011; Christensen 2012; Cottle 2011a; Ellis 2009b; Frosh 2011; Frosh & Pinchevsky 2009; Mortensen 2011; Robertson 2013; Robinson 2012). The compulsion to bear witness to atrocities committed in the Syrian conflict that began in 2011, for example, is a far cry from Baudrillardian claims about nonexistent wars.

There are significant elements of both continuity and change in this timeline. Visual democratization co-exists – at least in the accounts of critical scholars – with media constructions of terrorist threats that align with those of their governments. The changes that matter are both technological (radically impacting on how conflicts are reported, and by whom) and political. The political context of the wars covered by journalists in the twentieth century was one of international conflict, with a clear East–West divide that structured news values. The political context of the 'new wars' of the twenty-first century is global. Societies are perpetually at risk, the 'enemy' less often identified as a foreign state or government and more often as a terrorist, and, like the civilians witnessing it, using personal media to communicate his or her version of the violent act. Scholars such as Freedman & Thussu (2012) maintain that the global threat is represented, in an undifferentiated manner, as being militant Islam:

> Islamist groups in different parts of the world – al-Qaeda . . . in Afghanistan/Pakistan, Hezbollah in Lebanon, Hamas in Palestine, al-Shabab in Somalia, Chechen groups, Lashkar-eToiba in Kashmir and Jemaah Islamiyah in Indonesia – are all too often presented in the mainstream media as part of a seamless transnational terror network which links terrorist activities in such diverse locations as Madrid, Mumbai and Moscow. (Freedman & Thussu 2012: 2–3)

In this context, professional journalists are also embattled, fighting a 'rearguard action' to protect their 'historical position' as the legimate reporters of conflict (Miller 2011: 207). While terrorism is itself a communicative act, mainstream media outlets are pointed to as 'active agents in the actual conceptualization' of such events (Freedman & Thussu 2012: 10). It is through news reporting that disparate acts of violence are brought together in narrative wholes and, as with so many other political and societal phenomena, provide people with mental frameworks for understanding and remembering. In this respect, the story of mediated conflict is one characterized by continuity. In other respects, however, the explosion of digital media and increasing incidence of terrorism (and resultant official, if sometimes covert, political responses) combine to create a situation quite different from that prevailing in earlier historical periods. For this reason, Hoskins and O'Loughlin (2010) have argued that we are experiencing a 'genuinely paradigmatic shift'.

Scholarly perspectives

Robinson (2012) distinguishes between 'elite-driven theories' and 'neo-pluralist' accounts of conflict coverage. Somewhere in between are political economy perspectives on war reporting, an example of which is Thussu's critique of 'war as infotainment' (Thussu 2009).

Elites and bias

The first set of theories (elite-driven) are used to explain deferential coverage, evidence of which has been repeatedly tabled ever since Hallin's influential Vietnam study (Hallin 1986) with increasing insistence since 9/11. One key concept in this scholarly discourse is the 'indexing hypothesis', first proposed by Bennett in 1990 and still making a regular appearance in many political science studies. A variation on the broader notion of 'unwitting bias' mentioned in chapter 4, the hypothesis predicts that journalists will report conflict if political elites are divided (as they were in the final years of the Vietnam War, and again half a century later over whether to provide arms to the Syrian opposition), and 'index' the news to give the impression that the nation is behind an intervention if elite consensus prevails (which was confirmed by the Glasgow University Media Group in its pioneering study of Falklands War coverage, GUMG 1985). Wolfsfeld has used the example of Vietnam somewhat differently, to illustrate his idea that a power imbalance is created when a state is involved in armed conflict. Journalists in wartime and the organizations they work for are described in his 'political contest model' as an example of the 'media as faithful servant' ideal type, with military and political actors enjoying a privileged position in the relationship (Wolfsfeld 1997). Hahn's suggestion, over a decade later, that foreign correspondence has come to be dominated by conflict, crisis and war reporting, because it mirrors the agendas of governments, and because reporters tend to behave like 'bodyguards' or 'courtiers' when following their national leaders abroad (Hahn 2009: 497–8) indicates the continued utility of the model, at least in some contexts.

The concept of 'propaganda bias' was introduced in chapter 4, and propaganda is, perhaps unsurprisingly, a recurrent concept in accounts of conflict reporting. Whereas the indexing hypothesis and political contest model look to the tangible to explain news outcomes (someone either has information and controls it, or they don't), and relate to the first media role (the information-relayer), Herman and Chomsky (1988) emphasize the importance of ideology in shaping the understandings of journalists – and correspondingly of audiences – in ways that resemble those of political elites. Here, the task scholars set themselves is to explain 'how hegemony works' (Liebes 1997). In one respect, this puts them in the company of scholars who view journalists as playing the third role – maintaining the status quo, and treating the views of the dominant powers as though they were common sense. But the 'propaganda model' is concerned with the influence of economic power structures rather than discourse, so the fit is not perfect. What Herman and Chomsky insist (perhaps with more verve than verification) is that US governments have pursued foreign policies, some of them involving military interventions, that reflect the interests of big business – including those of the media industry.

Aware that propaganda is a contested concept, and noting that the term 'public relations' was coined to give more palatable connotations to the profession of propaganda that emerged in the twentieth century, Miller and Sabir (2012) identify four key aspects of the phenomenon, each of which is amenable to empirical inquiry. More than that: they argue that a 'proper' analysis must bring evidence to bear in the study of institutions (be they the people or organizations doing the propaganda work), doctrine (the philosophy 'which theorizes, codifies and organises propaganda efforts'), practice (what the institutions do and produce), and outcomes (which involves the impact of practices: Miller & Sabir 2012: 80). This analytical framework reflects their conviction that propaganda is a 'communicative practice'; that it is not something vague or generalized (as it is so often given the impression of being), but rather something that particular actors are responsible for making happen in specific situations. As the institutions in question are states, the analytical framework proposed by Miller and Sabir has a place beside other 'elite-driven theories'.

Neopluralist accounts of influence

What Robinson places under the rubric of 'neopluralist' accounts shares some features with the elite-fixated theories (and indeed, the names of some scholars turn up in both places). In both sets of accounts, it matters if and when elites are in disagreement over policy relating to conflict, or whether consensus prevails. In this case, however, the strategies in focus are not those of elites, but those of independent and oppositional actors seeking to exploit conflict situations and thus to challenge the elites. In the 'policy–media interaction model' proposed by Robinson (2002), possibilities arise for news media to challenge and even influence government officials (the 'CNN Effect') when there is a breakdown in elite consensus. The 'cascading activation model' (Entman 2003) posits a similar sort of influence: independent and oppositional news reporting is more likely when members of the government are not in agreement, and when mid-level officials question policy about events that are open to contestation. Unexpected and dramatic events are also at the heart of the 'event-driven news thesis', and provide 'legitimizing pegs' for 'relatively independent and critical news narratives' (Lawrence 2000). When civilian deaths occur beyond the control of governments involved in combat, or events take an unwanted turn, researchers have found that the opportunity arises for journalists to adopt a more critical stance. In the case of the 2003 Iraq invasion, Robinson found that such events resulted in reporting that was negotiated or oppositional (to use Hall's codes), even in media outlets that were otherwise strongly supportive: 'bad news' events, he concluded, have a uniform effect on the tone and slant of coverage in mainstream media across the board (Robinson 2011). The potential for such influence (whether it is the influence of reporting or of certain sorts of events) has grown, it is suggested, with the increasing use of social media and the rise of channels like Al Jazeera that make use of other sources than those customarily turned to by mainstream media (Robinson 2012).

Political economy perspectives

The notion of 'infotainment' recurs in a variety of contexts – popular and scholarly alike. It will be discussed and problematized in the next chapter, but because the argument that war reporting has become infotainment is central to Thussu's account of global news, it needs to be previewed here. Global media empires like that of Rupert Murdoch, which has Fox News in its stables, and global channels like CNN 'come alive' at times of war and conflict, according to Thussu. As they are predicated on the provision of live 24/7 programming and are in a perpetual state of competition with rival channels, television newsrooms tend to succumb

> to the sensationalization and trivialization of often complex situations and a temptation to highlight the entertainment value of news. Given the demand of television news for arresting and action-packed visuals and dramatic pictures, wars and civil conflicts are particularly susceptible to infotainment. (Thussu 2009: 113)

Where the theoretical perspectives sketched above sought explanations for the shape of conflict reporting in the political realm, Thussu's argument is typical of scholars working within the perspective of critical political economy. It is competition and commercial considerations, rather than information control by political elites, that is responsible for flawed and superficial accounts of conflict. Because of 'the fiercely competitive rating battle that television networks have to contend with, journalists are under tremendous pressure to make war reporting entertaining', he argues (Thussu 2009: 118). Correspondents are censured rather than censored, given that they tend to 'use unattributed sources, indulge in idle speculation or produce slanted reports influenced by rumour'. Editors and producers draw on the repertoire of entertainment media, using the best visuals rather than the best information, peppering reports with computer-game-style graphics, and filling the news hole not with well-researched reports from the field, but with so-called 'experts' exchanging views with newsreaders in the style of the chat show. 'Television news' is obsessed with 'high-tech' and the story goes missing (Thussu 2009: 114–16). The result is television news obsessed with the hi-tech, homogeneous and slick, spectacular coverage that is entertaining but devoid of expression. Audience members become de-sensitized to wars they are deprived of the opportunity to comprehend.

Media witnessing

Even before the Arab uprisings and the civil wars in Libya and Syria, Thussu's claims about high-tech obsessions were problematic (as are those about homogenization and global trends, given that the examples he draws on are Anglo-American, and Fox News is often the evidence cited). It could be argued – and often is – that television news has become obsessed with the opposite, and, rather than de-sensitization (or stupefication), audience members risk dizziness and nausea from the jerky, pixely, unslick, low-tech amateur footage that has become a recurrent feature of conflict reporting. Rather than elite strategies or economic pressures, scholars researching what is variously referred to as 'user-generated content', 'crowdsourcing' or 'citizen journalism' are more interested in the impact of technology, the actions of often impecunious non-elites, and the concept of 'media witnessing'.

In the influential anthology bearing that name, Frosh and Pinchevsky (2009) argue that bearing witness is an age-old practice, but that cameraphones and social media platforms have transformed people everywhere into 'dormant potential journalists' ready for 'activation' when events require it. The concept of witnessing, mentioned

Struggles to control the narrative were key battles in the conflict that broke out in the Ukraine in late 2013 – a conflict in which media witnessing played a key role. The 'orange' revolution is nestled in the helmet of this protester in Kiev in February 2014, his image shared on Flickr. Photograph: Christiaan Treibert. Reproduced under Creative Commons.

in chapter 5, makes it possible to 'glimpse the underlying connections between the phenomena of "embedded journalist" and "citizen journalism"' (Frosh & Pinchevsky 2009: 2–3). Rather than keeping news consumers distanced from sanitized conflicts, passively taking in the spectacle of war from the proverbial couch, the scholarly discourse of media witnessing sees 'ordinary people' being made part of the story, because they either produce the images used to tell it, or are implicated in its narrative strategies, connected to the news story through audience address. This theoretical approach to understanding what happens when conflict is mediated treats a given news report as a complex text, rather than a superficial or, as Thussu puts it, 'Foxified' media product. As Frosh & Pinchevsky explain,

> a television news report may depict witnesses to an event, bear witness to that event, and turn viewers into witnesses all at the same time. (Frosh & Pinchevsky 2009:1)

Hoskins and O'Loughlin (2010) also begin their treatise on war and media with the observation that there is something qualitatively new about how people connect to war in an age of globalization and advanced media technology. As with scholars working within the 'witnessing' discourse, connectivity is a recurrent, and central, term in their writing. It also has overtones of the 'manufacturing' critiques levelled by Baudrillard and Thussu, but the audiences in Hoskins and O'Loughlin's version are complicit rather than sidelined.

The changes in the relationship between media and war are so radical, and the ensuing problems so substantial, that they can scarcely be comprehended: the 'difficulty that governments, militaries, media organizations and other big institutions have had adapting to this world in the first years of the twenty-first century is hard to overstate'. They argue that conventional academic approaches are incapable of dealing with the paradigmatic shift that they have identified, and are interested in. They advocate instead the concept of 'diffused war' (a twin to the concept of 'diffused audience' discussed in chapter 5) to theorize the way everyone is connected through ubiquitous media, which 'constitutes the very condition of terror for us all'.

> Media enable a perpetual connectivity that appears to be the key modulator of insecurity and security today, amplifying our awareness of distant conflicts or close-to-home threats, yet containing these insecurities in comforting news packages. This connectivity is the principal mechanism through which media is weaponized. (Hoskins & O'Loughlin 2010: 2)

'Diffusion' is used to designate the changing character of war, rather than its causes (which are characterized more by continuity than change). Television is central to this account, despite the globalized, digitalized setting of the contemporary wars addressed by their theory, because it has 'utterly defined the vicarious experience of modern warfare' (Hoskins & O'Loughlin 2010: 4). The media have 'produced' warfare by determining how it is legitimized, contested and shaped. Whereas Baudrillard claimed that the Gulf War did not take place, Hoskins and O'Loughlin argue, in a way (and for similar reasons), that contemporary wars are waged in 'the media' as much as on the battlefield. A second concept which is key to their argument is thus 'mediatization', because 'media are becoming part of the practices of warfare to the point that the conduct of war cannot be understood unless one carefully accounts for the role of media in it' (Hoskins & O'Loughlin 2010: 4). What precisely is meant by the abstract term 'the media' is not as clear as desired in a book that calls for an analysis and understanding of the dynamics of diffused war, but the authors do offer some methodological reflections that shed light on empirical points of access (2010: 185–92). The concept of mediatization will, like infotainment, be discussed more fully in a later chapter. As the notion of 'diffused' builds on the work of Abercrombie and Longhurst (1998), mentioned in chapter 5, this theoretical contribution implicates audiences, including them in a relationship often described as having only elite axes (political–military–media). It is one of the things that makes the book such an important contribution to scholarship on mediated conflict.

Remembering war

A significant feature of news reporting that has not yet been mentioned is the recurrent tendency of journalists to frame contemporary conflicts with reference to bygone wars. When this happens, the third media role is in play. The key concept here is 'mediated historicity', which refers to how our sense of the past, 'and our sense of the ways in which the past impinges on us today', is nourished by 'an ever expanding reservoir of mediated symbolic forms' (Thompson 1995: 34). Societies are selective about what they forget and how they interpret what is remembered. As wars are experienced and thus remembered differently, depending on the historical circumstances, the sense that is made of current interventions also varies from one country to the next. Excellent opportunities to observe this are afforded by the analysis of commemorative events, such as the anniversary of the invasion of Normandy in June 1944.

D-Day, as the invasion is often referred to, is acknowledged to have been the turning point of World War II. On 6 June 1944, about 3.5 million Allied troops crossed the Channel from England to Normandy and drove the Nazis out of France. The majority of the troops came from the US, the UK and Canada, but Australians, New Zealanders, Czechs, Poles, Belgians, French, Dutch and Greeks also took part. The sixtieth anniversary of D-Day was the first to be attended by a German chancellor, and was celebrated shortly after US President Bush had proclaimed the 'liberation' of Iraq by Allied forces, and at a time when occupying forces and civilians continued to die in Fallujah, Najaf and Baghdad on a daily basis. News coverage of the event reflected rather different representations of the world in general, and international conflict in particular, in television news programmes targeting audiences in different parts of the world. British reporting emphasized the importance of taking to arms in defence of freedom, and of coming to the assistance of those oppressed by undemocratic regimes, be they led by Hitler or Saddam Hussein. Recurrent references to 'liberation', and expressions of pride in the brave men who had sacrificed so much for future generations, were a striking feature of reports made for a British public with a stake in the Iraq War. By contrast, the emphasis placed by Swedish and German national public service broadcasters, and by the global Deutsche Welle and Euronews channels, on the human cost of warfare, and the importance of reconciliation and partnership, spoke the language of EU politics. The globals, in particular, drew on stories of German soldiers who had married French and British women after the war, or British soldiers who had fallen in love with Germans. In contrast to the 'us against them' frame of the British reports, the lessons of D-Day were structured in these texts around the metaphor of mixed marriage. The European way of resolving conflict was no longer the centuries-old resort to arms, but the strategy of getting to know and respect – even love – the Other. Where BBC news coverage symbolized D-Day with a black-and-white logo featuring a gun, it was visually represented in Euronews reports by the passionate embrace of the French and German leaders (Robertson 2010: 104–36).

To think about

In June 2013, journalists working for the the *Guardian* newspaper in the UK reported first that a secret order issued by the US National Security Agency (NSA) had been requiring one of the country's largest telecommunications providers to supply the FBI with records of millions of private communications every day (Greenwald 2013), and then that the NSA was directly accessing the systems of giant internet companies under the 'PRISM' programme. US officials could collect not only telephone records, but also the content of personal communications sent on the internet, in e-mails, via Skype or file transfer. According to the *Guardian*, to which information about PRISM was leaked, Google and Facebook had joined the top-secret programme in 2009, YouTube in 2010, Skype and AOL in 2011 and Apple in 2012 (Greenwald & MacAskill 2013). Similar reports were broken by the *Washington Post*. It was noted that, a decade after Republican President George W. Bush declared a 'war on terror', the administration of Democratic President Barack Obama sanctioned the indiscriminate collection of data on citizens, whether or not they were suspected of any wrongdoing. A string of disclosures followed hard on the heels of these reports, alleging that the governments of other nations were using, and contributing to, the data mining. Several conflicts were put together in an editorial published as the news broke:

> Few Americans believe that they live in a police state; indeed many would be outraged at the suggestion. Yet the everyday fact that the police have the right to monitor the communications of all of its citizens – in secret – is a classic hallmark of a state that fears freedom as well as championing it. Ironically, the *Guardian's* revelations were published 69 years to the day since US and British soldiers launched the D-day invasion of Europe. The young Americans who fought their way up the Normandy beaches rightly believed they were helping free the world from a tyranny. They did not think that they were making it safe for their own rulers to take such sweeping powers as these over their descendants. (*Guardian* 2013)

While the internet giants 'flatly refused' to admit they had been deferential to secret political demands, established media were quick to publish the news under scandalized headlines. (The rest is history.) An instance of political contest, cascading activation, event-driven news, or evidence of a pluralistic media environment in which more and different voices challenge political and military elites? Or perhaps of well-established media outlets, prepared to make resources available for investigative journalism (or to cultivate sources and verify leaked information), playing the old-fashioned 'watchdog' role? Scholarship on 'Snowdengate' can draw on a flora of explanatory models, and time will tell whether it results in new concepts and theories of more general applicability. It is possible to get quite far simply by asking: is this an example of change (technological advances having made industrial-scale datamining possible) or continuity (the watchdog role having been played since before 1949, the year Orwell – himself a journalist – wrote *1984*)? One thing to think about is what the answer to this question might be.

Another is whether contemporary mediated conflict is best studied from the starting point of 'techno-wars', 'virtual conflicts' and Baudrillardian nonexistence, or from the authenticity claims of social media footage disseminated by citizen witnesses. There is a theoretical gap between the two foci, and the accounts of mediated conflict they generate can be confusingly contradictory in the absence of integrative analytical frameworks.

The Greek dramatist Aeschylus (525–456 BC) noted that truth is the first casualty in war. While most social scientists have come to acknowledge that truth does not exist in any absolute form (indeed, learning its multiplicity is the point of much social science), truth claims are the basis for the notion of journalistic objectivity first discussed in chapter 4. Is Aisha's portrait a true likeness of the Afghan conflict? How objective is Jodi Bieber's account? Were the editors of *Time Magazine* simply showing things the way they are when they decided to put Aisha's photograph on the front cover, or were they attempting to influence the opinions of readers and the policies of political elites, as critics contended?

The notion of unwitting bias ('the result of standard operating procedures and a reflection of what is instinctively known to be the stuff of news in a given journalism culture') was introduced in chapter 4. An illustration of what this means in practice has a direct bearing on discussions of conflict coverage. A few years after the Gulf War, senior British journalist Michael Buerk interviewed two cameramen who had both filmed the notorious 'Basra Road' incident.[5] As Buerk put it, 'The camera crews saw the reality. Their pictures defined the central issue of how far to attack a defeated enemy.' Susan Stein adopted a quietly defiant attitude.

> When I saw the scene before my eyes, I wanted to film it in such a way that it represented my feelings towards that situation. I felt very strongly about it. I felt this was the one chance we had of actually seeing the horror, if you like, the death and destruction that had taken place during the Gulf War. It was our one point of access. I was aware that there were other cameramen around, I was aware that Ian was filming, and so I shot in a slightly different way. I focussed more on the people who were killed in the road, more sort of unacceptable images for British television, because I thought it was an unacceptable event. I filmed it in a way which isn't necessarily immediately usable in news terms.

Ian Pritchard reacted differently, showing conformity to standard operating procedures and thereby committing the sin of unwitting bias.

> I was a bit annoyed with myself after the Basra Road, because I filmed it as I would have any news event really. I did the odd shot from the back and the side which alluded to the fact that there were dead people there, but didn't actually show the horror of it, because I produced material suitable for transmission rather than perhaps reflected what was actually there.

The contrast between the reactions of the two cameramen, and the idea of 'reflecting what was actually there' shows that the question posed by Robinson (2012: 345) is worth mulling over: 'precisely what kind of coverage would constitute impartial or balanced representation of war?' The question contains things to think about – such as whether 'impartial', 'balanced' and 'objective' reporting of war is always best.

Mediated conflict is not just a war story. Particularly in global, multicultural societies, the role played by media actors, outlets and institutions in instigating, inflaming and resolving conflicts of values and norms within political communities – local, national or global – is increasingly important, and increasingly challenged. Such concerns form part of the chapter on media freedom which is yet to come. But several of the scholars preoccupied with mediated conflict have noted the influence, in this context, of popular cultural narratives, computer games and the vast genre of war films (Gerbner & Gross 1976; Miller 2011; Sachleben & Yenerall 2012; Thussu 2009). Before building an analytical bridge between the theoretical and empirical concerns of the first part of the book, and the normative discussions of media freedom and power at the end of it, the next chapter will thus chart the terrain of the scholarly field of politics and popular culture.

8 Infotainment

The television screen is filled with images of turmoil. The constitutionally sanctioned president has fallen under the influence of religious elements and the head of the military finds himself compelled to intervene. He imprisons the president and assumes command. Reporting of the conflict is impeded. The reins of civilian power seem likely to be picked up by a figurehead of recent protests for democratic reform. He promises early elections, but outraged people demand the reinstatement of the president. Civil war threatens.

The summary of a news report filed from Egypt in July 2013, following the ouster of Mohammed Morsi? No: it is in fact the synopsis of an episode in the cult science-fiction series *Battlestar Galactica*.[1]

When the series was first broadcast in 2004, the prospect of 'Facebook revolutions' sweeping the Arab world was as futuristic as any science fiction plot. The 9/11 attacks were, however, a recent memory and the 'war on terror' was in full swing. In the parallel universe of *Battlestar Galactica* (BSG), the war being waged is between the few thousand people who have survived annihilation, and the inhuman Cylons who infiltrated their network, bombed the human colonies (killing 50 billion), and now wander among unwitting survivors, disguised as ordinary people but preparing more evil deeds. An uneasy alliance had been formed between the head of the government and the head of the military to save the last of the colonials – the people who left Earth at some time in the distant past and who will be returned to their home planet by a dying leader, according to an ancient religious prophecy. President Roslin, who has terminal cancer, uses her political skills to outmanoeuvre the military leader, Commander Adama, to make the prophecy come true. This is what prompts the commander to imprison the president, convinced as he is that she has lost her sense of judgement under the sway of religious advisers, and that her continuation in office endangers the long-term survival of the community. Audience members following the story from a safe spot on the couch, or embracing a screen on bedtops the world over, find themselves torn. The skilful characterization and sophisticated narrative techniques mean it is difficult to distinguish right from wrong, and heroes from villains. Viewers are compelled to ask themselves how they would react if the head of state imposed emergency rule and gave herself special powers, and if the military blocked the move with a coup. The issue presented to them is whether civil liberties and the separation of powers are inviolable, or whether collective security can sometimes require that they be suspended.

Earlier in this book, it was noted that some scholars are worried we are 'amusing ourselves to death', being 'dumbed down' and entertained rather than informed, with the standard of public discourse lowered and its scope narrowed as a consequence, and the health of the polity thereby endangered. The spectre of 'infotainment' is ritually

Napoleon and Britain's King George III represented as Gulliver and the King of Brobdingnag, characters from *Gulliver's Travels*, Swift's satirical novel of 1726. Image: Ann Ronan Picture Library. © Heritage Images / Corbis.

invoked in this context, and the associated argument that economic forces have an interest in cultivating public ignorance and apathy. This chapter critically assesses that concern, not by focusing on information deficits, but by considering some of the entertainment fare in circulation. The questions that serve as the red thread in what follows have theoretical, empirical and normative dimensions. Does infotainment necessarily preclude understanding? How is 'dumbing down' to be distinguished from the narrative and pedagogical strategies that are used in some media texts to make political problems more meaningful and memorable in an era of information overflow? The chapter questions the default position that information – the more exhaustive and in-depth the better – is always preferable to stories about politics that engage, and that encourage people to think and to question rather than just to get informed.

The connection between politics and popular culture is not new. Political satire has been around since ancient times. Medieval Arab poetry had its own satirical genre and Chaucer, Rabelais, Shakespeare and Swift (popular in their own day) could be scathing in their depictions of the powerful.

The music of the Romantic composers of the late eighteenth and early nineteenth centuries was deeply ideological and often had political themes (Wagner was a political activist – a radical who supported the 1848 revolutions, had to flee Germany to escape arrest and ended his days in political exile). Public consciousness about social inequality and political problems was raised by popular novels penned by the likes of Victor Hugo, George Eliot and Charles Dickens. Chapters were published in separate instalments, ending in cliffhangers, much the way that radio and then television series would later keep their audiences returning the following week for a new episode. The popularity of such novels and 'penny dreadfuls' in societies that were undergoing significant transformation (literacy was growing among the 'lower classes', and industrialization had given many the disposable incomes to purchase such literature) was identified as a threat to society, and the newspaper magnates and publishers who grew rich from the sales of such media were accused of profiting from people's predilection for escapism. From Roman gladiatorial sports and bear-baiting through to contemporary World Cup matches, sport has served as a form of social control and a way of confining aggression and competition between nations to the playing field (Delgado 2003: 293). Sometimes it has worked. Although Adorno and Horkheimer were worried about the frivolous influence of Hollywood on Americans in the 1930s (see chapter 5), popular culture was used to maintain political order in Franco's Spain, Mussolini's Italy, Stalin's Soviet Union and Hitler's Germany.[2]

What is newer, and perhaps more challenging, is the trend whereby the boundary between fact and fiction – between satire, 'genuine' politics and real news – is increasingly difficult to distinguish. The trend sees figures like *The Daily Show*'s Jon Stewart occupying a central position in political discourse, with a genre that has spread to other parts of the world not because of media capitalism's need to find new markets, but because the spirit and format fills a need in, say, post-revolution Egypt. When Mubarak was forced out of power, a heart surgeon called Bassem Youssef began mocking politicians and Egyptian media in a way that emulated Stewart, and posted his satires on YouTube. Within three months, he had 5 million hits and *Al Bernameg* (The Programme) was born. Apart from its popularity, its significance could be measured by the number of times the Egyptian chief prosecutor placed Youssef under arrest for insulting President Morsi, and by the fact that it was taken off the air after Morsi in turn was removed from power and replaced by Commander-in-Chief el-Sisi. Fans the world over were treated to a moment of tangible media globalization when Jon Stewart appeared on *Al Bernameg* shortly before the events referred to above (the deposing of Morsi, not the cylon attack). Stewart was escorted into the Egyptian studio like a foreign spy about to be interrogated, Youssef removed the black hood over the head of *The Daily Show* host and explained to the audience in Arabic: 'They say he is the Bassem Youssef of America. He imitates me.' A TV-couch chat in English followed, in the course of which the two comedians talked about the importance of tolerance and showed their mutual disdain for governments throughout the world that overstep their power. In a reference to Youssef's recurrent arrests, Stewart commented wryly: 'A joke has never ridden a motorcycle with a baton into a crowd. A joke has never fired tear gas into a park.'[3]

The quip is one answer to a question posed at the outset of this book: to whom does a certain state of affairs matter? While jokes may not fire tear gas, they often have clout. As Delli Carpini (2012: 9) notes, 'the potential power of entertainment media has not been lost on those interested in influencing the opinions, attitudes and behaviors of citizens'. Efforts to influence people through entertainment are one of the phenomena it can be instructive to study. It is also worth attending to the many ways that stories about politics can be told, and the many genres through which they are relayed (or encoded, to borrow vocabulary from chapter 5), and come to shape people's understandings. Instead of focusing on news (safe, secure ground when it comes to studies of political communication), this chapter is structured around other phenomena which should

Blurring the borders between politics and entertainment: Jon Stewart, host of *The Daily Show*, at The Rally to Restore Sanity in Washington, October 2010. Photograph: © Julie Dermansky / Corbis.

be taken into account when seeking to understand the power relationship explored in this book: celebrity politics, music, reality television, comedy and satire, drama, and science fiction and fantasy (SF). To this end, a variety of scholarly discourses on these narrative forms will be surveyed, and an overview provided of the sense that is made of how popular culture works politically. In focus is the tension between the arguments of scholars who are concerned that we are amusing ourselves to death, or being stupefied into passivity by those with an economic interest in keeping us distracted, and those who maintain that entertainment is a significant source of political information and understanding, and that satire has become an increasingly necessary complement to political journalism everywhere from North America to North Africa. It argues that 'infotainment' – a term that recurs in both scholarly literature and public discourse – need not have negative connotations.

Imagining politics

'To entertain' can mean quite different things, as Baym (2005: 274) points out. It can mean 'to interest, to amuse, to give pleasure', but it can also mean 'to engage with and consider'. While the political influence of entertainment media remains under-theorized and, as a form of political communication, has received far less attention than press and television news, it has been attracting an increasing amount of schol-arly attention in recent years (Corner & Pels 2003; Delli Carpini 2012; Herkman 2012; Jones & Baym 2010; Street 2012b; van Zoonen 2005). The following section provides a cursory inventory of contemporary entertainment phenomena that call for the atten-tion of scholars interested in mediated politics.

Celebrities and politics

An internet search on 'Angelina Jolie and politics' generates 35,800,000 hits.[4] In March 2013, she travelled to the Democratic Republic of Congo with British Foreign Secretary William Hague to draw international attention to the use of rape as an instrument of warfare, prior to the G8 summit that had the issue on its agenda. The initiative, which took the unlikely pair to Libya, Mali and the Syrian border, was one of many humanitarian issues with which the American film star has been associated.

Jolie is one example of a trend which has seen celebrities playing an increasingly prominent – and perhaps self-evident – role in political discourse. Bono and Bob Geldof spearheaded the 'charity supergroup' Band Aid to raise funds for the poverty-stricken in Africa in the 1980s, followed later by Live Aid, and are among the celebrities more recently associated with the Make Poverty History campaign.[5] Bruce Springsteen, Sting and Peter Gabriel have headed tours on behalf of Amnesty International. Performers have publicly supported presidential candidates throughout the world, and causes on both left (George Clooney was arrested during the Occupy Wall Street protests and in demonstrations against human rights violations in Sudan) and right (Charlton Heston was a leading figure in the US pro-gun lobby, and Jeremy Irons actively opposed the British government ban on fox-hunting). High-profile comedians regularly stage Comic Relief galas, and stars have been involved with fundraising to support victims of the Asian tsunami in 2004, Hurricane Katrina in 2005, the Haitian earthquake in 2010, the Philippine cyclone and the ongoing Syrian refugee crisis. Penelope Cruz, Elisabeth Canalis and Olivia Munn are among the actresses who have posed nude to publicize their anti-fur stance (peta.org). NGOs now have extensive teams of 'celebrity liaison workers' who are recruited to boost any given cause, and stars feature prominently on the websites of organizations like Amnesty, Oxfam and Greenpeace (Street 2012b: 77).

Driessens et al. (2012) use the word 'charitainment' to designate the phenomenon of moral causes being subordinated to the logic of entertainment media:

> Distress is packaged in amusing formats that motivate the audiences to give. Charity is turned into charitainment, compassion into a spectacle, thus reducing reality to a mediated abstraction. (2012: 712)

Where there are celebrities, there are fans, and fan culture is a phenomenon that interests an increasing number of scholars from a variety of fields. Van Zoonen has pointed to the connection between the fan and the engaged citizen, and to how electorates must be emotionally constituted, with affective bonds forged and maintained between voters, candidates and parties (Van Zoonen 2005: 66). It is to this 'affective dimension' of politics that celebrities, and the popular cultural forms with which they are associated, can contribute (Street 2012b: 81).

Music (mediated and otherwise)

Musicians featured prominently in the ranks of celebrities mustered above. But music has a political function even when performers are not household names. In countries like Senegal, 'music and politics go hand in hand' (Mossman 2013). Singer and guitarist Baaba Maael is a UN youth emissary; singer and percussionist Youssou N'Dour ran for president in 2012; and hip hop artist Sister Fa is one of the world's leading campaigners against female genital cutting.

The women of the Pussy Riot punk group and their well-publicized conflicts with the Putin regime, focused international attention on threats to civil liberties in contemporary Russia, although it is not clear whether their 'prayer' to the Virgin Mary to remove Putin from power was 'an artistic action with political aims or a political action with artistic means' (Jonson 2012).

The protest song has long organized responses to societal and political wrongs (Street 2012a). Originally associated with the emancipation of the slaves in the US and, later, with the turbulent 1960s in Western democracies (the death of troubadour Pete Seeger in 2014 occasioned a flurry of retrospectives that comprise rich research material), the protest song has more recently figured in authoritarian Middle Eastern contexts. Tawil-Souri (2011b) has written of the role of rap in Palestinian resistance to the Israeli occupation. The Tunisian rapper El Général posted a track on Facebook at the end of 2010, about corruption, unemployment, poverty, and President Ben Ali. Rais Le Bled went viral 'and the words of the song were on the lips of many as they demonstrated out on the streets across Tunisia' (Hebblethwaite 2011).

> Within hours, the song had lit up the bleak and fearful horizon like an incendiary bomb. Before being banned, it was picked up by local TV station Tunivision and al-Jazeera. El Général's MySpace was closed down, his mobile cut off. But it was too late. The shock waves were felt across the country and then throughout the Arab world. (Morgan 2011)

Music is also politics in contemporary Europe, where it reflects and shapes political and cultural identity. Voting in the Eurovision Song Contest goes farther than voting in the European Parliament elections. More people vote in it, for one thing. For another, EU citizens can only vote for politicians from their own states to represent them in the European Parliament (a British Conservative can only vote for a British party, not for a Finnish or Greek Conservative candidate; nor can a Swedish Green vote for a Green candidate from Germany). In their cultural as opposed to civic capacities, however, Europeans can vote for songs and singers from other European countries, and the 'Europe' of the contest includes Russia, Azerbaijan, Turkey and other countries off the European political map (Robertson 2014).

Docu-drama and reality TV

Explosive documentaries like Michael Moore's *Fahrenheit 911* (about the collusion of the news industry in the war on terror) and *Sicko* (about the health care industry in the US), Al Gore's *An Inconvenient Truth* (about global warming) and the internet phenomenon Kony2012 (about the forced recruitment of children by a rebel African militia group) have arguably had a more profound impact on people's ideas about politics and policy, and in some cases on official behaviour, than any number of news programmes. While powerful and engaging fact-based (although not always entirely factual) texts, it is not only their format that distinguishes them from other news and current affairs output. It is also their emphasis on drama and their eschewing of objectivity.

The boundaries between journalism and commentary, and between journalism and entertainment, have blurred in another media format – what Thussu calls the 'globally successful hybrid genre' of reality television. Its expansion in the late 1990s from the US and UK to the rest of the world 'is another indication of how market forces have changed broadcast journalism'. Reality television (a vivid example of infotainment, in the view of Thussu) combines tabloid journalism, documentary television and entertainment in what is deemed an unhealthy mix (Thussu 2009: 82).

One of the most interesting examples of the genre – and certainly a programme that has attracted considerable scholarly attention – is *Big Brother*. Created in the Netherlands, the programme format travelled to Germany, France and Spain. It was 'localized, cloned and copied' throughout the world, making its creator a millionaire, and Endemol, its production company, a global business leader (Thussu 2009: 85). Endemol chairman Peter Bazalgette has been cited as claiming that

> when the series was broadcast in Denmark for the first time in 2001, MPs and bureaucrats crashed their entire Internet connections as they were all logging on at once to watch [. . .] In Spain (where the programme was called *Gran Hermano*), a Basque separatist broke into the Big Brother house to stage a protest and in Poland, one housemate joined the programme with the aim of entering politics, and won a parliamentary seat in the 2001 general elections . . . In Colombia, President Alvaro Uribe became a surprise guest at the local version of *Big Brother* to promote a package of constitutional reforms. (Thussu 2009: 85)

There is a more subtle connection to politics than this obvious exploitation of the forum for the publicity purposes of individual politicians. Reality television shows like *Big Brother* contribute to the blurring of the boundary between public and private. Bazalgette has noted that general elections in the noughties suffered the greatest fall-off in voter participation since 1918, with turn-out particularly low among young people. He is well aware of the divergent views on increasing political apathy familiar from the literature reviewed earlier in this book: the pessimistic view that an apolitical generation represents a serious threat to participatory democracy, and a 'more sanguine' view that young people are just as concerned about social and ethical issues as their forebears, but feel estranged from organized politics, which are no longer controversial and have lost their edge. People are faced with seemingly endless choice and are defined through the goods and services they buy, but only get to choose their government once every few years. 'And that's all we get to choose', Bazalgette adds; 'We cannot express our views on individual issues.' In such contexts, the house of *Big Brother* takes the place of the house of Parliament. In both houses, a popularity contest takes place (and in many polities, the contest in both is televised). Both competitions benefit from the emotional as well as intellectual engagement of the voters, in the producer's view. Engagement is encouraged and enhanced when the voters feel that their active participation might affect the outcome.

> Paradoxically, though their dramas and routines are played out in apparent isolation from the world beyond their walls, the residents of both houses are dependent upon how they are seen and judged by those outside. The relationship between inside and outside the houses is one of performance and perception; exhibition and surveillance. Feeling misunderstood by the outside world, the inhabitants put their ears to the walls and listen for the sounds of public opinion – their lifeblood. (Coleman 2003: 6)

Another reality show with political ramifications and voter power is *Star Academy*. Based on the Spanish format *Operación Triunfo* and produced by the same Endemol of *Big Brother* fame, the show has been broadcast in over fifty countries and proven particularly influential in the Arab world, where reality television is so controversial 'that it has triggered street riots, contributed to high-level political resignations, compelled clerics to issue hostile *fatwas*, and fanned transnational media wars' (Kraidy 2009: 3). In 2004, *Star Academy* garnered the largest audience in the history of pan-Arab television, but was outflanked some years later by *Arab Idol*. In 2013, a young singer from a refugee camp in the Gaza Strip became the first Palestinian to win the televised competition, in which millions throughout the region took part by SMS voting. Overcoming Hamas opposition to a phenomenon thought inappropriate for Muslims, President Abbas instructed Palestinian embassies throughout the world to vote for 'the pride of the Palestinian and Arab nation'. A journalist with insights into the region explained the victory was politically significant, because

> for the past few years, Palestinians felt as if they had been dropped into a deep dark hole, away from international attention and from the consciousness and interest of fellow Arabs.[6]

Comedy and satire

Satire and elections go hand-in-hand. In 2012, Lego toys appeared on Moscow street corners and parks, carrying banners complaining about corruption and official

Press review of *Les Guignols de l'Info* on display in the workshop of *Les Guignols de l'Info* in Paris. *Les Guignols* is a take-off of the British satire show *Spitting Image* with political figures and celebrities portrayed by rubber puppets. Photograph: © Lor/For Picture/Corbis

malpractice, in an action that was declared illegal by the authorities, on the grounds that the toys were not Russian citizens (seriously). On the other side of the world, Joss Whedon, creator of the *Buffy the Vampire-slayer* series, urged Americans to vote for presidential candidate Mitt Romney as the right man to lead the country into the zombie apocalypse, with a mock political advert that is a good example of generic blurring in political communication.[7]

Following in the footsteps of *Spitting Image* (UK) and *Les Guignols* (France), *ZANEWS*, produced in Capetown, and *The XYZ Show*, made by an independent company in Nairobi, use puppets to lampoon the misdeeds of the politically powerful in ways that journalists find difficult.[8]

The run-up to the 2013 elections in Kenya witnessed what Reinl (2013) characterized as an 'explosion' of cartoons, television and street art mocking politicians. One observer described a graffiti image of a vulture-like politician on a Nairobi wall. The caricaturized parliamentarian was scoffing at tribespeople for voting for him, despite his greedy behaviour. The man running the gift shop in the building beside the image was interviewed as saying:

> It's about the way members of government put money in their pockets while the people die poor. The picture tries to educate. If people see it, maybe they will learn something – not to vote like they did before. (Reinl 2013)

The quotation illustrates the efficacy of humour in both supporting and undermining civic practices (Hirzalla et al. 2013; Sachleben & Yenerall 2012). Considerable attention has been paid in the US context to how satirical programmes provide ways of talking about political issues that resist the 'pundit talk' of mainstream media (Hirzalla et al. 2012: 49). Along with Bill Maher, Jay Leno, David Letterman and Matt Drudge, Steven Colbert and Jon Stewart have been identified as the 'new gatekeepers' in a context where journalism has been found wanting (Delli Carpini 2012: 10). According to Baym, *The Daily Show* interweaves two levels of discourse. It is news as well as entertainment; pop culture as well as current affairs. More than comedy, it is satire that plays the watchdog role, using humour 'to confront political dissembling and misinformation and to demand a measure of accountability'. As with *ZANEWS* and *The XYZ Show*, *The Daily Show* can say 'that which the traditional journalist cannot' (Baym 2005: 273, 2010).[9] The UK has an even longer and, some would suggest, richer tradition of political satire. This book opened with a scene from *Yes Minister*, considered by British politicians to be the best political comedy ever. (Margaret Thatcher was said to have enjoyed the programme and appreciated 'its realistic depiction of "what goes on in the corridors of power"': van Zoonen & Wring 2012: 269). It was widely noted that the foul-mouthed spin doctor in *The Thick of It*, which carried on the tradition, bore an uncanny resemblance to former UK Prime Minister Blair's director of communications and strategy, Alastair Campbell.

Years before comedian Beppe Grillo harvested a sufficiently large share of votes to cast Italian politics into turmoil after the 2013 elections, political scientists had conceded that power in Italy was 'mainly criticized by comedians that take the place of journalists in informing people about the logics of political power' (Poletti & Brants 2010: 333). Having been shunned by Italian television after accusing the political elite of corruption (accusations which subsequently proved to be true, and which ended the rule of Prime Minister Craxi in 1987), Grillo was forced to take to the internet where (by his own account) he could not be controlled. He turned his comic fury on Berlusconi, whom he dubbed 'Mr Muscle' (as in the poisonous cleaning fluid with the gleaming smile), and exploited popular frustration over the gulf between the political class and the electorate:

> between them and us. Between millions of citizens who have become invisible and politicians who just talk among themselves (quoted in Holmes 2006).[10]

Several authors have drawn attention to how social media is exploited in the critique of the powerful. In writing about Twitter fakes (the adoption by satirists of the identity of politicians), Wilson (2011: 457) suggests that the practice is a symptom of 'new counter-spaces' opening up to contest increased mainstream media control.

Drama

Political television fiction, some argue, makes it possible for audiences to learn, reflect upon and judge politics: it 'can function as a source of political imagination and understanding, complementing or even constrasting with the standard sources that journalism offers' (van Zoonen & Wring 2012: 265; see also Sellnow 2014). An example is the Danish political drama *Borgen*, which has proven extremely popular with viewers throughout Europe. The central figure is Prime Minister Birgitte Nyborg, who heads a coalition government. As the BBC Four controller explained, after deciding to buy the third series for a UK audience, 'strong characters coupled with delicately woven personal and political storylines have kept our audiences hooked on a Saturday night' (quoted in Frost 2013). An earlier and much celebrated example of political television drama is *The West Wing* (Riegert 2007).

On the big screen, films such as *JFK*, *W*, *The Candidate*, *The Queen*, *Iron Lady*, *The Lady* and *Frost/Nixon* have provided powerful narratives of politics and political dilemmas. Two Hollywood films with connections to current politics were said to have been made with the cooperation of the Obama administration: Kathryn Bigelow's *Zero Dark Thirty*, about the killing of Osama bin Laden, and Steven Spielberg's *Lincoln*, 'about a previous tall orator from Chicago who advanced the cause of race relations' (Lawson 2012). *Lincoln* had cultural resonance beyond the US. A Swedish editorialist, for example, used the Lincoln premiere as a point of departure for a rhetorical essay on contemporary politicians and power, praising the film for not offering a conventional depiction of a hero, but for depicting the marshes and trenches of politics in such a compelling manner. It is in *Lincoln*'s depiction of the tension between the short- and long-term goals of politics that the film is most fascinating, he wrote. Lincoln is a hero, in the eyes of history.

> The problem is that history takes a long time. A politician who uses similarly controversial methods is unlikely to become an icon during his own lifetime . . . What politician today, not least in Sweden, would risk applying such tunnel vision and go right through the wall for the ideas they feel most strongly about? Who would dare expose themselves to their opponents, their own party representatives, journalists, opinion pollsters, irate twitterers and cynical editorialists? (Helmersson 2013)

It is not only dramas about leaders that matter to politics, of course. Telenovelas are thought to bring considerable influence to bear on the way people imagine power relations, in the Latin American countries from which they emanate, but also in such places as Germany, Indonesia, Russia, Portugal, the Philippines, Egypt, India, Kenya, Tanzania, Canada and the USA (Delli Carpini 2012: 9). Lamuedra and O'Donnell (2012) have also argued that the immensely popular and long-running British soap opera *EastEnders* is a site for the imagination and maintenance of community, and for resistance to neoliberal hegemony (2012: 59, 72).

Science fiction and fantasy

This genre is so large and qualitatively different from drama per se, in some respects, that it deserves consideration in its own right, and has indeed received it of late, particularly in international relations quarters. SF image producers 'expand the spaces of political discourse' about politically sensitive or difficult topics by situating controversies in SF contexts. As Goulart and Joe (2008: 194) explain, depicting a contemporary real-world controversy 'as a conflict with aliens or robots in remote galaxies blunts the edge of ideas that might otherwise provoke instant condemnation or worse'. *Star Trek*, in its various incarnations and generations, is one enduring example (which has resulted in a suprising amount of political science literature, see e.g. Inayatullah 2003 and Neuman 2003); *Avatar* is another. The imagined futures need not be at the other end of the universe or involve unfamiliar life forms, as evidenced by such bleak visions of the future as *Children of Men*, *The Road* or *The Hunger Games*. Other games should be mentioned here too – notably the popular multiplayer online *World of Warcraft*, which could in some respects be said to form a global communicative space in its own right and which revolves around many of the lynchpins of international relations theory – be they anarchy and inter-ethnic conflict or deterrence and interdependence.

One thing that makes SF such a compelling source of insights is that the texts of different periods reflect understandings of politics and society, and the challenges facing both, at different times – the Zeitgeist, so to say. One insightful piece showed how the nation (in this case the US) was 'imagined' through television 'superwomen' such as Wonder Woman, The Bionic Woman and Isis in the 1970s – a period in which the US was suffering from 'a host of uncertainties about itself' (Clark 2009). The youthful and honest female superhero contained both the challenges of the burgeoning women's movement and constructed

> an imagined geography of the nation with an attendant political coherence and global superiority . . . the fantasy female superhero, a mediated figure of liberated womanhood, offered America an idealized image of itself during trying political, economic, and cultural times. (Clark 2009: 436)

Battlestar Galactica was born in this turbulent decade (i.e. at the end of the 1970s), and remade in the context of the even more vulnerable and globalized noughties. Against the backdrop of international terrorist attacks and the panicked efforts of governments to deal with them, the producers and writers fashioned a series around difficult and controversial questions, using what they called a 'different prism' through which characters are 'twisted' from the expected norm. In some situations, the 'good' humans that viewers have learned to invest in choose to behave in ways that would be considered immoral in the real world and present day. Protagonists are suicide bombers, for example, and use measures of questionable legality to stave off threats to the political community. The connection between organized religion and political and military actions is interrogated (BSG creator Ronald D. Moore, a political science graduate, told an interviewer that the Cylons 'have aspects of Al Qaeda, and they have aspects of the Catholic Church, and they have aspects of America'), and viewers are compelled to reflect on the fact that 'fundamentally decent people can behave in uncivil and immoral ways' in times of political and military conflict (Goulart & Joe 2008: 179–83).

It was not only *Battlestar Galactica* that challenged audiences to think twice about politics during the war on terror. The filmatization of the *Lord of the Rings* trilogy and J. K. Rowling's chronicles of the struggle of Harry Potter, and his friends and helpers, against the forces of evils (including the evils within themselves) spoke to a world of global conflict. More recently the successful *Hunger Games* trilogy has not only drawn on notions of centre and periphery familiar from world systems theory to explore themes of political oppression and anarchy (Weber 2013), but also critiqued the heavily mediated nature of the decadent society, and its fascination with reality shows and competitions.

Fantasy, claims Martin Hall (2006: 177) is a genre that mirrors the realist paradigm in international relations theory in its focus on the struggle between good and evil. Realism says that something has gone wrong in the world (Sauron or Voldemort are increasing their presence and power and preparing for war), and when this is recognized ('recognition is absolutely central' in both fantasy and international relations narratives, according to Hall) the wrongness can be named and measures devised to combat it. In the realist paradigm, that wrongness – the overriding threat – is the loss of sovereignty (Hall 2006: 189). SF is a genre for the globalized era.

Theoretical attempts to address such phenomena

How have scholars made sense of the sort of phenomena surveyed above, and their relation to politics? Broadly speaking, two approaches can be discerned.

One area of interest pertains to how established political actors use popular culture to garner support for, and interest in, their 'brand' (Holly 2008; Riegert 2007). Some scholars have argued that politics should be understood in terms of aesthetics, and as a competition in style between rival artists (Ankersmit 1996; Corner 2003; Corner & Pels 2003). In a helpful overview, Street (2012b) sorts out macro-level theories, which explain the intertwining of popular culture and political communication with reference to large-scale social and political transformations; meso-level theories focusing on the professionalization of political communication (and which refer to 'media logic' and spin); and theories which seek to explain changes in the nature of communication itself. Street argues that all these theories treat popular culture as a solution to a particular political problem, and focus on the political dimension of the relationship (Street 2012b: 79). These 'political' responses have been dealt with, to some extent, in chapter 3 and will be revisited later, so will not be dwelt upon further at this point.

A second broad approach is that of cultural studies. Rather than asking how politicians use popular culture, the question posed here is how popular culture can be political. Key concepts in this research strain are ideology, representation and, of course, culture, which refers to a general process of aesthetic and intellectual development, a way of life, and the artefacts produced by cultural activity (paintings, songs, novels, films, television series and so on). Stuart Hall has suggested that culture is simply about shared meanings – about people making sense of the world in similar ways. Social and political relations are given meaning by how they are represented in words, stories and images. Following what has been referred to as the 'cultural turn' in the social sciences, scholars have come to agree that meaning is produced or constructed, that meaning-makers have political power, and that the analysis of discourse is one point of access. What is studied in this approach is how language and representation produce meaning, but also

> how the knowledge which a particular discourse produces connects with power, regulates conduct, makes up or constructs identities and subjectivities, and defines the way certain things are represented, thought about, practised and studied. (Hall 2007:6)

This approach eschews universal and even general claims and conclusions, and focuses instead on specific discourses in particular times and places, or on certain 'regimes of representation'. Of interest here is the different sense made by readers of *Lord of the Rings* when it was first published in 1954 (or what it meant to Tolkein as he was writing it during World War II), and by viewers of the film first screened in 2001 (the year of the 9/11 attacks on the World Trade Center); or of the first *Star Trek* series broadcast on television in 1966, when the real world was bipolar, and the film that premiered in 2013, in a context of advanced globalization.

As Nexon and Neuman (2006) explain, politics 'relies upon, operates through, and produces representations'. They cite President Bush's famous 'war on terror' address as a representation of the al-Qaeda attacks that

> drew on representations from the media and intelligence communities about the attacks themselves, relied on representations of America and the world deeply ingrained in American political culture, and presented a representation of the meaning and significance of the attacks that it then tied to specific courses of actions, such as the imminent invasion of Afghanistan. (Nexon & Neuman 2006: 7–8)

A speech by a president (a Bush rather than a Roslin, that is) is best understood, in their account, as a 'first-order representation', while the sense made of an attack in an entertainment text (by a Roslin rather than a Bush) is a 'second-order representation'. The scholarly problem identified by Nexon and Neuman is that international relations theorists tend to view first-order representations unproblematically, as 'facts', and to overlook second-order representations and, crucially, the interplay between them.

Ideology is, as mentioned, a key concept in the study of popular culture. Storey (2001) explains that the concept is used to signal that cultural texts can present distorted images of reality, and to caution that the distortions tend to work 'in the interests of the powerful against the interests of the powerless'. Scholars like Thussu, not least when writing about 'infotainment', treat neoliberalism and media capitalism in ideological terms, concerned as they are that media audiences are blind to power exerted over them by Hollywood or Fox News accounts of the world (Miège 2011; Thussu 2009). Whether or not people are susceptible to such power, however, and suffer from 'false consciousness' is an empirical question. As will be recalled from chapter 5, the view that audiences can be 'active' and not just 'passive dopes' suggests that they can resist the preferred readings that discourse analysis locates in popular cultural texts about politics. Such analysis can also establish that some texts are polysemic, and present familiar tales of conflict and the struggle for survival through a 'different prism', to borrow Moore's phrase.

Entertaining possibilities

Another scholarly focus has thus been publics (or audiences or fans). The central question here is whether and how the blurring of the line between news and entertainment in recent years is influencing the political perceptions of the people who consume the sort of cultural products inventoried at the beginning of the chapter. Little is actually known about this, given the absence of sustained research into the effects of popular culture on political engagement (Delli Carpini 2012: 10; Street 2012b: 76) As with effects research in general (chapter 5 touched on this), some scholars have found that some people in some conditions at some times will adapt their political attitudes in light of some entertainment media. Wryly summing up the evidence provided by quantitative research, Delli Carpini has noted that we know that heavy use of entertainment media is correlated with lower levels of democratic engagement; that the awareness and opinions of people who consume entertainment media with explicitly political content correlate with the information and framing of such media; that there are significant variations in the influence of entertainment depending on form, content, genre and event; and that demographic, attitudinal and behavioural characteristics matter. In other words, a lot is known about little, and 'we cannot even say with any confidence whether and under what conditions entertainment media as a source of political information is more beneficial for political sophisticates or for the politically disengaged' (Delli Carpini 2012: 15).

A number of scholars (and perhaps the majority of those who have written about the influence of entertainment on citizens, according to Van Zoonen 2005) have pointed to the detrimental effect on politics of television in general and entertainment in particular. As the title of his influential book suggests, Postman (1987) is convinced we are amusing ourselves to death, while Putnam (1995) illustrates the decline in social capital that has accompanied the surge in entertainment consumption with the image of people 'bowling alone'. Some have also argued that entertainment television inculcates a belief that the real world is as threatening as that represented in crime shows and thrillers. Using the approach known as 'cultivation analysis', Gerbner et al. (1986) provided evidence that entertainment media provided largely homogeneous representations of the world, reflecting hegemonic political and economic agendas, that cultivated corresponding worldviews among heavy media users. The question is whether the hegemonic worldviews found in the US in the 1970s and 1980s have survived in the decentred world of contemporary globalization, and how well the approach works when making sense of what goes on in other cultures.

Other studies suggest that entertainment media can provide alternative sources of information about politics, both for those who do not follow the news, and for those who do (Delli Carpini 2012; Fox et al. 2007; Holbert et al. 2007; Jamieson &

Cappella 2008; LaMarre et al. 2009; Moy et al. 2005a, 2005b; Young 2004; Young & Tisinger 2006). Van Zoonen (2005) has made a particularly powerful case for he possibility that entertainment makes the work of being a citizen more enjoyable, and provides a meaningful connection between politics and the everyday lives of ordinary people. The argument has also been made that popular culture can provide more complex narratives than news reports, and can thus facilitate more sophisticated understandings of politics (Jones 2006, 2010; Scott et al. 2011).

Little of the research conducted on this topic is comparative (Bore 2011), which is regrettable, because as van Zoonen and Wring (2012: 275) note, 'television fiction itself is as much a product of political culture as it is able to affect that culture'. They note that the individual heroism that dominates much US political drama has an obvious relationship to the presidential system in which individuals have relatively more power. In Britain, on the other hand, where politicians are continually required to negotiate and compromise and are party animals more than handsome heroes occupying the moral high ground, the characters who populate political drama tend to be 'plain men of uncertain age – around 40 or over – somewhat grumpy, somewhat clumsy and hardly ever in full control over their situation'. While the Obamanesque 'yes we can' message emanates from American stories, the take-home message in British political drama is 'It's no use trying, unless you are an evil schemer' (van Zoonen & Wring 2012: 274–5). The cultural gap is, of course, an empirical question. This is well illustrated by the wildly (and globally) successful migration across the Atlantic of evil schemer Francis Urquhart, Chief Whip of the British Conservative Party and key figure in the 1990 BBC production of *House of Cards*, and his transformation into Frank Underwood, US Congressman and Democrat, in the 2013–15 Netflix remake.

To think about

In an essay of 1821, Shelley wrote that 'Poets are the unacknowledged legislators of the world.' Almost two centuries later, the Scottish Nationalist Party asked the novelist William McIlvanney 'to apply a dash of literary magic' to its White Paper on independence. A Scottish government source explained that the White Paper would be one of the most important documents in Scottish history, and inevitably redolent of civil service expertise and attention to detail. There was thus a perceived need for an interpretation,

> written for the people and designed to capture the imagination. It would seem appropriate to see this composed by one of Scotland's great literary talents. To win independence we need prose to inform, but also poetry to inspire. (McKenna 2013)

Poets and writers had strong words for independence a year later, although they were not in support of a government or nation-building, but of independence from Turkish state control of social media. When Prime Minister Erdogan imposed the ban on Twitter mentioned in an earlier chapter, and threatened to extend it, he said he would not leave the Turkish nation 'at the mercy of YouTube and Facebook'. Nobel laureates Orhan Pamuk and Elfriede Jelinek, together with prominent writers such as Margaret Atwood, Günter Grass and Zadie Smith, added their names to a protest letter from PEN International, calling Erdogan's move 'an unacceptable violation of the right to freedom of speech' (Flood 2014). The website of the international community of writers going by the PEN name is a useful site of primary source material, and highlights issues to be discussed towards the end of this book.[11]

Popular culture does not only have the potential to play the 'first role' of providing information about politics. It has as much, if not more, to do with the 'third role', explaining where the nation is situated in time and space and how the world works (Ashuri 2006; Frosh & Wolfsfeld 2006; Robertson 2010a; Sakota-Kokot 2011; Schubart 2007; Storey 2001). The experience can be painful as well as entertaining. In the months preceding the fifth anniversary of the death of Augusto Pinochet in December 2011, Chileans were drawn to a television drama about what happened in the eighteen years the former president ruled the country with an iron fist. The thriller *Los Archivos del Cardenal*, about a team of lawyers working with the Catholic church to expose the torture and killings that kept the Pinochet regime in power, narrated not only the crimes of the government, but also the failure of the Chilean media to play their watchdog role. The director of the series, Mauro Valdez, explained:

> We are telling the truth through fiction. I think it's been difficult to confront these issues. So I think the series has given us the opportunity to face this experience . . . Fiction is a legitimate genre for this. The aim is not so much to convey information as it is to describe the experience on the human level. This can't be done in a documentary. (Mauro Valdez, interviewed on *Listening Post*, Al Jazeera English, 26 November 2011)

Popular culture has affective power, speaking to emotions and engagement, as van Zoonen (2005) has argued. Political entertainment can also provide resources for the conversations about politics envisaged in deliberative theories of democracy (Baym 2005: 272). This chapter has suggested that satire and comedy can be seen as a response to the failure of journalism to confront serious issues in ways that match the job descriptions itemized in chapter 4, and that cultural workers are political actors in their own right. Seen this way, infotainment need not only be emblematic of enslavement to corporate interests. It can also be a weapon of civic self-defence. Something to think about when grinning at satirical critiques of politics on YouTube, curling up on the couch to watch *Game of Thrones*, or going to the cinema to watch the final instalment of *The Hunger Games*, is whether you are becoming more knowledgeable or more sceptical about politics, and what you remember, in what frame of mind.

9 Mediatization

In 1961, Adolf Eichmann went on trial in Israel, accused of war crimes and crimes against humanity for his role in organizing the Holocaust. The country followed the trial closely: 'it is in the air and the water, it is like dust on the trees', wrote one columnist. Indeed, it was *on* the air, as Pinchevski and Liebes (2010) point out, and the fact that it was broadcast on what was then the most important medium – radio – left an indelible impression on the event itself.[1] Many remembered the trial being broadcast live (although much of it was not) and listened to all over the place – at home and in public, in cafés and in offices, on streets and buses. A scholar later wrote that 'young and old could be seen radio in hand everywhere – in constant earshot of the broadcast', and a woman told interviewers that the trial 'emanated from every house; it was part of our lives'.

Something happened to the Holocaust, and to the relationship of ordinary Israelis to the concentration camp survivors in their midst, as a result of it being on the radio. Before the trial, people in Israel had chosen not to talk about the Nazi concentration camps, rendering the survivor 'a figure divested of language, a traumatized, speechless body' on the margins of a society whose collective identity was one of strength, not victimhood. When the testimonies that camp survivors gave at the trial were heard on the radio, they were transfigured by being literally disembodied – removed from the bodies of ghosts and put in a form that could be experienced and worked through collectively. At such moments, media like the radio 'redefine' the conditions under which events impacting on the body politic can be articulated in public (Pinchevski & Liebes 2010: 278). A return to defining moments such as these, and the scholarly work of making sense of them, opens a curtain on what too often cannot be seen. The way that media texts and technologies work on politics and society often remains invisible or is taken for granted, and this gets in the way of our understanding (Pinchevski & Liebes 2010: 265).

This chapter is about scholarly attempts to grasp and theorize the way that newspapers, radio, television and popular cultural artefacts, online and off, have become so 'pervasive and ubiquitous' that 'we become blind to that which shapes our lives the most' (Deuze 2011: 137). In other words, it is about attempts to make 'the media' (the time having come to think in terms of abstractions), and what they do, visible and thus comprehensible. A term used increasingly often in such scholarly work is 'mediatization'. The concept is not an easy one, and it can take some effort to master the literature on the subject, as it is used differently by different authors to refer to different processes and phenomena (some observable, others less so). The effort can be worth it, given the need to make sense of how media power has grown over time – or to ask whether it has simply changed. The aim of this chapter, then, is to set out why scholars of media and politics find the need for such a cumbersome concept, and to relate their work to that of other scholars who use different concepts to describe similar power relations and to make sense of parallel technological developments. Taken together, there are four broad perspectives in play, each with different research foci and assumptions: one with a political economy focus; a second that places technology at the centre of analysis; a third that concerns the negotiation of political and social power; and a fourth that involves discourse. It can be helpful to imagine key thinkers in this often meta-theoretical discourse as guests at a dinner party, and to give some thought to which of them should be seated beside or across from each other, as they have much in common, and which should be placed at opposite ends of the table, either to avoid disagreements that may get in the way of intellectual nourishment, or because they speak quite different scholarly languages, and will have little to talk about.

The concept

The word 'mediatize' is used, not infrequently, to refer to how something is now done with media technology instead of however it used to be done. One way of thinking about this is by substituting 'mediatization' with 'electrification'. The introduction of electric lighting certainly made it easier to read at night, but so did the gas lamp for people who had been used to reading by candlelight, or by the light of a fire or oil lamp. Electricity revolutionized society, but it does not explain why people read (and certainly not why they still read books that were penned by candlelight). It could be said that someone's reading of the *Guardian* has been mediatized, because they now read it on their iPad instead of on paper, or that their reading of *A Song of Ice and Fire* has been mediatized, because the person read *Game of Thrones* in book form and, getting around years later to *A Clash of Kings*, read it in iBooks (and consumed the rest of the story in the HBO version broadcast online). But while these might be examples of mediatization, they are not the sort that is of concern here.

Granted, one problem with this scholarly discourse is that it is not always clear what is of concern. For some, it is a fairly traditional matter of 'processes of communication between decision-makers and the citizens' (Kriesi 2013: 9) and of how media imperatives have become increasingly central to such processes (Herkman 2012: 375). For others, it is a matter of transformation and reconstitution. To continue a train of thought embarked on in an earlier chapter, Hoskins and O'Loughlin (2010: 5) maintain that war has been mediatized because 'the planning, waging and consequences of warfare do not reside outside the media'. Before returning to and thinking more about this more radically conceived development, the central features of what could be called the 'mediatization paradigm' should be set out. According to this paradigm (developed in large part by Scandinavian, German and Swiss scholars), mediatization refers to a meta-process in which the media become independent and powerful in their own right, and permeate all other spheres of society. Because of this pervasiveness, political and other actors have to adapt to 'media logic' (Asp 1986; Hjarvard 2007, 2008, 2009; Kepplinger 2002; Krotz 2007, 2009; Lundby 2008, 2009a, 2009b; Mazzoleni & Schulz 1999; Meyer 2002; Schulz 2004; Strömbäck 2008).

Hjarvard, who gives arguably the most cogent version of the theory as well as a helpful overview of its development, traces the idea back to the 1970s, and the work of authors such as Hernes (1978) and Altheide and Snow (1979, 1988), who didn't actually use the word 'mediatization', but who argued that media change impacted on 'both the inner workings of other social entities and their mutual relationships' (Hernes 1978: 181). Information was no longer a strategic resource, because it was now in abundance: it was attention that had taken its place (an argument later rehearsed by DeLuca and Peeples). In accounts that echoed those of earlier media theorists (Innis and McLuhan – see chapter 1), Altheide and Snow expressed concern that media formats were becoming more important than what they contained.

The Swedish media researcher Kent Asp is said to have been the first to use the word 'mediatization', to designate how a political system is compelled to adjust to the requirements of media reporting. A symptom of this influence was the increasing use of personalization techniques by politicians keen to win space in media coverage, who also showed a greater propensity for conflict behaviour, rather than striving for agreement with their political opponents (because conflict makes for better news). Mazzoleni and Schulz (1999) found evidence of the same adaptation strategies in Brazil (where Fernando Collor de Mello became, at forty, the youngest president in the country's history through the skilful use of television), the UK (where Tony Blair drew heavily on professional marketing techniques to popularize the 'New Labour' brand) and Italy (where, at the time, Silvio Berlusconi was transforming both the political and media landscape by building toll bridges across both). In the view of Mazzoleni and Schulz, politics that is no longer autonomous from the media is mediatized, although the trajectory described in this account is towards increasing media dependence rather than subsumption. Parliaments, parties and politicians continue to control the business of politics to a considerable extent, but its shape and tempo are determined by 'media logic' (Mazzoleni & Schulz 1999: 249).

In the years that followed, concerns about 'mediatized politics' were increasingly expressed by scholars in Europe, where the deregulation that had begun in the 1980s saw broadcasting move from public to private control. Some (e.g. Campus 2010; Strömbäck & Dimitrova 2011) have looked for the variable impact of deregulation on different European countries and on political systems such as that of the US, where it can seem to the outside observer that the media were never regulated in the first place. But the notion of mediatization has also been applied to consumption (Jansson 2002), the communication of science and biotechnology (Väliverronen 2001), cultural change (Hepp 2009), conflict (Cottle 2006a, 2006b), religion, language and society itself (Hjarvard 2007, 2008, 2009). Hjarvard has indeed suggested that a stage has been reached whereby 'the media have become mediatized',[2] which is easier to think about if a distinction is made between, for example, journalists (socialized according to certain professional norms) and the media organizations they work for (which might be more interested in profit than professionalism) and the media technology they use (with tweets from Taksim Square conveying news of clashes between Turkish protesters and police in less depth than a televised or newspaper report comprised of more than 140 characters).

Mediatization in theory and history

In his theory of mediatization, Hjarvard breaks down 'media logic' into specific elements, making it a concept that can be used in empirical analysis rather than a word used loosely to describe something that often remains vague. In so doing, he applies what he calls an 'institutional perspective' to the study of the interplay between the realm of the media and other parts of society. 'Media logic' in his theory refers to: modi operandi (both institutional and technological); the way material and symbolic resources are disseminated by the media; and how formal and informal rules help the media work (Hjarvard 2008: 113).

Hjarvard is also careful to use the term 'mediatization' to refer to a historical moment in the development of society and culture, or a historical situation, in which the social institution of the media has acquired autonomy and 'exerts a particularly predominant influence on other social institutions' (Hjarvard 2008: 110). Like Schulz (2004) and Strömbäck (2008), Hjarvard distinguishes between different phases. Somewhat confusingly, mediatization in such accounts seems to be both the meta-process of moving through these phases, and the final phase itself – the end of media history, to paraphrase Fukuyama (1992). Although Thompson and media theorists like Innis begin their accounts with the invention of the printing press, or even before, the first stage of development in Hjarvard's mediatization theory takes place later, in the period when the rise of the press helped to create a public space for democratic politics. As will be familiar from critiques of Habermas, this was a rather exclusive, and predominantly male, space. In the next phase, radio became the dominant medium, the media public became generalized, and the media began to take on the character of cultural institutions (which means they were no longer the extended arm of a special interest, and began to speak to and for the nation). In Europe, broadcast media were given the 'mission' of educating and enlightening – of playing the 'third role' – by socializing listeners and viewers to think of themselves as a national 'us'. In the next phase, the deregulation of the 1980s (the end of the public service broadcasting monopoly, the influx of commercial competitors and the discernible effects of the 'communications revolution' that introduced first cable and satellite and then digital technology) the media underwent a transition from 'cultural institution' to 'media institution'. Put differently, instead of being institutions that represented other institutions of politics and society in the public interest, the media became institutions in their own rights, and serving their own ends:

> That is not to say that the media have become private enterprises like any manufacturer of, say, furniture or bacon; they continue to perform collective functions in society. The media provide the communicative fora, both private and public, that other institutions depend on for their communication with the public and other institutions, and for their internal communication. The duality of having broken away from other institutions' operations, yet still serve collective communication functions in society give the media central importance to society as a whole. Therefore, the logic that guides the media cannot be reduced to the logic of the market alone . . . the media interact with all other social institutions, but from a position of greater autonomy than a pure market orientation would dictate. (Hjarvard 2008: 119)

Mediatization is not a universal process – it is easier to observe in modern, highly industrialized societies – but mediatization will affect more countries and regions as the parallel (or perhaps inter-related) process of globalization continues apace. Like globalization, it is an uneven process, with different trends on micro and macro levels, characterized by spurts. Following Pinchevsky and Liebes' train of thought, it is a transformation that becomes visible at certain moments, when the pressure that

A man holds a sign that says 'Facebook' during the 'Day of Departure' protest, in Tahrir Square, Cairo, Egypt on 4 Feb. 2011. Photograph: © Ron Haviv / VII / Corbis.

mounts as a result of seeping technological progress suddenly unleashes the floodgates of political change. The story of the Arab Spring is rarely told without reference to media technology and new media practices, and it is not by chance that this book's exploration of media and politics in a globalizing world began there. In some eyes, the iconic image of the traditionally clad man hailing a digital media platform with a handwritten cardboard sign captures the essence of this uneven, yet radicalizing process.

Unlike postmodernists – here Baudrillard's nonexistent Gulf War comes to mind – Hjarvard does not think that the only reality is a mediated one. Conventional ontological distinctions have not collapsed, in his account. But the distinction between the media construction of a 'new reality' and the 'old non-mediated reality' is no longer clear (Hjarvard 2008: 111–12). When a seventeen-year-old girl snapchats with friends she sat beside during a social science class earlier in the day, about a *House of Cards* episode they are watching at the same time on different laptops from bedrooms in different parts of town, their mediated interaction is no less authentic than the non-mediated interaction they had at school. In some ways it is more authentic, and perhaps even more intellectual.

As understood by Hjarvard, mediatization is 'the central concept in a theory of the both intensified and changing importance of the media in culture and society' (Hjarvard 2008: 113). He emphasizes that it must be well specified, comprehensive and coherent (and concedes that it often is not). Apart from describing developments in society, it must also demonstrate media impact on social institutions and human activity. Hjarvard is not alone in calling for empirical studies to test and illustrate the mediatization thesis (see, for example, Darras 2005 and Schrott 2009), but is one

of the few mediatization theorists to acknowledge that empirical work on this phenomenon has been far less sophisticated than theoretical contributions. Especially
when it comes to mediatized politics, these meta-theoretical ideas of social change
have been applied in studies of election reporting and personalization strategies that
could have been explained with reference to mid-range theories (such as several of
those mentioned in chapter 8) and concepts (including some of those that featured
in chapters 3 and 4).

Different theoretical perspectives, different explanations

Some scholars, then, invoke mediatization when they could get by with a less abstract
concept. On the other hand, there are many others in a variety of disciplines, interested in power relations and the impact of developments in media technology, who
do need a more abstract concept, but who choose not to use the word 'mediatization'. Within this motley group, four broad perspectives on the process – however it is
labelled – can be discerned, as mentioned in the introduction. Those whose research
is informed by the critical political economy approach are not pleased by what they
observe. Those who focus on the impact of technology can give the impression of
being awed, and at times even excited, by developments. Scholars who ask what
direction power flows, or how it is negotiated in specific situations, wear a puzzled
face, because the answers to the questions they pose are open. Scholars who ask
questions and contribute work that furthers an understanding of the role of discourse
seem to wear a pensive expression on their face. What they see could be cause for
concern, or not.

Political economy

Some scholars, then, observe the developments Hjarvard tries to encompass in
his theory, and one factor more than others catches their attention. Commercial
forces have emptied the media of information and replaced it with infotainment
(McChesney 2011, 2013; Thussu 2009), politicians have become commodified
(Jackson 2007), politics has become a performance (Jackson & Darrow 2005), politics
has become colonized (Meyer 2002) and ordinary people have become the victims of
political ignorance (Kaitatzi-Whitlock 2011).

The concerns expressed by Thussu in his critique of global news have already been
noted in chapters 7 and 8. These concerns are shared, he acknowledges, by journalists around the world, who are aware of 'the deleterious effect of marketization on
broadcast journalism' (i.e. who realize that the media have become mediatized,
as Hjarvard would put it). Like McChesney (2011, 2013) and others whose work is
based on economic trends, the problem in Thussu's view is that the present moment
is one of 'hyper-commercialism' and that 'almost every aspect of mediated communication is commodified' (Thussu 2009: 32). The commercialization of television
news has made entertainment a priority for broadcasters. Information has been
replaced with storytelling, and principles with personalities. Postman (1987) uses
the phrase 'amusing ourselves to death' and Thussu uses the term 'infotainment' to
describe and explain what some of the scholars mentioned in the previous section
call 'mediatization'.

For Thussu, this process is not just disappointing, it is cause for alarm. The 'marketization' of news diverts attention from the 'grim realities of neo-liberal imperialism . . . the intellectual and cultural subjugation by the tyranny of technology; of free-market capitalism and globalization of a profligate and unsustainable consumerist lifestyle' (Thussu 2009: 9). Infotainment is 'a conduit for the corporate colonization of consciousness, while public journalism and the public sphere have been undermined' (Thussu 2009: 11). Colonization is a word also used by Meyer, who argues that the prevailing political system in the West is now the 'mediacracy', as the media have changed the 'ontology of politics' (Meyer 2002); and by Kaitatzi-Whitlock, according to whom not only the news, but also politicians, have been commercialized and commodified (Kaitatzi-Whitlock 2011: 467). As will be recalled from chapter 5, her point is that citizens have become the victims of 'political ignorance', which 'is determined by the political economy of contemporary capitalism'. Colonization becomes possible when the media are emptied of political content and filled with entertainment. Although she does not use the word 'mediatization', Kaitatzi-Whitlock has the same fundamental change in her sights as those who do, arguing that the 'commercialization of television marks the most decisive turn toward the transmutation of the fundamental role of the media and inherently the political' (2011: 468).

Power

Unlike those who use words like 'colonization', some scholars consider the battle as yet undecided – or perhaps note that battles have been won and lost, but are not convinced that the war is over. Seen from this perspective, media power (even if not that of individual journalists) has grown over time, but so has that of other actors in society. The political realm can still be delineated from the realm of the media, and the territory occupied by each is continually open to border disputes.

The problem with the mediatization paradigm, Couldry argued some years ago, is that it sees the process in question as linear. But the process is much more complex than that, and the transformations that scholars are seeking to explain cannot be grasped with reference to a single logic. Something more heterogenous 'is simultaneously transforming the whole social space at once' (Couldry 2008: 375). Part of the complexity stems from the nature of the media themselves: they have a double essence, or 'articulation'. What we conceive of, and live with, are media that are at once a technology (that transmits messages) and the representational content of those messages (at which point Thompson might pull on Couldry's sleeve and remind him that they are also institutions, as noted in chapter 1). Couldry acknowledges that the sort of transformations mediatization scholars are making claims about are happening. But they are multipolar, and cannot be explained with reference to a single logic (such as that of the media). The concept of mediatization thus gets in the way of understanding the shifts in power that are occurring.

Drawing on Silverstone (2002), Couldry argued in several pieces that the familiar term 'mediation' suffices to describe how institutionalized media are involved in a fundamental, but uneven, way 'in the general circulation of symbols in social life'. The process in question (whether it is called 'mediation' or 'mediatization' or something else) has a two-day dynamic. The media transform their environments, and that transformation in turn transforms the conditions in which future media forms emerge and are used and understood (Couldry 2008: 380). What Couldry wants to capture is the variety of dynamics at work in media flows. To do so, it is necessary to appreciate that the 'space of media' is structured, and, because of that, interactions between certain 'sites' or 'agents' are closed off (Couldry 2008: 381). The relations entailed in this dynamic are not symmetrical, so what is at issue is a question of power (first discussed in chapter 2), and how and when and between which actors it shifts.

Because different types of transformation are at issue, Couldry maintains that different theoretical frameworks are needed. One such framework is the field theory introduced by Bourdieu and developed by a host of others (Benson & Neveu 2005; Bourdieu 2005; Hanitzsch 2011). In contrast to the single logic in focus in much mediatization scholarship, field theory is an attempt to make sense of social space with multiple poles. One of these is the 'journalistic field' which, like other fields, is structured by permanent relationships of inequality and governed by a particular logic (the *nomos*). The logic of the journalistic field, in many of these studies, is related to the professional values deeply rooted in different media cultures – not the market logic of political economy accounts and those of much mediatization research. (Bourdieu is, perhaps confusingly, nevertheless well known for his essay 'On television', written as a polemic rather than a piece of scholarship, which laments the sensationalizing and attention-grabbing propensity of the medium, and its danger to democracy.) As Hallin and Mancini and the contributors to their anthology established, the independence of journalists from particular interests, be they political or economic, is not a universal, but subject to cultural variation. The *nomos* of one particular field might be a lack of autonomy from the market, but that of another might be the opposite, and dependent on political interests: in field theory, this is an empirical question rather than a theoretical given. The notion of certain social domains having their own logic, and of competition between fields leading to the domination of one field (such as journalism) over others, captures a similar dynamic to that which Hjarvard seeks to theorize. Where field and mediatization theory part company is in the location of the journalistic field within a larger field of power. Some find field theory more helpful, given that what is broadly referred to as 'the media' is actually a collection of many different actors, who tend to be in contest with each other (journalists and owners, for example) as much as with actors from other fields. Field theory helps to make visible a situation, resulting from 'the growing significance of economic and technological imperatives', in which the boundaries of journalism have become 'destabilized' (Hanitzsch 2011: 479). It has also proven more useful to comparative research than mediatization theory has (see, for example, Benson 2005; Hallin 2005 and Hanitzch 2011).

A chair is pulled out and another scholar, familiar from the beginning of the book, returns to join the conversation at the chapter's metaphorical dinner party. Chadwick fits in well, and can speak to any of the others seated around the table, be they political scientists, media scholars or sociologists. But he gets on particularly well with Couldry, who nods as he agrees that a holistic approach to the role of communication in politics is needed, rather than a linear one. What Chadwick wants to describe and understand is a situation of 'in-betweenness', rather than a progression from one phase to the next. He wants to talk about complex interdependence rather than colonization or (put less dramatically) the preeminence of one force or logic. Reiterating a point made in chapter 1, he argues that 'hybridization' is the more helpful term because the flow of power is never unidirectional (Chadwick 2011: 7). It is more helpful because it can allow, for example, for 'the increasingly porous boundaries between "hard" news and "entertainment" genres in political communication', and treats this overlap as interesting rather than indicative of the end of civilization (or at least rational thought). Nor is the process simply a matter of economic domination. 'New' media have a particular power of their own and their use encourages 'subversive interaction' among audiences, who are in turn empowered. It is necessary to be creative when studying contemporary media systems, and how they interact with politics, insists Chadwick, and to do that scholars have to situate power and agency in the context of the 'integrated but conflict-ridden systems' in which people and technologies can be found, and not just profit-hungry multinational corporations. The reason it is so difficult to explain the process that everyone seeks to theorize is that it is one characterized by both integration and fragmentation. In contrast to the either/or imperative of the mediatization discourse, the notion of hybridization helps make visible the 'not only, but also' nature of interactions and 'the power struggles that criss-cross domains [that] are now defining features of political communication' (Chadwick 2011: 11).

Discourse

Hoskins and O'Loughlin contribute questions they think need to be addressed if the mediatization paradigm is to be developed by empirical research. How do media make political issues like war visible? How do they deliver them to audiences? How are the views of those audiences shaped by what they experience through the media and how do those views in turn shape the conduct of politics or, in their analysis, war? These are the sorts of questions that can be posed to media artefacts produced in the first phase of mediatization. A second set of questions interrogates the second phase of mediatization. Assuming (or observing) that the actors who engage in war (and by corollary other sorts of engagements that relate to politics) 'anticipate and shape media coverage of their actions, how do they design war for media, and how is media designed for war?' And given that, under mediatization, audiences are aware of the representational games being played, how do they find information that they consider believable and authoritative (Hoskins & O'Loughlin 2010: 19)? These sorts of questions are most easily answered by analysis of archived media reports, and of how people talk about what they learn from such reports (Philo & Berry 2004, 2011). Despite the keen interest in technological developments shown by Hoskins and O'Loughlin (of which more below), they can be placed at the table with scholars interested in discourse – like Thompson.

In chapter 8, Thompson's notion of 'mediated historicity' was mentioned in connection with reporting of the anniversary of the Normandy invasion. His related, and perhaps more central, concept of 'mediated worldliness' is most readily accessible through discourse analysis. It is also a way of designating the sense of 'new reality' that mediatization theory seeks to capture. As Couldry explained, 'the media' are both technology, and the representations or content disseminated by that technology. Both change, and these changes must be somehow grasped or rendered visible if social change is to be adequately accounted for. Society and politics are predicated on a sense of belonging to a collectivity. This sense is built on 'symbolic materials' that were there before. With media development, however, the nature of those pre-existing symbols changes in 'significant ways'. The increasingly mediated nature of society has altered the way people gain a sense of the past and of the world beyond their immediate experience (Thompson 1995: 33–4, 186). This change is gradual, rather one that can be assigned to clearly defined phases.

> If the media have altered our sense of the past, they have also created what we could call a 'mediated worldliness': our sense of the world which lies beyond the sphere of our personal experience, and our sense of our place within this world, are increasingly shaped by mediated symbolic forms . . . and as our sense of the world and our place within it becomes increasingly nourished by media products, so too our sense of the groups and communities with which we share a common path through time and space, a common origin and a common fate, is altered: we feel ourselves to belong to groups and communities which are constituted in part through the media. (Thompson 1995: 34–5)

Some of what mediatization theorists have attempted to grasp has been theorized by other scholars with recourse to the notion of 'media events'. Like Thompson, Scannell (2004) draws attention to how media discourse – that which conveys verbal, visual or symbolic representations – does things to experience. News, for example, has different temporalities – the 'immediate present' of live coverage or the 'historic present' of the evening broadcast that looks back on the most important events of the day (Scannell 2004: 573). To this could be added a 'new past', given that so many news reports are actually about historical events, with a commemoration or anniversary merely the current handle (Robertson 2010a). Scannell is not frowning, like the political economists. When reporting 'tumultuous events', we see the newsroom 'journeying forwards into the unknown, while looking back over its shoulder in a continuing effort to catch up with and make sense of what has just-now happened'. The concept of 'media events' in this context, he argues, is a 'corrective' to the oft-rehearsed claim that the presence of the media distorts and misrepresents events. The concept is associated with Dayan and Katz (1992) who theorized about 'liminal moments' in which all channels of communication merged into one and 'all eyes were fixed on the ceremonial centre'. The Eichmann trial is an obvious example, but the media spectacles of royal weddings are another which have figured in events research. Twenty years after their original work was published, Dayan said that something had changed. In globalizing societies, there is no longer a central narrative: media events have become conversations between voices from many places (Dayan 2010: 27–8). These two moments could be said to represent two different phases of mediatization, if that process is viewed in discursive terms.

Technology

Scholars in the fourth and final category have gleaming eyes rather than metaphorically furrowed brows. They draw attention to how media technology is transforming political as well as information landscapes; refer not to colonization but to diffusion; and speak not of newspaper death but of 'media life' (Deuze 2011).

It has been argued by some that being part of an audience is 'constitutive of everyday life', and that what were once distinct spheres of existence (being at home, or being at work, for example) have 'converged in and through our concurrent and continuous exposure to, use of, and immersion in media, information and communication technologies' (Abercrombie & Longhurst 1998; Deuze 2011: 137). As mentioned earlier, Deuze argues that the media have become invisible in their ubiquity, that we have become blind to what shapes our lives the most, and that we experience reality in mediated, rather than direct, form (2011: 140). The problem is that people have become more connected at the same time as they are increasingly left on their own. The symbolic forms referred to by Thompson multiply and circulate endlessly, giving people resources to imagine 'endless alternatives to and versions of' themselves, but exposing them to social pressure to 'stick to a version that was generated for them, for example as "citizens" for democracy or "consumers" for capitalism' (Deuze 2011: 145). Whether good or bad, or a problem for ordinary people rather than political elites, the notion of 'media life' seems to describe the same transformation as the mediatization paradigm. Understood this way, media

> should not be seen as somehow located outside of lived experience, but rather should be seen as intrinsically part of it. Our life is lived in, rather than with, media – we are living a media life. (Deuze 2007: 242)

This has not just happened to ordinary people in their everyday lives, according to this perspective. Chapter 7 set out the idea that it has also changed the experience and waging of war, which, according to Hoskins & O'Loughlin (2010: 4) has been 'utterly defined' by the medium of television. The media 'production' of warfare has shaped the way it is legitimated, contested and played out more than 'any discernible "original" or "authentic" experience'. It is not possible to understand or account for practices such as those of warfare unless a careful account is given of the role of the media in it, they argue: 'This is what it means to speak of war as mediatized' (Hoskins & O'Loughlin 2010: 4). Fields of perception are changing and leading in turn to changes in the culture of political and social practices such as these. Technological developments, which have made media portable, unprecedentedly accessible and transferable, have 'potentially profound effects in shaping current and future events and also in transforming those considered "settled" in collective memory' (Hoskins and O'Loughlin 2010: 9, 104–19). The idea is easy to relate to the live broadcast of the revolutionary events that took place in Tahrir Square in 2011, but it also applies to the live radio broadcast of the Eichmann trial and collective memories of the Holocaust and, revived in 2014, of World War. The third role of the media could thus be said to have a technological dimension. This depends, however, on whom you choose to sit beside and talk to at the theoretical dinner table. As the BBC camerawoman said, we see what we are prepared to see. This applies to the array of scholars who have tried to make sense of the meta-process increasingly referred to as mediatization, whatever vocabulary they choose, as well as those who listen to, read and work with their ideas.

To think about

In an influential essay that reflected on whether television had come to an end, and took stock of 'its impact on the world so far' (Katz & Scannell 2009), Katz put a large task on the research agenda. The challenge facing scholars, he argued, is to identify 'larger and more enduring' effects than dealt with in previous research (such as the 'effects tradition' in audience research presented in chapter 5 or the 'CNN Effect' that featured in chapter 7). The point is not whether television has succeeded in selling a given product (political or otherwise), but whether it has succeeded in 'implanting consumerism'. It is not whether Americans have become more interested in reality shows that matters, but whether the phenomenon of reality shows has spread to other countries, continents and cultures. From this vantage point, it is less interesting 'whether Kennedy or Nixon was the more skillful orator in the presidential debates of 1960 than the fact that this election campaign enabled voters in their living rooms to hear both sides of an argument – something that was quite unusual prior to the introduction of this broadcast form' (Katz 2009: 9). What is interesting, in other words, is how technological development interacts with political, social and economic change to produce specific outcomes in specific situations. Such outcomes might be easily observed (such was when Kennedy was elected president). Others – like the transfiguration of silent ghosts into witnesses of genocide by the radio broadcast of a trial – only become visible through the analysis of revealing events, with the benefit of hindsight or through certain theoretical glasses.

Like globalization, mediatization (or whatever it is to be called) is an uneven process, and often invisible, according to ideas presented in the last few pages. This means that it is not apparent always and everywhere. One thing to think about is how helpful such a concept is, and how necessary. Something is obviously happening that needs to be made sense of, but attempts to explore mediatization empirically are continually stymied or fail to get off the ground. How valuable is a concept around which there is so much confusion, and if it is difficult to operationalize in the sort of concrete, empirical research that its proponents (e.g. Hjarvard 2008, 2009; Darras 2005) as well as its critics insist is required?

Ultimately, however, what deserves thought is the invisibility of the media in daily life, and of the power relations they are predicated on and enable.

10 Media Freedom

In July 2012, a 13-minute low-budget film called *Innocence of Muslims* was posted on YouTube. It showed Christians being attacked by a Muslim mob in Egypt while police stood idly by, then recounted the life of the prophet Muhammad, using actors dressed as if for a Sunday-school play, performing amateurishly against obviously fake backdrops, in what appears to be an effort to emphasize the fact that it is a work of propaganda. Originally said to be the work of an Israeli businessman called Sam Bacile funded by money given by Jewish donors, it later transpired that the man behind the film was an Egyptian-American and convicted fraudster called Nakoula Basseley Nakoula. The film remained obscure for months (as had the infamous Muhammad cartoons, after their initial Danish publication in 2006). Then the film was translated into Arabic and publicized on *Al-Nas*, a popular Egyptian television show. The conservative hosts of *Al-Nas* told their viewers that *The Innocence of Muslims* was going to be broadcast in the US two days later, on the anniversary of 9/11, which was untrue. Violent protests broke out in Egypt and spread through the region (just as they had in other countries when clerics drew global attention to the Muhammad caricatures subsequent to their Danish publication), leaving hundreds injured and fifty dead. A Pakistani minister offered a reward for the person who killed Nakoula. Google took the film off YouTube in Egypt and Libya, sparking a different set of protests for different reasons. Freedom-of-speech advocates were concerned that Google was signalling it was possible to get something censored by threatening violence, which they considered wrong, regardless of whether the film was offensive. The argument was succinctly put by one policy analyst:

> If you don't support the freedom of speech of people like this to make deeply offensive, bigotted movies, you really don't support freedom of speech.[1]

Richard Gizbert, host of the *Listening Post* media magazine, remarked that propagandists no longer had to be clever or professional. The media, new and old, and the audience, were now doing their work for them.[2]

The episode features actors from all the categories that have featured in the book so far – political elites, media owners, journalists, activists and the man-on-the-street. It highlights the tensions inherent in the globalization process, and is a reminder of how communication can push people farther apart as well as bring them closer together. It is an example of how 'new' and 'old' media interact, with the former lowering thresholds for political influence and the latter amplifying the message. It is an artefact of popular culture and an instance of mediatized conflict. And it is a useful point of entry into the thicket of questions about the limits to freedom of information and expression throughout the world.

Earlier chapters of this book have ended with things to think about. This chapter is largely comprised of them. The stakeholders are all of the actors presented in Part Two, and the issue areas range from local and national to global politics. Before pulling the threads together in the concluding chapter, it can be instructive to unpack contemporary problems related to media freedom drawn from across the media-politics spectrum, and see which, if any, of the concepts, contentions and analytical frameworks presented in this book can further an understanding of a phenomenon at the heart of politics under globalization. It could be that some of the things to think about call for ways of thinking about them that are different from the theoretical tools encountered so far.

Political elites set the tone and police the parameters of what is acceptable to say, show and share in the mediated messages that circulate thoughout society. As outlined in chapter 3, their investment in the control of information flows and narratives is considerable. For them, curbing media freedom can be a problem (if they are well-meaning and troubled about how to ensure pluralism while safeguarding the rights of individuals in multicultural societies) or a possibility (if they want to use their political and legislative power to silence opponents and maintain the status quo).

Media owners wield considerable power and this can be both benign and malignant; a burdensome responsibility as well as a source of influence. In some political settings, the people running media outlets are faced with the problem of retaining editorial control and safeguarding the integrity of their publications and the safety of their staff while ensuring that publics get information that political elites would rather they didn't. In economically troubled times, they often lack the resources to compete with political actors. Some media owners have more ignoble agendas, and their problem is instead how to ensure profits and resist regulation, for example in the UK in the wake of the phone-hacking scandal and subsequent Leveson

The publication of the Leveson Report. Photograph: © sinister pictures / Demotix / Corbis.

inquiry recommendations that a Royal Charter be established for the self-regulation of the media industry. As media mogul Rupert Murdoch tweeted in August 2012, in the furore surrounding the publication of nude photos of Britain's Prince Harry in the *News of the World*:

> Need to demonstrate no such thing as free press in US. Internet makes mockery of these issues. 1st amendment please.

For public-service media, the problem is to retain autonomy from politicians' attempts to meddle in their charters; for journalists working for state-controlled media in authoritarian regimes and troubled democracies, it is to be able to do their job according to increasingly universal standards of objectivity. For correspondents everywhere, media freedom means being able to report without threat of reprisal (for them or their sources) or, in many cases, fear for their lives. It is a problem that they are not.

In the private sphere, ordinary people have to become media literate to be aware of, and protect themselves from, such infringements on reliable reporting. In countries with troubled democracies or other forms of governance, they are faced with the problem of sustained violations of their right to use social and other media to communicate what, and with whom, they choose. A tension exists in many countries between the protection of copyright and cultural property so ardently defended by the media industry, and the freedom of ordinary media users to record films, programmes and songs with home technology marketed by the same industry, and to share their recordings with friends. (The SOPA story related earlier in the book threw this tension into sharp relief.) A problem that is becoming increasingly evident, even in democratic countries, is how to maintain one's privacy and personal integrity while under state surveillance.

For people everywhere, on every level of society, in every actor category – including that of the scholar, be it student or professor – the problem is to determine where the line should be drawn between protection of the individual, and the right to freedom of expression and information.

Media freedom in theory

The notion that freedom of thought, expression and information is a basic human right dates back to the Enlightenment. The principle of tolerance is central: as Voltaire famously said: 'I disagree with what you say but I will defend to the death your right to say it.' Tolerance ensures the right to expression but also means that freedom of speech is not a licence to slander, mislead, or publish pornography. Nor is it a licence to reveal state secrets or harm the nation in other ways, according to some (Warburton 2009). The fates of Manning and Snowden – the one imprisoned for life, the other in exile, both for bringing to public attention information that the US wanted classified – are reminders of how polarized views on the topic can be, and that freedom is an essentially contested concept.

Leaving aside the issue of state interests for a moment, it must be acknowledged that, even if freedom of speech is a key feature of democracy, some speech can undermine it. This is the case with hate speech and the use of various media outlets by political extremists. Before shooting sixty-nine young Norwegians, Anders Behring

Breivik was free to disseminate his Islamophobic and misogynist views in a manifesto entitled '2083: A European Declaration of Independence', to anyone who could wade through the 1500-page document. (When this book went to print, it was still available online.) The problem of liberty has thus exercised a number of political philosophers. Isaiah Berlin, for example, distinguished between two sorts. 'Negative liberty' entails the right to be free from harm, which can be extrapolated to include freedom from intimidation, freedom from persecution, and freedom from arbitrary sanction by the state (Steel 2012: 21). 'Positive liberty' is freedom to, as opposed to freedom from. This principle is invoked by those who feel they have the right to see, hear and do what they like (upload an Islamaphobic manifesto or video, or download and share copyright-protected material). Being a liberal idea, the actor in mind is the individual. Problems arise when stakeholders are collectivities in social settings, rather than individuals in the privacy of their homes.

Steel has pointed out that there is a problem when it comes to applying ideas about individual rights to media organizations that in many cases are large commercial enterprises:

> It is my contention that freedom of the press should not be seen as merely the freedom of those rich enough to own a newspaper or media outlet to publish and be damned, rather it should be seen in the context of debates about journalism itself, its function, its history, its purported democratic role and its often complex sense of self-identity. (Steel 2012: 23)

This view has been challenged by combatants on the media–politics battlefield, as illustrated by the examples presented in what follows.

The view from the top

Most states have constitutional safeguards on freedom of the press and of expression. The First Amendment to the American Constitution is often invoked (by others than Rupert Murdoch), but a quarter of a century earlier, Sweden became the first country to introduce a constitutional law stipulating press freedom as a positive one (Tryckfrihetsförordningen – The Law on the Freedom of Printing – 1766). It has been said that this law forms the basis for all the world's Freedom of Information Acts.

In some political cultures and for some theorists and commentators, media freedom and pluralism are best safeguarded by public-service broadcasting systems, and cannot be left to the market. European Commissioner Viviane Reding, on the other hand, has insisted that 'deregulation and enhanced competition' have as their goals precisely 'freedom of opinion, freedom of media and media pluralism' (eu4journalists.eu). The fact that not all agree became painfully obvious when Turkish Prime Minister Erdogan issued a dire warning during the protests against the EU candidate country's government in June 2013:

> There is now a menace which is called Twitter . . . The best examples of lies can be found there. To me, social media is the worst menace to society.

This philosophy was translated into practice, as dozens of Twitter users were arrested for posting messages in support of anti-government protests. While Taksim Square was besieged by protesters, Turkish television broadcast documentaries about penguins, instead of news reports of police brutality. The reason was not philosophical or even entirely political: it was that Turkish media companies belong to conglomerates that include many other business interests, dependent on publicly financed contracts. The intimate relationship between the Erdogan regime and the media industry in Turkey has resulted in widespread self-censorship (AJE 2014; Melin 2013).

Constraints on media freedom – seen from the top – vary according to political context. The situation in Argentina is diametrically opposed to that in Turkey. As mentioned in chapter 3, Argentinian President Kirchner came into direct confrontation with Grupo Clarín when she tried to curb its power. Clarín, which has dominated the country's media landscape since the days of the dictatorship, controls 60 per cent of the cable market, 25 per cent of the internet market, a popular national and three regional television channels, ten radio stations, six newspapers and a news agency (Watts 2013). When the government introduced a new media law in 2009 with the aim of promoting media pluralism (i.e. of breaking up the Clarín monopoly), the moguls fought back. Using the media they owned, they argued that the government move amounted to 'persecution of free journalism'. It is a cry to be recalled when considering the case of Kenya, of which more in a moment.

The view from the front lines

As mentioned in chapter 4, the Committee to Protect Journalists, and Reporters without Borders, have reported the deaths of hundreds of journalists in dozens of countries, killed with impunity while trying to inform the public. According to CPJ Executive Director Joel Simon,

> the targeted killing of journalists serves as a silencing message to others, ensuring that sensitive issues are not subjected to public scrutiny. (BBC 2011a)

Ranked by unsolved killings proportional to the population, unsolved murders in the last decade include: Iraq (92), Somalia (10), Philippines (56), Sri Lanka (9), Colombia (11), Afghanistan (7), Nepal (6), Mexico (13), Russia (16), Pakistan (14), Bangladesh (5), Brazil (5), India (7). Murders of local journalists constitute the majority of unsolved cases. But foreign correspondents covering international conflicts also find themselves in the firing line, as has been spectacularly illustrated in Egypt, Libya, Syria, Afghanistan and elsewhere, and as reflected in the statistics presented in chapter 7.

Some are targeted by security forces, others by the opposition (CPJ 2011a). The safety of journalists in war zones is often given as the reason for curtailing media freedom. This was the case when France intervened in Mali in January 2013. Some journalists were allowed to embed with French forces, but were kept away from combat areas and their reporting was restricted to marginal logistic matters, while the Malian army barred journalists from many areas. Reporters working for local outlets and global newsrooms alike warned that the intervention was being waged as an 'invisible war'. Reporters without Borders said neither France nor Mali were acting to protect journalists, but instead to impose a media blackout, and argued that in times of conflict, it is up to journalists and the organizations they work for to determine the risks that should be taken to obtain information, not the military (RSF 2013; Ryan 2013).

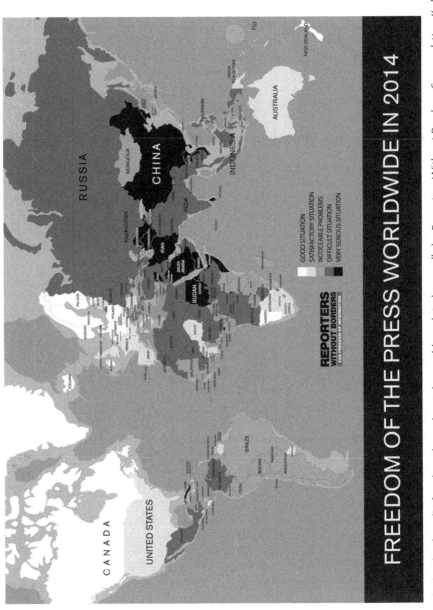

A map charting the levels of media freedom throughout the world, updated annually by Reporters Without Borders. Source: https://rsf.org/ index2014/data/carte2014_en.png.

Sometimes they fall victim to the 'mob'. The gang rape of CBS reporter Lara Logan in Tahrir Square in January 2011 made headlines around the world. The following year, Sonia Dridi, a journalist with France24, was sexually assaulted while broadcasting live from the same place. While both male and female journalists face the threat of arrest, violence and death, it has been observed that the freedom of women to report is curtailed in other ways. Fatima Tlisova, a journalist in North Caucasus, related how she was beaten on the head, ribs and stomach by two men who

> seemed to realise that I would not make a sound because the door to my flat was only a few yards away and, if I did scream, my children, who were sitting peacefully watching TV, would be the first ones to hear me. I could not risk them coming running out and getting attacked too. So I kept quiet and I let them beat me, without putting up any resistance. (quoted in Schmidt 2014: 188)

Schmidt, who encountered such stories on a regular basis in her capacity as former deputy editor for the *Index on Censorship* magazine, observed that a weapon used by Tlisova's attackers was her role as a mother (2014: 189).

The body of Saleem Shahzad was found the day before the CPJ 2011 Report was released. The Pakistani journalist had written about al-Qaeda's infiltration of the navy and had paid with his life. No one has been convicted of the murder (which was preceded by kidnapping and torture), although Human Rights Watch and US government officials claim there is reliable evidence that Pakistani intelligence officials are behind the killing. Journalists live dangerously in many parts of the world. In Kyrgyzstan, Alisher Saipov, a human rights activist and editor, was murdered in 2007, reputedly by the security service (Freedman 2012: 53).

Years after a pluralist political system was re-adopted in Kenya, and the country was deemed 'well past the era of extreme media repression', masked gunmen raided the offices of the country's oldest media company, beat up staff, confiscated computers thought to contain information that would compromise political elites, and took the Kenya Television Network off the air. According to Mudhai (2011: 675), it was later confirmed that the intruders had been acting on the instructions of John Michuki, Minister of Internal Security. In November 2013, a harsh new media law came into effect with stipulations for strict controls on broadcasting, and establishing a new Communications and Multimedia Appeals Tribunal with the power to impose heavy fines and bar journalists from working. The independent newspaper the *Daily Nation* said the Bill put Kenya 'in the same ranks with Zimbabwe, Cuba, Ethiopia and Kuwait', and that Parliament had 'written away the media's rights' (*Daily Telegraph* 2013).

The influence of oligarchs and what Hallin and Mancini (2004: 37) call the 'instrumentalization' of news media by entrenched local interests is more of a problem in new and fragile democracies. Many of the journalists Freedman interviewed in Kyrgyzstan were so worried about criminal libel laws and suits that they avoided covering controversial news and public affairs (Freedman 2012: 55). Independent journalists who question political and business interests are excluded from meetings and denied information. Foreign investors in Romanian, Serbian and Bulgarian media markets pulled out in 2010 because of what they called the 'widespread abuse of power'. The CEO of the WAZ Media Group, Bodo Hombach, has gone on record as saying:

Journalists from the foreign correspondence organization participate in a protest demanding the release of four Al Jazeera correspondents outside the Egyptian Embassy premises in Kenya's capital Nairobi, 4 February 2014. Photograph: © GEORGE PHILIPAS / Reuters / Corbis.

> Oligarchs in the Balkans are buying ever more often newspapers and magazines in order to exert political influence, not in order to win money. We cannot stand up to such market-destroying competition.[3]

Stetka (2012) has identified three types of instrumentalization in the CEE region. The first is the publishing of information that promotes other businesses run by the owner of a news outlet. Journalists working for such media organizations are not free to report what is in the public interest if it conflicts with the owner's business interests. The second sort of instrumentalization involves the exploitation of newspapers and radio and television channels to cover up corruption scandals involving the owners, by giving negative publicity to rivals to deflect attention from their own misdeeds (as happened with the Latvian oligarch Aivars Lembergs and the Romanian mogul Dan Voiculescu). The third is the promotion of political and business allies through the blackening of the reputations of opponents and competitors. Stetka (2012: 447) cites the example of the suppression of a report about the questionable financing of the ruling SMER Party in Slovakia shortly before the 2010 election, after one of the owners of the TV JOJ channel intervened. The economic power of owners of these and other concerns and empires means that direct intervention is seldom required: journalists engage in the practice of self-censorship. Media freedom need not be threatened by physical violence for media freedom to be at risk. It can be curtailed by indirect influences, the power to allocate resources and appoint staff, and through regulation and licensing (Davis 2007; Tworzecki & Semetko 2012).

In political science studies of clientelism, journalists are seen as playing one of two roles, according to Örnebring (2012). These are familiar from earlier chapters. One is to relay information. The other is to act as watchdog – to work against the forces of clientelism, by exposing its practices and networks. Örnebring advocates a definition of clientelism that is wider than classic political science definitions – more anthropological – that encompasses the informal practices of corruption. He also points to a need to take into account the fact that in many cultures, particularly fragile democracies, media owners either have personal connections to political and business elites, or are members of those elites themselves. In informal clientelistic networks, journalists, or the media companies they work for, take money from PR firms to write 'advertorials', i.e. reports that promote certain interests while pretending to be impartial. They can also do the opposite, and engage in *kompromat* or 'smearing'. Watchdogs such as Spinwatch (spinwatch.org) go to considerable lengths to document that such practices are rife in established democracies as well as new ones (Minton 2013).

In the private sphere

Attempts by states to control information flows do more than constrain and threaten journalists. Civilians are also involved in the battle for media freedom. Sometimes their freedom to use digital media is at threat; sometimes it is their privacy that is threatened, either by states exploiting developments in media technology, or by unscrupulous reporters and editors trampling personal integrity in the pursuit of profit.

Amendments to India's Information Technology Act, made in response to the 2008 Mumbai attacks, have led to an increasing number of arrests, and the prosecution of Indian citizens posting content online that is judged to be 'grossly harmful' or 'blasphemous'. Critics warn that such censorship of online speech could have global repercussions, as the Indian law affects one in six people on earth, and is a harbinger of future trends in internet governance (Harris 2014).

At the other end of the world, a columnist writing for a liberal newspaper lit a metaphorical candle, on All Soul's Day 2013, for Peter Forsskål, the Enlightenment thinker whose influential essay 'Thoughts about civic freedom' (Tankar om borgerliga friheten) had inspired Sweden's unique 1766 law. Apart from guaranteeing press freedom, Tryckfrihetsförordningen guarantees all citizens the right of access to public documents. (This was why WikiLeaks based its servers in Stockholm until Assange and Sweden fell out over his rape charge.) The columnist opined that this right of citizen access was being distorted. Instead of citizens monitoring the acts of the powerful, it was now the powerful who were using media to monitor citizens. What the surveillance scandals of 2013 had in common was that, in each case, governments and public authorities had stopped asking the question that Forsskål and other Enlightenment thinkers considered central: what intrusions into the freedom of the citizen are justified with reference to the common good (Wiman 2013)?

The issue is complicated (to say the least) by the debate taking place across the English Channel. Throughout the years of revelations about the *News of the World* phone-hacking scandal and trial in the UK, and the official inquiry headed by Lord Justice Leveson, Hacked Off campaigners called for tougher self-regulation by the British media. Arguing that editors and journalists would rise in public esteem by accepting the sort of self-regulation recommended by Leveson, it called on the press to embrace the Royal Charter of October 2013 that 'safeguards the press from political interference while also giving vital protection to the vulnerable' (http://hackinginquiry.org).

An argument in the *Observer* on 16 March 2014 opined that the argument in favour of the freedom of the press would become more intense, not least thanks to pressure from Hacked Off. The argument in favour of press freedom 'is generally pitched as the case for freedom from the state and freedom to hold the state to account', as the author put it (Hutton 2014). There are problems with taking this argument at face value: 'Holding the state to account and limiting its tentacles are a crucial part of the story, but only a part. The case for a free press is larger. It is about how to ensure as much true information as possible is disseminated in a free society.' Hutton pointed out that governments are the main, but not the only, suspects: 'private disseminators of information are not disinterested guardians of the public good. They, too, have political and social agendas. Nor are they guaranteed to behave ethically and professionally. Moreoever, private power has become steadily more potent, more unaccountable and more willing than ever to exert overt political force' (Hutton 2014).

On the dark side

Freedom of expression thus has a dark side, as argued by Hutton but also, in a different way, as illustrated by the portkey that opened the chapter. In many countries throughout the world, this freedom involves the liberty to polarize and to demonize opponents. Radio, a medium that for decades had the power to unify the nation, and in many places still has, has been used as a deadly instrument, spreading hate of rival ethnic groups in Rwanda in 1994, for example, and of homosexuals in Uganda. Hate radio is an entrenched phenomenon in the US, and figures like Rush Limbaugh, whose vitriolic tirades against 'feminazis' and 'sluts' like the Georgetown law student who lobbied for contraception to be covered by health insurance, have significant political clout. Concerns have been expressed that hate has been adopted in the US as a 'profit model' (NHMC 2012). But it exists in Poland too, in the form of Radio Maryja, driven by forces and motives other than profit. Founded by Father Rydzyk, the station is supported by Catholic clergy. Listeners can partake of xenophobic political commentary and warnings that freemasons, Jews, liberals and progressive Catholics are threatening the nation (Tworzecki & Semetko 2012: 422).

A moral panic surrounding freedom of expression in a digital environment was sparked by a current affairs programme broadcast in Sweden in 2013. The programme documented the increased tendency for women who engage in public debate to be subjected to virulent abuse and threats from anonymous commentators on Facebook posts and official company and media institution websites. On the programme, women working as journalists, writers and debaters read aloud the often shocking and threatening letters and comments they had received. Swedish women – and of course men – are not alone in having such experiences, but given that they live in a country ranked at the top of the press freedom index, there is reason to be concerned about how the parameters for democratic debate – the walls of the public sphere – have closed, and the ceiling been lowered by internet hate, if this is the trend in an ostensibly tolerant country.[4]

Wikipedia's appeal to protect free speech on the internet, on 18 January 2012. Reproduced with permission.

There are other dark corners, populated by actors who complicate the debate on media freedom. Nameless and faceless hactivists push the limits of media freedom by sabotaging the servers and websites of institutions and actors with whom they disagree. When US officials shut down Megaupload in January 2012 (federal prosecutors had accused the popular file-sharing site of costing copyright holders more than US$ 500 million in lost revenue), the hackers' group Anonymous launched an attack on the websites of the FBI and Department of Justice. Arguments can be made for criticizing the government move, but even stronger ones to question the use of sabotage to defend 'media freedom' when it comes into conflict with property rights.

The police action against Megaupload was among the largest criminal copyright cases ever brought by the US, the crime being 'misuse of public content storage' and facilitation of intellectual property crime. The site was not the only thing to go offline. The same week, thousands of websites took part in a blackout to protest against the Stop Online Piracy Act (SOPA) and the Protect Intellectual Property Act (PIPA), including Wikipedia. Critics of the proposed legislation argued that political elites were acting in the interests of corporate capital rather than in the defence of the information rights of the people, that parts of it violated the First Amendment, and that it would be the starting shot in a global trend of internet censorship. Neither of the Bills were passed.

Cultural differences

The cases that have featured here represent a range of different problems, confronting different actors in different settings. There is no universal agreement as to what constitute the key components of media freedom, or how or whether to safeguard them. Understandings of conflict of interest (between the rights to information and privacy rights, for example) vary from culture to culture. Nor is it always considered the most important of values. A poll conducted by the BBC in 2007 found that people in Singapore set much greater store by stability and prosperity than press freedom (Josephi 2010). There is also considerable national variation in views of the duty journalists may have to sustain national identity and, in the case of young countries like Kyrgyzstan, or countries with troubled pasts like Indonesia, to the national project itself (Freedman 2012: 58). The example of DSK in chapter 3 also built on the fact that the parameters of freedom of expression as opposed to the right of the individual to privacy are policed differently in, for example, the US and France. It has also been pointed out that the term 'freedom of expression' is understood differently in the Anglo-American and the German context (Hanusch 2009: 619). The European Broadcasting Union is clear about what media freedom means: it is about 'editorial independence, the protection of journalists and the unrestricted public access to information sources':

> Any threat to the independence and availability of these media, whether via govern-mental interference, the intimidation of journalists, a lack of transparency in owner-ship structures and concentration, overriding commercial interests, or deliberate attempts to block access to content, upsets the overall state of media freedom and pluralism in any European country. (EBU 2013)

Nevertheless, the world's largest alliance of public-service broadcasters concedes that media freedom is not something even EU member states have in common: it is promoted and challenged in different ways in different European countries.

There are other differences – for example, in views on the matter of who owns infor-mation. In December 2012, delegates from 190 countries met at the International Telecommunications Union (ITU) in Dubai to update an international treaty from 1988 on telecommunications.[5] Several governments made the case for leaving the management of the internet to private companies, while others proposed changes that would make it easier for states to censor it. Russian President Putin said he wants to use the ITU to 'maintain international control' over communication in the digital age and, as was discussed in chapter 3, many regimes are increasingly energetic when it comes to blocking information about what they are doing.

The differences cannot just be attributed to culture, however. They have more to do with the vantage point of a given actor, or set of actors, in the media–politics relation-ship. Critical voices being raised in and about one country – the UK – highlight the basic contradiction at the heart of the media freedom issue.

Observer columnist Nick Cohen, for example, has argued that the English legal system helps to suppress what the rich and powerful consider to be 'inconvenient truths' instead of defending investigative journalism and freedom of speech. When oligarchs migrated from newly capitalized states to the UK in the early noughties and journalists investigated and tried to report on their often questionable business dealings, they were prevented from doing so by libel laws.

> With an aristocratic prejudice against freedom of speech, the judges imposed costs and sanctions on investigative journalism that would have been hard to endure in

the best of times, but were unbearable after the internet had undermined the media's business models. Instead of aiming its guns at the worst of British writing, the law of libel aimed at the bravest. (Cohen 2012)

Cohen cites the example of journalists working for the Danish newspaper *Ekstra Bladet* who decided to investigate the meteoric rise of the Kaupthing bank in Iceland. They found that the bank had links with Russian oligarchs, was involved in tax havens, and was in trouble. The bank sued the newspaper in Denmark and lost, so took its suit to London instead, on the grounds that the Danish publication was available in the UK, thanks to its internet edition. *Ekstra Bladet*, unable to bear the legal costs, settled with Kaupthing before the case came to court, and was forced to print an apology. Several months later, Kaupthing collapsed and so did Iceland, its GDP falling by 65 per cent overnight. The United Nations subsequently declared that the restrictive British libel law was a global danger, and could 'affect freedom of expression worldwide on matters of valid public interest' (Smith 2009).

Guardian editor Alan Rusbridger recounts the bizarre meeting he had with a 'very senior' British government official who demanded the newspaper return or destroy material its correspondent Glenn Greenwald had obtained from Edward Snowden:

> I explained to the man from Whitehall about the nature of international collaborations and the way in which, these days, media organizations could take advantage of the most permissive legal environments. Bluntly, we did not have to do our reporting from London. Already most of the NSA stories were being reported and edited out of New York. And had it occurred to him that Greenwald lived in Brazil? The man was unmoved. And so one of the more bizarre moments in the *Guardian*'s long history occurred – with two GCHQ security experts overseeing the destruction of hard drives in the *Guardian*'s basement just to make sure there was nothing in the mangled bits of metal which could possibly be of any interest to passing Chinese agents. (Rusbridger 2013a)

On the other hand, as journalists in the UK writhed and argued about the fallout from the phone-hacking scandal, with the Prime Minister ordering a public inquiry (the 'Leveson') into the violations, by reporters and editors working for Rupert Murdoch, of legal and moral restrictions on the right of individuals to privacy, Barnett (2011) wrote about the confusion that prevailed between two entirely different models of journalism. One is the Clark Kent figure, the caped crusader 'committed to rooting out corruption, standing up for the bullied and the downtrodden and confronting evil'. The other is the pig in a raincoat described in chapter 4, who is the unscrupulous individual who exploits unsuspecting victims in the pursuit of profits for greedy newspaper owners. Barnett noted that 'many plaintive cries' could be heard insisting that 'the caped crusader must be protected at all costs'. And yet, as another observer pointed out, journalists are no different from members of parliament, the police and bankers: without independent scrutiny to hold them to account, there is a distinct risk that not only professional codes will develop, but also 'self-serving moral codes' that conflict with what is generally acceptable. As Marsh so pithily put it,

> the freedom to scrutinise the repressive organs of power and privilege is not the same as the freedom to scrutinise the reproductive organs of Premiership footballers. (Marsh 2011: 52).

If the Leveson inquiry and the public debate surrounding it is about anything at all, Barnett wrote,

> it should be about understanding the difference between freedom of speech and freedom from abusive and intrusive speech. (Barnett 2011: 15)

What that difference is, and how the distinction is to be drawn between the work of the caped crusader and of the pig in a raincoat, is more than a little difficult to define. Nor does it only involve scurrilous practices by journalists and their greedy employers. The public is also complicit, as was demonstrated in May 2011, when a British member of parliament, John Hemming, named footballer Ryan Giggs as the married man alleged to be having an affair with a former *Big Brother* contestant. Journalists working for mainstream media had been prevented from doing so by a gagging order. Hemming and other parliamentarians wanted to make the point that the actions of thousands of people posting details on Twitter of individuals involved in superinjunctions risked making the law 'look an ass'. For Hemming, the issue was 'enforceability of a law that clearly does not have public consent'. England's attorney general, Dominic Grieve, countered by saying

> The government believes freedom of speech is the cornerstone of our democracy and it is of the greatest importance that people should be able to discuss and debate issues as freely and openly as possible. This includes those occasions when freedom of speech is exercised provocatively, as it's supposed to be in a free country. Plainly, however, there are also occasions when an individual is entitled to have their privacy protected. There is a balance to be struck.

but acknowledged there were widely different views on what that balance should be (Mulholland 2011). The debate over media regulation in the UK – of the tension between press freedom and the freedom of the individual to keep their private life just that – provides a large portion of food for thought.

Are, then, curbs on media freedom always a bad thing? Was the freedom to publish the *Innocence of Muslims* film worth the fifty lives lost in the protests it sparked? Was it right of the German government to persuade Twitter to block the account of the neo-Nazi group Besseres Hannover, accused of threatening immigrants and distributing racist pamphlets at German schools? And if so, was it also right of the authorities in Pakistan to block Twitter because of messages deemed offensive to Islam? Keir Starmer, director of public prosecutions in England and Wales, has argued that new guidelines for policing social media in the UK would have a 'chilling effect' on free speech, and that high thresholds are needed (BBC News Technology, 11 October 2012). Is one of these views right and the others wrong? If so, on what grounds? Who should decide? The examples that have featured in the past few pages point to the tension between positive and negative freedom; between the freedom to use media institutions and technology in an appropriate way, without infringing on the freedom and rights of others. This is a scholarly problem, a political problem and a moral problem. With this chapter, the book has taken a step back from its comparative, empirical agenda, and opened a window on the more theoretical and general concerns with which it began. Something to think about is the role that journalists, editorialists, radio hosts and the producers of popular cultural texts should play in polities that are increasingly multicultural and heterogeneous, with all the religious and ethnic conflict that entails, in a world where information and media texts circulate seemingly freely and where the market rules as well as the state.

To think about

The US officially advocates a free internet. Former US Secretary of State Hillary Clinton invoked the First Amendment and the UN Declaration of Human Rights when she declared that the US stands for an internet where all of humanity has the same access to information and ideas. This entails the right of people everywhere to search, receive and share information in all media, without taking borders into account. In many respects, she said, 'information has never been so free', with information networks making even authoritarian governments more accountable. At the same time, she lamented the moves of states to build electronic barriers to citizen access to internet resources which, she emphasized, amounted to 'a new information curtain' being drawn across the world:

> Because amid this unprecedented surge in connectivity, we must also recognize that these technologies are not an unmitigated blessing. These tools are also being exploited to undermine human progress and political rights. Just as steel can be used to build hospitals or machine guns, or nuclear power can either energize a city or destroy it, modern information networks and the technologies they support can be harnessed for good or for ill. The same networks that help organize movements for freedom also enable al-Qaida to spew hatred and incite violence against the innocent. And technologies with the potential to open up access to government and promote transparency can also be hijacked by governments to crush dissent and deny human rights. (Clinton 2010)

Something to think about is whether and how those words fit with the actions, three years later, of the administration Clinton had served. In June 2013, the US revoked the passport of Edward Snowden and put pressure on states all over the world to deny him the right to political asylum, on the grounds that the man who had leaked documents about US surveillance of private individuals was not a whistleblower or dissident but a criminal.

Another thing to think about is how comparable the claims of government persecution and violation of media freedom are, when made by media actors such as Kenya's the *Standard*, on the one hand, and Argentina's Grupo Clarín, on the other. How is the scholar to make sense of universal principles being invoked in quite different contexts? Related to this, does globalization improve the prospects for media freedom worldwide (Greenwald lives in Brazil and the material for the British newspaper story was stored in First-Amendment-protected New York) or make it more difficult to safeguard (as the bizarre Kaupthing saga suggests)?

The power struggles involved in the promotion and policing of media freedom are familiar from previous decades, and indeed even centuries. The technology involved, however, has changed the rules of the game almost beyond recognition. Creators of SF narratives of politics such as those who featured in chapter 8, have forecast at regular intervals how technological advances would infringe on citizen rights. It is no coincidence that when the surveillance scandal broke, the name 'Orwell' was swiftly invoked.

There is a platitude, in accounts of media bias during wartime, that 'one man's terrorist is another man's freedom-fighter'. In the digital age, events have shown that one person's traitor is another one's freedom-of-information fighter. As the battle raged to control the PRISM narrative, Chelsea Manning was standing trial for having released classified documents into the global public sphere in the 'Cablegate' incident that opened this book. Analyses of the different ways Manning's actions and the trial were framed by political elites, journalists and activists, and were made sense of by citizens and audience members in different countries, will keep media scholars and political scientists – and their students – busy for years to come. There is much to think about.

11 Conclusion

Several days after the *Guardian* published Edward Snowden's revelations that the US was engaging in mass surveillance of ordinary citizens, causing a global outcry and demands from political leaders, activists and ordinary people the world over for openness and accountability, an appeal was published on the front page of Scandinavia's largest newspaper, *Dagens Nyheter* (DN). Editor-in-Chief Peter Wolodarski and a team of investigative reporters looked readers in the eye and asked them to 'help us scrutinize power'.[1]

> We need you to help us do our job. The biggest scoops come from people who have valuable information . . . Snowden's testimony became world news that has shaken the American administration and started an essential debate on the balance between combating terror and the right to a personal sphere. Many journalistic revelations happen this way... recent discoveries of corruption in the public sector and waste of tax money have a similar background: individual citizens get in touch and tell about wrongdoing. *Dagens Nyheter* invests considerable resources in investigative

Investigative reporters at the Swedish newspaper *Dagens Nyheter*, with Editor-in-Chief Peter Wolodarski (centre). Byline: Magnus Hallgren/DN/TT.

journalism. We follow up all the leads that come in and research them ourselves. All our sources are protected, as is their constitutional right. And while we're on the subject: DN's e-mail servers are not in the US, they're close to the newsroom. On the secure site https://dngranskar.dn.se you can leave an encrypted message, which can only be read by someone with a key. Get in touch. We need your help.

DN is not a new challenger to 'hegemonic' media: it was founded in 1864 and has for a century and a half occupied a central place in the mainstream of the national information flow and public debate. And yet this piece is strongly reminiscent of the portkey that opened the book – the appeal from 'counter-hegemonic' Al Jazeera to its viewers to help 'crowdsource Cablegate'. DN's Editor-in-Chief Peter Wolodarski bears little resemblance to Commander Adamo, but just as *Battlestar Galactica* managed to elude conquest by technologically superior Cylons and their backdoors thanks to Adamo's determination to keep the ship's computer network separate from the system that connected all the others, Wolodarski could promise to protect people willing to help him maintain the balance of power because his newspaper's servers were housed locally. Whereas the British politician in *Yes Minister* said there was no need to scramble, because word of a coup was on the news, the Swedish newspaper, like WikiLeaks, encrypted tips from the public and whistleblowers precisely so that they could make the news.

Grasping a portkey like this enables a journey back in time, to the oft-invoked golden (or in some accounts mythical) age when journalists were watchdogs who protected the public from the abuse of power, and not the 'pigs in raincoats' who fell into disgrace after a global media mogul, rather than an American president, was found guilty of phone-hacking. Like the even older and hardly less mainstream *Guardian*, DN has responded to the economic crisis in the newspaper industry by prioritizing investigative journalism, rather than sacrificing it, which runs counter to what the reader of much literature on the subject might be led to expect. These newspapers are by no means the only such media institutions to do so, nor are their reporters the only watchdogs in a field of pigs. As commercial media, they are obviously not uninterested in profit, and there are myriad examples, in Sweden and the UK as in the rest of the world, of media power being misused, but it is worth bearing in mind that reports of newspaper death, to paraphrase Mark Twain, are sometimes exaggerated. The story of the media–politics relationship has many chapters about continuity.

But a portkey like this also transports us to the sometimes SF-like present, so marked by change as to make it hard to conceive of a more altered future. Old media like the *Guardian* and *Dagens Nyheter* continue to appear on doormats and newsstands in paper form, but are more often accessed virtually. When Snowden revealed his identity, the famous interview was published in the newspaper in video format. Just a few years before, it was only in Hogwarts and in the wizard world's *Daily Prophet* that photographs talked and moved from frame to frame. Another element of change (even if it no longer feels new) is the direct appeal to readers to take part in newsgathering. The DN piece is a typical example of the trend discussed in several chapters of the news having become a process rather than a product, never finished and continually altered and updated by readers and viewers as well as journalists and editors.

What you see depends on where you stand

This book has been structured around the insight that the media–politics relationship, and the problems and potential it entails, looks different from the vantage point of different sets of actors. The research fields related to each of these – their central concepts, questions, methods and primary source material – are shaped by the objects of analysis (and vice versa). The narratives of media and politics can thus often be contradictory and confusing.

Journalist Nik Gowing argues that what he calls 'the tyranny of real time' affects 'all of the professions – whether media, government, military or diplomats – who are dealing with information', especially at times of crisis (which seems to be most of the time, under globalization). All of these sorts of actors, whatever their position,

> are confounded by the very basic necessity to filter and validate information at high speed. It is an imperfect skill, where expectations – especially of the audience – exceed our capabilities to validate and confirm reports, at least in the first few minutes or hours. (Gowing 2003: 235)

Ordinary people are, it could be argued, similarly tyrannized, by the multitude of demands posed by postmodern society, and the same overabundance of information that needs to be filtered. It may also be a task that exceeds their capabilities, requiring, as it does, management of the daily reinforcement of narrative understandings of the way the world works. The imaginative architecture that is involved varies, just as the styles of houses differ from country to country, and the different materials from which they are constructed.

One thing that is different about mediated life under globalization is that the houses are increasingly made of glass. Thompson's classic theory of media and modernity, which has featured here and there throughout the book, suggests, among other things, that a 'transformation of visibility' has taken place. Political leaders have become familiar because we see them regularly on television, and have learned to think of them as figures in a shared world that is visible to everyone. The example of *Big Brother* served to illustrate how this transformation extends to popular as well as political culture, and Snowdengate is an important reminder of how it has come to intrude into the private sphere of ordinary people.

There are cultural differences in the rate and degree of this transformation, and how it is controlled. Chapter 3 illustrated how the legal right to privacy in France is absolute, in contrast to the US, where press freedom takes precedence over the individual's right to privacy. In Thompson's narrative, publicity is traced back to the days of the *ancien régime* when the king and queen held court in bed. Centuries later, and deep into globalization, the royal bed was still in the limelight, when reporters from all over the world camped outside a London hospital in July 2013, waiting for a woman's very private work to result in a very public announcement of the birth of the third in line to the British throne. A year before, Sweden's heir to the throne beat the paparazzi by publishing the first picture of her newborn daughter on the Royal Court's Facebook page (www.facebook.com/kungahuset). Meyrowitz (2009) was quoted as saying that television 'humanized' the image of elites, and lowered them to the level of the common person. Developments in media technology have encouraged the 'personalization' of politics, redirecting the gaze to individual politicians and their characteristics rather than what they stand for, or why (when their policies are shaped by other forces). The possibility was discussed that political elites have lost control over their images or 'brands', as Admiral Roughead would say, but also the opposite – that they have increased their control over the political narrative, and in many cases the media outlets that shape it.

Journalistic strategies have also been discussed. The question of which ideals and interests they should serve has been posed in relatively abstract terms by political theorists (Muhlmann 2010), but need also to be discussed in relation to specific examples. Professionals from the same country and same end of the market have argued in these pages about whether professional standards are on the decline or higher than ever before, suggesting that caution is in order before generalizing to other media outlets and cultures. On a typical round of the apps on a common device, dialogues were encountered that touched on the impact of technology, changing journalistic role conceptions and news values, the tension between politicization and professionalism, and the question of whether newswork is abetted or undermined by crowdsourcing. It has been emphasized throughout that such issues are empirical questions.

Quite a few pages have been devoted to 'ordinary people' ('the people formerly known as the audience'). Political scientists may have found themselves uncomfortable with this, and more used to studying elites, bureaucrats and activists. But ordinary people are part of the media–politics relationship and the study of how they relate to mediated politics, and to the changing media technology involved in that mediation, yields insights into how society works. Citizens, voters (dutiful or uninformed), members of the public, consumers whose behaviour is shaped by economic forces or individuals who form a diffused or extended audience, or part of the viewertariat that adapts to new technology rather than to market forces: whatever they are called, the study of what these people do with media messages is part of the study of politics and power. It is important to put our own experiences and practices under the magnifying glass, and ask what they say about power relations at all levels. Thompson argued that people on the receiving end of media messages have limited or 'strictly circumscribed' possibilities to intervene in or contribute to the processes in which the messages and symbolic forms in these flows are produced. Production, he suggested, takes place without input or 'cues' from receivers. The audience or public has relatively little power, and readers and viewers are 'left to their own devices'. These ideas were challenged by competing notions of active and diffused audiences. As Gillespie (2005: 3) explains, the question of audience power is not just a personal matter. Our media practices are social and socially stratified, and understanding them 'gives us important insights into how media reproduce relations of power and identities'.

Continuity and change

Couldry's point of departure is that we live in a converged media environment in which stories told with images or video captured on mobile devices are compiled and circulated via 'single' sites like YouTube or Facebook. He maintains that having an online presence has become 'expected of well-functioning citizens'. The personal becomes public, and the opposite: people (especially young ones) learn to control their own public images. By 'holding back' personal narratives from such sites, it is argued, young people are 'protecting an older private/public boundary rather than tolerating a shift in that boundary because of significant social pressure to have an online presence' (Couldry 2008: 383). Digital media forms could contribute to 'a wider democratization of media resources and possibly to the conditions of democracy itself', vastly extending the number of people who could contribute to the public sphere.

Even with the sort of technological advances considered at various points in the book, however, the public, as conceived of by Mills over half a century ago, is still far from being realized – perhaps farther than ever. Some of the scholars encountered on this trip across a sprawling intellectual landscape insist that new technologies have no significant impact on whether an opinion formed in discussion could be materialized in an effective action, or whether a rationally formed and deliberated opinion is controlled by authorities. But technological developments have made it possible for 'virtually as many people to express opinions as to receive them' and have made the news junkie a happy person. According to one perspective that has been put forward, the proliferation of personal media is seen as having the potential to empower people and enhance their knowledge of and participation in politics. From another perspective, such developments have been seen as undermining the preconditions for shared political cultures and public communicative spaces.

Views differ, then, on whether things are looking up for the audience, or getting worse – not to mention whether its members are best understood as passive and ignorant, or as active and well informed. Widespread concern has been noted, particularly on the part of political scientists, that people are no longer participating in traditional politics to the extent they once were, and are less likely as time goes by to belong to established parties or social movement organizations. Young people, in particular, are thought to be uninformed about what elites consider to be relevant issues, and are perceived as being politically apathetic. In contrast to these, more optimistic scholars have turned to look at new forms of engagement. They see different things, think different things are relevant, and think about them differently. Nor are they particularly interested in civic cultures of duty-bound citizens. They look out into the world of primary source material and see instead a web of networks replacing traditional political associations.

Outdated, heavily critiqued, arguably inappropriate to a globalizing world: the concept of the public sphere cropped up in several different locations on this intellectual map. Habermas conceived of this sphere as coming into being when engaged citizens discuss matters of mutual political concern, and as existing somewhere between the private sphere and the state. It is in this space that public opinion is formed and expressed – opinion that serves both to legitimate and to check the power of the state. Habermas laments the turn away from text and the increasing incidence of media spectacle. But spectacle is central to much mediated activism, and indeed to the performance of politics itself. One thing readers have been asked to think about is whether image does rule out rational thought, or provides an alternative way of reflecting on politics.

Different ages of political communication have been covered in these pages, beginning with the days when people in democracies throughout the world tended to vote in predictable ways, either for the party that represented their social class, or for the one that represented their values, or both. The second 'age' of dealignment followed. People started to vote in unpredictable ways, choosing issues rather than platforms, and making decisions based on the appeal of leaders' personality traits rather than the track record or manifesto of the party headed by those leaders. This was to the extent that people continued to vote at all: in the second age, the uninformed voter was replaced by the cynic as the villain of the piece. People started consuming the world in separate rooms, on individual devices, no longer required to tune into the same channel and thus no longer liable to discuss those mediated messages with each other. Now, mobile technology has taken us out of our homes, and while we continue to consume media messages privately – on personal devices and with headphones – we do so increasingly in public. And in these public spaces, it has been argued, we are using the same technology not just to take in messages about the world, but to record and disseminate such messages ourselves.

Whatever the changes that technology, developments in society and politics, and globalization bring, we still need to think of ourselves in terms of conceptualizations of the public. But publicity is being reconceptualized, it has been suggested. Once about reasoned debates, the notion has come to refer to activities that attract the interest or attention of many. The refeudalization of the public sphere discussed in an earlier chapter is not being caused by new media forms, so neither will new media forms bring about a defeudalization. What is needed instead is an attempt to change interpretations of the public sphere and public opinion in a way that allows for the original meaning of publicity: the personal right to communicate in public; the mediation between the state and civil society; and public surveillance of the government (Splichal 2009: 404). Not the other way around.

German protesters show their solidarity with whistleblower Edward Snowden and demonstrate against NSA surveillance, 27 July 2013. Photograph: © David von Blohn / NurPhoto / Corbis.

Understanding media globalization and its problems

Part of that reconceptualization entails the requirement to think of ourselves as cosmopolitan publics as well as citizens of states, however multicultural they may have become. In an age when global media place images of suffering civilians before our eyes, we cannot exclude the requirement to feel empathy and responsibility for distant others. When they relay and comment on UN reports that show global warming could spiral out of control if the world does not cut pollution, we cannot ignore the fact that there are no more important politics than those which transcend borders. But who is to be held to account? Contemporary movements for the environment (and economic justice and human rights) appeal to global publics through global media, 'new' and 'old', because when political representation is found wanting, media representation offers an alternative.

Remarkably, a substantial amount of research on media reporting under globalization continues to take national problems and relations as the point of departure, displaying traits of what Beck dismissed almost a decade ago as 'methodological nationalism'. But, as Cottle (2011b: 85) has argued, media coverage, even when it is nationally based and focused, can be seen to futher globalization and to contribute to 'a sense of globality' partly because of the nature of the problems in focus. 'The complexities and contingenices of these global crisis enactments, however, have barely begun to be recognized and theorized in terms of comparative, sustained investigations', he notes (Cottle 2011b: 90). One thing to think about is how to contribute to filling this research gap.

Another issue to be pursued is whether war in a globalizing world is depicted as entertaining or deadly serious, and whether coverage of it is manipulated by political, military or economic elites. Is technological development making war more abstract or bringing us into direct contact? Is the story of mediated conflict characterized more by continuity or change? Is contemporary mediated conflict best studied from the starting point of 'techno-wars', 'virtual conflicts' and Baudrillardian non-existence, or from the authenticity claims of social media footage disseminated by citizen witnesses and placed on our Facebook pages where they cannot be ignored? It has been argued that there is a theoretical gap between different foci in accounts of mediated conflict, and the accounts consequently generated can be confusingly contradictory in the absence of integrative analytical frameworks.

Hoskins and O'Loughlin (2010) maintain it is impossible to exaggerate the changes in the relationship between media and war – so radical and problematic are they. Together with research on activism, this account of mediated conflict provided perhaps the most compelling evidence of change in these pages. The concept of diffusion – be it the diffused audience or the diffused war – helps make sense of how people are both connected and terrorized by ubiquitous media, which, it will be recalled, Hoskins and O'Loughlin argue constitute 'the condition of terror'. While Baudrillard claimed that the Gulf War did not take place, Hoskins and O'Loughlin argue that contemporary wars are real, but mediatized. I suggest that the process known as mediatization is more difficult and abstract than the literature sometimes makes out. At its most helpful, the concept can grasp the way in which technological development interacts with political, social and economic change in a similar way to globalization. And, like globalization, it is uneven and often invisible, making it difficult to deal with empirically.

Media freedom is difficult too, but on a normative rather than empirical level. Kant understood what has been translated as freedom of the press (or 'pen') to be freedom of the citizen to publish with the aid of the press, as opposed to the freedom of the publisher to make a profit. But the safeguarding of negative freedom – the freedom to avoid harm – has been rendered increasingly difficult in multicultural, globalizing societies. Sakr reflects on the possibility that having a wide range of transnational television outlets increases the space available for cultural clashes and intercultural incomprehension to be overcome. In contrast to the protracted confrontation over Salman Rushdie's *The Satanic Verses*, the Danish cartoon crisis was defused relatively quickly. Sakr (2008: 295) notes that Rushdie's book was published before the era of Arab satellite TV. She sees Arab satellite channels as offering the tools that could make it possible for well-meaning people from different cultures to identify common ground, engage in persuasion, and acknowledge the other's point of view. A task for further research is to compare how media outlets in different countries in a globalizing world deal with ethnic and cultural diversity, and who the Other in global news might be.

The clash of media cultures that became evident in the row between the Italian government and Swedish television over the anti-Berlusconi, pro-public-service television campaign, and the sight of DSK doing the 'perp walk' at the beginning of chapter 3, serve as reminders of how different the media–politics relationship can be even in countries in the same political union. The DSK example also highlighted a normative question. Where should the line be drawn between public and private – when it comes to ownership, when it comes to visibility, and when it comes to the tension between the needs of political elites to provide security and the freedom of the individual to personal integrity? And how much pressure should be put on national governments by other states – be they friend or foe – and by transnational bodies like the EU and UNESCO, to ensure common ethical denominators and respect for the right to information and expression? Infringements on media freedom from Turkey to Kenya, and the alarming mortality rate of journalists the world over, make this a compelling question.

This is what the attempt to get to grips with the media–politics relationship entails, I think: moving from a specific manifestation of the power struggle to theoretical attempts to make sense of it, resulting in concepts to be applied to real-world conditions and events in comparative empirical analysis, before ending up in normative issues of public and private, freedom and, again – always – power.

And finally

Quite some time ago, I did research on the peace movement for my doctoral thesis in political science. I began using newspaper reports as background material (peace movement documents and political party conference proceedings were the primary sources) until I realized that the German newspaper articles seemed to be reporting an entirely different controversy from the British ones. The basic facts were the same, but the stories were quite different. The British news discourse was about the need to stand up to a foreign bully (that would be the Russians), a lesson learned when resisting the Nazis in World War II. The German news discourse was framed by experiences of the war, too, but it was reversed. It emphasized the importance of acting upon one's convictions and standing up to one's own government when it seemed to be doing something wrong in the name of its citizens (be it a government headed by Hitler or by Chancellor Kohl, who was set to allow the deployment of a new generation of nuclear weapons on German soil). When my thesis was finished, it included a comparative news analysis. Media reports had become my primary source material instead of background information, and I had learned how revealing a comparison of different national frames could be.

A few years later, I ran into a political scientist from another university in the same small country I live and work in, who asked me if I was still studying the media. The question was posed by others from the same discipline and country regularly over the years. The answer is yes: I still study 'the media'. That is another way of saying that I study globalization, cultural integration, democracy, representation, citizenship, identity, the public sphere, ideology, participation, and enough other things to keep me busy for decades to come. Above all, I still study power and the political. I no longer work in a political science department though.

Studying 'the media' means having an infinite supply of portkeys through which to journey into these conceptual worlds – a supply that is replenished daily. It means being able to explore abstract, difficult ideas by relating them to things we use and do in our everyday lives. It means taking a moment from installing a new app or setting up a new device to think about how quickly things are changing.

There is no doubt that the political and media landscapes we wander through are changing in radical ways. In the corridors of power, political leaders from Obama to Ahmadinejad have exploited new media technologies in a bid to master turbulent political landscapes. On the streets and in cyberspace, people have mobilized to challenge such elites, protesting against political decisions in Washington and Tehran, in Cairo, Cancún, Copenhagen and Istanbul, in response to appeals circulated on Fox News, Twitter, Facebook and the blogosphere. In newsrooms all over the world, journalists are rethinking their use of technology and their relations with the public – a public that may no longer exist in any recognizable form, with audiences fragmented beyond recognition and 'ordinary' people using media to produce as well as receive political messages. All this is taking place in front of an open curtain, and in many cases using an open microphone, as actors on all levels rework their relation to media and politics in real time, in dialogue with others. Our job is to make sense of this landscape, or at least find ways of seeing it, even though it changes before our eyes.

The perceptive reader will have noticed that use of the first-person has crept into the final paragraphs of this book. I have been encouraged by several people, as the book manuscript has grown and been tweaked, to be clearer about where I stand on the problems, theories and research presented in these pages. I have resisted, because it's not for me to tell you *what* to think. The way I have conceived of my role has been to provide insights, ideas and resources that might tell you *how* to think – a role I am happy to continue playing if you care to continue the conversation on the book's companion website, mediapolitics.net. If you have ever visited the Metropolitan Museum of Art in New York City, you might have joined a tour given by one of the volunteers who takes delight in showing you parts of the collection they are particularly

Former US President Ronald Reagan, British Prime Minister Margaret Thatcher and Soviet leader Mikhail Gorbachev, represented and displayed at Madame Tussaud's in London. Photograph: Wikimedia Commons.

keen on. My job, in writing this book, has been to show you around, like one of the Met's enthusiasts, stopping in front of artefacts I find particularly interesting, and going on about them for a while. By doing so, I have perhaps stood in the way of you seeing other artefacts on the far side of the room, and refrained from mentioning the stockpiles in the store rooms. I might have pointed you to a portkey that landed you in the wrong place, to return to the metaphor pressed into service at the outset. Another guide may well have paused in front of quite different exhibits, or asked the curator to adjust the spotlights to illuminate quite different things. The guide doesn't matter: what matters is that you linger in the museum, explore it yourself, and revisit it from time to time, in case things have moved, or look different in another light.

The editor-in-chief of *Dagens Nyheter* and his team of investigative journalists made it clear that they want and need help with their work. The portkey that returns us to where we started is a clear illustration of Chadwick's idea that we have to pay careful attention to who actually does the powerful work in a hybridized, globalized, media-saturated environment, and makes the idea easier to grasp. That is the point of portkeys, and a reminder of why they are useful in a different kind of work – the scholarly work of making science out of the banal, of relating theory to everyday life, and the real world we inhabit (be it physical or mediated). The red thread running through this book has been the continual need to relate the theoretical to the empirical, and vice versa. Concepts, ideas and abstractions are useful – indeed essential – if we are to find a path through the forest of media artefacts. They might work as glasses or as compasses or as maps or, in particularly dense and dark parts of the woods, as flashlights. But they can narrow our field of vision too. So it is equally essential to leave the guide and the guidebook, to wander off the trail and look for other patterns in the media ecology and political landscape, and think about how different the map might look if they were on it. The Research guide at the end of the book provides some suggestions as to where to begin wandering.

Appendix: Research guide

The following pages contain suggestions for further reading, topics and primary source material for research projects related to the themes discussed in the book. Additional ones can be found on the companion website, mediapolitics.net. Before pursuing a particular topic in more depth, however, it can be a good idea to give some thought to your approach to doing research.

Designing your study

Begin your project creatively, guided by your interests and the trajectory that suits your research personality. It might be top-down. A concept, theory or academic debate might have caught your interest (agenda-setting or framing, perhaps), and you would like to work more with the literature pertaining to it, for example by following up on the phenomenon in question in a setting not dealt with in the secondary sources (applying it to attempts by the 'yes' and 'no' sides to control the narrative over Scottish independence, for example). In other words, it might suit you best to start with 'theory' and work down to an empirical application. Or your research personality might be better suited to a bottom-up approach instead. For example, a particular case (Russia Today's coverage of the Ukrainian crisis) or text (the Uganda Media Law, or *Captain America: The Winter Soldier* or Russell Brand's political manifesto) might have caught your interest, and you would like to analyse it and work upwards, to relate it to a theory or scholarly debate (like cultural regulation or infotainment or celebrity politics). It is worthwhile giving yourself some time to explore different possibilities, and to avoid closing off particular avenues of inquiry too soon. It is usually a good idea to start by identifying your general interest and then begin the scholarly task of putting words around it – words that get closer and closer to the vocabulary of the scholarly discussion and the discourse of methods textbooks. Proceed step-by-step, getting a dialogue going between the secondary sources (theory and previous research) and primary sources (empirical material). At each step of your research, let questions propel the inquiry forward. This will make your work more transparent, and your written reports more interesting to read.

Research interest and material

The first step involves formulating answers to some preliminary questions. What is your research interest? What sort of empirical material could you use to pursue this interest? Where can you get hold of it? This work generally involves brainstorming.

A common question is how much material to analyse. Some authors, like Chouliaraki (2006) have written influential books based on a few news reports and, in one of the essays in *Mythologies*, Barthes (1957/1993) got quite far by analysing the front cover of one news magazine. On the other hand, if your ambition is to say something about 'global media coverage of the Syrian conflict', then you will have validity problems if your sample includes a few reports published on the websites of one or two news channels. That said, the most common tendency is to be overly ambitious. To do justice to the magnitude of media reports about politics we encounter on a daily basis, large samples are needed, but if you feel compelled to use a methodology such as critical discourse or narrative analysis, you will run into difficulties – unless you have a decade for your project and someone prepared to read a 300–page report of your research. It is possible to analyse thousands of news reports if a simple methodology is employed to code superficial features, and you are clear about what conclusions can be drawn from such indicators. The right amount of material for your project depends on what you intend to do with it.

Research problem and aim

Formulating the aim or putting the research problem into words is often the hardest part of the project, with the exact wording tweaked as the research progresses. Your ideas are liable to change the more you read, and especially as you dig into your empirical material. As your hands get dirtier, make sure the aim you have formulated doesn't stay pristine, untouched in the proposal. Go back to it often, pick it up and turn it over until it is familiar and well worn. Keep interrogating it.

A well-formulated aim contains the answer to two questions:

1   What are you going to do in your study?
2   Why are you going to do it?

These two seemingly innocent questions can actually be quite difficult to answer, but the success of your project hangs on thinking about them and trying to formulate a clear response. The answer to the question 'what?' relates to the empirical material and analytical approach you will be using. The answer to the question 'why' relates your study to the broader academic discussion, or secondary sources (in some cases, 'theory'). To ensure that you produce an analysis, and not just description, there should be a puzzle involved – a question you don't know the answer to. What is it that we don't know the answer to at the outset? What knot are you trying to unravel by doing this study?

You should ask yourself what the focus of your research really is. When first answering this question, you might be tempted to give quite a vague answer. For example, you might say that you will be using Euronews and that your project is about the media and European identity. But what does that mean? Will this be a study of Euronews, or is your project about the notion of European identity as such, or about the media's role in cultivating identity (in which case, why Euronews and not the Eurovision Song Contest)? Is it a normative argument about how things should be (in which case your study should rest heavily on theoretical and perhaps even philosophical sources)? Are you aiming to map out the way things are (by analysing Euronews reports or doing a reception study, if you can find people who watch it) or are you hoping to do a study of the reasons behind this state of affairs (by interviewing journalists or analysing policy documents)? Your project might involve all these things, but in that case, you should establish a hierarchy of importance. One might just be the hook or point of entry to your inquiry; another could serve as a reflective note to finish your paper with; while another is what you actually spend your project finding out about.

When it comes to answering the 'why' question, it can be useful to bear in mind that explaining why your study is interesting is usually, although not always, a matter of situating the project in the context of the relevant scholarly discussion (which tends to get referred to, sometimes misleadingly, as Theory). The connection to an academic debate can be more or less intense. For example, sometimes the research question is generated by inconsistencies or gaps within a well-researched area. One example of that would be if previous research in a certain area leads us to expect that 'y' follows pattern 'x', but we've found that it actually follows pattern 'z' instead: how can that be or what does this imply? If previous research implies that we should expect national broadcasters to follow a certain pattern in their reaction to extra-Parliamentary protest, how can we understand the apparently completely different reaction of this particular French or Russian or Indian television news programme to that particular lobby or social movement? Posing questions such as these, and offering preliminary answers, is a good way of making a 'why' start to happen.

Another type of 'why' arises when insights from previous research are applied to fresh material. This could be material that for some reason has remained unexplored (radio seen in light of mediatization theory, or the visual strategies of the suffragettes), or material that has resulted from new developments (does the time-honoured theory of agenda-setting work when the medium is Twitter rather than newspapers?) or an unforeseen event or unprecedented phenomenon (like WikiLeaks or the Snowden disclosures). Sometimes you can create a niche of 'unexplored material' by placing empirical material (a film like *World War Z* or *Noah* perhaps) that normally belongs in one sub-disciplinary discussion (say, cinema studies) in what might seem like a completely different academic discussion (say, political science or security studies).

Analytical approach

Once your research focus has become clearer, you should start thinking about how to answer the questions you have posed. This means honing in on what material you will be using, and what you will be doing with it. 'I will apply discourse analysis to French and British reporting of the Syrian conflict' is not a helpful answer to the question of what your analytical approach will be. For your sake, and that of your reader(s), you should be clear about what material you are using, and why you have chosen it – in general, and in particular. The answer to the 'in general' question might concern why you chose to compare two countries (for example, because France and the UK are very similar in important ways, except for the issue you are investigating, or because they are different in important ways, for example in that they represent different Hallin-and-Mancini models), and you are using, for example, newspaper editorials or a blog to explore how that issue is problematized by an important actor (i.e. a leading newspaper or minister or activist) in that country. Telling your reader(s) why you have chosen this material in particular might involve explaining why you are using only editorials instead of news articles, and why you are looking at the specific dates you have chosen for analysis.

Next: you have to be clear about what are you going to do with the material. What criteria are you applying to it, what questions are you asking of it? The criteria or questions have to be specific enough in themselves, or sufficiently well explained, for the reader to be able to understand how you will know the answer to a question when you see it, or will be able to assess whether a given criterion has been fulfilled. For example, how will you be able to identify 'expressions of national identity' in your primary sources? What features does war reporting in a given medium have to display for you to be able to conclude that it is 'infotainment', in the way Thussu uses the term? What qualities does a given selection of news texts have to have for you to be able to distinguish 'hard' from 'soft' or to conclude that 'dumbing down' is going on?

It is important to make sure there is a clear connection between research problem (or aim) and method (or analytical approach). Is the material appropriate (does it make sense to look at editorials if you are trying to study spin-doctoring)? Is the general method appropriate (will a discourse analysis of a radio programme be able to tell you anything about the journalist's intentions)?

The academic debate ('theory')

It is important to be able to work with secondary sources, and not just show that you are able to place your project in the context of an academic debate. This need not mean getting bogged down with sophisticated and complex 'Theory' – unless you want to, of course.

What does 'working with' secondary sources entail, then? Among other things, it means:

- critically discussing the works you have chosen, both in terms of their own merits and in terms of their usefulness to your study;
- relating the different texts you have chosen to each other, synthesizing them;
- approaching them with questions, just as you would your empirical material. What are you looking for? When you have answered one particular question (e.g. 'how do Author X and Author Y understand the relation between media and power in general?'), you need to pose another ('what has Researcher Z found out about the relationship between power and Spanish media?'), and then another ('how could those Spanish findings be related to the situation in the country I am studying?');
- incorporating your discussion in the expression of your research problem/aim, applying it to your own empirical investigation, and reflecting on what you have learned when you get to the end of your project and are reflecting on it in the conclusion of your paper or thesis.

In what follows, secondary sources related to the problematics presented in each chapter of the book are listed, together with suggestions for primary sources that can be analysed to explore these issues. New research is being published every month, and can be accessed in electronic form through scholarly journals subscribed to by most university libraries.

Research topics

Researching media and globalization

There is no shortage of good, comprehensive works on globalization, but Barrie Axford's *Theories of Globalization* (Polity, 2013) is a good place to start, or any of the volumes on the subject by Anthony McGrew and David Held (see the 'Global Transformations' website, www.polity.co.uk/global/). Luke Martell's *The Sociology of Globalization* (Polity, 2010) provides an accessible introduction to the topic from a different disciplinary point of entry. A bigger challenge – well worth the effort – is Manuel Castells' magisterial *Information Age* trilogy (*The Information Age: Economy, Society and Culture* – see Castells 1996, 1997 and 1998 in the Bibliography, but look for the new editions as they have been revised).

Media globalization is one aspect of cultural globalization. An introduction to this is provided by Paul Hopper in *Understanding Cultural Globalization* (Polity, 2007). Older but influential texts are worth a read: John Tomlinson's *Globalization and Culture* (Polity, 1999), for example, as well as Jan Nederveen Pieterse's *Globalization and Culture: Global Melange* (Rowman & Littlefield, 2003) and Arjun Appadurai's *Modernity at Large: Cultural Dimensions of Globalization* (University of Minnesota Press, 1996/2003).

A website replete with primary source material relating to cultural globaliza-tion (or links to it) is that of UNESCO: www.unesco.org/new/en/culture/themes/culture-and-development/the-future-we-want-the-role-of-culture/globalization-and-culture/. To follow the development of policy debates over time, see:

- UNESCO, *The Power of Culture*, 1998. www.powerofculture.nl/uk/archive/report/background.html
- UNESCO, Universal Declaration on Cultural Diversity, 2 November 2001. http://unesdoc.unesco.org/images/0012/001271/127160m.pdf
- UNESCO, Convention on the Protection and Promotion of the Diversity of Cultural Expressions, Paris, 20 October 2005.
- http://portal.unesco.org/en/ev.php-URL_ID=31038&URL_DO=DO_TOPIC&URL_SECTION=201.html
- UNESCO, *World Report on Cultural Diversity*, 2009.

For an introduction to media globalization specifically, Jack Lule's *Globalization and Media: Global Village of Babel* (Rowman & Littlefield, 2012) is one starting point; another is Terry Flew's *Understanding Global Media* (Palgrave, 2007). My own *Global News: Reporting Conflicts and Cosmopolitanism* (Peter Lang, forthcoming 2015) provides an overview of the field of global media studies. For political economy perspectives, with more critical stances on media globalization, there is an anthol-ogy edited by Thomas McPhail, *Global Communication: Theories, Stakeholders, and Trends* (Wiley-Blackwell, 2014), Edward Herman and Robert McChesney's *Global Media: The New Missionaries of Global Capitalism* (Bloomsbury, 2001) and *The Myth of Media Globalization* by Kai Hafez (Polity, 2007), in addition to the works refer-enced in chapter 1 and elsewhere in the book.

The notion of the public sphere, I have suggested, is a communicating door between political science and media studies. Ingrid Volkmer's *The Global Public*

Sphere: Public Communication in the Age of Reflexive Globalization (Polity, 2014) critiques and updates the Habermasian ideal of a national public sphere, and uses case studies to reflect on how well the term works in a global context. A related title is *Transnationalizing the Public Sphere* (Polity, 2014) by Kate Nash and Nancy Fraser.

Studying global television is a compelling way of exploring larger theoretical issues. The imagery and narrative techniques deployed in television journalism are mechanisms which have the potential of bringing the world closer to viewers on other continents, and making them comfortable with the diversity that characterizes a world of transborder flows. Or they can do precisely the opposite, and strengthen the mechanisms that keep the world at arm's length through Othering practices. What does content tell us about getting the balance 'right'? Many global broadcasters have reasonably extensive archives on their websites, with material that can be used for such analyses. Good companion reading is the anthology edited by Akiba Cohen, *Foreign News on Television: Where in the World is the Global Village?* (Peter Lang, 2013).

Recent Marshall McLuhan anniversaries have yielded retrospectives that speak to this book's change-and-continuity theme. 'Of mediums and messages' can be accessed on the Al Jazeera English website, www.aljazeera.com/programmes/listen-ingpost/2013/04/20134683632515956.html, and a talk on 'McLuhan at 100' by Paul Levinson can be found on YouTube and www.youtube.com/watch?v=FVX5m7P0Zsg). An example of how Hallin & Mancini's concepts and comparative approach can be applied in current technological settings is provided by Matthew Powers and Rodney Benson in an article in the *International Journal of Press/Politics*, 19(2), 2014, entitled 'Is the Internet Homogenizing or Diversifying the News?' (see Bibliography for complete details).

Current facts and figures about audiovisual outlets and use, that can be used in comparative studies of European media, are to be found on the website of the European Audiovisual Observatory (a public-service organization funded by the Council of Europe): www.obs.coe.int.

Researching media power

Two must-read books on media power are Manuel Castells' *Communication Power* (Oxford University Press, 2009) and Nick Couldry's *The Place of Media Power: Pilgrims and Witnesses of the Media Age* (Routledge, 2000). Doris Graber's classic *Media Power in Politics* (CQ Press, 1984) is still available in electronic format. Other useful texts are *Contesting Media Power*, edited by Nick Couldry and James Curran (Rowan & Littlefield, 2003) and Ciaran McCullagh's *Media Power: A Sociological Introduction* (Palgrave, 2002).

For the empirical focus of chapter 2, see Benedetto Brevini, Arne Hintz and Patrick McCurdy (2013) *Beyond WikiLeaks: Implications for the Future of Communications, Journalism and Society* (Houndmills: Palgrave).

The *Guardian* has kept an archive of WikiLeaks-related material, which can be accessed at the www.theguardian.com/media/wikileaks. At the time of publication, WikiLeaks website was still up and running: www.wikileaks.org. Both are excellent sources of empirical material.

Researching political elites

One aspect of the relationship between political elites and journalists that deserves more study is that of gender. To explore this in different national contexts, start with a book by Karin Ross entitled *Women, Politics, Media: Uneasy Relations in Comparative Perspective* (Hampton Press, 2002) and then look for studies such as the following:

Adcock, C. (2010) 'The politician, the wife, the citizen and her newspaper: Rethinking women, democracy and media(ted) representation', *Feminist Media Studies* 10(2): 135–60.

Banwart, M. C., Bystrom, D. G. & Robertson, T. (2003) 'From the primary to the general election: A comparative analysis of candidate media coverage in mixed-gender 2000 races for governor and US senate', *American Behavioral Scientist* 46(5): 658–76.

Braden, M. (1996) *Women, Politicians and the Media*. Lexington: University of Kentucky Press.

Gidengil, E. & Everitt, J. (2005) 'Conventional coverage / unconventional politicians: Gender and media coverage of Canadian leaders' debates 1993, 1997, 2000', *Canadian Journal of Political Science* 36(3): 559–77.

Kahn, K. F. (1994) 'The distorted mirror: Press coverage of women candidates for statewide office', *Journal of Politics* 54: 154–73.

Policy documents, reports, press releases and White Papers published by the European Union are a rich source of primary source materials. Examples include:

- European Broadcasting Union. 'Audiovisual services and GATS negotiations. EUB contribution to the public consultation on requests for access to the EU market', 17 January 2003
- European Commission. 'WTO members' requests to the EC and its Member States for improved market access for services', Consultation Document of 12 November 2002
- European Commission. 'Action plan to improve communicating Europe'. ec.europa.ed
- European Commission. 'On implementing the information and communication strategy for the European Union', Brussels, 20 April, COM(2004)196 final, http://eur-lex.europa.eu/LexUriServ/site/en/com/2004/com2004_0196en01.pdf
- European Commission. 'The Commission's contribution to the period of reflection and beyond: Plan D for Democracy, Dialogue and Debate', COM(2005)494 final. www.ec.europa.eu
- European Commission. 'White Paper on a European communication policy', COM(2006)35 final, ec.europa.eu
- European Parliament and Council. Directive 2007/65/EC, 11 December 2007. *Official Journal of the European Union* L332/27.

A more global source is the website of the International Telecommunications Union (ITU), a UN agency with the mandate to promote connectivity: www.itu.int/en/Pages/default.aspx. For national views, check out the websites of ministries and departments of culture worldwide.

A wide variety of topics suggest themselves for research projects on this aspect of the media–politics relationship. Here are a few suggestions:

- Compare analyses of the DSK affair in media from different countries, using online archives or your local or university library. (You might want to compare DSK reports with those on the Clinton–Lewinsky or similar scandals.) In their interpretation of the issues involved, can different norms pertaining to the media–politics relationship be detected?
- Analyse speeches, press releases and similar communications by political elites and use a framing analysis to explore their perspectives on the problems and potential originating in the changing media landscape. Examples cited in this chapter can be explored in more detail (EC press releases, speech by Admiral Roughead, address to the G8 summit by President Sarkozy, Pope Benedict's speech). A framing analysis, at its most basic, involves posing questions to the text (e.g. a speech): what is the problem (as defined by the speaker); whose problem is it (that of the organization, national government, security services, international community, etc.); and what is the solution?
- Locate policy documents online and do a comparison of the media policies of different states (check the government website or that of the culture minister or equivalent), the EU, UNESCO and so on. Framing analysis could be helpful here too, as policymakers tend to explain their strategies (what is the solution?) after describing the situation (what is the problem?).
- Pick a media event and analyse the image-making of the political leader. (Incidentally, you can see Kennedy's 'Ich bin ein Berliner' speech on YouTube.)
- Search online news reports for the name of a president or prime minister in a given country. How often do details of his or her private life come up and to what effect are they deployed? Compare this with the 'private' components of the public image of a leader in a different political cultural setting.
- Keep an eye on regulatory steps and the public debate about such issues as file-sharing, the FRA law, SOPA, etc. What are the arguments in favour of and against liberalization/restriction? How are they distributed according to the political affiliation of advocate and critics, or across cultures?
- Do a case study of the policy, public or media debate surrounding a media regulation issue – such as Turkish media regulation against the background of the country's EU membership aspirations, the principles involved in media reform in Yemen since the 2011 uprising, or the role of political elites in the UK debate following the Leveson inquiry.

Researching journalists

For further reading on journalism in a global perspective, Silvio Waisbord's *Reinventing Professionalism: Journalism and News in Global Perspective* (Polity, 2013) is a good place to start. An article by Carpentier and Trioen provides a good overview and problematization of the concept of objectivity, and ideas about what sort of material can be used to study it: Carpentier, N. & Trioen, M. (2010) 'The particularity of objectivity: A post-structuralist and psychoanalytical reading of the gap between objectivity-as-a-value and objectivity-as-a-practice in the 2003 Iraqi War coverage', *Journalism* 11(3): 311–28.

Hanitzsch and Mellado ('What shapes the news around the world? How journalists in eighteen countries perceive influences on their work', *International Journal of Press/Politics* 16(3): 408), whose research was reviewed in chapter 4, reasoned as follows: 'If there is such a thing as global homogenization of news work, we would then expect organizational, professional and procedural influences, as well as the influence of reference groups, to be perceived of relatively similar importance across the countries.' Using this expectation as a point of departure, a research project could be designed around the question: does that apply to the country I live, or work, or study in?

Larsen studied how programme directors and the CEOs of news organizations portray the public service mission discursively 'and the institutional reflexivity that is communicated through the institutions' official documents' (Larsen (2010) 'Legitimation strategies of public service broadcasters: The divergent rhetoric in Norway and Sweden', *Media, Culture & Society* 32(2): 269). This was done by combining insights from policy documents with how CEOs talk about their mission – an approach that could be replicated in countries outside the Nordic region. Interviews and surveys can also be used to access differences in values, and thus role perceptions. Data can be generated by asking journalists (or, as did Sanders et al., journalism students - (2008) 'Becoming journalists: A comparison of the professional attitudes and values of British and Spanish journalism students', *European Journal of Communication* 23(2): 133–52) what their background is, why they chose to become a journalist, and what kind, and what their views are on news media role and ethics. Answers can be solicited by telephone, e-mail, skype or freeware like SurveyMonkey.

Many journalists have published memoirs or narratives about a particular experience, and these can be useful sources of insight, and antidotes, in some cases, to scholarly theories about news values. An excellent example is Kate Adie's *The Kindness of Strangers* (London: Headline Publishing, 2002). Other primary source materials are (as mentioned in chapter 4) the motivations of the juries, over time, of the World Press Photo Awards, and the winning photographs themselves. These can be found on the award's website: www.worldpressphoto.org.

Other primary sources that can be used for research on the perspective of media actors include documents (policies, press releases, reports) from organizations such as the European Broadcasting Union (EBU, http://www3.ebu.ch/home) and journalist federations around the world. News content itself is a great, and easily accessible, primary source, which can be studied using any one of a number of methods, such as framing analysis. The book entitled *Doing News Framing Analysis: Empirical and Theoretical Perspectives* by Paul D'Angelo and Jim Kuyper (Taylor & Francis 2010) is a useful guide.

Researching publics and audiences

Which texts you choose for further reading on 'the people formerly known as the audience' depends on which of the perspectives on 'us' surveyed in chapter 5 you might have found most useful or convincing. Follow the references given in that chapter. The anthology edited by Marie Gillespie, entitled *Media Audiences* (Open University, 2005) is very pedagogical, and has been appreciated by many students.

Classics to put on the list include Ien Ang's *Watching Dallas* (Routledge, 1985); Alasuutaari's *Rethinking the Media Audience: The New Agenda* (Sage, 1999); Kirsten

Drotner's 'Media ethnography' (*Communications* 19(1): 87–103, 1994); and David Morley's *The 'Nationwide' Audience* (BFI, 1980).

Questions that can be explored in research on this actor include: what media sites do people turn to first? Do they talk about politics, and if so, how: face-to-face or via some sort of chat site? Are they interested in local, national or global issues? Views on infotainment (do they like *Young Turks* and *The Daily Show*?) and celebrity politics? It is unlikely that most readers of this book will have the opportunity to do large-scale public surveys as part of their research projects. Focus group interviews are a fruitful alternative.

The 1938 broadcast by Orson Welles that had people fleeing the city, terrified that Martians were invading, and which recurs in many accounts of media effects, was called *War of the Worlds* and can be accessed on YouTube: https://www.youtube.com/watch?v=W6YNHq1qc44.

Researching activists

Chapter 6 was about the influence of media forms and texts on political activism, and attempts by scholars to grasp and understand the relationship between media technology and actors, on the one hand, and protesters, on the other, in the context of social and political change. The triptych of mediated dissent presented at the beginning served as a portkey because it pointed to change in power relations under globalization, and highlighted the role of media technology and representation in that relationship. Another portkey is also comprised of primary source material, and as such could form the basis for a research project. A discussion between a journalist – Paul Mason, author of the influential *Why It's Kicking Off Everywhere* and *Why It's Still Kicking Off* – and activist respondents in Occupy Everything provides foot for thought about this relationship. It is a useful exchange, because it deals with the global dimension, is a conversation between journalist and activist(s), and highlights the role of new technology. Both exist in book form, but can also be accessed as blogs:

www.bbc.co.uk/blogs/newsnight/paulmason/2011/02/twenty_reasons_why_its_kic king.html
www.scribd.com/doc/79641340/Occupy-Everything-Reflections-on-why-it's-kicking -off-everywhere.

For further reading on this topic, I would recommend Peter Dahlgren's *Media and Political Engagement: Citizens, Communication and Democracy* (Cambridge University Press, 2009) and Coleman and Blumlers' *The Internet and Democratic Citizenship: Theory, Practice, and Policy* (Cambridge University Press, 2009). Papers presented at social media panels at the European Consortium of Political Research conference in Reykjavik in 2011 included thought-provoking texts by Cammaerts, DeLuca and Peeples, Bennett and Segerberg, Morozov, and Bimber (www.ecpr.eu).

One way of researching mediated activism is to analyse mainstream news reports of protest, and comparing how different protest issues, taking place in different places, fit into the narrative frameworks of media outlets in different political cultures. Events of the last five years provide ample material.

Activist websites comprise another research resource. Analyses could involve inquiring into how they formulate the communicative challenges facing their organization and what strategies they use to overcome them. A good place to start to get ideas is Put People First (www.putpeoplefirst.org.uk). Not to be missed is Anonymous (http://anonnews.org) The appendix in Lim (2013) provides addresses for Malaysian video-sharing websites, for those interested in analysing video activism that advocates human rights and social and political justice (J. B. Y. Lim (2013) 'Video blogging and youth activism in Malaysia', *The International Communication Gazette* 75(3): 300–21). Mishal Husain's documentary on the role of cameras and satphones in the Syrian uprising is still available on the BBC website: www.bbc.co.uk/news/magazine-14914765.

Finally, the researcher interested in mediated activism could take up the gauntlet laid down by Cammaerts, who notes that a crucial aspect of mediation that 'is under-developed and needs to be articulated further' is the relationship between the mediation of protest performances and audiences/publics. We urgently need a more detailed understanding 'of how protest and its mediation is received and decoded in different ways by increasingly fragmented populations; those in whose name protest is often staged' (Cammaerts, (2012) 'Protest logics and the mediation opportunity structure', *European Journal of Communication* 27(2): 131).

Researching mediated conflict

Hoskins and O'Loughlin devote a chapter of *War and Media: The Emergence of Diffused War* (Polity, 2010) to methods: this is a good place to start if you are interested in pursuing this topic further. An article published by Michael Griffin in 2010, 'Media images of war' (*Media, War & Conflict* 3(1): 7–41) contains a useful review of iconic moments in media–military/politics relations in times of war. Also recommended is the March 2014 special issue of *Index on Censorship* (43(1)) devoted to the use of propaganda in war. This and other publications, be they scholarly texts or media reports, that take the 2014–18 centenary of World War I as the point of departure for retrospectives of a century of warfare, provide rich sources of material to write about.

Researching infotainment

Where to start? Secondary sources pertaining to politics and popular culture are to be found in a wide range of scholarly fields and when it comes to primary source material – well, the sky is the limit.

You should read Barthes (*Mythologies*, Vintage, 1957/1993). It's fun, it's a key text, and it's available on several online sites if you google it. An anthology edited by Stuart Hall is also a good introduction to issues of representation that are both political and grounded in the field of cultural studies: *Representation: Cultural Representations and Signifying Practices* (Sage, 2007). Deanna Sellnow's *The Rhetorical Power of Popular Culture* (Sage, 2013) is highly recommended. It is a reader-friendly introduction to the different theories that guide the different analytical approaches to the study of popular culture – not least its political aspects – with examples of student essays that use each approach.

As for more specific topics, a list follows with some suggestions to give you a few ideas. Plunder these authors' reference lists while you're at it.

- on reality TV:
  - Graham, T. & Hajru, A. (2011) 'Reality TV as a trigger of everyday political talk in the net-based public sphere', *European Journal of Communication* 26(1): 18–32
- on political satire:
  - Jones, J. P. & Baym, G. (2010) 'A dialogue on satire news and the crisis of truth in postmodern political television', *Journal of Communication Inquiry* 34(3): 278–94
  - Kuipers, G. (2011) 'The politics of humour in the public sphere: Cartoons, power and modernity in the first transnational humour scandal', *European Journal of Cultural Studies* 14(1): 63–80
  - special issue of *Popular Communication* devoted to political satire around the world (10(1–2))
- on film & television, politics, national identity and globalization:
  - Castelló, E. (2009) 'The nation as a political stage. the theoretical approach to television fiction and national identities', *The International Communication Gazette* 71(4): 303–20
  - Narine, N. (2010) 'Global trauma and narrative cinema', *Theory, Culture & Society* 27(4): 119–45
  - Sachleben, M. & Yenerall, K. M. (2012) *Seeing the Bigger Picture. American and International Politics in Film and Popular Culture.* New York: Peter Lang
  - Shapiro, M. (2009) *Cinematic Geopolitics.* Routledge
  - Wodak, R. (2010) 'The glocalization of politics in television: Fiction or reality?' *European Journal of Cultural Studies* 13(1): 43–62
  - Van Zoonen, L. (2005) *Entertaining the Citizen: When Politics and Popular Culture Converge.* Lanham: Rowman & Littlefield
- on music:
  - Street, J. (2012) *Music & Politics.* Cambridge: Polity.
- on celebrities, media spectacle, charitainment:
  - Nash, K. (2008) 'Global citizenship as show business: The cultural politics of Make Poverty History', *Media, Culture & Society* 30(29): 167–81
- on SF, anthologies by:
  - Hassler, D. M. & Wilcox, C. (2008) *New Boundaries in Political Science Fiction.* Columbia: University of South Carolina Press
  - Nexon, D. & Neuman, I. B. (2006) *Harry Potter and International Relations.* Lanham: Rowman & Littlefield
  - Weldes, J. (2003) *To Seek Out New Worlds: Exploring Links between Science Fiction and World Politics.* Houndmills: Palgrave Macmillan

Check out the films and documentaries mentioned in this appendix – most of them are available on the internet and can be analysed as primary source materials. For the political scientist a bit wary of venturing over to the dark side, terra firma is provided by speeches by politicians and newspaper editorials that can be analysed to suss out popular cultural references and access the 'regimes of representation' these might reveal (Nexon & Neuman 2006). Ask questions such as that posed by Street (2012b): 80): 'what does this or that film or television program communicate about contemporary politics? How is politics portrayed; what sort of values are associated with it?'

Or follow the course charted by van Zoonen & Wring (2012: 276), who point out that we need to know more about the 'particular perceptions, motives and reflections of political fiction screen writers and producers' as well as how audiences intepret politics as a result of the stories they consume through political fiction.

Still stuck for primary sources to analyse? All the episodes of *The XYZ Show*, and information about the independent broadcasting company behind the Kenyan satire, are available online at https://buni.tv/xyzshow. The views, words and actions of prominent poets and writers who use their position as cultural workers to engage in politics can be accessed through PEN International: wwwpen-international.org. Stephen Fry's open letter calling for a boycott of the 2014 Winter Olympics is still of interest, after the flame has been quenched: www.stephenfry.com/2013/08/07/an-open-letter-to-david-cameron-and-the-ioc/.

And do an internet search once a month or so, to see what political cause George Clooney has been arrested for, how he has described his action, and how that has been framed in mainstream media reports.

Researching mediatization

If you are interested in the scholarly views of those who use the 'm-word', an up-to-date volume is the one by H. Kriesi, S. Lavenex, F. Esser, J. Matthes, M. Bühlmann and D. Bochsler, *Democracy in the Age of Globalization and Mediatization* (Houndmills: Palgrave Macmillan, 2013). Another text is the anthology edited by Lundby: *Mediatization: Concept, Changes, Consequences* (Peter Lang, 2009).

If mediatization is a process, and one which unfolds in distinct stages, then historical research is needed, with particular attention to how media technology shapes public debate about politics. Chadwick ('The Hybrid Media System', paper presented at the ECPR General Conference in Reykjavik, 25 August 2011) concluded that 'the construction of political news is now a much more fluid and dynamic process than it was during the heyday of linear broadcast television'. The research agenda he sketches gives some ideas for studies. It involves tracing who does what, when, where and to whom (a difficult but not impossible task, he says); documenting the difference made by discrete actions; conducting detailed narrative case studies to 'capture rich and useful data in this emerging environment' as well as using more quantitative approaches to the same ends.

Above all, work is needed that shows how mediatization theory can be made amenable to meaningful empirical research.

Researching media freedom

John Steel's *Journalism and Free Speech* (Routledge, 2012) is a good place to start if you want to read and think more about this topic. But it can be instructive to work backwards, through classic texts from the Enlightenment (mentioned in chapter 10) to follow this train of thought in a historical context. A key dimension for research here is comparative. Ideas about freedom of expression are rooted in a historical European context: how universal are they, and should they be?

Primary source material can be found on the websites of champions of media freedom:

- Reporters without Borders (https://en.rsf.org) (the *World Press Freedom Index 2014* can be downloaded as a PDF from https://rsf.org/index2014/en-index2014.php)
- Committee to Protect Journalists (https://www.cpj.org)
- *Index on Censorship* (www.indexoncensorship.org). One research focus could be motivations for The Freedom of Expression Awards, which celebrate 'extraordinary people and organizations who are champions to free expression'. Motivations for the 2014 nominees can be accessed at: 'Nominees', www.indexoncensorship.org/freedom-expression-awards-2014/. Another interesting document is the *Index* policy paper: *Time to Step Up: The EU and Freedom of Expression* can be downloaded from indexoncensorship.org. IoC claims the report shows the EU fails to honour the values it claims to uphold
- Freedom House (www.freedomhouse.org)
- the National Hispanic Media Coalition, which monitors hate radio in the US (www.nhmc.org)
- the European Broadcasting Union policy paper on media freedom (http://www3.ebu.ch/files/live/sites/ebu/files/Knowledge/Publication%20Library/EBU-Viewpoint-MediaFreedom_EN.pdf)
- the Open Government Partnership (www.opengovpartnership.org)

Media reaction to the Leveson Report also says a good deal about different actor views on press freedom. See, for example: www.bbc.com/news/uk-21797513.

Finally, the weekly programme *Listening Post*, broadcast by Al Jazeera English and available online and as a podcast, is a good way of keeping up on issues relating to media freedom in parts of the world that may elude your daily field of vision: www.aljazeera.com/programmes/listeningpost.

Notes

1 INTRODUCTION

1 www.itu.com
2 And it is not even Europeans who get to vote in European Parliament elections, but citizens of the nation-states that are members of the European Union.

2 POWER IN MEDIA SOCIETIES

1 It was a quite different sort of problem from his subsequent legal wrangles around accusations of sexual misconduct in Sweden. This chapter does not deal with those events.
2 The issue of freedom of information is explored in more depth in chapter 10.
3 www.guardian.co.uk/world/interactive/2012/jan/26/european-stereotypes-europa
4 www.eurovision.tv.

3 POLITICAL ELITES

1 Other languages have better ways of dealing with the distinction, but the study of political communication has been dominated by native English-speakers, so the linguistic evolution of this word has led to a conceptual evolution beyond North America and the UK as well.
2 He refused, and, at the time of writing, the story could still be accessed on his blog: http://brux elles.blogs.liberation.fr/coulisses/2007/07/fmi-sarkozy-pro.html.
3 Jon Henley, interviewed on *Listening Post*, Al Jazeera English, 4 June 2011; www.aljazeera.com/programmes/listening post.
4 Scholars who have studied the relationship between gender, media and politics have documented how men and women 'attract different kinds of media attention, not just in tone and content but, as importantly, in volume and therefore visibility' (Ross & Comrie 2011: 970).
5 Ron Deibert, Director of the Citizen Lab http://citizenlab.org, and Canada Centre for Global Security Studies, at the Munk School of Global Affairs at the University of Toronto www.munk school.utoronto.ca/canadacentre.
6 E-mail correspondence with a former press secretary to an EU Commissioner.
7 Address at the SIDA Development Talks in Stockholm on 26 October 2011.
8 Anne-Marie Slaughter, former head of political planning at the US State Department and professor of political science and IR at Princeton University, warned in 2012 of work by many regimes to build 'electronic walls' around their citizens in an ongoing information war.

4 JOURNALISTS

1 Mats Svegfors, 'Kvalitetsjournalistiken på snabb reträtt i Sverige', *Dagens Nyheter* debatt, 10 February 2013
2 'Onödigt svarta rubriker', unsigned editorial, *Dagens Nyheter*, 11 February 2013.
3 *South2North*, Al Jazeera English, 11 February 2013, broadcast at 04:30 GMT, www.aljazeera.com/programmes/south2north/2013/02/201325114146879356.html.
4 Ryan Gallagher, 'Defence giant builds "Google for spies" to track social networking users', *Guardian,* 11 February 2013.
5 Revelations that reporters working for Rupert Murdoch's *News of the World* had unlawfully and unethically tapped the phones of politicians, celebrities and ordinary people (including a kidnapped schoolgirl later found dead) threw British journalism into disarray in 2011 and led to a public inquiry headed by Lord Justice Leveson, that recommended restrictions on the freedom

of journalists. The influential 1980s current affairs satire *Spitting Image* carried a sketch in which newspaper reporters were depicted as pigs that wore raincoats, carried shorthand notebooks, turned over unsuspecting victims, and behaved obsequiously towards owners and editors who swore and bullied. The image found its way back into public debate as a result of the Newscorp scandal (see Barnett 2011: 14–15).

6   Public trust in the BBC suffered a blow when it was established in 2012 that television personality Jimmy Savile was a serial abuser, and that the BBC had been aware of such claims but had stopped a *Newsnight* investigation that would have clashed with a Savile tribute, scheduled for Christmas 2011, shortly after his death.

7   Roger Tooth, photo editor of the *Guardian*, interviewed on *Listening Post*, Al Jazeera, 24 November 2011.

8   Mohammed Safi was speaking at a seminar at the Swedish Institute of International Affairs in Stockholm, 22 November 2012.

9   Interview conducted by Nika Bender.

10 https:/www.cpj.org, https://en.rsf.org. This problem will be returned to in chapter 10.

5 THE PEOPLE FORMERLY KNOWN AS THE AUDIENCE

1   www.youtube.com/watch?v=oP-rkzJ6yZw.

2   Susan Stein, interviewed by Michael Buerk on 'The Eye of the Storm', a documentary written and presented by Michael Buerk for the Australian Broadcasting Corporation, first broadcast in 1993 and subsequently aired by broadcasters throughout the world.

3   (The news junkie is a close relative of the 'monitorial citizen', who expends considerable energy in keeping abreast of breaking news, but who is better at 'surveilling' the information environment than acquiring purposeful knowledge (Schudson 1998: 310).

6 ACTIVISTS

1   The *Time Magazine* representation of the protester can be seen here: http://content.time.com/time/person-of-the-year/2011/

2   'Twenty reasons why it's kicking off everywhere', www.bbc.co.uk/blogs/newsnight/paul mason/2011/02/twenty_reasons_why_its_kicking.html.

3   Elisa Davoglio, activist, quoted in Hultquist (2011).

4   The platform is hosted by a company based in California. According to the media director of the company that bought LiveJournal, Anton Nosik, Russian police can check up on the blogger if the blog has a Russian host, but can't get to blogs on LiveJournal without approaching their counterparts in Sacramento. 'The typical answer from the state of California is: "no can do"' (quoted in Greenall 2012).

5   See DeLuca and Peeples (2002: 127) for an interesting list overview of its various appearances.

6   The point was made in the call for a workshop on transnational protest, which was convened by Donatella della Porta and Alice Mattoni.

7 MEDIATED CONFLICT

1   Jodi Bieber interviewed on *Listening Post*, Al Jazeera English, 24 November 2011.

2   Ibid.

3   Griffin (2010: 9) makes the point about textbooks. Hallin (1986) is among those who argue that television news, which 'loves drama', requires conflict. Hess (1996) and Perlmutter (1998) maintain that violence – not least visual evidence – is what makes news most newsworthy.

4   A full transcript of a videotaped speech can still be found on the Al Jazeera website, www.aljazeera.com/archive/2004/11/200849163336457223.html.

5   This refers to the attack, on 26–27 February 1991, on retreating Iraqi military personnel and others escaping Kuwait, by US and Canadian forces.

8 INFOTAINMENT

1   The series was, in fact, originally aired in 1978. References to *Battlestar Galactica* in this chapter – and the vast majority of the scholarly literature on the subject – are to the more influential and popular remake that aired from 2004 to 2009. The episode opening this chapter is 'Kobol's Last Gleaming', part 2, season 1.

2 Cultural artefacts from the latter two political contexts, Sergei Eisenstein's *Battleship Potemkin* (1925) and Leni Riefenstahl's *Triumph des Willens* (1935) can both be viewed in their entirety on YouTube.

3 www.youtube.com/watch?v=kEO2Rd3sJbA, www.youtube.com/watch?v=LyDOAQNsTrI.

4 The number varies depending on the day and the search engine, but it is never small.

5 www.looktothestars.org/charity/make-poverty-history.

6 Rula Amin, Al Jazeera, www.aljazeera.com/news/middleeast/2013/06/201362219549114855.html.

7 www.youtube.com/watch?v=6TiXUF9xbTo.

8 www.xyzshow.com,http://zanews.co.za. Another example is Jeff Dunham's puppet 'Achmed the Dead Terrorist'. Martin (2011: 235) argues that 'Achmed is rendered palatable as a tool of humor and critique by his already-dead status. He cannot constitute a danger – or make the audience uncomfortable – if he is already deceased.' He is an example of how terrorism has been reflected in popular culture in the last decade in various ways (2011: 233).

9 Young & Tisinger (2006) found that watching *The Daily Show* complements and reinforces rather than substitutes for traditional news consumption (Delli Carpini 2012: 14). Holbert et al. (2007) found, on the basis of experimental research, that the order of watching *The Daily Show* and the ordinary news (CNN) affected the gratification participants received from the latter.

10 For the importance of the internet to Grillo's success see also Hooper (2013).

11 www.pen-international.org/newsitems/leading-international-writers-join-pen-in-calling-for-greater-freedom-of-expression-in-turkey.

9 MEDIATIZATION

1 All quotations in the Eichmann trial 'portkey' are taken from their excellent 'Severed Voices' essay; see Bibliography for complete details.

2 Hjarvard was speaking at a research seminar at the Department of Journalism, Media and Communication, Stockholm University, 14 October 2010.

10 MEDIA FREEDOM

1 Matthew Duss, Center for American Progress, interview on Al Jazeera's *Listening Post*.

2 www.aljazeera.com/programmes/listeningpost.

3 www.handelsblatt.com/unternehmen/it-medien/waz-gruppe-konzernchef-hombach-sagt-dem-balkan-ade/3505254.html.

4 An excerpt from the programme, 'Män som näthatar kvinnor', the name of which is a paraphrase of the original Swedish title of Stieg Larsson's crime thriller *The Girl with the Dragon Tatoo* (literally 'Men Who Hate Women') can be seen on YouTube: https://www.youtube.com/watch?v=k_pLmq8d7Mk. An official version with English subtitles, entitled 'Surfing the Web of Hate' can be obtained at http://svtsales.com/programme-sales/surfing-the-web-of-hate.

5 www.itu.int/en/wcit-12/Pages/default.aspx.

11 CONCLUSION

1 The Swedish word *granska* does not translate easily into English: 'scrutinize' is often used, but this suggests something more scholarly, less active and engaged than the practice of *granskande journalistik*. What is almost always invoked by this term is the 'watchdog' role of the journalist. The text was published on 12 June 2013.

Bibliography

Abercrombie, N. & Longhurst, B. (1998) *Audiences: Towards a Theory of Performance and Imagination*. London: Sage.

Adams, W. C. (1986) 'Whose lives count? Television coverage of natural disasters', *Journal of Communication* 36: 113–22.

Adcock, C. (2010) 'The politician, the wife, the citizen and her newspaper: Rethinking women, democracy and media(ted) representation', *Feminist Media Studies* 10(2): 135–60.

Ahlin, P. (2004) 'Den globaliserade fotbollen är lokal', *Dagens Nyheter*, 14 February, p. A2.

Adie, K. (2002) *The Kindness of Strangers*. London: Headline Publishing.

Aitkenhead, D. (2014) 'David Hare: "The security services are running the country, aren't they?"', *The Guardian*, 21 February.

AJE (2014) 'Turkey: The media sub-plot', Al Jazeera English, *Listening Post*, 25 January, www.aljazeera.com/programmes/listeningpost/2014/01/turkey-media-sub-plot-201412575710632142.html.

AJE (2013) 'More than one million join Brazil protests', www.aljazeera.com/news/americas/2013/06/201362022328194879.html.

AJE (2011a) 'Help Al Jazeera to search WikiLeaks cables', http://english.aljazeera.net/news/americas/2011/09/20119214591524307.html.

AJE (2011b) 'About the Transparency Unit', http://transparency.aljazeera.net/en.

AJE (2010a) 'Corporate profile', http://english.aljazeera.net/aboutus/2006/11/2008525185555444449.html.

AJE (2010b) 'Code of ethics', http://english.aljazeera.net/aboutus/2006/11/2008525185733692771.html.

Akhtar, S. (2013) 'Celebrities add colour to Indian politics', Al Jazeera, 20 October, http://www.aljazeera.com/indepth/2013/10/celebrities-add-colour-indian-politics-2013101415415991691.html, accessed 25 February 2014.

Al-Sadi, M. (2012) 'Al Jazeera Television: Rhetoric of deflection', *Arab Media*, 15, Spring, www.arabmediasociety.com/?article=786.

Alasuutaari, P. (ed.) (1999) *Rethinking the Media Audience*. London: Sage.

Alexander, J., Giesen, B. & Mast, J. L. (eds.) (2006) *Social Performance*. Cambridge: Cambridge University Press.

Allan, S. & Thorsen, E. (2011) 'Journalism, public service and BBC News Online', in G. Meikle & G. Redden (eds.) *News Online: Transformations and Continuities*. Houndmills: Palgrave Macmillan, pp. 20–37.

Allern, S. (2011) 'PR, politics and democracy', *Central European Journal of Communication* 4, No. 1 (6): 125–39.

Allern, S. & Pollack, E. (eds.) (2012) *Scandalous! The Mediated Construction of Political Scandals in Four Nordic Countries*. Gothenburg: Nordicom.

Al Maskati, N. A. (2012) 'Newspaper coverage of the 2011 protests in Egypt', *The International Communication Gazette* 74(4): 342–66.

Althaus, S. L. (2003) 'When news norms collide, follow the lead: New evidence for press independence', *Political Communication* 20(3): 381–414.

Altheide, D. (2006) *Terrorism and the Politics of Fear*. Lanham: AltaMira Press.

Altheide, D. L. & Snow, R. P. (1988) 'Toward a theory of mediation', in J. A. Anderson (ed.) *Communication Yearbook* 11: 194–223.

Altheide, D. L. & Snow, R. P. (1979) *Media Logic*. Beverly Hills: Sage.

Åman, J. (2011a) 'Revolutioner: Ny teknik tjänar även diktatorer', *Dagens Nyheter*, 13 February, p. 2.

Åman, J. (2011b) 'Internet: Inget område för biståndsamatörism', *Dagens Nyheter*, 18 February, p. 2.

Amay, H. (2010) 'Citizenship, diversity, law and *Ugly Betty*', *Media, Culture & Society* 32(5): 801–17.

Andén-Papadopoulos, K. (2009) 'Body horror on the internet: US soldiers recording the war in Iraq and Afghanistan', *Media, Culture & Society* 31: 921–38.

Andén-Papadopoulos, K. & Pantti, M. (eds.) (2011) *Amateur Images and Global News*. London: Intellect Press.

Anderson, B. (1983/2006) *Imagined Communities*. London and New York: Verso.

Anderson, N. (2011) 'Tweeting tyrants out of Tunisia: the global internet at its best', *Ars Technica* 15 January, http://arstechnica.com.

Andrejevic, M. (2007) 'Surveillance in the digital enclosure', *The Communication Review* 10: 295–317.

Andrews, K. & Briggs, M. (2006) 'The dynamics of protest diffusion: Movement organization, social networks and news media in the 1960 sit-ins', *American Sociological Review* 71(5): 752–77.

Ang, I. (1985) *Watching Dallas*. London: Routledge.

Ankersmit, F. (1996) *Aesthetic Politics*. Stanford: Stanford University Press.

Anonymous (2011) 'Anonymous and the global correction', www.aljazeera.com/indepth/opinion/2011/02/201121321487750509.html.

Anstead, N. & O'Loughlin, B. (2011) 'The emerging viewertariat and BBC *Question Time*: television debate and real-time commenting online', *The International Journal of Press/Politics* 16(4): 440–62.

Antony, M. G. & Thomas, R. J. (2010) '"This is citizen journalism at its finest": YouTube and the public sphere in the Oscar Grant shooting incident', *New Media & Society* 12(8): 1280–96.

Appadurai, A. (1996) *Modernity at Large: Cultural Dimensions of Globalisation*. London: University of Minnesota Press.

Ashuri, T. (2006) 'Television tension: National versus cosmopolitan memory in a co-produced television documentary', *Media, Culture and Society* 29(1): 31–51.

Asp, K. (1986) *Mäktiga massmedier: studier i politisk opinionsbildning*. Stockholm: Akademilitteratur.

Atton, C. & Mabweazara, H. (2011) 'New media and journalism practice in Africa: An agenda for research', *Journalism* 12(6): 667–73.

Auter, P. J., Arafa, M. & Al-Jaber, K. (2005) 'Identifying with Arabic journalists. How Al-Jazeera tapped parasocial interaction gratifications in the Arab world', *Gazette: The International Journal for Communication Studies* 67(2): 189–204.

Axford, B. (2013) *Theories of Globalization*. Cambridge: Polity.

Axford, B. & and Huggins, R. (2007) 'The European information society: A new public sphere?' in C. Rumford (ed.) *Cosmopolitanism and Europe*. Liverpool: Liverpool University Press.

Ayed, N. (2013) 'Egyptian comedian tests the limits of post-revolution satire', CBC News online, 3 March, www.cbc.ca/newsworld/egyptian-comedian-tests-the-limits-of-post-revolution-satire-1.1333984.

Babak, B. (2007) *The CNN Effect in Action: How the News Media Pushed the West Toward War in Kosovo*. Basingstoke: Palgrave Macmillan.

Bachrach, P. & Baratz, M. S. (1962) 'Two faces of power', *The American Political Science Review* 56(4): 947–52.

Bagdikian, B. (2004) *The New Media Monopoly*. Boston: Beacon Press.

Bahry, L.Y. (2001) 'The new Arab media phenomenon: Qatar's Al-Jazeera', *Middle East Policy* 8(2): 88–99.

Bailey, M. (2007) 'Rethinking public service broadcasting: The historical limits to publicness', in R. Butsch (ed.) *Media and Public Spheres*. Houndmills: Palgrave Macmillan, pp. 96–108.

Bakir, V. (2011) 'Torture and intelligence in the War on Terror: The struggle over strategic political communication', *Global Media and Communication* 7(3): 239–43.

Balabanova, E. & Balch, A. (2010) 'Sending and receiving: The ethical framing of intra-EU migration in the European press', *European Journal of Communication* 25(4): 382–97.

Banaji, S. & Al-Ghabban, A. (2006) '"Neutrality comes from inside us": British-Asian and Indian perspectives on television news after 11 September', *Journal of Ethnic and Migration Studies* 32(6): 1005–26.

Banwart, M. C., Bystrom, D. G. & Robertson, T. (2003) 'From the primary to the general election: A comparative analysis of candidate media coverage in mixed-gender 2000 races for governor and US senate', *American Behavioral Scientist* 46(5): 658–76.

Barker, C. (1999) *Television, Globalization and Cultural Identities*. Buckingham: Open University Press.

Barkman, C. (2011) 'En räddare i nöden', *Dagens Nyheter*, 20 March, pp. B2–3.

Barn, R. (2013) 'Social media and protest – the Indian Spring?' Huffington Post, 9 January, www. huffingtonpost.co.uk/professor-ravinder-barn/india-social-media-and-protest_b_2430194.html.

Barnett, S. (2011) 'Crusaders or pigs in raincoats?' *British Journalism Review* 22(3): 13–15.

Barnhurst, K. G. (2011) 'The new "media affect" and the crisis of representation for political communication', *International Journal of Press/Politics* 16(4): 573–93.

Barthes, R. (1957/1993) *Mythologies*. London: Vintage.

Baudrillard, J. (1991/1995) *The Gulf War Did Not Take Place*. Bloomington:Indiana University Press.

Baum, M. & Potter, P. (2008) 'The relationship between mass media, public opinion and foreign policy: Toward a theoretical synthesis', *Annual Review of Political Science* 11: 39–66.

Bauman, Z. (2007) *Liquid Times*. Cambridge: Polity.

Baumann, G., Gillespie, M. & Sreberny, A. (2011) 'Transcultural journalism and the politics of translation: Interrogating the BBC World Service', *Journalism* 12(2): 135–42.

Baumgartner, J. C. & Morris, J. S. (2006) 'The *Daily Show* effect: Candidate evaluations, efficacy, and american youth', *American Politics Research* 34(3): 341–67.

Baym, G. (2010) *From Cronkite to Colbert: The Evolution of Broadcast News*. Boulder: Paradigm Publishers.

Baym, G. (2005) '*The Daily Show*: Discursive integration and the reinvention of political journalism', *Political Communication* 22 (3): 259–76.

BBC (2012a) 'US "launched Flame cyber attack on Sarkozy's office"', www.bbc.co.uk/news/world-europe-20429704, 21 November 2012.

BBC (2011a) 'Anger as Wikileaks releases all US cables unredacted', http://news.bbc.co.uk/news/world-us-canada-14765837?print=true.

BBC (2011b) 'Google chairman warns of censorship after Arab Spring', www.bbc.co.uk/news/world-us-canada-13935470?print=true.

BBC (2011c) 'Russian Twitter political protests "swamped by spam"', www.bbc.co.uk/news/technology-16108876.

BBC (2011d) 'Journalists' killings "go unpunished" in 13 countries', www.bbc.co.uk/news/world-us-canada-13611500, 1 June.

BBC (2010) 'France considers Google tax plan', http://news.bbc.co.uk/go/pr/fr/-/2/hi/technology/8448389.stm, 8 January.

Beck, U. (2006) *The Cosmopolitan Vision*. Cambridge: Polity.

Beck, U. (2002) 'The silence of words and political dynamics in the world risk society', *Logos* 1(4): 1–18.

Becker, K. (1996) 'Pictures in the press: Yesterday, today, tomorrow', in U. Carlsson (ed.) *Medierna i samhället: Igår, idag, imorgon*. Gothenburg: Nordicom Sverige, pp. 177–200.

Beckett, A. (2014) 'Tony Blair: From New Labour hero to political embarrassment', *The Guardian*, 26 February, www.theguardian.com/politics/2014/feb/26/tony-blair-new-labour-hero-political-embarrassment-murdoch.

Benedict XVI (2011) 'Truth, proclamation and authenticity of life in the digital age', www.vatican.va/holy_father/benedict_xvi/messages/communications/documents/hf_ben-xvi_mes_20110124_45th-world-communications-day_en.html.

Benjamin, W. (1936) 'The work of art in the age of mechanical reproduction', www.marxists.org/reference/subject/philosophy/works/ge/benjamin.htm.

Benkler, Y. (2006) *The Wealth of Networks: How Social Production Transforms Markets and Freedoms*. New Haven, CT: Yale University Press.

Bennett, T. (2005) 'The media sensorium: Cultural technologies, the senses and society', in M. Gillespie (ed.) *Media Audiences*. Maidenhead: Open University Press, pp. 51–96.

Bennett, W. L. (2014) 'Press–government relations in a changing media environment', in K. Kenski &

K. H. Jamieson (eds.) *The Oxford Handbook of Political Communication*. Oxford: Oxford University Press.

Bennett, W. L. (2010) Inaugural lecture, Olof Palme Professorship, Dept of Political Science, Stockholm University.

Bennett, W. L. (2004) *News: The Politics of Illusion*. New York, Longman.

Bennett, W. L. (2003a) 'New media power: The internet and global activism', in N. Couldry & J. Curran (eds.) *Contesting Media Power: Alternative Media in a Networked World*. Lanham: Rowman and Littlefield, pp. 17–38.

Bennett, W. L. (2003b) 'Communicating global activism: Strengths and vulnerabilities of networked politics', *Information, Communication & Society* 6(2): 143–68.

Bennett, W. L. (1990) 'Toward a theory of press–state relations in the US', *Journal of Communication* 40(2): 103–27.

Bennett, W. L. & Paletz, D. L. (eds.) (1994) *Taken by Storm: The Media, Public Opinion, and US Foreign Policy in the Gulf War*. Chicago: University of Chicago Press.

Bennett, W. L. & Segerberg, A. (2013) *The Logic of Connective Action. Digital Media and the Personalization of Contentious Politics*. Cambridge: Cambridge University Press.

Bennett, W. L. & Segerberg, A. (2012) 'The logic of connective action: Digital media and the personalization of contentious politics', *Information, Communication & Society* 15(5): 739–68.

Bennett, W. L. & Segerberg, A. (2011) 'Digital media and the personalization of collective action: Social technology and the organization of protests against the global economic crisis', *Information, Communication & Society* 14(6): 770–99.

Bennett, W. L. & Segerberg, A. (2009) *Collective Action Dilemmas with Individual Mobilization through Digital Networks*. Center for Communication and Civic Engagement Working Paper 2. Seattle: University of Washington, http://ccce.com.washington.edu/projects/assets/working_papers/Bennett_Segerberg_CCCE.WP.pdf

Bennett, W. L., Breunig, C. & Givens, T. (2008) 'Communication and political mobilization: Digital media use and protest organization among anti-Iraq war demonstrators in the U.S.', *Political Communication* 25: 269–89.

Bennett, W. L., Freelon, D. G., Hussain, M. H. & Wells, C. (2012) 'Digital media and youth engagement', in H. Semetko & M. Scammell (eds.) *The Sage Handbook of Political Communication*. London: Sage, pp. 127–40.

Bennett-Jones, O. (2011) 'How cameras hidden in pens outflanked the Syrian regime', BBC News, http://newsvote.bbc.co.uk/mpapps/pagetools/print/news.bbc.co.uk/2/hi/programmes/from_our_own_correspondent/9470481.stm.

Benson, R. (2010) 'What makes for a critical press? A case study of French and U.S. immigration news coverage', *International Journal of Press/Politics* 15(1): 3–24.

Benson, R. (2005) 'Mapping field variation: Journalism in France and the United States', in R. Benson & E. Neveu (eds.) *Bourdieu and the Journalistic Field*. Cambridge: Polity, pp. 85–112.

Benson, R. & Hallin, D. (2007) 'How states, markets and globalization shape the news: The French and US national press, 1965–97', *European Journal of Communication* 22(1): 27–48.

Benson, R. & Neveu, E. (2005) 'Introduction: Field theory as a work in progress', in R. Benson & E. Neveu (eds.) *Bourdieu and the Journalistic Field*. Cambridge: Polity, pp. 1–28.

Berger, G. (2011) 'Empowering the youth as citizen journalists: A South African experience', *Journalism* 12(6): 708–26.

Berger, G. (2009) 'How the internet impacts on international news: Exploring paradoxes of the most global medium in a time of "hyperlocalism"', *The International Communication Gazette* 71(5): 355–71.

Berlin, I. (1969) *Four Essays on Liberty*. Oxford: Oxford University Press.

Beutin, L. (2012) 'When artists are out of work: Handmade Protest Signs in the Digital Revolution Era'. Paper presented at the ICA, Phoenix, 25 May.

Biltereyst, D. & Meers, P. (2011) 'The political economy of audiences', in J. Wasko, G. Murdock & H. Sousa (eds.) *The Handbook of Political Economy of Communication*. Oxford: Blackwell, pp. 415–35.

Bimber, B. (2012) 'Digital media and citizenship', in H. Semetko & M. Scammell (eds.) *The Sage Handbook of Political Communication*. London: Sage, pp. 115–26.

Bimber, B., Flanagin, A. & Stohl, C. (2005) 'Reconceptualizing collective action in the contemporary media environment', *Communication Theory* 15(4): 365–88.

Bjurwald, L. (2011) 'Public service: Äntligen på väg mot framtiden', *Dagens Nyheter*, www.dn.se/ledare/signerat/public-service-antligen-pa-vag-mot-framtiden.

Blondheim, M. & Liebes, T. (2009) 'Television news and the nation: The end?' *The ANNALS of the American Academy of Political and Social Science*, 625(1): 182–95.

Blumler, J. G. & Gurevitch, M. (1995) *The Crisis of Public Communication*. London: Routledge.

Blumler, J. G. & Gurevitch, M. (1981) 'Politics and the press: An essay in role relationships', in D. Nimmo & K. Sanders (eds.) *Handbook of Political Communication*. Beverley Hills: Sage, pp. 467–93.

Blumler, J. G. & Kavanagh, D. (1999) 'The third age of political communication: Influences and features', *Political Communication* 16(3): 209–30.

Borger, J. (2013) 'NSA files: why the Guardian in London destroyed hard drives of leaked files', *The Guardian*, 20 August.

Bore, I.-L. (2011) 'Transnational TV comedy audiences', *Television & New Media* 12(4): 347–69.

Booth, P. (2010) *Digital Fandom*. New York: Peter Lang.

Boudana, S. (2011) 'A definition of journalistic objectivity as a performance', *Media, Culture & Society* 33(3): 385–98.

Boudana, S. (2010) "On the values guiding the French practice of journalism: Interviews with thirteen war correspondents", *Journalism* 11(3): 293–310.

Bourdieu, P. (2005) 'The political field, the social science field, and the journalistic field', in Benson, R. & Neveu, E. (eds.) *Bourdieu and the Journalistic Field*. Cambridge: Polity, pp. 29–47.

Bourdon, J. (2007) 'Unhappy engineers of the European soul: The EBU and the woes of pan-European television', *The International Communication Gazette* 69(3): 263–80.

Boyd-Barret, O. (2010) 'Assessing the prospects for an Asian re-configuration of the global news order', *Global Media and Communication* 6(3): 346–56.

Boyd-Barret, O. (2004) 'Judith Miller, The *New York Times* and the propaganda model', *Journalism Studies* 5(4): 435–49.

Boyle, J. (2003) 'The second enclosure movement and the construction of the public domain', *Law and Contemporary Problems* 66: 33–74.

Braden, M. (1996) *Women, Politicians and the Media*. Lexington: University of Kentucky Press.

Bradshaw, P. (2012) '*Innocence of Muslims*: a dark demonstration of the power of film', *The Guardian*, www.guardian.co.uk/film/filmblog/2012/sep/17/innocence-of-muslims-demonstration-film.

Braman, S. (2010) 'Mediating the public through policy', in Papathanassopoulos, S. & Negrine, R. (eds.) *Communications Policy: Theories and Issues*. Basingstoke: Palgrave Macmillan, pp. 22–48.

Brand, R. (2013) 'We no longer have the luxury of tradition', *New Statesman*, 24 October, www.newstatesman.com/politics/2013/10/russell-brand-on-revolution.

Brants, K. (1998) 'Who's afraid of infotainment?' *European Journal of Communication* 13(3): 313–35.

Brants, K., de Vrees, C., Möller, J. & Van Praag, P. (2010) 'The real spiral of cynicism? Symbiosis and mistrust between politicians and journalists', *International Journal of Press/Politics* 15(1): 25–40.

Brors, H. (2010) 'Ambassadörens okunnighet det pinsamma i avslöjandet', *Dagens Nyheter*, 3 December, p. 10.

Brown, M. & Michaels, S. (2014) 'Elton John to Putin: I will show you gay people victimised under Russian law', *The Guardian*, 23 January, www.theguardian.com/world/2014/jan/23/elton-john-vladimir-putin-russian-gay-legislation.

Brevini, B. (2010) 'Towards PSB 2.0? Applying the PSB ethos to online media in Europe: A comparative study of PSBs' internet policies in Spain, Italy and Britain', *European Journal of Communication* 25(4): 348–65.

Brevini, B., Hintz, A. & McCurdy, P. (2013) *Beyond WikiLeaks: Implications for the Future of Communications, Journalism and Society*. Houndmills: Palgrave.

Brewer, P. R. (2006) 'National interest frames and public opinion about world affairs', *Press/Politics* 11(4): 89–102.

Brors, H. (2011) 'Ungern ändrar sin medielag', *Dagens Nyheter*, 17 February.

Brown, S. (2003) *Crime and Law in Media Culture*. Buckingham: Open University Press.

Brüggeman, M. (2005) 'How the EU constructs the European public sphere', *Javnost – The Public* 12(2): 57–74.

Brundson, C. & Morley, D. (1978) *Everyday Television: Nationwide*. London: British Film Institute.

Bruns, A. (2011) 'News produsage in a pro-am mediasphere: why citizen journalism matters', in G. Meikle & G. Redden (eds.) *News Online: Transformations and Continuities*. Houndmills: Palgrave Macmillan, pp. 132–47.

Bryne, C. (2003) 'War reporting "changed forever" says the BBC', www.guardian.co.uk/media/2003/mar/31/iraqandthemedia.iraq.

Buckingham, D. (2000) *The Making of Citizens: Young People, News and Politics*. London: Routledge.

Burns, M. & N. Brügger (eds.) (2012) *Histories of Public Service Broadcasters on the Web*. New York: Peter Lang.

Butsch, R. (ed.) (2007) *Media and Public Spheres*. Houndmills: Palgrave Macmillan.

Cammaerts, B. (2012) 'Protest logics and the mediation opportunity structure', *European Journal of Communication* 27(2). 117–34.

Campus, D. (2010) 'Mediatization and personalization of politics in Italy and France: The cases of Berlusconi and Sarkozy', *International Journal of Press/Politics* 15(2): 219–35.

Cao, X. (2008) 'Political comedy shows and knowledge about primary campaigns: The moderating effects of age and education', *Mass Communication & Society* 11(1): 43–61.

Cappella, J. & Jamieson, K. H. (1997) *Spiral of Cynicism: The Press and the Public Good*. Oxford: Oxford University Press.

Carey, J. W. (1992) *Communication as Culture*. London: Routledge.

Carpenter, S. (2010) 'A study of content diversity in online citizen journalism and online newspaper articles', *New Media & Society* 12(7): 1064–84.

Carpentier, N. (2011) *Media and Participation. A Site of Ideological–Democratic Struggle*. Bristol: Intellect Books.

Carpentier, N. & Trioen, M. (2010) 'The particularity of objectivity: A post-structuralist and psycho-analytical reading of the gap between objectivity-as-a-value and objectivity-as-a-practice in the 2003 Iraqi War coverage', *Journalism* 11(3): 311–28.

Carruthers, S. L. (2000) *The Media at War: Communication and Conflict in the Twentieth Century*. Basingstoke: Palgrave Macmillan.

Cassel, M. (2013) 'Concern for free speech in Egypt', Al Jazeera, 6 July, www.aljazeera.com/indepth/features/2013/07/20137613173543260.html.

Castelló, E. (2009) 'The nation as a political stage. The theoretical approach to television fiction and national identities', *The International Communication Gazette* 71(4): 303–20.

Castells, M. (2012) *Networks of Outrage and Hope*. Cambridge: Polity.

Castells, M. (2009) *Communication Power*. Oxford: Oxford University Press.

Castells, M. (2007) 'Communication, power and counter-power in the network society', *International Journal of Communication* 1(1): 238–66.

Castells, M. (2000) 'Materials for an exploratory theory of the network society', *British Journal of Sociology* 51(1): 5–24.

Castells, M. (1998) *End of Millenium*. Oxford: Blackwell.

Castells, M. (1997) *The Power of Identity*. Oxford: Blackwell.

Castells, M. (1996) *The Rise of the Network Society*. Oxford: Blackwell.

Chadwick, A. (2011) 'The Hybrid Media System'. Paper presented at the ECPR General Conference in Reykjavik, 25 August.

Chadwick, A. (2009) 'Web 2.0: New challenges for the study of e-democracy in an era of informational exuberance', *I/S: A Journal of Law and Policy for the Information Society* 5(1): 11–41.

Chadwick, A. (2006) *Internet Politics: States, Citizens, and New Communication Technologies*. Oxford and New York: Oxford University Press.

Chalaby, J. (2010) 'The rise of Britain's super-indies: Policy-making in the age of the global market', *The International Communication Gazette* 72(8): 675–93.

Chalaby, J. K. (2009) *Transnational Television in Europe: Reconfiguring Global Communications Networks*. London: I. B. Taurus.

Chalaby, J. K. (2005) *Transnational Television Worldwide: Towards a New Media Order*. London: I. B. Taurus.

Champagne, P. (2005) 'The "double dependency": The journalistic field between politics and markets', in R. Benson & E. Neveu (eds.) *Bourdieu and the Journalistic Field*. Cambridge: Polity, pp. 48–63.

Champagne, P. & Marchetti, D. (2005) 'The contaminated blood scandal: Reframing medical news', in R. Benson & E. Neveu (eds.) *Bourdieu and the Journalistic Field*. Cambridge: Polity, pp. 113–34.

Chan, J. M. & Lee, C. C. (1984) 'The journalistic paradigm on civil protests: A case study of Hong Kong', in A. Arno & W. Dissanayake (eds.) *The News Media in National and International Conflict*. Boulder: Westview Press, pp. 183–202.

Chang, T.-K., Southwell, B., Lee, H. M., & Hong, Y. (2012) 'A changing world, unchanging perspectives: American newspaper editors and enduring values in foreign news reporting', *The International Communication Gazette* 74(4): 367–84.

Charles, N. & Smith, D. (2010) 'Editorial introduction: Imagining the political', *The Sociological Review* 58(4): 527–9.

Chouliaraki, L. (2006) *The Spectatorship of Suffering*. London: Sage.

Christensen, C. (2012) 'Thoughts on revolution, state aid and liberation technologies', *Irish Studies in International Affairs* 23(1): 37–45.

Christensen, C. (2011) "Wikileaks: Losing suburbia", *Le Monde Diplomatique*, 5 September, http://mondediplo.com/blogs/wikileaks-losing-suburbia.

Christensen, C. (2010) 'Three digital myths', *Le Monde Diplomatique*, 9 August, http://mondediplo.com/blogs/three-digital-myths.

Christensen, C. (2008) 'Uploading dissonance: YouTube and the US occupation of Iraq', *Media, War & Conflict* 1(2): 155–75.

Christensen, M. (2010) 'Notes on the public sphere on a national and post-national axis: Journalism and freedom of expression in Turkey', *Global Media and Communication* 6(2): 177–97.

Chulov, M. (2013) 'Wife breaks silence over Spanish journalist's kidnap in Syria', *The Guardian*, 10 December, www.theguardian.com/world/2013/dec/10/spanish-journalist-javier-espinosa-kidnap-syria

Ciaglia, A. (2013) 'Politics in the media and media in politics: A comparative study of the relationship between the media and political systems in three European countries', *European Journal of Communication* 28(5): 541–55.

Clark, A. M. & Werder, O. (2007) 'Analyzing international radio stations', *The International Communication Gazette* 69(6): 525–37.

Clark, J. S. (2009) 'Liberating bicentennial America: Imagining the nation through TV superwomen of the seventies', *Television & New Media* 10(5): 434–54.

Clark, L. S. (2009) 'Theories: Mediatization and media ecology', in K. Lundby (ed.) *Mediatization: Concept, Changes, Consequences*. New York: Peter Lang, pp. 85–100.

Clausen, L. (2004) 'Localizing the global: "Domestication" processes in international news production'. *Media, Culture and Society* 26(1): 25–44.

Clinton, H. R. (2010) 'Remarks on internet freedom', address at the Newseum, Washington, 21 January, www.state.gov/secretary/rm/2010/01/135519.htm.

Cohen, A. (2013) *Foreign News on Television: Where in the World is the Global Village?* New York: Peter Lang.

Cohen, B.C. (1963) *The Press and Foreign Policy*. Princeton: Princeton University Press.

Cohen, N. (2012) *You Can't Read This Book: Censorship in an Age of Freedom*. London: Fourth Estate.

Cohen, S. (1972) *Folk Devils and Moral Panics: The Creation of the Mods and Rockers*. London: MacGibbon & Key.

Cohen, S. & Young, J. (eds.) (1973) *The Manufacture of News*. London: Constable.

Coleman, S. (2003) 'A tale of two houses: The House of Commons, the Big Brother house and the people at home', Hansard Society, www.acteurspublics.com/files/epublic/pdf/scoleman-a-tale-of-two-houses.pdf.

Coleman, S. & Blumler, J. G. (2012) 'The internet and citizenship: Democratic opportunity structure or more of the same?' in H. Semetko & M. Scammell (eds.) *The Sage Handbook of Political Communication*. London: Sage, pp. 141–152.

Coleman, S. & Blumler, J. G. (2009) *The Internet and Democratic Citizenship: Theory, Practice, and Policy*. Cambridge & New York: Cambridge University Press.

Coleman, S. & Ross, K. (2010) *The Media and the Public: 'Them' and 'Us' in Media Discourse*. Malden: Wiley-Blackwell .

Collins, R. (2011) 'Content online and the end of public media? The UK, a canary in the coal mine?' *Media, Culture & Society* 33(8): 1202–19.

Coman, I. & Gross, P. (2012) 'Uncommonly common or truly exceptional? An alternative to the political system-based explanation of the Romanian mass media', *International Journal of Press/Politics* 17(4): 457–79.

Committee to Protect Journalists (2011a) 'CPJ condemns attacks on press in Libya, Yemen and Egypt, www.cpj.org/2011/03/cpj-condemns-attacks-on-press-in-libya-yemen-and-e.php, 9 March.

Committee to Protect Journalists (2011b) 'Tunisia must end censorship on coverage of unrest', open letter to President Zine Abidine Ben Ali, 5 January, www.cpj.org/2011/01/tunisia-must-end-censorship-on-coverage-of-unrest.php.

Considine, A. (2011) 'For activists, tips on safe use of social media', *The New York Times*, 1 April, www.nytimes.com/2011/04/03/fashion/03noticed.html?_r=0.

Converse, P. E. (1962) 'Information flow and the stability of partisan attitudes', *Public Opinion Quarterly* 26(4): 578–99.

Cook, T. (1998) *Governing with the News*. Chicago: University of Chicago Press.

Coombs, W. T. & Holladay, S. J. (2007) *It's Not Just PR: Public Relations in Society*. Oxford: Blackwell.

Corner, J. (2003) 'Mediated persona and political culture' in J. Corner & D. Pels (2003) *Media and the Restyling of Politics: Consumerism, Celebrity and Cynicism*. London: Sage, pp. 67–84.

Corner, J. & Pels, D. (2003) *Media and the Restyling of Politics: Consumerism, Celebrity and Cynicism*. London: Sage.

Corner, J., Richardson, K. & Parry, K. (2013) 'Comedy, the civic subject, and generic mediation', *Television & New Media* 14(1): 31–45.

Cornia, A. (2010) 'The Europeanization of Mediterranean journalistic practices and the Italianization of Brussels: Dynamics of interaction between EU institutions and national journalistic cultures', *European Journal of Communication* 25(4): 366–81.

Cottle, S. (2011a) 'Transnational protests and the media: New departures, challenging debates', in S. Cottle & L. Lester (eds.) *Transnational Protests and the Media*. New York: Peter Lang.

Cottle, S. (2011b) 'Taking global crises in the news seriously: Notes from the dark side of globalization', *Global Media and Communication* 7(2): 77–95.

Cottle, S. (2009) *Global Crisis Reporting: Journalism in the Global Age*. Maidenhead: McGraw Hil l/ Open University Press.

Cottle, S. (2008) 'Reporting demonstrations: The changing media politics of dissent', *Media, Culture and Society* 30(6): 853–72.

Cottle, S. (2006a) *Mediatized Conflict*. Maidenhead: Open University Press.

Cottle, S. (2006b) 'Mediatized rituals: Beyond manufacturing consent', *Media, Culture & Society* 28(3): 411–32.

Cottle, S. (ed.) (2003) *News, Public Relations and Power*. London: Sage.

Cottle, S. & Rai, M. (2008) 'Global 24/7 news providers: Emissaries of global dominance or global public service?' *Global Media and Communication* 4(2): 157–81.

Couldry, N. (2009) 'Does "the media" have a future?' *European Journal of Communication* 24(4): 437–49.

Couldry, N. (2008) 'Mediatization or mediation? Alternative understandings of the emergent space of digital storytelling', *New Media & Society* 10(3): 373–91.

Couldry, N. (2005) 'The extended audience: Scanning the horizon', in M. Gillespie (ed.) *Media Audiences*. Maidenhead: Open University Press, pp. 183–222.

Couldry, N. (2003) 'Beyond the hall of mirrors: Some theoretical reflections on the global contestation of media power', in N. Couldry & J. Curran (eds.) *Contesting Media Power: Alternative Media in a Networked World*. Lanham: Rowman & Littlefield, pp. 39–54.

Couldry, N. (2001) 'The hidden injuries of media power', *Journal of Consumer Culture* 1(2): 155–74.

Couldry, N. (2000) *The Place of Media Power*. London: Routledge.

Couldry, N. & Curran, J. (eds.) (2003) *Contesting Media Power* Rowan & Littlefield

Couldry, N. & McCarthy, A. (eds.) (2004) *MediaSpace: Place, Scale and Culture in a Media Age*. London: Routledge.

Couldry, N., Hepp, A. & Krotz, F. (eds.) (2010) *Media Events in a Global Age*. Abingdon: Routledge.

Couldry, N., Livingstone, S. & Markham, T. (2007) 'Connection or disconnection? Tracking the mediated public sphere in everyday life', in R. Butsch (ed.) *Media and Public Spheres*. Houndmills: Palgrave Macmillan, pp. 28–42.

CPJ (2011a) 'Journalists under physical assault in Egypt', http://cpj.ord/2011/02/journalists-under-physical-assault-in-egypt.php.

Crawford, K. (2011) 'News to me: Twitter and the personal networking of news', in G. Meikle & G. Redden (eds.) *News Online: Transformations and Continuities*. Houndmills: Palgrave Macmillan, pp. 115–31.

Crouch, C. (2004) *Post-Democracy*. Cambridge: Polity.

Curran, J., Salovaara-Moring, Coen, S. & Iyengar, S. (2010) 'Crime, foreigners and hard news: A cross-national comparison of reporting and public perception', *Journalism* 11(1): 3–19.

Curtin, M. (2010) 'Comparing media capitals: Hong Kong and Mumbai', *Global Media and Communication* 6(3): 263–70.

D'Angelo, P. & Kuyper, J. (2010) *Doing News Framing Analysis: Empirical and Theoretical Perspectives*. Taylor & Francis.

D'Arma, A. (2011) 'Global media, business and politics: A comparative analysis of News Corporation's strategy in Italy and the UK', *The International Communication Gazette* 73(8): 670–84.

Dagens Nyheter (2013) 'De lata utopisterna', *Dagens Nyheter*, 28 October (unsigned editorial), www.dn.se/ledare/huvudledare/de-lata-utopisterna.

Dahlberg, L. & Siapera, E. (2007) *Radical Democracy and the Internet*. Houndmills: Palgrave.

Dahlgren, P. (2009) *Media and Political Engagement: Citizens, Communication, and Democracy*. Cambridge: Cambridge University Press.

Dahlgren, P. (1995) *Television and the Public Sphere: Citizenship, Democracy and the Media*. London: Sage.

Dahlgren, P. & Olsson, T. (2007) 'From public sphere to civic culture: Young citizens' internet use', in R. Butsch (ed.) *Media and Public Spheres*. Houndmills: Palgrave Macmillan, pp. 198–209.

Dailey, K. (2012) 'Michelle Obama: Her four-year evolution', *BBC News Magazine*, www.bbc.co.uk/news/magazine-1943100, 4 September.

Daily Telegraph (2013) 'Kenyan press outraged at controversial media law', 1 November, www.telegraph.co.uk/news/worldnews/africaandindianocean/kenya/10420218/Kenyan-press-outraged-at-controversial-media-law.html.

Darras, E. (2005) 'Media consecration of the political order', in R. Benson & E. Neveu (eds.) *Bourdieu and the Journalistic Field*. Cambridge: Polity, pp. 156–73.

Dauncey, H. (2012) 'French videogaming: What kind of culture and what support?' *Convergence: The International Journal of Research into New Media Technologies* 18(4): 385–402.

David, C. C. (2013) 'ICTs in political engagement among youth in the Philippines', *The International Communication Gazette* 75(3): 322–37.

Davis, A. (2007) *The Mediation of Power: A Critical Introduction*. London and New York: Routledge.

Davis, D. (2008) 'Science fiction narratives of mass destruction and the politics of national security', in D. M. Hassler & C. Wilcox (eds.) *New Boundaries in Political Science Fiction*. Columbia: University of South Carolina Press, pp. 145–56.

Dawson, R. (2010) 'Launch of the newspaper extinction timeline for every country in the world', http://rossdawsonblog.com/weblog/archives/2010/10/launch_of_newsp.html, 31 October.

Dayan, D. (2010) 'Beyond media events: Disenchantment, derailment, disruption', in N. Couldry, A. Hepp & F. Krotz (eds.) *Media Events in a Global Age*. Abingdon and New York: Routledge, pp. 25–31.

Dayan, D. (2009) 'Sharing and showing: Television as monstration', *The ANNALS of the American Academy of Political and Social Science*, 625(1): 19–31.

Dayan, D. & Katz, E. (1992) *Media Events: The Live Broadcasting of History*. Cambridge and London: Harvard University Press.

De Bens, E. & Østbye, H. (1998) 'The European newspaper market', in D. McQuail & K. Siune (eds.) *Media Policy: Convergence, Concentration and Commerce*. London: Sage, pp. 7–22.

De Nelson, S. A. (2008) 'Understanding the press imaging of "terrorist"', *The International Communication Gazette* 70(5): 325–37.

De Vreese, C. H. (2005) 'The spiral of cynicism reconsidered', *European Journal of Communication* 20(3): 283–301.

Dean, J. (2009) *Blog Theory: Feedback and Capture in the Circuits of Drive*. Cambridge: Polity.

Deans, J. (2013) 'MediaGuardian lists digital consumer as most powerful industry figure', *The Guardian*, 1 September, www.theguardian.com/media/2013/sep/01/mediaguardian-digital-consumer-most-powerful.

Dehghan, S. K. (2013) 'Iran's artists warn US and European sanctions are affecting their work', *The Guardian*, 31 October, www.theguardian.com/world/2013/oct/31/iran-artists-sanctions-affecting-work.

Deibert, R. et al. (2010) 'Cyclones in Cyberspace: Information Shaping and Denial in the 2008 South Ossetia War'. Paper presented at the International Studies Association conference in New Orleans.

Dekavalla, M. (2012) 'Constructing the public at the royal wedding', *Media, Culture & Society* 34(3): 296–311.

Delgado, Fernando (2003) 'The fusing of sport and politics. Media constructions of U.S. versus Iran at France '98', *Journal of Sport and Social Issues* 27(3): 293–307.

Della Porta, D. & Mosca, L. (2009) 'Searching the net', *Information, Communication & Society* 12(6): 771–92.

Delli Carpini, M. X. (2012) 'Entertainment media and the political engagement of citizens', in H.A. Semetko & M. Scammell (eds.) *The Sage Handbook of Political Communication*. London: Sage, pp. 9–21.

DeLuca, K. M. & Peeples, J. (2002) 'From public sphere to public screen: Democracy, activism, and the "violence" of Seattle', *Critical Studies in Media Communication* 19(2): 125–51.

Deuze, M. (2011) 'Media life', *Media, Culture & Society* 33(1): 137–48.

Deuze, M. (2008) 'The changing context of news work: Liquid journalism and monitorial citizenship', *International Journal of Communication* 2(5): 848–65.

Deuze, M. (2007) *Media Work*. Cambridge: Polity.

Deuze, M. (2005) 'What is journalism? Professional identity and ideology of journalists reconsidered', *Journalism* 6(4): 442–63.

Deuze, M. (2002) 'National news cultures: A comparison of Dutch, German, British, Australian and US journalists', *Journalism and Mass Communication Quarterly* 79(1): 134–49.

Deuze, M. & Fortunati, L. (2011) 'Journalism without journalists: On the power shift from journalists to employers and audiences', in G. Meikle & G. Redden (eds.) *News Online: Transformations and Continuities*. Houndmills: Palgrave Macmillan, pp. 164–77.

Devereux, E. (2003) *Understanding the Media*. London: Sage.

Dickinson, E. (2011) 'The first WikiLeaks revolution', *Foreign Policy*, 13 January, http://wikileaks.foreignpolic.com/posts/2011/01/13/wikileaks_and_the_tunisia_protests.

Djerf-Pierre, M. (2000) 'Squaring the circle: Public service and commercial news on Swedish television 1956–99', *Journalism Studies* 1(2): 239–60.

Dong, F. (2012) 'Controlling the internet in China: The real story', *Convergence: The International Journal of Research into New Media Technologies* 18(4): 403–25.

Donsbach, W. & Patterson, T. E. (2004) 'Political news journalists: Partisanship, professionalism, and political roles in five countries', in F. Esser & B. Pfetsch (eds.) *Comparing Political Communication: Theories, Cases and Challenges*. Cambridge: Cambridge University Press, pp. 251–70.

Downey, J. & Stanyer, J. (2010) 'Comparative media analysis: Why some fuzzy thinking might help. Applying fuzzy set qualitative comparative analysis to the personalization of mediated political communication', *European Journal of Communication* 25(4): 331–47.

Doyle, G. (2010) 'From television to multi-platform', *Convergence: The International Journal of Research into New Media Technologies* 16(4): 431–49.

Doyle, J. (2009) 'Climate action and environmental activism: The role of environmental NGOs and grassroots movements in the global politics of climate change', in T. Boyce & J. Lewis (eds.) *Climate Change and the Media*. New York: Peter Lang, pp. 103–16.

Drezner, D. W. (2010a) ''Weighing the scales: The internet's effect on state–society relations', *Brown Journal of World Affairs*, 16(2): 31–44.

Drezner, D. W. (2010b) 'What should scholars and foreign policy wonks do with WikiLeaks?' *Foreign Policy*, 2 December, www.foreignpolicy.com/posts/2010/11/29/what_should_scholars_and_foreign_policy_wonks_do_with_wikileaks.

Driessens, O., Joye, S. & Biltereyst, D. (2012) 'The X-factor of charity: A critical analysis of celebrities' involvement in the 2010 Flemish and Dutch Haiti relief shows', *Media, Culture & Society* 34(6): 709–25.

Drotner, K. (1994) 'Media ethnography', *Communications* 19(1): 87–103.

Drotner, K. (1992) 'Modernity and media panics', in M. Skovmand & K. C. Schroder (eds.) *Media Cultures: Reappraising Transnational Media*. London: Routledge, pp. 42–62.

Dutta, M. J. & Pal, M. (2007) 'The internet as a site of resistance: The case of the Narmada Bachao Andolan', in S. C. Duhé (ed.) *New Media and Public Relations*. New York: Peter Lang, pp. 203–15.

Duval, J. (2005) 'Economic journalism in France', in R. Benson & E. Neveu (eds.) *Bourdieu and the Journalistic Field*. Cambridge: Polity, pp. 135–56.

DW (2011) 'Authoritarian regimes eliminate the freedom of the Internet', Deutsche Welle Global Media Forum, Human Rights in a Globalized World / Challenges for the Media Conference, Bonn, 20–22 June.

EBU (2013) 'Media freedom and pluralism', http://www3.ebu.ch/files/live/sites/ebu/files/Knowledge/Publication%20Library/EBU-Viewpoint-MediaFreedom_EN.pdf.

EBU (2011) 'About the EBU', www.ebu.ch/en/about/index.php.

EBU (2003) 'Audiovisual services and GATS negotiations: EBU contribution to the public consultation on requests for access to the EU market', www.ebu.ch/CMSimages/en/leg_pp_gats_170103_tcm6-4388.pdf.

EC (2006) 'White Paper on a European Communication Policy' COM(2006)35 final, http://eur-lex.europa.eu/LexUriServ/LexUriServ.do?uri=COM:2006:0035:FIN:EN:PDF.

EC (2005a) 'Action plan to improve communicating Europe by the Commission', Communication to the Commission of 20 July, SEC(2005) 985 final, http://europa.eu/legislation_summaries/institutional_affairs/decisionmaking_process/l10102_en.htm

EC (2005b) 'The Commission's contribution to the period of reflection and beyond: Plan D for Democracy, Dialogue and Debate', COM (2005) 494 final, http://eur-lex.europa.eu/smartapi/cgi/sga_doc?smartapi!celexplus!prod!DocNumber&type_doc=COMfinal&an_doc=2005&nu_doc=494&lg=en.

EC (2004) 'On implementing the information and communication strategy for the European Union', Brussels, 20 April, COM(2004) 196 final, http://eur-lex.europa.eu/LexUriServ/site/en/com/2004/com2004_0196en01.pdf, accessed 25 September 2011.

EC (2002). 'WTO members' requests to the EC and its Member States for improved market access for services', consultation document, 12 November, http://trade.ec.europa.eu/doclib/docs/2004/march/tradoc_112335.pdf.

Eco, U. (1979) *The Role of the Reader: Explorations in the Semiotics of Texts*. Bloomington: Indiana University Press.

Edmonds, R. (2009) *The State of the News Media 2009.* Pew Project for Excellence in Journalism, http://stateofthemedia.org/2009/.

EFJ (2012) 'European jobs crisis damaging journalism: EFJ stands in support of ETUC day of action', http://europe.ifj.org/en/articles/european-jobs-crisis-damaging-journalism-efj-stands-in-support-of-etuc-day-of-action.

Ekecrantz, J., Olsson, T., Pollack, E. & Sahlstrand, A. (1994) 'Journalistik som kommunikation: Tre Tidstablåer', in C. von Feilitzen, H. Strand, S. Ross, T. Holmqvist, J. Fornäs & U. Carlsson (eds.) *Kommunikationens korsningar.* Gothenburg: Nordicom-Sverige pp. 109–46.

Ekman, Mattias (2013a) 'Högerextrema, våldsbejande och antidemokratiska budskap på internet', in *Extremistiska, våldsbejakande och antidemokratiska budskap på internet.* Stockholm: Statens Medieråd.

Ekman, Mattias (2013b) 'Sanitising Fascism: Online Video Activism of the Swedish Far Right'. Paper presented at the IAMCR Annual Conference, Dublin, 25–29 June, Community Communication Section.

Ekström, A. (2012) 'Exhibiting disasters: Mediation, historicity and spectatorship', *Media, Culture & Society* 34(4): 472–87.

El-Ibiary, R. (2011) 'Questioning the Al-Jazeera effect: Analysis of Al-Qaeda's media strategy and its relationship with Al-Jazeera', *Global Media and Communication* 7(3): 199–204.

El-Nawawy, M. & Powers, S. (2010) 'Al-Jazeera English: A conciliatory medium in a conflict-driven environment?' *Global Media and Communication* 6(1): 61–84.

Elliot, C. (2013) 'The readers' editor on … interpreting social media reports from Egypt', *The Guardian*, 24 February, www.theguardian.com/commentisfree/2013/feb/24/social-media-reports-egypt-middle-east.

Ellis, J. (2009a) 'The performance on television of sincerely felt emotion', *The ANNALS of the American Academy of Political and Social Science*, 625(1): 103–15.

Ellis, J. (2009b) 'Mundane witness', in P. Frosh & A. Pinchevsky (eds.) *Media Witnessing: Testimony in the Age of Mass Communication.* Houndmills: Palgrave Macmillan, pp. 73–88.

Elmelund-Præstekær & Wien, C. (2008) 'What's the fuss about? The interplay of media hypes and politics', *Press/Politics* 13(3): 247–66.

Entman, R. M. (2004) *Projections of Power: Framing News, Public Opinion and US Foreign Policy.* Chicago: University of Chicago Press.

Entman, R. M. (2003) 'Cascading activation: Contesting the White House's frame after 9/11', *Political Communication* 20: 415–23.

Esbjörnsson, E. (2013) 'Ny medielag: UD har all anledning att följa utvecklingen i Kenya', *Dagens Nyheter*, 2 November.

Essa, A. (2011) 'In search of an African revolution', Aljazeera.net 21 Feb, www.aljazeera.com/indepth/features/2011/02/201122164254698620.html.

Esser, F. (1999) '"Tabloidization" of news: A comparative analysis of Anglo-American and German press journalism', *European Journal of Communication* 14(3): 291–324.

Esser, F. (1998) 'Editorial structures and work in British and German newsrooms', *European Journal of Communication* 13(3): 375–405.

Esser, F. & Hemmer, K. (2008) 'Characteristics and dynamics of election news coverage in Germany" in J. Strömbäck and L. Kaid (eds.) *The Handbook of Election News Coverage Around the World.* London: Routledge, pp. 289–307.

Esser, F. & Spanjer, B. (2005) 'News management as news', *Journal of Political Marketing* 4(4): 27–57.

Esser, F., Reinemann, C. & Fan, D. (2001) 'Spin doctors in the United States, Great Britain, and Germany: Meta-communication about media manipulation', *Harvard International Journal of Press/Politics* 6(4): 16–45.

Esser, F., de Vreese, C. H., Strömbäch, J., et al. (2012) 'Political information opportunities in Europe: A longitudinal and comparative study of thirteen television systems', *The International Journal of Press/Politics* 17(3): 247–74.

Etling, B., Kelly, J., Faris, R. & Palfrey, J. (2010) 'Mapping the Arabic blogosphere: Politics and dissent online', *New Media & Society* 12(8): 1225–43.

Ettema, J., Whitney, D. C. & Wackman, D. B. (1987/1997) 'Professional mass communicators', in D. Berkowitz (ed.) *Social Meanings of News*. Thousand Oaks: Sage, pp. 31–51.

European Parliament and Council (2007) Directive 2007/65/EC, 11 December, *Official Journal of the European Union* L332/27.

Fahmy, S. (2010) 'Contrasting visual frames of our times: A framing analysis of English- and Arabic-language press coverage of war and terrorism', *The International Communication Gazette* 72(8): 695–717.

Fandy, M. (2007) *(Un)Civil War of Words: Media and Politics in the Arab World*. New York: Praeger.

Fenton, N. & Witschge, T. (2011) '"Comment is free, facts are sacred": Journalistic ethics in a changing mediascape', in G. Meikle & G. Redden (eds.) *News Online: Transformations and Continuities*. Houndmills: Palgrave Macmillan, pp. 148–63.

Figenschou, T. (2013) *Al Jazeera and the Global Media Landscape*. Abingdon: Routledge.

Figenschou, T. (2010a) 'Young, female, Western researcher vs. senior, male, Al Jazeera officials: Critical reflections on accessing and interviewing media elites in authoritarian societies', *Media, Culture & Society* 32(6): 961–78.

Figenschou, T. (2010b) 'A voice for the voiceless? A quantitative content analysis of Al-Jazeera English's flagship news', *Global Media and Communication* 6(1): 85–107.

Filkins, D. (2010) 'TV channel draws viewers, and threats, in Iran', *The New York Times*, 19 November, www.nytimes.com/2010/11/20/world/middleeast/20afghan.html?_r=1.

Fiske, J. (1987) *Television Culture*. London: Methuen.

Fiske, J. & Hartley, J. (1978/2003) *Reading Television*. London & New York: Methuen.

Flew, T. (2007) *Understanding Global Media*. Houndmills: Palgrave.

Flew, T. & Wilson, J. (2010) 'Journalism as social networking: The Australian youdecide project and the 2007 federal election', *Journalism* 11(2): 131–47.

Flood, A. (2014) 'Turkey's Twitter ban fires authors'rage over free speech', *The Guardian*, 28 March.

Forssberg, J. (2012) 'Nördlobbyns stora seger', *Expressen*, 3 September, www.expressen.se/ledare/johannes-forssberg/johannes-forssberg-nordlobbyns-stora-seger/.

Fox, J. R., Koloen, G. & Sahin, V. (2007) 'No joke: A comparison of substance in *The Daily Show* with Jon Stewart and broadcast network television coverage of the 2004 presidential election campaign', *Journal of Broadcasting and Electronic Media* 51: 213–27.

Fraley, T. (2007) 'The revolution will be televised: Free speech TV, democratic communication and the public sphere', in R. Butsch (ed.) *Media and Public Spheres*. Houndmills: Palgrave Macmillan, pp. 175–84.

Franklin, B. (2004) *Packaging Politics: Political Communication in Britain's Media Democracy*. London: Arnold.

Franklin, B. (1997) *Newszak and News Media*. London: Arnold.

Fraser, N. (2007) 'Transnationalizing the public sphere: On the legitimacy and efficacy of public opinion in a post-Westphalian world', *Theory, Culture & Society* 24(4): 7–30.

Freedland, J. (2011) 'We owe the internet for changing the world: Now let's learn how to turn off', *The Guardian*, 22 February, www.guardian.co.uk/commentisfree/2011/feb/22/internet-learn-to-turn-off/print.

Freedman, D. & Thussu, D. K. (eds.) (2012) *Media and Terrorism: Global Perspectives*. London: Sage.

Freedman, E. (2012) 'Deepening shadows: The eclipse of press rights in Kyrgyzstan', *Global Media and Communication* 8(1): 47–64.

Freelon, D. G. (2010) 'Analyzing online political discussion using three models of democratic communication', *New Media and Society* 12(7): 1172–90.

Friedland, L. A., Long, C. C., with Shin, Y. J. & Kim, N. (2007) 'The local public sphere as a networked space', in R. Butsch (ed.) *Media and Public Spheres*. Houndmills: Palgrave Macmillan, pp. 43–57.

Friesen, N. & Hug, T. (2009) 'The mediatic turn', in K. Lundby (ed.) *Mediatization: Concept, Changes, Consequences*. New York: Peter Lang, pp. 63–83.

Fröhlich, R. (2010) 'Research note: The coverage of war: Do women matter? A longitudinal content analysis of broadsheets in Germany', *European Journal of Communication* 25(1): 59–68.

Fröhlich, R. & Holtz-Bacha, C. (eds.) (2003) *Journalism Education in Europe and North America: An International Comparison*. Creskill: Hampton Press.

Frosh, P. (2011) 'Phatic morality: Television and proper distance', *International Journal of Cultural Studies* 14: 383–400.

Frosh, P. (2009) 'The face of television', *The ANNALS of the American Academy of Political and Social Science*, 625(1): 87–102.

Frosh, P. & Pinchevsky, A. (2009) "Why media witnessing? Why now?" in P. Frosh & A. Pinchevsky (eds.) *Media Witnessing: Testimony in the Age of Mass Communication*. Houndmills: Palgrave Macmillan, pp. 1–19.

Frosh, P. & Wolfsfeld, G. (2006) 'ImagiNation: News discourse, nationhood and civil society', *Media, Culture & Society* 29(1): 105–29.

Frost, V. (2013) 'BBC buys series 3 of Danish political drama *Borgen*', *The Guardian*, 17 February.

Frydén Bonnier, M. (2007) 'Europeanization in European news broadcasts? A comparative study of Euronews and Rapport'. Master's thesis, Department of Political Science, Stockholm University.

Fukuyama, F. (1992) *The End of History and the Last Man*. New York: Avon Books.

G20–G8 (2011), Address by the president of the French Republic, opening of the G8 forum, May, www.g20-g8.com/g8-g20/g8/english/live/news/opening-of-the-e-g8-forum.1270.html.

Gahran, A. (2011) 'How Al Jazeera is putting audio updates from Egypt online fast', Knight Digital Media Center, www.knightdigitalmediacenter.org.

Gamson, W. A. (2004) 'Bystanders, public opinion and the media', in D. A. Snow, S. H. Soule & H. Kriesi (eds.) *The Blackwell Companion to Social Movements*. Oxford: Blackwell, pp. 242–61.

Gamson, W. A. & Wolfsfeld, G. (1993) 'Movements and media as interacting systems', *Annals of the American Academy of Political and Social Science* 526: 114–27.

Gans, H. J. (2011) 'Multiperspectival news revisited: Journalism and representative democracy', *Journalism* 12(1): 3–13.

Garber, M. (2011a) 'Nick Kristof turns to Facebook to report from Egypt', Nieman Journalism Lab, 30 January, www.niemanlab.org/2011/01/nick-kristof-turns-to-facebook-to-report-from-egypt/.

Garber, M. (2011b) 'The Egypt list: Sulia curates content by curating expertise', Nieman Journalism Lab, 1 February, http://feedproxy.google.com/-r/NiemanJournalismLab/-3/1ka_o9Spb9s.

Garlough, C. (2012) 'Grassroots political communication in India: Women's movements, vernacular rhetoric and street play performance', in H. Semetko & M. Scammell (eds.) *The Sage Handbook of Political Communication*. London: Sage, pp. 484–93.

Garnham, N. (2000) *Emancipation, the Media, and Modernity: Arguments about the Media and Social Theory*. Oxford: Oxford University Press.

Gemmill, M. A. & Nexon, D. H. (2006) 'Children's crusade: The religious politics of Harry Potter', in D. Nexon & I. B. Neuman (eds.) *Harry Potter and International Relations*. Lanham: Rowman & Littlefield, pp. 79–100.

Geraghty, L. (2008) 'A truly American Enterprise: *Star Trek*'s post-9/11 politics' in D. M. Hassler & C. Wilcox (eds.) *New Boundaries in Political Science Fiction*. Columbia: University of South Carolina Press, pp. 157–66.

Gerbner, G. (1992) 'Persian Gulf War: The movie', in H. Mowlana, G. Gerbner & H. Schiller (eds.) *The Triumph of the Image: The Media's War in the Persian Gulf – A Global Perspective*. Boulder: Westview Press, pp. 243–65.

Gerbner, G., Gross, L., Morgan, M. & Signorielli, N. (1986) 'Living with television: The dynamics of cultivation process', in J. Bryant & D. Zillman (eds.) *Perspectives on Media Effects*. Hillsdale: Erlbaum Associates, pp. 17–40.

George, L. (2007) 'What's fit to print: The effect of ownership concentration on product variety in daily newspaper markets', *Information Economics and Policy* 19(3/4): 285–303.

Georgiou, M. & Silverstone, R. (2007) 'Diasporas and contra-flows: Beyond nation-centrism', in D. K. Thussu (ed.) *Media on the Move: Global Flow and Contra-flow*. London & New York: Routledge, pp. 33–48.

Giddens, A. (1994) *The Consequences of Modernity*. Cambridge: Polity.

Gidengil, E. & Everitt, J. (2005) 'Conventional coverage / unconventional politicians: Gender and media coverage of Canadian leaders' debates 1993, 1997, 2000', *Canadian Journal of Political Science* 36(3): 559–77.

Gilbert, D. (2011) 'Politics and PR: Do they gel?' *Publicity Update*, 7 November, www.publicityupdate. co.za/?IDStory=42992.

Gilboa, E. (2005) 'The CNN effect: The search for a communication theory of international relations', *Political Communication* 22: 27–44.

Gillespie, M. (ed.) (2005) *Media Audiences*. Maidenhead: Open University Press.

Gitlin, T. (2001) *Media Unlimited*. New York: Metropolitan Books.

Gitlin, T. (1980) *The Whole World is Watching: Mass Media in the Making and Unmaking of the New Left*. Berkeley / Los Angeles: University of California Press.

Gladwell, M. (2010) 'Small change: Why the revolution will not be tweeted', *The New Yorker*, 4 October, http://www.newyorker.com/magazine/2010/10/04/small-change-3.

Glanville, J. (2010) 'New frontiers', *Index on Censorship* 39: 3–5.

Glanz, J. & Lehren, A. (2013) 'N.S.A. dragnet included allies, aid groups and business elite', *The New York Times*, 20 December, http://www.nytimes.com/2013/12/21/world/nsa-dragnet-included-allies-aid-groups-and-business-elite.html?pagewanted=all&_r=0.

Glaser, M. (2008) 'Semi-pro journalism teams give alternative view of U.S. elections', Media Shift/ Digging Deeper, www.pbs.org/mediashift/2008/03/semi-pro-journalism-teams-give-alternative-view-of-us-elections073.html.

Goff, P. M. (2006) 'Producing Harry Potter: Why the medium is still the message', in D. Nexon & I. B. Neuman (eds.) *Harry Potter and International Relations*. Lanham: Rowman & Littlefield, pp. 27–44.

Goggin, G. (2011) 'The intimate turn of mobile news', in G. Meikle & G. Redden (eds.) *News Online: Transformations and Continuities*. Houndmills: Palgrave Macmillan, pp. 99–114.

Gokul, T. G. (2011) 'Covering crises: Indian news channels and the Mumbai terror attacks', *Global Media and Communication* 7(3): 269–74.

Golding, P. & Elliott, P. (1979) *Making the News*. London: Longman.

Goulart, W. & Joe, W. Y. (2008) 'Inverted perspectives on politics and morality in *Battlestar Galactica*', in D. M. Hassler & C. Wilcox (eds.) *New Boundaries in Political Science Fiction*. Columbia: University of South Carolina Press, pp. 179–97.

Gowing, N. (2003) 'Journalists and war: The troubling new tensions post 9/11', in D. Thussu & and D. Freedman (eds.) *War and the Media*. London: Sage, pp. 231–40.

Graber, D. (1984) *Media Power in Politics*. CQ Press.

Graham, T. & Hajru, A. (2011) 'Reality TV as a trigger of everyday political talk in the net-based public sphere', *European Journal of Communication* 26(1): 18–32.

Gravengaard, G. (2012) 'The metaphors journalists live by: Journalists' conceptualisation of news-work', *Journalism* 13(8): 1064–82.

Greenall, R. (2012) 'LiveJournal: Russia's unlikely internet giant', *BBC News Magazine* 1 March, www.bbc.co.uk/news/magazine-17177053.

Greenwald, G. (2013) 'NSA collecting phone records of millions of Verizon customers daily', *The Guardian*, 6 June, www.guardian.co.uk/world/2013/jun/06/nsa-phone-records-verizon-court-order.

Greenwald, G. & MacAskill, E. (2013) 'NSA taps in to internet giants' systems to mine user data, secret files reveal', *The Guardian*, 7 June, www.guardian.co.uk/world/2013/jun/06/us-tech-giants-nsa-data.

Griffin, M. (2010) 'Media images of war', *Media, War & Conflict* 3(1): 7–41.

Gripenberg, P. (2011) 'Ericsson både hjälper och stjälper Mellanösterns diktatorer', *Dagens Nyheter*, 5 December, p. 21.

Guardian, The (2013) 'Civil liberties: American freedom on the line', editorial, 7 June, www.guardian. co.uk/commentisfree/2013/jun/06/civil-liberties-american-freedom-on-the-line.

Guardian, The (2010) 'Afghanistan: the war logs', www.guardian.co.uk/world/the-war-logs.

Guardian, The (2007) 'The looting of Kenya', www.guardian.co.uk/world/2007/aug/31/kenya.top stories3.

GUMG (Glasgow University Media Group) (1985) *War and Peace News*. Milton Keynes: Open University Press.

Gunaratne, S. A. (2007) 'A systems view of "international" communication, its scope and limitations', *Global Media and Communication* 3: 267-71.

Gupta, M. (n.d.) Interview with Johan Lindén, http://archive.eurescom.eu/message/message Oct2005/Interview_with_Johan_Linden_from_SVT.asp.

Gurevitch, M., Coleman, S. & Blumler, J. (2009) 'Political communication – old and new media relationships', T*he ANNALS of the American Academy of Political and Social Science*, 625(1): 164-81.

Habermas, J. (1996) *Between Facts and Norms*. Cambridge MA: MIT Press.

Habermas, J. (1962/1989) *The Structural Transformation of the Public Sphere*. Oxford and Cambridge: Polity/Blackwell.

Hafez, K. (2011) 'Global journalism for global governance? Theoretical visions, practical constraints', *Journalism* 12(4): 483-96.

Hafez, K. (2007) *The Myth of Media Globalization*. Cambridge: Polity.

Hahn, O. (2009) 'Transatlantic foreign reporting and foreign correspondents after 9/11: Trends in reporting Europe in the United States', *International Journal of Press/Politics* 14(4): 497-515.

Hall, M. (2006) 'The fantasy of realism, or mythology as methodology', in D. Nexon & I. B. Neuman (eds.) *Harry Potter and International Relations*. Lanham: Rowman & Littlefield, pp. 177-94.

Hall, S. (ed.) (2007) *Representation: Cultural Representations and Signifying Practices*. London: Sage.

Hall, S. (2000) 'The Multicultural Question'. The Pavis Lecture 2000, 19 October, The Open University, Milton Keynes, http://stadium.open.ac.uk/stadia/preview.php?s=1&whichevent=49

Hall, S. (1992) 'The West and the rest: Discourse and power", in S. Hall & B. Gieben (eds.) *Formations of Modernity*. Milton Keynes and Cambridge: Open University / Polity, pp. 275-331.

Hall, S. (1982) 'The rediscovery of ideology: The return of the repressed in media studies', in M. Gurevitch, T. Bennett, J. Curran & J. Wollacott (eds.) *Culture, Society and the Media*. London: Methuen, pp. 56-90.

Hall, S. (1980/1994) 'Encoding/Decoding', in D. Graddol & O. Boyd-Barrett (eds.) *Media Texts: Authors and Readers*. Clevedon: Open University, pp. 200-11.

Hallin, D. C. (2005) 'Field theory, differentiation theory, and comparative media research', in R. Benson & E. Neveu (eds.) *Bourdieu and the Journalistic Field*. Cambridge: Polity, pp. 224-43.

Hallin, D. C. (1986) *The Uncensored War: The Media and Vietnam*. Berkeley: University of California Press.

Hallin, D. C. (1984) 'The media, the war in Vietnam and political support: A critique of the thesis of an oppositional media', *The Journal of Politics* 46(1): 2-24.

Hallin, D. & Mancini, P. (2011) *Comparing Media Systems Beyond the Western World*. Cambridge: Cambridge University Press.

Hallin, D. & Mancini, P. (2004) *Comparing Media Systems: Three Models of Media and Politics*. Cambridge: Cambridge University Press.

Hallin, D. & Papathanassopoulos, S. (2002) 'Political clientelism and the media: Southern Europe and Latin America in comparative perspective', *Media, Culture & Society* 24(2): 175-95.

Halloran, J., Elliott, P. & Murdock, G. (1970) *Demonstrations and Communication: A Case Study*. London: Penguin.

Hamelink, C. (2007) 'The professionalisation of political communication: Democracy at stake?' in R. Negrine, C. Holtz-Bacha, P. Mancini & S. Papatha (eds.) *The Professionalisation of Political Communication*. Bristol: Intellect.

Hamilton, E. (2011) 'Öppna SVT:s arkiv och satsa på internet-tv', *Dagens Nyheter*, 22 February, p. 6.

Handley, R. L. & Rutigliano, L. (2012) 'Journalistic field wars: Defending and attacking the national narrative in a diversifying journalistic field', *Media, Culture & Society* 34(6): 744-60.

Hanitzsch, T. (2011) 'Populist disseminators, detached watchdogs, critical change agents and opportunist facilitators: Professional milieus, the journalistic field and autonomy in 18 countries', *The International Communication Gazette* 73(6): 477-94.

Hanitzsch, T. & Hanusch, F. (2012) 'Does gender determine journalists' professional views? A reassessment based on cross-national evidence', *European Journal of Communication* 27(3): 257-77.

Hanitzsch, T. & Mellado, C. (2011) 'What shapes the news around the world? How journalists in eighteen countries perceive influences on their work', *International Journal of Press/Politics* 16(3): 404–26.

Hanusch, F. (2009) 'A product of their culture: Using a value systems approach to understand the work practices of journalists', *The International Communication Gazette* 71(7): 613–26.

Harcup, T. (2011) 'Alternative journalism as active citizenship', *Journalism* 12(1): 15–31.

Harding, L. (2014) 'Writing the Snowden files: "The paragraph began to self-delete"', *The Guardian*, 20 February, www.theguardian.com/books/2014/feb/20/edward-snowden-files-nsa-gchq-luke-harding.

Harrington, S. (2011) 'The uses of satire: Unorthodox news, cultural chaos and the interrogation of power', *Journalism* 13(1): 38–52.

Harris, M. (2014) 'Index around the world', *Index on Censorship* 43(1): 186–7.

Harris, P. (2011) 'Murdoch's fight to stay afloat in US as sharks circle News Corp', *Guardian Weekly*, 16 July, http://www.theguardian.com/media/2011/jul/16/rupert-murdoch-news-corp-profits.

Hartley, J. (2007) '"Reality" and the plebiscite' in K. Riegert (ed.) *Politicotainment: Television's Take on the Real*. New York: Peter Lang, pp. 21–58.

Hartley, J. (1999) *Uses of Television*. London: Routledge.

Hartley, J. (1992) *The Politics of Pictures*. New York: Routledge.

Harvey, D. (1990) *The Condition of Postmodernity*. Cambridge: Blackwell.

Hasian, M. (2013) '*Zero Dark Thirty* and the critical challenges posed by populist postfeminism during the global War on Terrorism', *Journal of Communication Inquiry* 37(4): 322–43.

Hassler, D. M. & Wilcox, C. (2008) *New Boundaries in Political Science Fiction*. Columbia: University of South Carolina Press.

Hebblethwaite, C. (2011) 'Is hip hop driving the Arab Spring?' BBC News Online, www.bbc.co.uk/news/world-middle-east-14146243.

Heidelberg Institute for International Conflict Research (2013) Conflict Barometer 2012, www.hiik.de/en/konfliktbarometer/pdf/ConflictBarometer_2012.pdf.

Heikkilä, H. (2007) 'Beyond "insofar as" questions: Contingent social imaginaries of the European public sphere', *European Journal of Communication* 22(4): 427–41.

Heikkilä, H. & Kunelius, R. (2006) 'Journalists imagining the public sphere'. *Javnost – The Public* 13(4): 63–80.

Held, David (2002) 'Cosmopolitanism: Ideas, realities and deficits', in D. Held & A. McGrew (eds.) *Governing Globalization: Power, Authority and Global Governance*. Cambridge: Polity, pp. 305–23

Hellström, M. (2010) 'Gamla hotbilder hämnar kontakten med Ryssland', *Dagens Nyheter*, 30 May, p. 6.

Helmersson, R. (2013) 'Politikern som maktmaskin', *Dagens Nyheter*, 24 January, www.dn.se/ledare/signerat/politikern-som-maktmaskin.

Hencke, D. (2011) 'Privacy? It's a dangerous myth', *British Journalism Review* 22(3): 43–8.

Hepp, A. (2009) 'Differentiation: Mediatization and cultural change', in K. Lundby (ed.) *Mediatization: Concept, Changes, Consequences*. New York: Peter Lang, pp. 139–57.

Herbert, D. (2005) 'Media publics, culture and democracy', in M. Gillespie (ed.) *Media Audiences*. Maidenhead: Open University Press, pp. 97–136.

Herkman, J. (2012) 'Convergence of intermediality? Finnish political communication in the New Media Age', *Convergence: The International Journal of Research into New Media Technologies* 18(4): 369–84.

Herman, E. & Chomsky, N. (1988) *Manufacturing Consent: The Political Economy of the Mass Media*. New York: Pantheon.

Herman, E. & McChesney, R. (2001) *Global Media: The New Missionaries of Global Capitalism*. Bloomsbury.

Hernes, G. (1978) 'Det mediavridde samfunn', in G. Hernes (ed.) *Forhandlingsekonomi og blandningsadministrasjon*. Bergen: Universitetsforlaget, pp. 181–95.

Hess, S. (1996) *International News and Foreign Correspondents*. Washington: Brookings Institution.

Higgins, M. (2008) *Media and Their Publics*. Maidenhead: Open University Press.

Hilsum, L. (2011) 'Not finally . . . Subjective views on matters journalistic', *British Journalism Review* 22(3): 5–7.

Hirzalla, F., Van Zoonen, L. & Müller, F. (2013) 'How funny can Islam controversies be? Comedians defending their faiths on YouTube', *Television & New Media* 14(1): 46–61.

Hjarvard, S. (2010) 'The views of the news: The role of political newspapers in a changing media landscape', *Northern Lights* 8: 25–48.

Hjarvard, S. (2009) 'Soft individualism: Media and the changing social character' in K. Lundby (ed.) *Mediatization: Concept, Changes, Consequences*. New York: Peter Lang, pp. 159–77.

Hjarvard, S. (2008) 'The mediatization of society: A theory of the media as agents of social and cultural change', *Nordicom Review* 29(2): 105–34.

Hjarvard, S. (2007) 'Changing Media, Changing Language: The Mediatization of Society and the Spread of English and Medialects'. Paper presented to the 57th ICA Conference, San Francisco, CA, 23–28 May.

Hollander, B. A. (2005) 'Late night learning: Do entertainment programs increase political campaign knowledge for young viewers?' *Journal of Broadcasting and Electronic Media* 49(4): 402–15.

Holbert, R.L., Lambe, J. L., Dudo, A. D. & Carlton, K. A. (2007) 'Primacy effects of *The Daily Show* and national TV news viewing: Young viewers, political gratifications, and internal political self-efficacy', *Journal of Broadcasting & Electronic Media* 51(1): 20–38.

Holbert, R. L., Pillion, O., Tschida, D. A., et al. (2003) '*The West Wing* as endorsement of the U.S. presidency: Expanding the bounds of priming in political communication', *Journal of Communication* 53(3): 427–43.

Holly, W. (2008) 'Tabloidisation of political communication in the public sphere', in R. Wodak & V. Koller (eds.) *Handbook of Communication in the Public Sphere*. Berlin: Moutin de Gruyter, pp. 317–41.

Holmes, S. (2006) 'Meeting Italy's silenced satirist', BBC News Online, http://news.bbc.co.uk/2/hi/europe/6187504.stm.

Hooghe, M. (2002) 'Watching television and civic engagement: disentangling the effects of time, programs and stations', *Harvard International Journal of Press/Politics* 7(2): 84–104.

Hooper, J. (2013) 'Beppe Grillo's Five Star Movement becomes Italy's election success story', *The Guardian*, 25 February, www.theguardian.com/world/2013/feb/25/beppe-grillo-italy-election-success.

Hopkins, N. & Taylor, M. (2013) 'Alan Rusbridger and the home affairs select committee: The key exchanges', *The Guardian*, 3 December, www.theguardian.com/world/2013/dec/03/rusbridger-home-affairs-nsa-key-exchanges.

Hopper, P. (2007) *Cultural Globalization*. Cambridge: Polity.

Hoskins, A. & O'Loughlin, B. (2010) *War and Media: The Emergence of Diffused War*. Cambridge & Malden: Polity.

Hultquist, C. (2011) 'Nyckeln till framgång', *Dagens Nyheter*, 21 February, p. 18.

Husain, M. (2011) 'Syrian unrest: The exiles keeping the uprising online', *BBC News Magazine*, 14 September, www.bbc.co.uk/news/magazine-14914765.

Hutton, W. (2014) 'Why I've decided to sign up to the campaign for real press freedom', *The Observer*, 14 March.

Hyde, M. (2014) 'Let's point a satellite at GCHQ and the NSA, and see how they feel', *The Guardian*, 28 February.

Iawbuchi, K. (2007) 'Contra-flows or the cultural logic of uneven globalization?' in D. K. Thussu (ed.) *Media on the Move: Global Flow and Contra-flow*. London and New York: Routledge, pp. 67–83.

Ilavarasan, P. V. (2013) 'Community work and limited online activism among India youth', *The International Communication Gazette* 75(3): 284–99.

Inayatullah, N. (2003) 'Bumpy space: Imperialism and resistance in *Star Trek: The Next Generation*', in J. Weldes (ed.) *To Seek Out New Worlds: Exploring Links between Science Fiction and World Politics*. Houndmills: Palgrave Macmillan, pp. 53–75.

ITU (International Telecommunications Unit) (2011) www.itu.int/en/Pages/default.aspx.

Ivison, D. (ed.) (2010) *The Ashgate Research Companion to Multiculturalism*. Farnham and Burlington, VT: Ashgate.

Iyengar, S. & McGrady, J. (2007) *Media Politics*. New York: Norton.

Jackson, J. D. (2007) 'Selling politics: The impact of celebrities' political beliefs on young Americans', *Journal of Political Marketing* 6(4): 67–83.

Jackson, J. D. & Darrow, T. I. A. (2005) 'The influence of celebrity endorsements on young adults' political opinions', *Harvard International Journal of Press Politics* 10(2): 80–98.

Jameson, F. (1991) *Postmodernism, or, The Cultural Logic of Late Capitalism*. London: Verso.

Jamieson, K. H. & Cappella, J. N. (2008) *Echo Chamber: Rush Limbaugh and the Conservative Media Establishment*. Oxford: Oxford University Press.

Jankowski, N. W. (2012) 'Foreword: Public service broadcasters and the Web. Interplay of convenience, necessity, and challenge', in M. Burns & N. Brügger (eds.) *Histories of Public Service Broadcasters on the Web*. New York: Peter Lang, pp. xi–xvi.

Jansson, A. (2002) 'The mediatization of consumption: Towards an analytical framework of image culture', *Journal of Consumer Culture* 2(1): 5–31.

Jayyusi, L. (2007) 'Internationalizing media studies: A view from the Arab world', *Global Media & Communication* 3: 251–5.

Jenkins, H. (2010) 'Towards a new civic ecology: Addressing the grand challenges', Center for Future Civic Media, http://henryjenkins.org/2010/10/towards_a_new_civic_ecology.html.

Jenkins, H. (2008) *Convergence Culture. Where Old and New Media Collide*. New York and London: New York University Press.

Jenkins, H. (2007) 'Transmedia storytelling 101', www.henryjenkins.org.

Jenkins, S. (2013) 'Empire of digital chip meets nemesis: The law of diminishing political returns', *The Guardian*, 24 October, www.theguardian.com/commentisfree/2013/oct/24/simon-jenkins-digital-revolution-surveillance.

Jensen, K. B. (ed.) (2002) *A Handbook of Media and Communication Research*. London: Routledge.

Jensen, R. B. (2011) 'British military media strategies in modern wars', *Global Media and Communication* 7(3): 193–7.

Jhally, S. (1982) 'Probing the blindspot: The audience commodity', *Canadian Journal of Political and Social Theory* 6(1–2): 204–10.

Jhally, S. & Livant, B. (1986) 'Watching as working: The valorization of audience consciousness', *Journal of Communication* 36: 124–43.

Johansson, S. (2007) ' "They just make sense": Tabloid newspapers as an alternative public sphere' in R. Butsch (ed.) *Media and Public Spheres*. Houndmills: Palgrave Macmillan, pp. 83–95.

Johnson, T. (2010) 'Wikileaks and challenges to internet freedom', interview with Adam Segal, Council on Foreign Relations, www.cfr.org, publication 23661.

Johnstone, J. W. C., Slawski, E. J. & Bowman, W. W. (1976) *The News People: A Sociological Portrait of American Journalists and their Work*. Urbana: University of Illinois Press.

Jones, J. (2010) *Entertaining Politics: Satiric Television and Political Engagement*, 2nd edition. Plymouth: Rowman & Littlefield.

Jones, J. (2006) 'A cultural approach to the study of mediated citizenship', *Social Semiotics* 16(2): 365–83.

Jones, J. P. & Baym, G. (2010) 'A dialogue on satire news and the crisis of truth in postmodern political television', *Journal of Communication Inquiry* 34(3): 278–94.

Jonson, L. (2012) 'Pussy Riots metoder har gamla anor', *Svenska Dagbladet*, 12 August, http://www.svd.se/kultur/understrecket/pussy-riots-metoder-har-gamla-anor_7427648.svd.

Josephi, B. (ed.) (2010) *Journalism Education in Countries with Limited Media Freedom*. New York: Peter Lang.

Juris, J. (2004) 'Networked social movements: Global movements for global justice', in M. Castells (ed.) *The Network Society*. Northampton: Edward Elgar, pp. 341–62.

Kahn, K. F. (1994) 'The distorted mirror: Press coverage of women candidates for statewide office', *Journal of Politics* 54: 154–73.

Kaitatzi-Whitlock, S. (2011) 'The political economy of political ignorance', in J. Wasko, G. Murdock

& H. Sousa (eds.) *The Handbook of Political Economy of Communications*. Oxford: Blackwell, pp. 458–81.

Kalan, J. (2013) 'Technology holds key to fair Kenya elections', Al Jazeera, www.aljazeera.com/indepth/features/2013/01/2013115132332780404.html.

Kaldor, M. (2001) *New and Old Wars. Organized Violence in a Global Era*. Cambridge: Polity.

Kalyango, Y. & Eckler, P. (2010) 'International journalists' expectations from the US media coverage of Hurricane Katrina', *Journalism* 11(3): 277–92.

Kampf, Z. (2011) 'Journalists as actors in social dramas of apology', *Journalism* 12(1): 71–87.

Kampfner, J. (2013) 'MI5 chief Andrew Parker is right to enter the Prism debate: But why the cheer-leading from the rightwing press?' *The Guardian*, 9 October, www.theguardian.com/commentis-free/2013/oct/09/mi5-chief-andrew-parker-prism-debate.

Karlsson, M. (2012) 'Charting the liquidity of online news: Moving towards a method for content analysis of online news', *The International Communication Gazette* 74(4): 385–402.

Karlsson, M. (2011) 'The immediacy of online news, the visibility of journalistic processes and a restructuring of journalistic authority', *Journalism*, 12(3): 279–95.

Karlsten, E. (2012) 'Informationskriget pågår parallellt', *Dagens Nyheter*, 20 November, www.dn.se/nyheter/emanuel-karlsten-informationskriget-pagar-parallellt.

Katz, E. (1980) 'On conceptualising media effects', *Studies in Communication* 1: 119–41.

Katz, E., Blumler, J. G. & Gurevitch, M. (1973–4) 'Uses and gratifications research', *The Public Opinion Quarterly* 37(4): 509–23.

Katz, E. & Scannell, P. (eds.) (2009) 'The end of television? Its impact on the world (so far)'. *The ANNALS of the American Academy of Political and Social Science*, 625(1): 6–18.

Kavoori, A. P. (2007) 'Thinking through contra-flows: Perspectives from post-colonial and transna-tional cultural studies', in D. K. Thussu (ed.) *Media on the Move.: Global Flow and Contra-flow*. London & New York: Routledge, pp. 49–64.

Keller, B. (2013) 'Is Glenn Greenwald the future of news?' *The New York Times*, 27 October, www.nytimes.com/2013/10/28/opinion/a-conversation-in-lieu-of-a-column.html?pagewanted=all.

Kellner, D. (1995) *Media Culture*. New York: Routledge.

Kendall, B. (2010) 'Wikileaks: site list reveals US sensitivities', www.bbc.co.uk/news/11932041.

Kendall, L. (2008) 'Beyond media producers and consumers: Online multimedia productions as interpersonal communication', *Information, Communication and Society* 11(2): 207–20.

Kepplinger, H. M. (2002) 'Mediatization of politics: Theory and data', *Journal of Communication* 52(4): 972–86.

Kevin, D., Pellicanò, F, & Schneeberger, A. (2013) 'Television News Channels in Europe'. European Audiovisual Observatory, www.obs.coe.int/documents/205595/264629/European+news+Market+2013+FINAL.pdf/116afdf3-758b-4572-af0f-61297651ae80.

Khazan, O. (2013) 'Meet Egypt's Jon Stewart, who is now under investigation for satire', *The Washington Post*, 2 January, www.washingtonpost.com/blogs/worldviews/wp/2013/01/02/egypt-bassem-youssef-jon-stewart-investigation/.

Kim, H. S. (2012) 'War journalists and forces of gatekeeping during the escalation and the de-escalation periods of the Iraq War', *The International Communication Gazette* 74(4): 323–41.

Kingsley, P. (2014a) 'Egypt's censorship of comedian Bassem Youssef sends "wrong message"', *The Observer*, 26 January, www.theguardian.com/world/2014/jan/26/egypt-censorship-bassem-youssef-tv-satirist.

Kingsley, P. (2014b) 'Threats, assaults and arrests . . . the perils of reporting from Egypt', *The Guardian*, 7 February, www.theguardian.com/world/2014/feb/07/threats-charges-reporting-egypt.

Kingsley, P. (2013) 'Meet Egypt's Jon Stewart', *The Guardian* (iPad edition), 6 March.

Kitzinger, J. (2000) 'Media templates: patterns of association and the (re)construction of meaning over time', *Media, Culture and Society* 22: 61–84.

Kleinsteuber, H. J. (2001) 'Habermas and the public sphere: From a German to a European perspec-tive', *Javnost – the Public* 8(1): 95–108.

Klinenberg, E. & Benzecry, C. (2005) 'Introduction: Cultural production in a digital age', *The ANNALS of the American Academy of Political and Social Science* 597: 6–18.

Knight, E. (2012) 'Fairfax shakes up operations as sweeping changes unveiled', *The Age*, 18 June, www. smh.com.au/business/fairfax-shakes-up-operations-as-sweeping-changes-unveiled-20120618-20 k7p.html.

Knightley, P. (2003) *The First Casualty: The War Correspondent as Hero, Propagandist and Myth-Maker from the Crimea to Iraq*. London: André Deutsch.

Köcher, R. (1986) 'Bloodhounds or missionaries: Role definitions of German and British journalists', *European Journal of Communication* 1(1): 43–64.

Kolmer, C. & Semetko, H. (2009) 'Framing the Iraq War: Perspectives from American, UK, Czech, German, South African, and Al-Jazeera news', *American Behavioural Scientist* 52(5): 643–56.

Koopmans, R. (2004) 'Movements and media', *Theory & Society* 33: 367–91.

Kperogi. F. A. (2011) 'Cooperation with the corporation? CNN and the hegemonic cooptation of citizen journalism through iReport.com', *New Media & Society* 13(2): 314–29.

Kraidy, M. (2009) *Reality Television and Arab Politics: Contention in Public Life*. Cambridge: Cambridge University Press.

Kriesi, H. (2013) 'Introduction – the new challenges to democracy", in H. Kriesi, S. Lavenex, F. Esser, J. Matthes, M. Bühlmann & D. Bochsler, *Democracy in the Age of Globalization and Mediatization*. Houndmills: Palgrave Macmillan, pp. 1–16.

Kriesi, H., Lavenex, S., Esser, F., Matthes, J., Bühlmann, M. & Bochsler, D. (2013) *Democracy in the Age of Globalization and Mediatization*. Houndmills: Palgrave Macmillan.

Krotz, F. (2009) 'Mediatization: A concept with which to grasp media and societal change', in K. Lundby (ed.) *Mediatization: Concept, Changes, Consequences*. New York: Peter Lang, pp. 21–40.

Krotz, F. (2007) 'The meta-process of "mediatization" as a conceptual frame', *Global Media and Communication* 3(3): 256–60.

Kuipers, G. (2011) 'The politics of humour in the public sphere: Cartoons, power and modernity in the first transnational humour scandal', *European Journal of Cultural Studies* 14(1): 63–80.

Kumar, S. (2010) 'Google Earth and the nation state: Sovereignty in the age of new media', *Global Media and Communication* 6(2): 154–76.

Kunelis, R. & Sparks, C. (2001) 'Problems with a European public sphere: An introduction', *Javnost – the Public* 8(1): 5–20.

LaMarre, H .L., Landreville, K. D. & Beam, M. A. (2009) 'The irony of satire: Political ideology and the motivation to see what you want to see in the Colbert Report', *International Journal of Press/ Politics* 14(2): 212–31.

Lamuedra, M. & O'Donnell, H. (2012) 'Community as context: EastEnders, public service and neoliberal ideology', *European Journal of Cultural Studies* 16(1): 58–76.

Lamy, A. (2011) 'Post-9/11 era: To the end of a period', *Global Media and Communication* 7(3): 287–91.

Lanchester, J. (2013) 'The Snowden files: Why the British public should be worried about GCHQ', *The Guardian*, 3 October, www.theguardian.com/world/2013/oct/03/edward-snowden-files-john-lanchester.

Landreville, K. D., Holbert, R. L. & LaMarre, H. L. (2010) 'The influence of late-night TV comedy on political talk: A moderated-mediation model', *International Journal of Press/Politics* 15(4): 482–98.

Larsen, H. (2010) 'Legitimation strategies of public service broadcasters: The divergent rhetoric in Norway and Sweden', *Media, Culture & Society* 32(2): 267–83.

Larsson, L. (2005) *Opinionsmakarna: En studie om PR-consulter, journalistik och demokrati*. Lund: Studentlitteratur.

Lauk, E. (2008) 'How will it all unfold? Media systems and journalism cultures in post-communist countries', in K. Jakubowicz & M. Sükösd (eds.) *Finding the Right Place on the Map: Central and Eastern European Media Change in a Global Perspective*. Bristol: Intellect Books, pp. 193–212.

Lawrence, R. G. (2000) *The Politics of Force: Media and the Construction of Police Brutality*. Berkeley: University of California Press.

Lawson, M. (2012) 'Hollywood won't decide the US election', *The Guardian*, 30 August, www.guardian.co.uk/film/shortcuts/2012/aug/29/hollywood-us-election-spielberg-lincoln.

Lax, S. (2007) 'Digital radio and the diminution of the public sphere' in R. Butsch (ed.) *Media and Public Spheres*. Houndmills: Palgrave Macmillan, pp. 109–21.

Leapman, M. (2011) 'Murdoch: How it all began', *British Journalism Review* 9(22:3): 11–13.

Lenas, S. (2014) 'Soran Ismail tystnar i Sveriges Radio', *Dagens Nyheter*, 12 February, http://www.dn.se/kultur-noje/soran-ismail-tystnar-i-sveriges-radio/

Lester, L. (2010) *Media and Environment*. Cambridge: Polity.

Lester, L. & Hutchins, B. (2009) 'Power games: Environmental protest, news media and the internet', *Media, Culture & Society* 31(4): 579–95.

Lewis, J., Inthorn, S. & Wahl-Jorgensen, K. (2005) *Citizens or Consumers? What the Media Tell Us about Political Participation*. Maidenhead: Open University Press.

Liebes, T. (1998) 'Television's disaster marathons: A danger for democratic processes?' in T. Liebes and J. Curran (eds.) *Media, Ritual and Identity*. London: Routledge, pp. 71–84.

Liebes, T. (1997) *Reporting the Arab–Israeli Conflict: How Hegemony Works*. London: Routledge.

Liebes, T. & Katz, E. (1990) *The Export of Meaning: Cross-Cultural Readings of 'Dallas'*. New York and Oxford: Oxford University Press.

Lierouw, L. (2011) *Alternative and Activist New Media*. Oxford: Polity.

Lilleker, D. G. (2006) *Key Concepts in Political Communication*. London: Sage.

Lim, J. B. Y. (2013) 'Video blogging and youth activism in Malaysia', *The International Communication Gazette* 75(3): 300–21.

Lindén, J. (2011) *TV-ledning i konkurrens: En studie av Sveriges Televisions publicistiska ledning 1997–2000*. Stockholm: IMS, SU.

Lindén, J. (2005) '"Media and telecom need to cooperate more". Interview on convergence with Johan Lindén from Sveriges Television', Eurescom mess@age, http://archive.eurescom.eu/message/messageOct2005/interview_with_Johan_Linden_from_SVT.asp.

Lindgren, S. & Lundström, R. (2011) 'Pirate culture and hacktivist mobilization: The cultural and social protocols of #Wikileaks on Twitter', *New Media & Society* 13(6): 999–1018.

Lingenberg, S. (2006) 'The audience's role in constituting the European public sphere: A theoretical approach based on the pragmatic concept of John Dewey', in N. Carpentier, P. Pruulmann-Vengerfeldt, K. Nordenstreng, M. Hartmann, P. Vihalemm & B. Cammaerts (eds.) *Researching Media, Democracy and Participation*. Tartu: University of Tartu Press, pp. 121–34.

Livant, B. (1982) 'Working at watching: A reply to Sut Jhally', *Canadian Journal of Political and Social Theory* 6(1–2): 211–15.

Livant, B. (1979) 'The audience commodity: On the blindspot debate', *Canadian Journal of Political and Social Theory* 6(1–2): 211–15.

Livingstone, S. (2009) 'On the mediation of everything: ICA presidential address 2008', *Journal of Communication* 59: 1–18.

Livingstone, S. (2005) 'Media audiences, interpreters and users', in M. Gillespie (ed.) *Media Audiences*. Maidenhead: Open University Press, pp. 9–50.

Löblich, M. & Pfaff-Rüdiger, S. (2011) 'Network analysis: A qualitative approach to empirical studies on communication policy', *The International Communication Gazette* 73/7: 630–47.

Loewe, P. (2011) 'Berlusconis medier till motoffensiv efter åtalet', *Dagens Nyheter*, 17 February, p. 24.

Long, P. & Wall, T. (2009) *Media Studies. Texts, Production and Context*. Harlow: Pearson Longman.

Lorenzo-Dus, N. & Bruan, A. (2011) 'Recontextualising participatory journalists' mobile media in British television news: A case study of the live coverage and commemorations of the 2005 London bombings', *Discourse and Communication* 5(1): 23–40.

Lotz, A.D. (2009) 'What is U.S. television now?' *The ANNALS of the American Academy of Political and Social Science* 625(1): 49–59.

Louw, E. (2005) *The Media and Political Process*. London: Sage.

Loveluck, L. (2014) 'Al-Jazeera journalists appeal for support as Egypt trial starts', *The Guardian*, 20 February, www.theguardian.com/world/2014/feb/20/al-jazeera-journalists-appeal-egypt-trial-terrorism.

Lugo-Ocando, J. & Canizálex, A. (2011) 'When magical realism confronted virtual reality: online news and journalism in Latin America', in G. Meikle & G. Redden (eds.) *News Online: Transformations and Continuities.* Houndmills: Palgrave Macmillan, pp. 69–83.

Lukes, S. (1974/2005). *Power: A Radical View.* Basingstoke: Palgrave Macmillan.

Lule, J. (2012) *Globalization and Media: Global Village of Babel.* Rowman & Littlefield.

Lundby, K. (2009a) 'Introduction: "mediatization" as key', in K. Lundby (ed.) *Mediatization: Concept, Changes, Consequences.* New York: Peter Lang, pp. 1–18.

Lundby, K. (2009b) 'Media logic: Looking for social interaction', in K. Lundby (ed.) *Mediatization: Concept, Changes, Consequences.* New York: Peter Lang, pp. 101–19.

Lundby, K. (2008) 'Editorial: Mediatized stories: Mediation perspectives on digital storytelling', *New Media & Society* 10(3): 363–71.

Lunghi, A. & Wheeler, S. (eds.) (2012) *Occupy Everything. Reflections on Why It's Kicking Off Everywhere.* Wivenhoe: Minor Compositions.

Lunt, P. (2009) 'Television, public participation, and public service: From value consensus to the politics of identity', in E. Katz & P. Scannell (eds.) *The End of Television? Its Impact on the World (So Far). The ANNALS of the American Academy of Political and Social Science,* 625(1): 128–38.

Lunt, P. & Pantti, M. (2007) 'Popular culture and the public sphere: Currents of feeling and social control in talk shows and reality TV' in R. Butsch (ed.) *Media and Public Spheres.* Houndmills: Palgrave Macmillan, pp. 162–74.

Mabweazara, H. M. (2011) 'Between the newsroom and the pub: The mobile phone in the dynamics of everyday mainstream journalism practice in Zimbabwe', *Journalism* 12(6): 692–707.

Machado-Borges, T. (2007) 'Brazilian telenovelas, fictionalized politics, and the merchandising of social issues', in K. Riegert (ed.) *Politicotainment: Television's Take on the Real.* New York: Peter Lang, pp. 151–80.

Machiavelli, N. (1532/1978) *The Prince.* Harmondsworth: Penguin.

Machill, M. (1998) 'Euronews: The first European news channel as a case study for industry development in Europe and for spectra of transnational journalism research', *Media, Culture & Society* 20(3): 427–50.

Machill, M., Köhler, S. & Waldhasuer, M. (2007) 'The use of narrative structures in television news: An experiement in innovative forms of journalistic presentation', *European Journal of Communication* 22(2): 185–205.

Machill, M., Beiler, M. & Fischer, C. (2006) 'Europe – topics in Europe's media', *European Journal of Communication* 2(1): 57–88.

Makinnen, V. (2011) 'Google versus Nicolas Sarkozy at G8', WordPress, http://contadorwanarua.wordpress.com/2011/05/24/google-versus-nicolas-sarkozy-at-eg8/.

Manning, P. (2001) *News and News Sources: A Critical Introduction.* London: Sage.

Marchetti, D. (2005) 'Mapping field variation: Journalism in France and the United States', in R. Benson & E. Neveu (eds.) *Bourdieu and the Journalistic Field.* Cambridge: Polity, pp. 85–112.

Mardell, M. (2011) 'Raw politics of the US election', BBC News online, http://newsvote.bbc.co.uk/mpapps/pagetools/print/news.bbc.co.uk/2/hi/programmes/from_our_own_correspondent/9568353.stm.

Markham, T. & Couldry, N. (2007) 'Tracking the reflexivity of the (dis)engaged citizen: Some methodological reflections', *Qualitative Inquiry* 13(5): 675–95.

Marsden, C. & Verhulst, S. (1999) *Convergence in European Digital TV Regulation.* London: Blackstone Press.

Marsh, K. (2011) 'Our only hope is to stand – and deliver', *British Journalism Review* 22(3): 49–55.

Marshall, T. H. (1992 [1950]) 'Citizenship and social class', in T. H. Marshall & T. Bottomore (eds.) *Citizenship and Social Class.* London: Pluto, pp. 3–51.

Martell, L. (2010) *The Sociology of Globalization.* Cambridge: Polity.

Martin, E. (2011) 'Terrorism, humor, and American popular culture', *Global Media and Communication* 7(3): 233–7.

Martin, J. D. (2011) 'News use and political socialization among young Jordanians', *International Communication Gazette* 73(8): 706–31.

Mason, P. (2012) *Why It's Kicking Off Everywhere: The New Global Revolutions.* London: Verso.

Mason, R. (2013) 'Lord Steel criticises culture of spin and tweeting in modern politics', *The Guardian*, 31 October, www.theguardian.com/politics/2013/oct/31/lord-steel-criticises-culture-spin-docto rs-twitter-politics.

Matheson, D. (2005) *Media Discourses. Analysing Media Texts*. Maidenhead: Open University Press.

Matheson, D. and Allan, S. (2009) *Digital War Reporting*. Cambridge and Malden: Polity.

Mayhew, L. (1997) *The New Public: Professional Communication and the Means of Social Influence*. Cambridge: Cambridge University Press.

Mazzoleni, G. & Schulz, W. (1999) 'Mediatization of politics: A challenge for democracy', *Political Communication* 16: 247–61.

McCarthy, J. D., McPhail, C. & Smith, J. (1996) 'Images of protest', *American Sociological Review* 6(3): 478–99.

McChesney, R. W. (2013) *Digital Disconnect: How Capitalism is Turning the Internet Against Democracy*. New York: The New Press.

McChesney, R. W. (2011) 'The crisis of journalism and the Internet', in G. Meikle & G. Redden, (eds.) *News Online: Transformations and Continuities*. Houndmills: Palgrave Macmillan, pp. 53–68.

McCombs, M. E. & Shaw, D. L. (1972) 'The agenda-setting function of mass media'. *Public Opinion Quarterly* 36: 176–87.

McCullagh, C. (2002) *Media Power: A Sociological Introduction*. Houndmills: Palgrave.

McCurdy, P. (2010) 'Breaking the spiral of silence: Unpacking the "media debate" within global justice movements. A case study of Dissent! and the 2005 Gleneagles G8 summit', *Interface: A Journal for and about Social Movements* 2(2): 42–67.

McKenna, K. (2013) 'SNP task for Scottish writer', *The Observer*, 14 July.

McKnight, D. (2010) 'A change in the climate? The journalism of opinion at News Corporation', *Journalism* 11(6): 693–706.

McLaughlin, L. (2007) 'Transnational feminism and the Revolutionary Association of the Women of Afghanistan', in D. K. Thussu (ed.) *Media on the Move: Global Flow and Contra-flow*. London & New York: Routledge, pp. 221–36.

McLeod, J. M. & Lee, N.-J. (2012) 'Social networks, public discussion and civic engagement: A socialization perspective', in H. Semetko & M. Scammell (eds.) *The Sage Handbook of Political Communication*. London: Sage, pp. 197–208.

McLuhan, M. (1964/2003) *Understanding Media: The Extensions of Man*. Berkeley: Gingko Press.

McNair, B. (2011) 'Managing the online news revolution: The UK experience', in G. Meikle & G. Redden (eds.) *News Online: Transformations and Continuities*. Houndmills: Palgrave Macmillan, pp. 38–52.

McNair, B. (2006) *Cultural Chaos: Journalism, News and Power in a Globalised World*. London: Routledge.

McNair, B. (2000) *Journalism and Democracy: An Evaluation of the Political Public Sphere*. London: Routledge.

McNamee, J. (2010) 'Out of sight, out of mind', *Index on Censorship* 39(1): 108–17.

McPhail, T. (ed.) (2014) *Global Communication: Theories, Stakeholders, and Trends*. Oxford: Wiley-Blackwell.

McQuail, D. (2010) *McQuail's Mass Communication Theory*. London: Sage.

McQuail, D., Golding, G. & De Bens, E. (eds.) (2005) *Communication Theory and Research*. London: Sage.

Meikle, G. & Redden, G. (2011) 'Introduction: Transformation and continuity', in G. Meikle & G. Redden (eds.) *News Online: Transformations and Continuities*. Houndmills: Palgrave Macmillan, pp. 1–19.

Melin, A. S. (2013) 'Största möjliga tystnad', *Dagens Nyheter*, 26 July, www.dn.se/ledare/signerat/ storsta-mojliga-tystnad.

Mellado, C. & Humanes, M. L. (2012) 'Modeling perceived professional autonomy in Chilean journalism', *Journalism* 13(8): 985–1003.

Meraz, S. (2011) 'The fight for "how to think": Traditional media, social networks, and issue interpretation', *Journalism*, 12(1): 107–27.

Meraz, S. (2009) 'The many faced "you" of social media', in Z. Papacharissi (ed.) *Journalism and Citizenship: New Agendas in Communication*. New York & Abingdon: Routledge, pp. 123–47.

Meyen, M. & Scheu, A. (2011) 'The role of external broadcasting in a closed political system: A case study of the German post-war states', *Global Media and Communication* 7(2): 115–28.

Meyer, D. (2012) 'The US election: A vote for the status quo', BBC Online, 7 November, www.bbc.co.uk/news/20216166.

Meyer, T. (2002) *Media Democracy. How the Media Colonize Politics*. Cambridge: Polity.

Meyrowitz, J. (2009) 'We liked to watch: Television as progenitor of the surveillance society', *The ANNALS of the American Academy of Political and Social Science*, 625(1): 32–48.

Meyrowitz, J. (1985) *No Sense of Place: The Impact of Electronic Media on Social Behavior*. New York: Oxford University Press.

Miège, B. (2011) 'Theorizing the cultural industries: Persistent specificities and reconsiderations', in J. Wasko, G. Murdock & H. Sousa (eds.) *The Handbook of Political Economy of Communications*. Oxford: Blackwell, pp. 83–108.

Miles, H. (2005) *Al-Jazeera: How Arab TV News Challenged the World*. New York: Abacus.

Miller, J. (2011) 'Wars and their journalisms', *Global Media and Communication* 7(3): 205–10.

Miller, D. & Sabir, R. (2012) 'Counterterrorism as counterinsurgency in the UK "war on terror"', in D. Whyte & S. Poynting (eds.) *Counter Terrorism and State Political Violence*. London: Routledge.

Mills, C. W. (1956/2000) *The Power Elite*. Oxford: Oxford University Press.

Minton, A. (2013) 'News report: Scaring the living daylights out of people', Spinwatch, 27 March, www.spinwatch.org/index.php/issues/lobbying/item/5458-the-local-lobby-and-the-failure-of-democracy.

Mody, B. (2010) 'Towards contextually grounded comparative scholarship', *Global Media and Communication* 6(3): 246–52.

Moe, H. (2010) 'Everyone a pamphleteer? Reconsidering comparisons of mediated public participation in the print age and the digital era', *Media, Culture & Society* 32(4): 691–700.

Monbiot, G. (2013) 'It's business that really rules us now', *The Guardian*, 11 November, www.theguardian.com/commentisfree/2013/nov/11/business-rules-lobbying-corporate-interests.

Moorcraft, P. & Taylor, P. M. (2007) 'War watchdogs or lapdogs?' *British Journalism Review* 18(4): 39–50.

Morgan, A. (2011) 'From fear to fury: How the Arab world found a voice', *The Guardian*, 27 February, www.guardian.co.uk/music/2011/feb/27/egypt-tunisia-music-protests.

Morley, D. (1980) *The Nationwide Audience: Structure and Decoding*. London: British Film Institute.

Morozov, E. (2009) 'The brave new world of slacktivism', *Foreign Policy*, 19 May, http://neteffect.foreignpolicy.com/posts/2009/05/19/the_brave_new_world_of_slacktivism.

Morris, N. & Waisbord, S. (2001) 'Rethinking media globalization and state power', in N. Morris & S. Waisbord (eds.) *Media and Globalization: Why the State Matters*. New York: Rowman & Littlefield, pp. vii–xvi.

Mortensen, M. (2011) 'When citizen photojournalism sets the news agenda: Neda Agha Soltan as a Web 2.0 icon of post-election unrest in Iran', *Global Media and Communication* 7(1): 4–16.

Mossman, K. (2013) 'Unkindest cut gives African rapper cause', *The Observer*, 17 February.

Mouffe, C. (1997) *The Return of the Political*. London: Verso.

Moy, P., Xenos, M. A. & Hess, V. K. (2005a) 'Priming effects of late-night comedy', *International Journal of Public Opinion Research* 18(2): 198–210.

Moy, P., Xenos, M.A. & Hess, V.K. (2005b) 'Communication and citizenship: Mapping the political effects of infotainment', *Mass Communication and Society* 8(2): 111–31.

Moyo, L. (2011) 'Blogging down a dictatorship: Human rights, citizen journalists and the right to communicate in Zimbabwe', *Journalism* 12(6): 745–60.

Moyo, L. (2010) 'The global citizen and the international media: A comparative analysis of CNN and Xinhua's coverage of the Tibetan crisis', *The International Communication Gazette* 72(2): 191–207.

Mozorov, E. (2011) 'Repressing the internet, Western-style', *The Wall Street Journal*, 13 August, http://online.wsj.com/news/articles/SB10001424053111903918104576502214236127064.

Morozov, E. (2009) 'Iran: Downside to the "Twitter revolution"', *Dissent* 56(4): 10–14.

Mudhai, O. F. (2011) 'Immediacy and openness in a digital Africa: Networked-convergent journalisms in Kenya', *Journalism* 12(6): 674-91.

Muhlmann, G. (2010) *Journalism for Democracy*. Cambridge: Polity.

Mulholland, H. (2011) 'Ryan Giggs named as footballer at the centre of privacy row', *The Guardian*, 23 May, www.guardian.co.uk/politics/2011/may/23/ryan-giggs-named-footballer-injunction-row.

Murdock, G. (1990/2005) 'Television and citizenship: In defence of public broadcasting', in A. Tomlinson (ed.) *Consumption, Identity and Style: Marketing, Meanings and the Packaging of Pleasure*. London & New York: Routledge, pp. 77-101.

Nacos, B. L. (2008) *Terrorism and Counterterrorism: Understanding Threats and Responses in the Post 9/11 World*. New York: Penguin.

Napoli, P. M. (2010) 'Revisiting "mass communication" and the "work" of the audience in the new media environment', *Media, Culture & Society* 32(3): 505-16.

Narine, N. (2010) 'Global trauma and narrative cinema', *Theory, Culture & Society* 27(4): 119-45.

National Hispanic Media Coalition (NHMC) (2012) 'American hate radio: How a powerful outlet for democratic discourse has deteriorated into hate, racism and extremism', http://nhmc.org/american_hate_radio_nhmc.pdf.

Nash, K. (2008) 'Global citizenship as show business: The cultural politics of Make Poverty History', *Media, Culture & Society* 30(29: 167-81.

Nash, K. & Fraser, N. (2014) *Transnationalizing the Public Sphere*. Cambridge: Polity.

Naughton, J. (2013) 'Twitter and the transformation of democracy', *The Guardian*, 14 September, www.theguardian.com/commentisfree/2013/sep/14/twitter-flotation-facebook-politics-social-network.

Negrine, R. (2008) *The Transformation of Political Communication: Continuities and Changes in Media and Politics*.Houndmills: Palgrave Macmillan.

Negroponte, N. (1995) *Being Digital*. New York: Vintage Books.

Neuman, I. B. (2003) ' "To know him was to love him. Not to know him was to love him from afar": Diplomacy in *Star Trek*', in J. Weldes (ed.) *To Seek Out New Worlds: Exploring Links between Science Fiction and World Politics*. Houndmills: Palgrave Macmillan, pp. 31-52.

Neuman, W. R., Just, M. R. & Crigler, A. N. (1992) *Common Knowledge. News and the Construction of Political Meaning*. Chicago: University of Chicago Press.

Neveu, E. (2005) 'Bourdieu, the Frankfurt School, and cultural studies: On some misunderstandings', in R. Benson & E. Neveu (eds.) *Bourdieu and the Journalistic Field*. Cambridge: Polity, pp. 195-213.

Nevéus, I. (2011) 'Putins parti till attack i slutspurten', *Dagens Nyheter*, 3 December, pp. 8-9.

Nexon, D. H. & Neuman, I. B. (eds.) (2006) *Harry Potter and International Relations*. Lanham: Rowman & Littlefield.

Nguyen, A. (2011) 'Marrying the professional to the amateur: strategies and implications of the OhmyNews model', in G. Meikle & G. Redden (eds.) *News Online. Transformations and Continuities*. Houndmills: Palgrave Macmillan, pp. 195-209.

Nightingale, V. (2007) 'Lost in space: Television's missing publics' in R. Butsch (ed.) *Media and Public Spheres*. Houndmills: Palgrave Macmillan, pp. 185-97.

Nisbet, E. C., Nisbet, M. C., Scheufele, D. A. & Shanahan, J. E. (2004) 'Public diplomacy, television news, and Muslim opinion', *Press/Politics* 9(2): 11-37.

Nohl, A.-M. (2011) 'Cosmopolitanization and social location: Generational differences within the Turkish audience of the BBC World Service', *European Journal of Cultural Studies* 14(3): 321-38.

Norris, P. (2000) *A Virtuous Circle: Political Communications in Postindustrial Societies*. Cambridge: Cambridge University Press.

Norris, P. & Inglehart, R. (2009) *Cosmopolitan Communications: Cultural Diversity in a Globalized World*. Cambridge: Cambridge University Press.

Norton-Taylor, R. & Cobain, I. (2013) 'Ten reasons not to trust claims national security is being threatened by leaks', *The Guardian*, 16 October, www.theguardian.com/uk-news/2013/oct/16/national-security-leaks-gchq-nsa-intelligence-agencies.

NPR (2010) 'Entering the secret world of Wikileaks', www.npr.org/templates/story/story.php?storyId=128485967.

Nyabola, N. (2014) 'Why do Western media get Africa wrong?', Al Jazeera English, 2 January, www.aljazeera.com/indepth/opinion/2014/01/why-do-western-media-get-africa-wrong-2014115 2641935954.html.

Nye, J. (2010) 'Soft power and public diplomacy in the 21st century' http://soundcloud.com/british council/joseph-nye.

Nye, J. (2004) *Soft Power*. New York: Public Affairs.

O'Brien, J. (2011) 'Privacy? It's secrecy by stealth', *British Journalism Review* 22(3): 31–5.

O'Reilly, T. (2007) 'What is Web 2.0: Design patterns and business models for the next generation of software', http://ssrn.com/abstract=1008839.

Oliphant, R. (2010) 'The charge of the bucket brigade', www.mn.ru/comments/20100603/187859836. html/http://waytomoscow.com/news_current.php?part_id=21&id=38.

Oliver, P. E. & Maney, G. (2000) 'Political processes and local newspaper coverage of protest events', *American Journal of Sociology* 106: 463–505.

Orgad, S. (2012) *Media Representation and the Global Imagination*. Cambridge: Polity.

Orgad, S. (2008) ' "Have you seen Blomberg?" Satellite news channels as agents of the new visibility', *Global Media and Communication* 4(3): 301–27.

Örnebring, H. (2013) 'Anything you can do, I can do better? Professional journalists on citizen journalism in six European countries', *The International Communication Gazette* 75(1): 35–53.

Örnebring, H. (2012) 'Clientelism, elites, and the media in Central and Eastern Europe', *The International Journal of Press/Politics* 17(4): 497–515.

Örnebring, H. (2009) *The Two Professionalisms of Journalism: Journalism and the Changing Context of Work*. RISJ Working Paper 2, http://reutersinstitute.politics.ox.ac.uk/publications/risj-chal lenges/.

Örnebring, H. (2007) 'A Necessary Profession for the Modern Age? Nineteenth-century news, journalism and the public sphere', in R. Butsch (ed.) *Media and Public Spheres*. Houndmills: Palgrave Macmillan, pp. 71–82.

Orstadius, K. (2013) 'Hundratals miljoner till försvarets signalspaning', *Dagens Nyheter*, 10 November, www.dn.se/nyheter/sverige/hundratals-miljoner-till-forsvarets-signalspaning/.

Ostertag, S. (2010) 'Establishing news confidence: A qualitative study of how people use the news media to know the news-world', *Media, Culture & Society* 32(4): 597–614.

Owen, A. S. (1999) 'Oppositional voices in China Beach: Narrative configurations of gender and war', in D. K. Mumby (ed.) *Narrative and Social Control: Critical Perspectives*. London: Sage, pp. 207–31.

Painter, J. (2008) *Counter-Hegemonic News. A Case Study of Al-Jazeera English and Telesur*. Oxford: Reuters Institute.

Pantti, M. (2005) 'Masculine tears, feminine tears – and crocodile tears. Mourning Olof Palme and Anna Lindh in Finnish newspapers', *Journalism* 6(3): 357–77.

Papacharissi, Z. (2010) *A Private Sphere: Democracy in a Digital Age*. Cambridge: Polity.

Papacharissi, Z. (2002) 'The virtual sphere: The internet as a public sphere', *New Media & Society* 4: 9–27.

Papathanassopoulos, S. (2005) 'Europe: An examplary landscape for comprehending globalization', *Global Media & Communication* 1(1): 46–50.

Parameswaran, R. (2010) 'The rise of China and India: Promising new teaching and research directions for global media studies', *Global Media and Communication* 6(3): 285–90.

Parthasarathi, V. (2010) 'Deciphering Chindia: Two accents of media governance', *Global Media and Communication* 6(3): 329–36.

Patterson, C. (2011) 'Government intervention in the Iraq war media narrative through direct coercion', *Global Media and Communication* 7(3): 181–16.

Patterson, T. (2000) 'The United States: News in a free-market society', in R. Gunther & A. Mugham (eds.) *Democracy and the Media*. Cambridge: Cambridge University Press, pp. 241–65.

Patterson, T. E. & Donsbach, W. (1996) 'News decisions: Journalists as partisan actors', *Political Communication* 13(4): 455–68.

Pels, D. (2003) 'Aesthetic representation and political style: Re-balancing identity and difference in media democracy', in J. Corner & D. Pels (eds.) *Media and the Restyling of Politics*. London: Sage, pp. 41–66.

Perlmutter, D. (1998) *Photojournalism and Foreign Policy: Icons of Outrage in International Crisis*. Westport: Prager.

Peters, C. (2011) 'Emotion aside or emotional side? Crafting an "experience of involvement" in the news', *Journalism* 12(3): 297–316.

Peters, J. D. (2009) 'Witnessing', in P. Frosh & A. Pinchevsky (eds.) *Media Witnessing: Testimony in the Age of Mass Communication*. Houndmills: Palgrave Macmillan, pp. 23–48.

Petley, J. (2011) 'Privacy: Watchdogs turned attack dogs', *British Journalism Review* 22(3): 36–42.

Pfetsch, B. & Voltmer, K. (2012) 'Negotiating control: Political communication cultures in Bulgaria and Poland', *International Journal of Press/Politics* 17(4): 388–406.

Philo, G. & Berry, M. (2011) *More Bad News from Israel*. London: Pluto Press.

Philo, G. & Berry, M. (2004) *Bad News from Israel*. London: Pluto Press.

Pieterse, J. N. (2009) 'Representing the rise of the rest as threat: Media and global divides', *Global Media and Communication* 5(2): 221–37.

Pieterse, J. N. (2003) *Globalization and Culture: Global Melange*. Rowman & Littlefield, 2003.

Pinchevski, A. & Liebes, T. (2010) 'Severed voices: Radio and the mediation of trauma in the Eichmann trial', *Public Culture* 22(2): 265–91.

Pintak, L. (2009) 'Arab media and the Al-Jazeera effect', in T. McPhail (ed.) *Global Communication: Theories, Stakeholders, and Trends*, 3rd edition. Malden and Oxford: Wiley-Blackwell, pp. 290–304.

Pintak, L. & Setiyono, B. (2011) 'The mission of Indonesian journalism: Balancing democracy, development, and Islamic values', *International Journal of Press/Politics* 16(2): 185–209.

Plesner, U. (2009) 'An actor-network perspective on changing work practices', *Journalism* 10(5): 604–26.

Plunkett, J. (2013) '*Borgen* could get British makeover in return of political drama on TV', *The Guardian*, 25 October, http://www.theguardian.com/tv-and-radio/2013/oct/25/borgen-british-makeover-political-drama-tv

Poletti, M. & Brants, K. (2010) 'Between partisanship and cynicism: Italian journalism in a state of flux', *Journalism* 11(3): 329–46.

Postman, N. (1987) *Amusing Ourselves to Death*. London: Methuen.

Powers, M. & Benson, R. (2014) 'Is the internet homogenizing or diversifying the news? External pluralism in the U.S., Danish, and French press', *The International Journal of Press/Politics* 19(2): 246–65.

Preston, P. (2009) *Making the News. Journalism and News Cultures in Europe*. Abingdon: Routledge.

Price, M. E. (2009) 'End of television and foreign policy', *The ANNALS of the American Academy of Political and Social Science* 625(1): 196–204.

Price, M. E. (1996) *Television, the Public Sphere and National Identity*. Oxford and New York: Oxford University Press.

Prior, M. (2006) *Post-Broadcast Democracy: How Media Choice Increases Inequality in Political Involvement and Polarizes Elections*. Cambridge: Cambridge University Press.

Puddington, A. (2013) 'Freedom in the world 2013: Democratic breakthroughs in the balance', www.freedomhouse.org/sites/default/files/FIW%202013%20Overview%20Essay%20for%20Web_0.pdf.

Putnam, R. (1995) 'Bowling alone: America's declining social capital', *The Journal of Democracy* 6(1): 65–78.

Raboy, M. (2002) 'Media policy in the new communications environment', in M. Raboy (ed.) *Global Media Policy in the New Millennium*. Luton: University of Luton Press.

Rantanen, T. (2013) 'A critique of the systems approaches in comparative media research: A Central and Eastern European approach', *Global Media and Communication* 9(3): 257–77.

Rantanen, T. (2005) *The Media and Globalization*. London: Sage.

Rao, U. (2010a) *News as Culture: Journalistic Practices and the Remaking of Indian Leadership Traditions*. New York and Oxford: Berghahn Books.

Rao, U. (2010b) 'Neoliberalism and the rewriting of the Indian leader', *American Ethnologist* 37(4): 713–25.

Reding, V. (2009) 'EU film support goes global', press release, 9 January 2009, http://europa.eu/rapid/pressReleasesAction.do?reference=IP/09/26&format=HTML&aged=0&language=EN&guiLanguage=en.

Reinardy, S. (2011) 'Newspaper journalism in crisis: Burnout on the rise, eroding young journalists' career commitment', *Journalism* 12(1): 33–50.

Reinl, J. (2013) 'Kenyan satire takes aim at "corrupt leaders"', www.aljazeera.com/indepth/features/2013/02/2013217105233247915.html.

Resende, F. & Paes, A.B. (2011) 'The Arab conflicts and the media discourse: A Brazilian perspective', *Global Media and Communication* 7(3): 215–19.

Rettberg, J. W. (2008) *Blogging*. Cambridge and Malden: Polity.

Reynolds, P. (2011) 'A glimpse of journalism's future', BBC News, 23 February, www.bbc.co.uk/news/world-middle-east-12536855.

Rhoads, C. & Fassihi, F. (2011) 'Iran vows to unplug internet', *The Wall Street Journal*, http://online.wsj.com/article/SB10001424052748704889404576277391449002016.html.

Richardson, K. & Meinhof, U. M. (1999) *Worlds in Common? Television Discourse in a Changing Europe*. London: Routledge.

Richter, A. (2008) 'Post-Soviet perspectives on censorship and freedom of the media: An overview', *International Communication Gazette* 70(5): 307–24.

Riegert, K. (ed.) (2007) *Politicotainment. Television's Take on the Real*. New York: Peter Lang.

Rippon, P. (2011) 'Sofa-lising with Newsnight', www.bbc.co.uk/blogs/theeditors, 27 May.

Robertson, A. (forthcoming 2015) *Global News: Reporting Conflicts and Cosmopolitanism*. New York: Peter Lang.

Robertson, A. (2014) 'Euromedia: Integration and cultural diversity in a changing media landscape', in T. McPhail (ed.) *Global Communication*, 4th edition. Oxford: Wiley-Blackwell, pp. 164–80.

Robertson, A. (2013) 'Connecting in crisis. New and old media and the Arab Spring', *International Journal of Press/Politics* 18: 325–41.

Robertson, A. (2012) 'Narratives of resistance: Comparing global news coverage of the Arab awakening', *New Global Studies* 6(2): article 3.

Robertson, A. (2010a) *Mediated Cosmopolitanism: The World of Television News*. Cambridge and Malden: Polity.

Robertson, A. (2010b) 'Providing an insight into the lives of others', in *Euromed Intercultural Trends: The Anna Lindh Report*. Alexandria: The Anna Lindh Foundation, www.euromedalex.org/trends/report/2010/main.

Robertson, A. (1992) *National Prisms and Perceptions of Dissent: The Euromissile Controversy Reflected in Opinion and the News in the UK and FRG 1980–83*. Edsbruk: Akademitryck.

Robertson, A. & Levin, P. (2010) 'Europe as other: Difference in global media discourse', *Statsvetenskaplig tidskrift* 112(1): 85–90.

Robinson, J. P. & Martin, S. (2009) 'Of time and television', *The ANNALS of the American Academy of Political and Social Science*, 625(1): 74–86.

Robinson, M. J. (1976) 'Public affairs television and the growth of political malaise: The case of "The Selling of the Pentagon"', *American Political Science Review* 70(2):409–32.

Robinson, P. (2012) 'News media and war', in H. A. Semetko & M. Scammell (eds.) *The Sage Handbook of Political Communication*. London: Sage, pp. 342–55.

Robinson, P. (2011) 'Pockets of Resistance: Theorising Media–State Relations and the Case of the British Media and the 2003 Iraq Invasion'. Paper presented at the ISA, Montreal, 17 March.

Robinson, P. (2002) *The CNN Effect: The Myth of News, Foreign Policy and Intervention*. London: Routledge.

Robinson, P., Goddard, P., Parry, K., Murray, C. & Taylor, P. M. (2010) *Pockets of Resistance: British News Media, War and Theory in the 2003 Invasion of Iraq*. Manchester: Manchester University Press.

Rooke, R. (2009) *European Media in the Digital Age: Analysis and Approaches*. Harlow: Pearson/Longman.

Rosen, J. (2006) 'The people formerly known as the audience', Huffington Post, 30 June, www.huffing-tonpost.com/jay-rosen/the-people-formerly-known_1_b_24113.html.

Rosen, J. (2008) 'A most useful definition of citizen journalism', http://archive.pressthink.org/2008/07/14/a_most_useful_d_p.html.

Rosenberry, J. & St. John III, B. (eds.) (2010) *Public Journalism 2.0: The Promise and Reality of a Citizen-Engaged Press*. London: Routlege.

Rosenstiel, T. (1993) *Strange Bedfellows: How Television and the Presidential Candidates Changed American Politics*. New York: Hyperion.

Ross, K. (2002) *Women, Politics, Media: Uneasy Relations in Comparative Perspective*. Hampton Press.

Ross, K. & Carter, C. (2011) 'Woman and news: A long and winding road', *Media, Culture & Society* 33(8): 1148–65.

Ross, K. & Comrie, M. (2012) 'The rules of the (leadership) game: Gender, politics and news', *Journalism* 13(8): 969–84.

Roughead, G. (2011) Speech given at the Institute for Public Relations Strategic Communications Summit, 6 June, reproduced on www.damniwish.com/2011/08/please-read-this-a-very-impor tant-speech-about-social-media-in-america.html.

Rozhnov, K. (2011) 'Social media capitalise on Russia's history of censorship', BBC News, 24 March, www.bbc.co.uk/news/business-12834226.

(RSF) Reporters Without Borders (2013) 'France and Mali urged to let journalists into war zones', 17 January, http://en.rsf.org/mali-france-and-mali-urged-to-let-17-01-2013,43920.html.

(RSF) Reporters Without Borders (2011a) 'Wave of arrests of bloggers and activists', 7 January, http://en.rsf.org/spip.php?page=imprimir_articulo&id_article=39238.

(RSF) Reporters Without Borders (2011b) 'Internet censorship and attacks on journalists amid major street protests, 26 January, http://en.rsf.org/egypt-internet-censorship-and-attacks-on-26-01-2011,39400.html.

(RSF) Reporters Without Borders (2011c) "Nawaat: Reporters Without Borders awards the 2011 Netizen Prize to Tunisian bloggers', 11 March, http://en.rsf.org/nawaat-reporters-without-borders-11-03-2011,39776.html.

RT (2009) 'Corporate profile', www.russiatoday/com/About_Us/Corporate_Profile.html.

Ruddock, A. (2001) *Understanding Audiences: Theory and Method*. London: Sage.

Rugh, W. (2004) *Arab Mass Media*. London: Praeger.

Ruigrok, N. & van Atteveldt, W. (2007) 'Global angling with a local angle: How U.S., British, and Dutch newspapers frame global and local terrorist attacks', *The Harvard International Journal of Press/Politics* 12(1): 68–90.

Ruiz, C., et al. (2011) 'Public Sphere 2.0? The democratic qualities of citizen debates in online newspapers', *The International Journal of Press/Politics* 16(4): 463–87.

Rusbridger, A. (2013a) 'David Miranda, schedule 7 and the danger that all reporters now face', *The Guardian*, 19 August, www.theguardian.com/commentisfree/2013/aug/19/david-miranda-schedule7-danger-reporters.

Rusbridger, A. (2013b) 'What now for the surveillance state?', *The Guardian*, 2 December, www.theguardian.com/world/2013/dec/02/alan-rusbridger-surveillance-state-spies-gchq-nsa.

Rusbridger, A. (2009) 'I've seen the future and it's mutual', *British Journalism Review* 20(3): 19–26.

Russell, A. (2011) *Networked: A Contemporary History of News in Transition*. Cambridge: Polity.

Ryan, Y. (2013) 'Mali journalists despair over "invisible war"', Al Jazeera, 27 January, www.aljazeera.com/indepth/features/2013/01/2013127154355125483.html.

Ryfe, D.M. (2009) 'Broader and deeper. A study of newsroom culture in a time of change', *Journalism* 10(2): 197–216.

Sabry, T. (2005) 'What is "global" about Arab media?', *Global Media & Communication* 1: 41–6.

Sachleben, M. & Yenerall, K. M. (2012) *Seeing the Bigger Picture. American and International Politics in Film and Popular Culture*. New York: Peter Lang.

Sakota-Kokot, T. (2011) 'Fiction film and the "real" world', *Global Media and Communication* 7(3): 221–6.

Sakr, N. (2008) 'Diversity and diaspora: Arab communities and satellite communication in Europe', *Global Media and Communication* 4(3): 277–300.

Sakr, N. (2007) 'Challenger or lackey? The politics of news on Al-Jazeera', in D. K. Thussu (ed.) *Media on the Move: Global Flow and Contra-flow*. London and New York: Routledge, pp. 116–32.

Sambrook, R. (2013) 'Why journalists need the Open Government Partnership to help them', *The Guardian*, 20 October, www.theguardian.com/media/media-blog/2013/oct/20/journalists-open-government-partnership.

Sampedro, V. (2011) 'Introduction: New trends and challenges in political communication', *International Journal of Press/Politics* 16(4): 431–9.

Samuels, D. (2010) 'The shameful attacks on Julian Assange', *The Atlantic*, www.theatlantic.com/international/print/2010/12/the-shameful-attacks-on-julian-assange/67440/.

Sanders, K. (2003) *Ethics and Journalism*. London: Sage.

Sanders, K., Crespo, M. J. C. & Holtz-Bacha, C. (2011) 'Communicating governments: A three-country comparison of how governments communicate with citizens', *The International Journal of Press/Politics* 16(4): 523–47.

Sanders, K., Hanna, M. Berganza, M. R. & Aranda, J. J. S. (2008) 'Becoming journalists: A comparison of the professional attitudes and values of British and Spanish journalism students', *European Journal of Communication* 23(2): 133–52.

Sandvoss, C. (2007) 'Public sphere and publicness: Sport audiences and political discourse', in R. Butsch (ed.) *Media and Public Spheres*. Houndmills: Palgrave Macmillan, pp. 58–70.

Sarrica, M., Fortunati, L., O'Sullivan, J., et al. (2010) 'The early stages of the integration of the internet in EU newsrooms', *European Journal of Communication* 25(4): 413–22.

Scammell, M. (2010) 'Freedom is not a Luxury', *Index on Censorship* 39(1): 155–67.

Scannell, P. (2004) 'What reality has misfortune?' *Media, Culture & Society* 26(4): 573–84.

Scannell, P. (1996) *Radio, Television and Modern Life*. Oxford: Blackwell.

Schaefer, D. J. & Karan, K. (2010) 'Problematizing Chindia: Hybridity and Bollywoodization of popular Indian cinema in global film flows', *Global Media and Communication* 6(3): 309–16.

Schiller, D. (2007) *How to Think About Information*. Urbana: University of Illinois Press.

Schiller, D. (1999) *Digital Capitalism: Networking the Global Market System*. Cambridge, MA: MIT Press.

Schiller, H. (1969) *Mass Communications and American Empire*. New York: A. M. Kelley.

Schiller, J. Z. (2007) 'On becoming the media: Low power FM and the alternative public sphere' in R. Butsch (ed.) *Media and Public Spheres*. Houndmills: Palgrave Macmillan, pp. 122–35.

Schirato, T. & Webb, J. (2003) *Understanding Globalization*. London: Sage. Schlesinger, P. (2007) 'A cosmopolitan temptation?' *European Journal of Communication* 22(4): 413–26.

Schlesinger, P. (2003) 'The Babel of Europe? An essay on networks and communicative spaces', ARENA Working Paper 22/03, www.sv.uio.no/arena/english/research/publications/arena-publications/workingpapers/working-papers2003/wp03_22.pdf.

Schlesinger, P. & Tumber, H. (1994) *Reporting Crime: The Media Politics of Criminal Justice*. Oxford: Clarendon Press.

Schmidt, N. (2014) 'Women on the frontline', *Index on Censorship* 43(1): 188–9.

Schönbach, K., de Ridder, J. & Lauf, E. (2001) 'Politicians on TV news: Getting attention in Dutch and German election campaigns', *European Journal of Political Research* 39: 519–31.

Schrøder, K. C. & Phillips, L. (2007) 'Complexifying media power: A study of the interplay between media and audience discourses on politics', *Media, Culture & Society* 29(6): 890–915.

Schrott, A. (2009) 'Dimensions: Catch-all label or technical term', in K. Lundby (ed.) *Mediatization: Concept, Changes, Consequences*. New York: Peter Lang, pp. 41–61.

Schubart, R. (2007) 'Storytelling for a nation: Spielberg, memory, and the narration of war', in K. Riegert (ed.) *Politicotainment: Television's Take on the Real*. New York: Peter Lang, pp. 267–88.

Schudson, M. (2005) 'Autonomy from what?' in R. Benson & E. Neveu (eds.) *Bourdieu and the Journalistic Field*. Cambridge: Polity, pp. 214–23.

Schudson, M. (2001) 'The objectivity norm in American journalism', *Journalism* 2(2): 149–70.

Schudson, M. (1998) *The Good Citizen: A History of American Civic Life*. New York: The Free Press.

Schudson, M. (1978) *Discovering the News: A Social History of American Newspapers*. New York: Basic Books.

Schulz, W. (2004) 'Reconstructing mediatization as an analytical concept', *European Journal of Communication* 19(1): 87–101.

Scola, N. (2010) 'Drezner's guide to thinking about civil society 2.0', techPresident, 9 November, http://techpresident.com/blog-entry/drezners-guide-thinking-about-civil-society-20.

Scott, M., Street, J. & Inthorn, S. (2011) 'From entertainment to citizenship: A comparative study of the political uses of popular culture by first-time voters', *International Journal of Cultural Studies* 14(5): 499–514.

Segerberg, A. & Bennett, W. L. (2011) 'Social media and the organization of collective action: Using Twitter to explore the ecologies of two climate change protests', *The Communication Review* 14(3): 197–215.

Seib, Philip (2008) *The Al Jazeera Effect: How the New Global Media are Reshaping World Politics*. Dulles: Potomac Books.

Sellnow, D. (2014) *The Rhetorical Power of Popular Culture*. London: Sage.

Semetko, H., de Vreese, C. & Peter, J. (2000) 'Europeanised politics – Europeanised media? European integration and political communication', *West European Politics* 23(4): 121–41.

Semetko, H., Blumler, J., Gurevitch, M., Weaver, D. H., Barkin, S. & Wilhoit, G. C. (2001) *The Formation of Campaign Agendas: A Comparative Analysis of Party and Media Role in Recent American and British Elections*. Hillsdale: Lawrence Erlbaum.

Seo, H. (2011) 'Media and foreign policy: A comparative study of journalists' perceptions of press-government relations during the six-party talks', *Journalism* 12(4): 467–81.

Servaes, J. (1999) *Communication for Development: One World, Multiple Cultures*. Cresskill: Hampton Press.

Shafer, R. & Freedman, E. (2009) 'Press constraints as obstacles to establishing civil societies in Central Asia', *Journalism Studies* 10(6): 851–69.

Shapiro, M. (2009) *Cinematic Geopolitics*. Routledge

Shaw, I. S. (2009) 'Towards an African journalism model: A critical historical perspective', *The International Communication Gazette*, 71(6): 491–510.

Shehata, A. (2010a) 'Pathways to politics: How media system can influence socioeconomic gaps in political participation', *International Journal of Press/Politics* 15(3): 295–318.

Shehata, A. (2010b) 'Marketing journalistic independence: Official dominance and the rule of product substitution in Swedish press coverage', *European Journal of Communication* 25(2): 123–37.

Shepperson, A. & Tomaselli, K. G. (2009) 'Media in Africa: Political, cultural and theoretical trajectories in the global environment', *The International Communication Gazette* 71(6): 473–89.

Shi, A. (2005) 'The taming of the shrew: Global media in a Chinese perspective', *Global Media & Communication* 1: 33–6.

Shiels, M. (2010) 'Cyber-sabotage and espionage top 2011 security fears', BBC News online, www.bbc.co.uk/news/technology-12056594.

Shirky, C. (2003) 'Power laws, weblogs, and inequality": Clay Shirky's writings about the internet', www.shirky.com.

Shimpach, S. (2007) 'Representing the public of the cinema's public sphere' in R. Butsch (ed.) *Media and Public Spheres*. Houndmills: Palgrave Macmillan, pp. 136–48.

Shoemaker, P. J. & Reese, S. D. (1996) *Mediating the Message: Theories of Influence on Mass Media Content*. White Plains: Longman.

Shu, X. (2010) 'Lords of misrule', *Index on Censorship* 39(1): 47–51.

SIDA (2012) 'Support to actors working for democracy and freedom of expression', www.sida.se/English/Partners/Civil-society-organisations/About-cooperation-with-civil-society/Support-to-actors-working-for-democracy-and-freedom-of-expression/.

Sifry, M. (2011) 'Exclusive excerpt: Wikileaks, Assange, and why there's no turning back', Huffington Post, 9 February, www.huffingtonpost.com/2011/02/09/wikileaks-assange-transparency_n_820348.html.

Silverstone, R. (2007) *The Media and Morality*. Cambridge: Polity.

Silverstone, R. (2005) 'Mediation and communication', in C. Calhoun, C. Rojek & B. Turner, (eds.) *The International Handbook of Sociology*. London: Sage, pp. 188–207.

Silverstone, R. (2002) 'Complicity and collusion in the mediation of everyday life', *New Literary History* 33(5): 745–64.

Silverstone, R. (1990) 'Television and everyday life: Towards an anthropology of the television audience', in M. Ferguson (ed.) *Public Communication: The New Imperatives*. London: Sage, pp. 173–89.

Simonson, P. (2010) *Refiguring Mass Communication*. Urbana, Chicago and Springfield: University of Illinois Press.

Siune, K. & Hultén, O. (1998) Does public broadcasting have a future?' in D. McQuail & K. Siune (eds.) *Media Policy: Convergence, Concentration and Commerce*. London: Sage, pp 23–37.

Skjerdal, T. S. (2011) 'Journalists or activists? Self-identity in the Ethiopian diaspora online community', *Journalism* 12(6): 727–44.

Sklar, R. (1987) 'Developmental democracy', *Comparative Studies in Society and History* 29(4): 686–714.

Slade, C. (2010) 'Media and citizenship: Transnational television cultures reshaping political identities in the European Union', *Journalism* 11(6): 727–63.

Slaughter, A.-M. (2012) 'Kallt krig om information', *Dagens Nyheter*, 29 August.

Smedsrud, J. (2011) 'Kannibalisme på avismarkedet? Strategiske valg i fem medie- og avishus', Master's Thesis, Oslo University, http://urn.nb.no/URN:NBN:no-29002.

Smith, A. (2009) 'A crackdown coming on British libel suits?' *Time World*, www.time.com/time/world/article/0,8599,1940242,00.html.

Smith, V. (2010) 'The "brittle" compact between military and the media', in R. Lance & J. Mair (eds.) *Afghanistan, War and the Media: Deadlines and Frontlines*. Suffolk: Arima Publishing, pp. 42–8.

Smythe, D. (1997) 'Communications: Blindspot of western Marxism', *Canadian Journal of Communications* 1(3): 1–27.

Smythe, D. (1981) *Dependency Road*. Norwood: Ablex.

Socolow, M. J. (2010) '"We should make money on our news": The problem of profitability in network broadcast journalism history', *Journalism* 11(6): 675–91.

Soffer, O. (2009) 'The competing ideals of objectivity and dialogue in American journalism', *Journalism* 10(4): 473–91.

Splichal, S. (2009) '"New" media, "old" theories: Does the (national) public melt into the air of global governance?' *European Journal of Communication* 24(4): 391–405.

Splichal, S. (2006) 'In search of a strong European public sphere: Some critical observations on conceptualizations of the publicness and the (European) public sphere', *Media, Culture & Society* 28(5): 695–714.

Spyridou, L-P., Matsiola, M., Veglis, A. & Dimoulas, C. (2013) 'Journalism in a state of flux: Journalists as agents of technology innovation and emerging news practices', *The International Communication Gazette* 75(1): 76–98.

Sreedharan, C., Thorsen, E. & Allan, S. (2011) 'Wikileaks and the changing forms of information politics in the network society', in E. Downey and M. A. Jones (eds.) *Public Service and Web 2.0 Technologies: Future Trends in Social Media*. IGI Global, pp. 167–80.

Statham, P. (2008) 'Making Europe news: How journalists view their role and media performance', *Journalism* 9(4): 398–422.

Stanyer, J. (2007) *Modern Political Communication*. Cambridge: Polity.

Steel, J. (2012) *Journalism and Free Speech*. London: Routledge.

Steensen, S. (2009) 'The shaping of an online feature journalist', *Journalism* 10(5): 702–18.

Steiner, L. (2009) 'Gender in the newsroom', in K. Wahl-Jorgensen & T. Hanitzsch (eds.) *Handbook of Journalism Studies*. London: Routledge, pp. 116–29.

Sterling-Folker, J. & Folker, B. (2006) 'Conflict and the nation-State: Magical mirrors of Muggles and refracted images', in D. Nexon & I. B. Neuman (eds.) (2006) *Harry Potter and International Relations*. Lanham: Rowman & Littlefield, pp. 103–26.

Stetka, V. (2012) 'From multinationals to business tycoons: Media ownership and journalistic autonomy in Central and Eastern Europe', *The International Journal of Press/Politics* 17(4): 433–56.

Stevenson, N. (2003) *Cultural Citizenship. Cosmopolitan Questions.* Maidenhead: Open University Press.

Stevenson, N. (2002) *Understanding Media Cultures: Social Theory and Mass Communication.* London: Sage.

Stevenson, N. (1999) *The Transformation of the Media: Globalisation, Morality and Ethics.* London: Longman.

Stiernstedt, J. (2010) 'Början till slutet för ett fritt internet', *Dagens Nyheter*, 6 December, pp. 8–9.

Stone, B. (2010) 'Exclusive: Biz Stone on Twitter and activism', *The Atlantic*, 19 October, www.theatlantic.com/technology/archive/2010/10/exclusive-biz-stone-on-twitter-and-activism/64772/.

Storey, J. (2001) *Cultural Theory and Popular Culture: An Introduction.* Harlow: Pearson.

Storr, J. (2011) 'The disintegration of the state model in the English speaking Caribbean: Restructuring and redefining public service broadcasting', *The International Communication Gazette* 73(7): 553–72.

Straubhaar, J. (2010) 'Chindia in the context of emerging cultural and media powers', *Global Media and Communication* 6(3): 253–62.

Straubhaar, J. (2008) *World Television: From Global to Local.* London: Sage.

Street, J. (2012a) *Music & Politics.* Cambridge: Polity.

Street, J. (2012b) 'Popular culture and political communication', in H. A. Semetko & M. Scammell (eds.) *The Sage Handbook of Political Communication.* London: Sage, pp. 75–84.

Street, J. (2001) *Mass Media, Politics and Democracy.* Houndmills: Palgrave.

Ström, P. (2011) *Storebror på Facebook: Integritet och risker på sociala medier.* Stockholm: Stiftelsen Den Nya Välfärden.

Strömbäck, J. (2011) 'Mediatization of politics: Towards a conceptual framework for comparative research', in E. Bucy & R. L. Holbert (eds.) *Sourcebook of Political Communication Research.* Abingdon: Routledge, pp. 367–82.

Strömbäck, J. (2008) 'Four phases of mediatization: An analysis of the mediatization of politics', *International Journal of Press/Politics* 13(3): 228–46.

Strömbäck, J. & Dimitrova, D. V. (2011) 'Mediatization and media interventionism: A comparative analysis of Sweden and the United States', *International Journal of Press/Politics* 16(1): 30–49.

Strömbäck, J. & Esser, F. (2009) 'Shaping politics: Mediatization and media interventionism', in K. Lundby (ed.) *Mediatization: Concept, Changes, Consequences.* New York: Peter Lang, pp. 205–23.

Strömbäck, J. and Kaid, L. (eds.) (2008) *The Handbook of Election News Coverage Around the World.* New York and London: Routledge.

Strömbäck, J. & Shehata, A. (2010) 'Media malaise or a virtuous circle? Exploring the causal relationships between news media exposure, political news attention and political interest', *European Journal of Political Research* 49: 575–97.

Su, W. (2010) 'New strategies of China's film industry as soft power', *Global Media and Communication* 6(3): 317–22.

Sunstein, C. (2001a) *Republic.com.* Princeton: Princeton University Press.

Sunstein, C. (2001b) 'The daily we'. *Boston Review.* http://bostonreview.net/BR26.3/sunstein.php.

Suriowecki, J. (2004) *Wisdom of the Crowds.* London: Little Brown.

Svegfors, M. (2013) 'Kvalitetsjournalistiken på snabb reträtt i Sverige', *Dagens Nyheter*, 10 February, www.dn.se/debatt/kvalitetsjournalistiken-pa-snabb-retratt-i-sverige/.

Svegfors, M. & Benkö, C. (2011) 'Detta vill Sveriges Radio, men vad vill riksdagen?' Press release, 24 February, http://sverigesradio.se/sida/artikel.aspx?programid=2938&artikel=4367701.

Svegfors, M. & Benkö, C. (2010) 'Journalistik 3.0: Medieormen ömsar skinn', http://sverigesradio.se.

Tang, L. & H. Sampson (2012) 'The interaction between mass media and the internet in non-democratic states: The case of China', *Media, Culture & Society* 34(4): 457–71.

Tawil-Souri, H. (2011a) 'The hi-tech enclosure of Gaza', Bitzeit University Working Paper 2011/18, http://ssrn.com/abstract=1764251.

Tawil-Souri, H. (2011b) 'Where is the political in cultural studies? In Palestine', *International Journal of Cultural Studies* 14(5): 467–82.

Taylor, M. & Hopkins, N. (2013) 'GCHQ faces legal challenge in European court over online privacy', *The Guardian*, 3 October, www.theguardian.com/uk-news/2013/oct/03/gchq-legal-challenge-europe-privacy-surveillance.

Taylor, P. M. (1997) *Global Communications, International Affairs and the Media Since 1945*. London: Routledge.

Taylor, P. M. (1991) *War Photography: Realism in the British Press*. London: Routledge.

Teer-Tomaselli, R., Wasserman, H. & de Beer, A. S. (2007) 'South Africa as a regional media power', in D. K. Thussu (ed.) *Media on the Move: Global Flow and Contra-flow*. London & New York: Routledge, pp. 153–64.

Tharoor, Ishaan (2011) 'Clinton applauds Al Jazeera, rolls eyes at U.S. media', *Time*, http://globalspin.blogs.time.com/2011/03/03/clinton-applauds-al-jazeera-rolls-eyes-at-u-s-media, 7 March.

Thinkbox (2011) 'Social TV: One screen good, two screens better', www.thinkbox.tv/server/show/nav.1400.

Thompson, E. P. (1968) *The Making of the English Working Class*. Harmondsworth: Pelican.

Thompson, J. B. (1995) *The Media and Modernity. A Social Theory of the Media*. Cambridge: Polity.

Thompson, K. (ed.) (1997) *Media and Cultural Regulation*. London: Sage / Open University.

Thorpe, V. (2014) 'Vivenne Westwood: Climate change, not fashion, is now my priority', *The Guardian*, 8 February, www.theguardian.com/lifeandstyle/2014/feb/08/vivienne-westwood-arctic-campaign.

Thornborrow, J. & Montgomery, M. (2010) 'Special issue on personalization in the broadcast news interview' (editorial), *Discourse & Communication* 4(2): 99–104.

Thussu, D. K. (2009) *News as Entertainment: The Rise of Global Infotainment*, 2nd edition. London: Sage.

Thussu, D. K. (2008) *International Communication: Continuity and Change*, 2nd edition. New York: Oxford University Press.

Thussu, D. K. (2007) 'Mapping global media flow and contra-flow', in D. K. Thussu (ed.) *Media on the Move: Global Flow and Contra-flow*. London and New York: Routledge, pp. 11–32.

Thussu, D. K. & Freedman, D. (2003) *War and the Media: Reporting Conflict 24/7*. London: Sage.

Tilly, C. (2005) *Popular Contention in Great Britain 1758–1834*. Boulder: Paradigm.

Tilly, C. (1986) *The Contentious French*. Cambridge, MA: Harvard University Press.

Tilt, B. & Xiao, Q. (2010) 'Media coverage of environmental pollution in the People's Republic of China: Responsibility, cover-up and state control', *Media, Culture & Society* 32(2): 225–45.

Toepfl, F. (2013) 'Why do pluralistic media systems emerge? Comparing media change in the Czech Republic and in Russia after the collapse of communism', *Global Media and Communication* 9(3): 239–56.

Tomlinson, J. (1999) *Globalization and Culture*. Cambridge: Polity.

Trenz, H.-J. (2004) 'Media coverage on European governance', *European Journal of Communication* 19(3): 291–319.

Triandafyllidou, A., Wodak, R. & Krzyzanowski (eds.) (2009) *The European Public Sphere and the Media: Europe in Crisis*. Basingstoke: Palgrave Macmillan.

Tuman, J. (2003) *Communicating Terror: The Rhetorical Dimensions of Terrorism*. London: Sage.

Tumber, H. (2004) 'Prisoners of news values? Journalists, professionalism, and identification in times of war', in S. Allan & B. Zelizer (eds.) *Reporting War: Journalism in Wartime*. London and New York: Routledge, pp. 190–205.

Tunstall, J. (2008) *The Media Were American*. New York and Oxford: Oxford University Press.

Tworzecki, H. & Semetko, H.A. (2012) 'Media use and political engagement in three new democracies: Malaise versus mobilization in the Czech Republic, Hungary and Poland', *The International Journal of Press/Politics* 17(4): 407–32.

Ullah, M. S. (2013) 'ICT changing youths' political attitudes and behaviors in Bangladesh', *The International Communication Gazette* 75(3): 271–83.

UNESCO (2009) 'World report on cultural diversity', www.unesco.org/new/en/culture/resources/report/the-unesco-world-report-on-cultural-diversity/.

UNESCO (2005) Convention on the Protection and Promotion of the Diversity of Cultural Expressions, Paris, 20 October, http://portal.unesco.org/en/ev.php-URL_ID=31038&URL_DO=DO_TOPIC&URL_SECTION=201.html.

UNESCO (2001) Universal Declaration on Cultural Diversity, 2 November, http://unesdoc.unesco.org/images/0012/001271/127160m.pdf.

UNESCO (1998) 'The power of culture', www.powerofculture.nl/uk/archive/report/background.html.

Ürper, D. C. (2011) 'Rival discourses on the "war on terror": Afghanistan and Iraq wars in the opinion columns of liberal and Islamist newspapers in Turkey', *Global Media and Communication* 7(3): 275–79.

Urrichio, W. (2009) 'Contextualizing the broadcast era: Nation, commerce, and constraint', *The ANNALS of the American Academy of Political and Social Science*, 625(1): 60–73.

Usher, Nikki (2011) 'How Egypt's uprising is helping redefine the idea of a "media event"', Nieman Journalism Lab, 8 February, www.niemanlab.org/2011/02/how-egypts-uprising-is-helping-redefine-the-idea-of-a-media-event.

Valadbaygi, S. (2010) 'Power to the people', *Index on Censorship* 39(1): 138–41.

Väliverronen, E. (2001) 'From mediation to mediatization: The new politics of communicating science and biotechnology', in U. Kivikuru & T. Savolainen (eds.) *The Politics of Public Issues*. Helsinki: Department of Communication, University of Helsinki, pp. 157–77.

Van Aelst, P., Sehata, A. & Van Dalen, A. (2010) Members of Parliament: Equal competitors for media attention? An analysis of personal contacts between MPs and political journalists in five European countries', *Political Communication* 27(3): 310–25.

Van Dalen, A. (2012) 'Structural bias in cross-national perspective: How political systems and journalism cultures influence government dominance in the news', *The International Journal of Press/Politics* 17(1): 32–55.

Van Dalen, A., Albaek, E. & De Vreese, C. (2011) 'Suspicious minds: Explaining political cynicism among political journalists in Europe', *European Journal of Communication* 26(2): 147–62.

Van de Donk, W., Loader, B. D., Nixon, P. G. & Rucht, D. (eds.) (2004) *Cyberprotest: New Media, Citizens and Social Movements*. Chicago: University of Chicago Press.

Van de Steeg, M. (2002) 'Rethinking the conditions for a public sphere in the European Union', *European Journal of Social Theory* 5(4): 499–519.

Van Zoonen, L. (2005) *Entertaining the Citizen: When Politics and Popular Culture Converge*. Lanham: Rowman & Littlefield.

Van Zoonen, L. (1998) 'One of the girls? The changing gender of journalism', in C. Carter, G. Branston & S. Allan (eds.) *News, Gender and Power*. London: Routledge, pp. 33–46.

Van Zoonen, L. & Wring, D. (2012) 'Trends in political television fiction in the UK: Themes, characters and narratives, 1965–2009', *Media, Culture & Society* 34(3): 263–79.

Viner, K. (2009) 'Internet has changed foreign policy forever', *The Guardian*, 19 June, www.guardian.co.uk/politics/2009/jun/19/gordon-brown-internet-foreign-policy.

Volkmer, I. (2014) *The Global Public Sphere: Public Communication in the Age of Reflexive Globalization*. Cambridge: Polity.

Volkmer, I. (2003) 'The global network society and the global public sphere', *Development* 46(1): 9–16.

Voltmer, K. (ed.) (2006) *Mass Media and Political Communication in New Democracies*. London: Routledge.

von Seth, R. (2011) 'The language of the press in Soviet and post-Soviet Russi: Creation of the citizen role through newspaper discourse', *Journalism* 13(1): 53–70.

von Twickel, N. (2010) 'Russia Today uses controversy to seek viewers', *The St. Petersburg Times* 1557, 19 March, www.sptimes.ru/index.php?action_id=2&story_id=30993.

Vulliamy, E. & Wainwright, R. (2014) 'Farewell, Pete Seeger', *The Observer*, 2 February, http://www.theguardian.com/music/2014/feb/02/pete-seeger-farewell-american-folk-singer-rufus-wainwright.

Waisbord, S. (2013) *Reinventing Professionalism: Journalism and News in Global Perspective.* Cambridge: Polity.

Waisbord, S. (2000) *Watchdog Journalism in South America: News, Accountability, and Democracy.* New York: Columbia University Press.

Walgrave, S., Bennett, L., Van Laer, J. & Breunig, C. (2011) *Mobilization: An International Journal* 16(3): 325–49.

Walker, S. (2014) 'Russian cable news channel TV Rain under threat after "political attack"', *The Guardian*, 29 January, www.theguardian.com/world/2014/jan/29/russia-news-channel-tv-rain-under-threat.

Wall, M. (2010) 'In the battle(field): The US military, blogging and the struggle for authority', *Media, Culture & Society* 32(5): 863–72.

Warburton, N. (2009) *Free Speech: A very short introduction.* Oxford: Oxford University Press.

Ward, D. (2002) *European Union Democratic Deficit and the Public Sphere: An Evaluation of EU Media Policy.* Amsterdam: IOS Press.

Ward, D. (2001) 'The democratic deficit and European Union communication policy. An evaluation of the Commission's approach to broadcasting', *Javnost – the Public* 8(1): 75–94.

Ward, J. & de Vreese, C. (2011) 'Political consumerism, young citizens and the Internet', *Media, Culture & Society* 33(3): 399–413.

Warshaw, D. A. (2011) 'Conan 2.0', Fortune Tech, 10 February, http://tech.fortune.cnn.com/2011/02/10/conan-2-0.

Washbourne, N. (2010) *Mediating Politics.* Maidenhead: McGraw Hill / Open University.

Watt, N., Millar, S. & Hopkins, N. (2013) 'UK debate grows over "Orwellian" NSA and GCHQ surveillance', *The Guardian*, 9 October, www.theguardian.com/world/2013/oct/09/debate-grows-orwellian-nsa-technology.

Watts, J. (2013) 'Argentina's president and Grupo Clarín go head-to-head over media law', *The Guardian*, 20 August, www.theguardian.com/world/2013/aug/20/argentina-supreme-court-media-law.

Weaver, D. H. (1998) 'Journalists around the world: Commonalities and differences', in D. H. Weaver (eds.). *The Global Journalist: News People around the World.* Cresskill: Hampton.

Weaver, D. H. & Wilhoit, G. C. (1998) *The Global Journalist: News People around the World.* Cresskill: Hampton Press.

Weaver, D. H.& Wilhoit, G. C. (1996) *U.S. News People at the End of an Era.* Mahwah: Lawrence Erlbaum.

Weaver, D. H., Beam, R. A., Brownlee, B. J., Voakes, P. S. & Wilhoit, G. C. (2007) *The American Journalist in the 21st Century: US News People at the Dawn of a New Millennium.* Mahwah: Lawrence Erlbaum.

Webb, R. (2013) 'Russell, choosing to vote is the most British kind of revolution there is', *New Statesman*, 30 October, www.newstatesman.com/2013/10/russell-brand-robert-webb-choosing-vote-most-british-kind-revolution-there.

Weber, C. (2013) *International Relations Theory: A Critical Introduction.* Abingdon: Routledge.

Weiss, A. S. & Domingo, D. (2010) 'Innovation processes in online newsrooms as actor-networks and communities of practice', *New Media and Society* 12(7): 1156–71.

Weldes, J. (2003) *To Seek Out New Worlds. Exploring Links between Science Fiction and World Politics.* Houndmills: Palgrave Macmillan.

Wessler, H. & Adolphsen, M. (2008) 'Contra-flow from the Arab world? How Arab television coverage of the 2003 Iraq war was used and framed on Western international news channels', *Media, Culture & Society* 30(4): 439–61.

Wessler, H. & Schultz, T. (2007) 'Can the mass media deliberate? Insights from print media and political talk shows', in R. Butsch (ed.) *Media and Public Spheres.* Houndmills: Palgrave Macmillan, pp. 15–27.

Wetzstein, I. (2010) 'Mediated conflicts: Capacities and limitations of "mediative journalism" in public diplomacy processes', *The International Communication Gazette* 72(6): 503–20.

White, D. M. (1950) 'The gatekeeper: A case study in the selection of news', *Journalism Quarterly* 27: 383–90.

White, M. (2013) 'Data debate stirs up spooks, pinkos and Julians', *The Guardian*, 31 October, www. theguardian.com/world/2013/oct/31/mps-debate-spying-julians

Whitehurst, T. (2011) 'The patch effect: What AOL's new venture could mean for hyperlocal news', Reynolds Journalism Institute, January, www.rjionline.org/projects/skube/stories/patch-effect/ part-1.php.

Widholm, A. (2011) 'Europe in transition: Transnational television news and European identity', Stockholm University, Department of Journalism, Media and Communication (JMK), doctoral thesis.

Wikileaks (2011) 'What is Wikileaks?' http://wikileaks.ch/About.html.

Wikileaks (2010) 'About Wikileaks', http://213.251.145.96/about.html.

Williams, R. (1983) *Keywords*. London: Fontana.

Williams, R. (1974/2003) *Television: Technology and Cultural Form*. London and New York: Routledge.

Willsher, K. (2014) 'Magazine promises to remove claims of François Holland affair from website', *The Guardian*, 10 January.

Wilson, G. (2011) 'Our next step in News blogging', www.bbc.co.uk/blogs/theeditors, 11 May.

Wilson, J. (2011b) 'Playing with politics: Political fans and Twitter faking in post-broadcast democracy', *Convergence* 17(4): 445–61.

Wilson, T. (2009) *Understanding Media Users: From Theory to Practice*. Malden: Wiley-Blackwell.

Wiman, B. (2013) 'Tänd ett ljus i helgen för en av upplysningens hjältar', *Dagens Nyheter*, 3 November, www.dn.se/kultur-noje/bjorn-wiman-tand-ett-ljus-i-helgen-for-en-av-upplysningens-hjaltar.

Wines, M. (2010) 'China's censors misfire in abuse-of-power case', *The New York Times* 17 November, www.nytimes.com/2010/11/18/world/asia/18li.html.

Winiarski, M. (2010a) 'Så ska USA stoppa skadorna efter Wikileaks avslöjande', *Dagens Nyheter*, 3 December, p. 23.

Winiarski, M. (2010b) 'Hot om nya läckor skrämmer USA', *Dagens Nyheter*, 7 December, pp. 8–9.

Winseck, D. (2008) 'Information Operations "Blowback". Communication, propaganda and surveillance in the global War on Terrorism', *The International Communication Gazette* 70(6): 419–41.

Wintour, P., Mason, R. & Roberts, D. (2013) 'Guardian's NSA revelations: spies to go under spotlight', *The Guardian*, 10 October, www.theguardian.com/world/2013/oct/10/guardian-nsa-spies.

Wodak, R. (2010) 'The glocalization of politics in television: Fiction or reality?', *European Journal of Cultural Studies* 13(1): 43–62.

Wojcieszak, M.E. (2007) 'Al Jazeera: A challenge to traditional framing research', *The International Communication Gazette* 69(2): 115–28.

Wolfsfeld, G. (1997) *Media and Political Conflict*. New York: Cambridge University Press.

Wolodarski, P. (2014) 'Moskvas män: sjuter medan Putin ser på OS', *Dagens Nyheter*, 23 February, www.dn.se/ledare/signerat/peter-wolodarski-moskvas-man-skjuter-medan-putin-ser-pa-os.

Wolodarski, P. (2013a) 'Journalistiken flyttar åter ner i garaget', *Dagens Nyheter*, 13 October, www. dn.se/ledare/kolumner/peter-wolodarski-journalistiken-flyttar-ater-ner-i-garaget.

Wolodarski, P. (2013b) 'Marschen från torget till den smala åsiktsgränden', *Dagens Nyheter*, 15 December, www.dn.se/ledare/signerat/marschen-fran-torget-till-den-smala-asiktsgranden.

Wolodarski, P. (2010) 'Den avklädda världspolisen', *Dagens Nyheter*, 5 December, p. 4.

Wring, D. (2005) *The Politics of Marketing the Labour Party*. Houndmills: Palgrave Macmillan.

Wu, Y. (2007) 'Blurring boundaries in a "Cyber-Greater China": Are internet bulletin boards constructing the public sphere in China?' in R. Butsch (ed.) *Media and Public Spheres*. Houndmills: Palgrave Macmillan, pp. 210–22.

Xin, X. (2011) 'Web 2.0, citizen journalism and social justice in China', in G. Meikle & G. Redden (eds.) *News Online: Transformations and Continuities*. Houndmills: Palgrave Macmillan, pp. 178–94.

Xin, X. (2010) 'Chindia's challenge to global communication: A perspective from China', *Global Media and Communication* 6(3): 296–301.

Xu, X. (2005) *Demystifying Asian Values in Journalism*. Singapore: Marshall Cavendish.

Young, D. G. (2004) 'Late night comedy in Election 2000: Its influence on candidate trait ratings and the moderating effects of political knowledge and partisanship', *Journal of Broadcasting and Electronic Media* 48(1): 1–22.

Young, D. G. & Tisinger, R. M. (2006) 'Dispelling late-night myths: news consumption among late-night comedy viewers and the predictors of exposure to various late-night shows', *The Harvard International Journal of Press/Politics* 11(3): 113–34.

Yunchao, W. (2010) 'The art of censorship', *Index on Censorship* 39(1): 53–7.

Yusha'u, M. J. (2011) 'News framing of the "Detroit Bomber" in the Nigerian press', *Global Media and Communication* 7(3): 281–6.

Zaller, J. (1992) *The Nature and Origins of Mass Opinion*. Cambridge: Cambridge University Press.

Zednik, R. (2002) 'Inside Al Jazeera', *Columbia Journalism Review* 2, www.cjr.org/issues/2002/2/war-zednik.asp.

Zelizer, B. (2005) 'The culture of journalism' in J. Curran & M. Gurevitch (eds.) *Mass Media and Society*, 4th edition. London: Hodder Arnold.

Zelizer, B. (1993) 'American journalists and the death of Lee Harvey Oswald: Narratives of self-legitimation', in D. K. Mumby (ed.) *Narrative and Social Control: Critical Perspectives*. London: Sage, pp. 189–206.

Zelizer, B. & Allan, S., eds. (2002) *Journalism after September 11*. London: Routledge.

Zhang, W. (2013) 'Redefining youth activism through digital technology in Singapore', *The International Communication Gazette* 75(3): 253–70.

Zhang, H. (2011) 'The globalization of Chinese television: The role of the party-state', *The International Communication Gazette* 73(7): 573–94.

Zolo, D. (1992) *Democracy and Complexity*. Cambridge: Polity.

Zukin, C. et al. (2006) *A New Engagement? Political Participation, Civic Life, and the Changing American Citizen*. Oxford: Oxford University Press.

Zunguzungu (2010) 'Julian Assange in Berkeley', http://zunguzungu.wordpress.com/2010/12/12/julian-assange-in-berkeley/.

Index

Page numbers in *italics* denote an illustration

Media and Politics in a Globalizing World